T0212662

Security and the Networked Society

Mark A. Gregory • David Glance

Security and the Networked Society

Foreword by Margaret Gardner AO and Robyn Owens

 Springer

Mark A. Gregory
RMIT University
Melbourne, VIC, Australia

David Glance
University of Western Australia
Crawley, WA, Australia

ISBN 978-3-319-34701-1 ISBN 978-3-319-02390-8 (eBook)
DOI 10.1007/978-3-319-02390-8
Springer Cham Heidelberg New York Dordrecht London

Printed on acid-free paper

Springer is part of Springer Science+Business Media (www.springer.com)

A special thank you to Susan Lagerstrom-Fife at Springer who supported this book from the outset. The authors would like to thank The Conversation (http://www.theconversation. edu.au) and Technology Spectator (http://www.technologyspectator.com.au). Special thanks goes to the editors who assisted with the preparation of the material included in this book: From The Conversation Andrew Jaspan, Misha Ketchell, Helen Westerman, Matt De Neef, Paul Dalgarno, Bella Counihan, Gillian Terzis and Charis Palmer and from Technology Spectator Supratim Adhikari and Harrison Polites. Thanks also to our universities RMIT University and University of Western Australia for supporting The Conversation and enabling us to develop our writing and ideas.

Foreword

The digital era has brought the world, in all its variety and constant change, closer to us, as physical boundaries become less important. We benefit from the multiple connections and the speed with which we can make them. We struggle with the way this changes fundamentally so many aspects of our lives.

This collection of articles about the impacts—positive and negative—that these advances in digital technologies are having on our lives had its origins in The Conversation.

The Conversation, of which RMIT University is a Strategic Partner, provides a means by which academics and researchers can provide their views and expertise direct to the public. It allows faster and broader communication of the ideas and assessments of researchers. It is shaping public debate and discourse and hopefully deepening our public conversations.

This collection of material from The Conversation is a thoughtful consideration of where such technologies may take us in the future. And it is itself a demonstration of how far such technologies have taken us already.

Professor Margaret Gardner AO
Vice-Chancellor and President
RMIT University

The use of technology has always been a driving force in the growth and development of humanity. Although it is now easy to see the general pervasiveness of digital technologies and their overall impact within various societies around the world, we can now capture the exact points in time when new technologies are created and how they develop as they come into contact and are modified by their users. As a result of this, our understanding of the significance of sentinel events in the story of technology and society in recent years has been better than for any other time in history. This collection of articles synthesizes the detail and significance of the important inflexions in the growth of social networks, smartphone use, cybercrime, hacking, and cyber security. For anyone making sense of how governments and societies first experienced the collective hacktivism of Anonymous, for example, the articles in this book capture stories of their rise into, and from, prominence. Since first being published, the articles presented in this book have been viewed collectively about 300,000 times and have provoked wide-ranging discussion amongst their readers. Taken collectively, they form an extremely valuable resource for those wanting to understand where technology is likely to take us in the future.

Professor Robyn Owens
Deputy Vice-Chancellor (Research)
The University of Western Australia

Contents

Chapter 1
Introduction

During man's history, the advent of technology has been pivotal in driving grand transformations of society. The Industrial Revolution (1760–1820) however, occurred over more than a century and affected predominately western civilization. The personal computing and Internet revolution has in 30 years produced a far greater impact and on a global scale.

This revolution has accelerated after connecting potentially every human being on the planet to each other over the Internet through portable devices. We now share more with each other than at any time in history.

Companies facilitating this transformation were not in existence 15 years ago and we are still witnessing their full impact as their platforms and products enable uprisings and revolutions of their own.

With the advent of the pervasiveness of mobile devices and the interconnectedness of the Internet has come with it the darker side of hackers, cyber criminals, cyber terrorists and the general threat of cyber war.

Governments have struggled to create legislation and formulate regulations to bring order to the online world whilst protecting the essence of the Internet that has made it the invaluable resource it has become.

This essence, to some brings anonymity, privacy and security. For others these same attributes displays a lack of an effective government and law enforcement presence leaving the door wide open for criminal activity to flourish online.

World actors including nations, international organizations, terrorists, and vigilantes have all exploited the Internet to further their own ambitions. Information theft, leaking of personal and national secrets, tax dodging, price gouging and law breaking have all occurred as a result of the growth of the Internet.

The Internet has also brought hope, education and awareness to the masses. Through the Internet people around the world can learn about and influence events as though they were actually physically participating.

Governments have a role to play in promoting the use of technology whilst ensuring technology does not become a vehicle for criminal activity. Sound

M.A. Gregory and D. Glance, *Security and the Networked Society*,
DOI 10.1007/978-3-319-02390-8_1, © Springer International Publishing Switzerland 2013

government policy is often a tradeoff between consumer and business interests. Careful preparation of legislation and regulation provides certainty.

Failure by government to update legislation and regulation in a timely manner can have catastrophic consequences because technology advances occur frequently and subsequent advances in cyber-warfare and cyber-crime keep pace.

A key aspect of society's use of technology has been the tradeoff between access to applications and customer security and privacy. Government, security agencies, business, and other organizations are now collecting data as quickly as possible and in ever increasing amounts. How to manage this data avalanche has become known as big data and mining for information has become a growth industry.

The progression of the technological revolution that is happening around us is not even. Drawing links between signature events sometimes only have relevance after the fact but at each juncture, the relevance and meaning of an event needs to be described and placed in the context of the day.

This collection of articles attempts to do exactly this. The articles were written because they captured significant events that reflected, shaped and defined trends and movements involving technology and society. We have grouped these articles into chapters that reflect attributes the articles share. This however artificially separates events that are in fact linked. The rise of Anonymous as a hacking/activist collective for example defined our understanding of this movement. But hacktivism is intertwined with cyber-crime, cyber terrorism and government, and everyone's use of the Internet. This in turn reflects the pervasiveness of the Internet in every aspect of our lives.

The period of time that this book covers saw several significant events occur. There was the rise of Anonymous, LulzSec and others who redefined the notion of groups of people with a common cause and who drove hacktivism to be a global phenomenon. At the same time, cyber-crime continued its inexorable rise and companies and governments struggled to deal with it. Distinguishing cyber-crime from cyber war was another recent problem. Ongoing state-based cyber-attacks were recognized for the first time and have now become part of the realities of using the Internet. From the consumer perspective, the move to mobile eclipsed the desktop PC for the first time and smartphones rapidly approached dominating the mobile phone market. This move coincided with the rise in social media use with platforms like Facebook, Twitter and Google+ bringing into question this new mode of interaction and sharing. Personal privacy became a central issue underpinning a general move by companies taking advantage of knowing as much about their users as possible whilst battling any attempts to remain anonymous.

Finally, this period of time saw Apple become the most valuable company in the world, fueled by sales of it mobile devices. That a technology company should become the most valuable company is not surprising considering its relative impact on society. Exactly how this has come to be is another thread in the narrative that follows.

Chapter 2
Hacking

With the rise in importance of the Internet in our lives came the opportunity for some to exploit this for their own gain. Hacking rose to prominence as the resources they targeted became more valued. Hackers sought opportunities to control sites and make a statement by attacking governments, businesses and organisations that they disagreed with. Other hackers did it for the financial gain and rewards. And yet another group hacked on behalf of government and defense to attack their enemies or learn their secrets.

The rise of Anonymous as a collective involving themselves in "causes" redefined the coordination of people with common interests on the Internet. Their high profile operations have spurred a growth in interest in hackers generally but also in the role of experts whose role it is to secure government, business and organizations against hackers.

The collected articles in this chapter explore both sides of this ongoing and escalating battle.

2.1 Hacking, Cracking and the Wild, Wild Web

14 April 2011

M.A. Gregory and D. Glance, *Security and the Networked Society*,
DOI 10.1007/978-3-319-02390-8_2, © Springer International Publishing Switzerland 2013

Is it time to get tougher on hackers, whatever their motivations? *Source*: **pixabay CC0[1]**

PRIVACY—Who are hackers and what do they want from you?

Pop culture would have us believe they live in dank basements, wear black leather from head to toe and have pseudonyms such as Warlock or Neo.

Hacking and film have long gone hand in hand. Pre-internet we had the appropriately-named Gene Hackman in The Conversation, a 1974 movie focusing on the violation of people's privacy.

Post-internet, the names trip easily off the tongue: The Matrix; The Score; Swordfish; GoldenEye; Tron; Hackers—each one revisits the theme of hacking, reworks it, reinforces the same key imagery.

Perhaps the film that most inspired the modern hacker genre was WarGames, the 1983 film in which a teenage hacker, played by a dew-faced Matthew Broderick, inadvertently leads the world to the brink of nuclear war.

A real-life echo of this comes in the shape of Gary McKinnon,[2] the Scottish systems administrator who faces charges of hacking into 97 US military and NASA computers over a 13-month period between 2001 and 2002.

And then of course there's Julian Assange, the WikiLeaks founder, who graduated from one-time teenage hacker to (notorious) world celebrity.

---

[1] Man despair problem null one binary code, pixabay, http://pixabay.com/en/man-despair-problem-null-one-65049/, 21 December 2012.

[2] Fresh evidence made public to help Enfield hacker Gary McKinnon's fight against extradition, http://www.enfieldindependent.co.uk/news/localnews/8923549.Lords_to_debate_fate_of_Enfield_hacker_Gary_McKinnon/, Accessed online 14 April 2011.

2.1.1 Who's Hacking Who?

Governments, private companies and criminal organisations are all involved in hacking to some extent and for different reasons.

Certain newspapers,[3] as we've learned recently, are not immune to the charms of listening in to the private affairs of others.

2.1.2 The Wild, Wild Web

In terms of corruptibility, the digital network we now take for granted is like the American Wild West of the 1860s.

It was designed to facilitate information flow over digital links and the idea that these links could be used for illicit activities may not even have crossed the minds of the engineers who built it.

In some ways, the current system is extremely hacker-friendly, and there would need to be a major infrastructure rebuild before hacking could be stamped out.

2.1.3 Colour-Coded Hacking

Broadly speaking, hackers fall into three camps:

1) **White hackers**

A so-called "white-hat" will inform an organisation if a security weakness is found in that organisation's systems.

Organisations such as the Australian Computer Emergency Response Team[4] (AusCERT) fill a white hat role in the hacker world. In one sense, they perform a defensive role: they are the good-guys of the hacking world.

2) **Grey hackers**

These are less clear-cut than the above (hence the fact they occupy something of a "grey" area in the hacking world).

Often, they act on the spur of the moment. Depending on the situation, they might exploit or warn an organisation if a weakness is found in their system. Are they our friends or enemies? That just depends.

3) **Black hackers**

These will act to exploit any weakness in a network or an organisation's systems for gain. This could mean collecting and selling intellectual property or personal information.

---

[3] News of the World phone hacking: John Whittingdale seeks public enquiry, http://www.guardian.co.uk/media/2011/apr/13/news-of-the-world-phone-hacking, Accessed online 14 April 2011.

[4] AusCERT, http://www.auscert.org.au/, Accessed online 14 April 2011.

It could also mean infecting an organisation's systems with a malicious virus. Black hackers may be individuals, organisations or governments.

And then there's something quite different, known as:

2.1.4 Crackers

For many, hacking is about learning new skills to gain a better understanding of how the digital network operates. Hacking, to crackers, is a hobby, a chance to be part of a group activity.

Will they graduate 1 day to black leather pants and dank basements? It's perfectly possible.

Sadly, for every "good" hacker there are countless others who act from less than noble motives, and follow well-worn paths to reach their goals.

2.1.5 Hack Attacks

The most common types of these are:

1) **Distributed Denial of Service or DDoS**
   Simply put, this involves hackers overloading a site's server with too many requests. There's nothing particularly sophisticated about this type of attack, but it's one of the most effective if executed on a large scale.
2) **Website hacking**
   This involves hackers bypassing the security parameters of a website, gaining access to its administrator panel, then adding or removing information (e.g. adding a page that carries a personal message from the hacker, or adding sexually explicit images on a site's landing pages).
   Viruses are, in their own way, a form of hacking.

2.1.6 Stuxnet

A particularly frightening example of these types of attacks was last year's "Stuxnet" attacks.[5]

This highly sophisticated computer worm infection infiltrated systems in Iranian nuclear plants, halting scheduled operations between June and September.

Which, in some way, brings us back to WarGames and, in my mind at least, the Wild West.

---

[5] A Declaration of Cyber-War, http://www.vanityfair.com/culture/features/2011/04/stuxnet-201104, Accessed online 14 April 2011.

In the Wild West, destruction caused by outlaws, over many years, led to the introduction of new laws, and the end of a free-for-all mentality to shared and relied-upon resources.

Has the time now arrived to impose tougher laws on hacking?

Read more on this topic:

Location, location: who's watching you (and why)?[6]

2.2   Anonymous, Child Porn and the Wild, Wild Web

28 October 2011

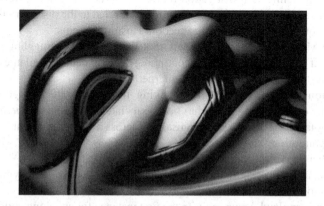

Is it right for hackers, regardless of public support, to take the law into their own hands?
Source: **AnonymousMXPT CC0**[7]

High-profile hacktivist group Anonymous[8] has turned its attention to fighting child pornography.

As a sign of what it pledges will become more widespread, the group this month launched an attack on[9] a server by the name of Freedom Hosting. In doing so, the group claimed to have temporarily disabled more than 40 child pornography sites on a hidden network while publishing a list of more than 1,500 of those sites' usernames online.

---

[6]Location, location: who's watching you (and why)?, http://theconversation.edu.au/location-location-whos-watching-you-and-why-691, Accessed online 14 April 2011.

[7]AnonymousMXPT, Flickr, http://www.flickr.com/photos/anonymousmxpt/8261353788/sizes/l/in/photostream/, Accessed online 21 December 2012.

[8]Anonymous (group), Wikipedia, http://en.wikipedia.org/wiki/Anonymous_(group, Accessed online 28 October 2011.

[9]Hacker group Anonymous' new target: Child pornography websites, TheWeek, http://theweek.com/article/index/220708/hacker-group-anonymousnew-target-child-pornography-websites, Accessed online 28 October 2011.

Similar denial-of-service (DDoS) attacks,[10] we can assume, will follow in what anonymous is calling Operation Darknet, or #OpDarknet.

The move on Freedom Hosting forced the company to switch to back-up systems, although this was not effective—Anonymous attacked again and forced Freedom Hosting offline.

In a statement posted online,[11] Anonymous claims to have evidence of Freedom Hosting's guilt: "For this," the statement reads, "Freedom Hosting has been declared #OpDarknet Enemy Number One".

The group claims: "The owners and operators at Freedom Hosting are openly supporting child pornography and enabling pedophiles (sic) to view innocent children, fuelling their issues and putting children at risk of abduction, molestation, rape, and death."

Anonymous claims its investigation into the "darknet", including websites that permit the operators and users to hide their identities, led to the discovery that many of the child pornography links led to Freedom Hosting systems.

At a time when police and governments around the world are struggling to combat cyber crime, it's interesting to see the continuing development of vigilante activism. The Wild West has been re-born on the internet.

Anonymous is well-known[12] for hacking into corporate and government websites. The ever-evolving group has been associated with civil disobedience and hacktivism—targeting attacks on organisations across a spectrum of entertainment, religious organisations and businesses.

"To catch a Predator" Anonymous YouTube video[13]

Of course, as is apparent in the name, one of the key goals of Anonymous is for its members to remain hidden from sight.

Society may applaud Anonymous in the first instance for attacking child pornographers, but concern must surely be raised that Freedom Hosting has been attacked in this manner without charge, trial and conviction.

In the YouTube video above, an eerie blend of voices representing Anonymous state: "Many of us have lingering traumatic images of the material that these pedophiles (sic) were hiding on the darknet.

"Anonymous took a pledge to defend the defenseless (sic) and fight for the fallen [...] The darknet is a vast sea of many providers. However, we fully intend to make it uninhabitable for these disgusting degenerates to exist."

The group's online statement regarding the DDoS attack reads: "By taking down Freedom Hosting, we are eliminating 40+ child pornography websites, among these

---

[10]Zombie computers, cyber security, phishing … what you need to know, http://theconversation. edu.au/zombie-computers-cyber-security-phishing-what-you-need-to-know-1671,   Accessed online 28 October 2011.

[11]#OpDarknet Major Release and Timeline, http://pastebin.com/T1LHnzEW, Accessed online 28 October 2011.

[12]Anonymous, http://theconversation.edu.au/pages/anonymous, Accessed online 28 October 2011.

[13]"To catch a Predator" Anonymous: The fight against child pornography Operation Darknet (#OpDarknet), http://www.youtube.com/watch?v=TcNimk1SJvA, Accessed online 28 October 2011.

is *Lolita City*, one of the largest child pornography websites to date containing more than 100 GB of child pornography."

Clearly the guns are out of their holsters. Anonymous has vowed to continue to act, possibly because its members believe government is not doing enough to halt the transmission of child pornography over the internet.

And yet if the group had actual evidence of a criminal offence being committed by organisations utilising Freedom Hosting, most people might expect them to hand this information to the police and be prepared to support the investigation.

This matter should be followed closely to see what response there is from Freedom Hosting—not least by the authorities, who should investigate whether the Anonymous claims are correct.

2.3 Fear and Loathing in Las Vegas: Tipping a Black Hat to the DefCon Hackers

8 August 2011

Las Vegas has a long association with people on the fringe of society but even Hunter S. Thompson's characters Raoul Duke and his drug-soaked Samoan lawyer[14] would have found visitors to the DefCon hacker conference[15] at the extreme edge of these fringes.

As the late, great Gonzo journalist would have put it: "There was madness in any direction, at any hour. You could strike sparks anywhere."

This year's DefCon, named after the US military's "defense readiness condition"[16], was held from August 4 to August 7.

It followed on from the Black Hat 2011 conference, also held in Las Vegas (from July 30 to August 4), which brought together academics, professional security experts and hackers alike.

Of the two conferences, Black Hat is probably the more serious (and tamer).

This year, Black Hat was in the news thanks to demonstrations of how to electronically and remotely unlock and start a Subaru Outback.[17]

The hack[18] involved a man-in-the-middle attack[19] with the hackers setting up their own GSM network[20] to intercept messages sent to the car's management systems and reading the contents before passing them on.

---

[14]Fear and Loathing in Las Vegas, http://en.wikipedia.org/wiki/Fear_and_Loathing_in_Las_Vegas, Accessed 8 August 2011.

[15]DEF CON Hacking Conference, http://www.defcon.org/, Accessed 8 August 2011.

[16]DEFCON, http://en.wikipedia.org/wiki/DEFCON, Accessed 8 August 2011.

[17]Hackers break into Subaru Outback via text message, http://www.engadget.com/2011/08/04/hackers-break-into-subaru-outback-via-text-message/, Accessed 8 August 2011.

[18]Hacking, cracking and the wild, wild web, http://theconversation.edu.au/hacking-cracking-and-the-wild-wild-web-738, Accessed 8 August 2011.

[19]Man-in-the-middle attack, http://en.wikipedia.org/wiki/Man-in-the-middle_attack, Accessed 8 August 2011.

[20]GSM, http://en.wikipedia.org/wiki/GSM, Accessed 8 August 2011.

Access codes gathered in this way could then be used to control the car, opening the doors and starting the engine. Known as "war-texting"[21], the technique can be used with a wide variety of equipment including security cameras and power- and water-supply sensors.

Another development that attracted some coverage was the (theoretical) ability to hack a person's insulin pump[22] and get it to administer a fatal dose.

Also at Black Hat, researchers from Carnegie Mellon University[23] demonstrated how they could use facial recognition software[24] on Facebook profile photos[25] (and photos from other sites) to identify people and gather a considerable amount of information about those identified.

Less well-publicised were talks on how to set up and defend a crisis map,[26] which are increasingly being used to collate information from social media[27] to establish an accurate picture of what is happening during crises such as Egyptian uprising.

Governments would have a huge interest in disrupting these services if they thought they were being used for the benefit of those involved in the revolution.

2.3.1   DefCon

Where Black Hat is a more serious and security-oriented conference, DefCon is more of a social event, with a greater emphasis on hacking than traditional security applications.

The conference was founded in 1993 by "Dark Tangent"[28] (Jeff Moss) as a party for hackers. Since then it has grown more than 15,000 attendees.

Journalists attending DefCon were warned[29] to leave credit cards at home, to not use their telephones and not to connect to any wireless network unless it was using a secure connection.

---

[21] Link no longer goes to specified page, https://www.isecpartners.com/storage/docs/presentations/iSEC_BH2011_War_Texting.pdf, Accessed 8 August 2011.

[22] Black Hat: Insulin pumps can be hacked, http://www.scmagazine.com/black-hat-insulin-pumps-can-be-hacked/article/209106/, Accessed 8 August 2011.

[23] Face-matching with Facebook profiles: How it was done, http://news.cnet.com/8301-31921_3-20088456-281/face-matching-with-facebook-profiles-how-it-was-done/, Accessed 8 August 2011.

[24] Facial recognition technology, http://theconversation.edu.au/pages/facial-recognition-technology, Accessed 8 August 2011.

[25] Facebook and facial recognition – you've been tagged http://theconversation.edu.au/facebook-and-facial-recognition-youve-been-tagged-1776, Accessed 8 August 2011.

[26] Link no longer goes to specified page, http://www.blackhat.com/docs/webcast/usa11preview_chamales.pdf, Accessed 8 August 2011.

[27] Crisis management: using Twitter and Facebook for the greater good, http://theconversation.edu.au/crisis-management-using-twitter-and-facebook-for-the-greater-good-2439, Accessed 8 August 2011.

[28] Jeff Moss (hacker), http://en.wikipedia.org/wiki/Jeff_Moss_%28hacker%29, Accessed 8 August 2011.

[29] DEF CON: The event that scares hackers, http://edition.cnn.com/2011/TECH/web/08/05/def.con.hackers/index.html?npt=NP1&on.cnn=1, Accessed 8 August 2011.

Within hours of the conference opening, hackers had interfered with the software controlling the lifts and, allegedly, ATM machines, poker machines, the public address system and lighting at the venue.

While conferences such as DefCon are primarily male-dominated affairs—around 90 % of attendees at this year's event—a 10-year-old girl known as CyFi,[30] founder of DefCon Kids[31] caused a bit of a stir after revealing a security exploit she had found.

She found the zero-day exploit[32] in games on iPhones and Android devices. The exploit allowed CyFi to "speed up" time in Farm-style games where rewards and achievements only occur after a certain period of time.

2.3.2 Government Hackers

This year's DefCon also saw an appearance by representatives from the US National Security Agency[33] (NSA) and other secret service organisations, groups that were actively recruiting "cyber warriors"[34] from conference attendees and speakers.

As cyber security[35] increasingly becomes a major area of concern for nations around the world, recruitment in this area has risen accordingly.

Such attention has not necessarily been welcomed by the hacker community. An open letter was published last week,[36] calling for hackers not to "sell out" to the NSA.

And of course no article on hacking would be complete without a mention of LulzSec and Anonymous,[37] the current hacktivists du-jour.

Obligingly, DefCon hosted a discussion panel[38] featuring an at-times heated discussion about the groups' activities.

---

[30] 10 year old girl hacker CyFi reveal her first zero-day in Game at #DefCon 19, http://thehackernews.com/2011/08/10-year-old-girl-hacker-cyfi-reveal-her.html, Accessed 8 August 2011.

[31] DEFCON Kids, http://www.defconkids.org/, Accessed 8 August 2011.

[32] Zero Day Exploits - Holy Grail Of The Malicious Hacker, http://netsecurity.about.com/od/newsandeditorial1/a/aazeroday.htm, Accessed 8 August 2011.

[33] Welcome to the National Security Agency, http://www.nsa.gov/, Accessed online 1 July 2013.

[34] Zakaria, Tabassum, Defcon Hacker Convention: Government Cybersecurity Experts Looking To Recruit Top Hacking Brass In Las Vegas, http://www.huffingtonpost.com/2011/08/02/defcon-hacker-convention-government-cybersecurity_n_915853.html? Accessed online 1 July 2013.

[35] Cyber security, http://theconversation.com/topics/cyber-security, Accessed online 1 July 2013.

[36] DJ Pangburn, An Open Letter to Defcon Hackers: Don't Sell Out to the NSA, http://www.deathandtaxesmag.com/127506/an-open-letter-to-defcon-hackers-dont-sell-out-to-the-nsa/, Accessed online 1 July 2013.

[37] Wright, Craig S, Are Anonymous and LulzSec about to hack PayPal for WikiLeaks? http://theconversation.com/are-anonymous-and-lulzsec-about-to-hack-paypal-for-wikileaks-2582, Accessed online 1 July 2013.

[38] Takahashi, Dean, Defcon panel: Anonymous is here. LulzSec is here. They're everywhere, http://venturebeat.com/2011/08/06/defcon-panel-anonymous-is-here-lulzsec-is-here-theyre-everywhere/, Accessed online 1 July 2013.

There was some suggestion that the hackivists should focus their efforts on unearthing corruption or child exploitation web sites, rather than hacking for fun[39] or other, less noble, reasons.

It was suggested there were members of LulzSec and Anonymous both in the audience and generally attending the conference.

In many ways, these conferences highlight that it is possibly not the widely-publicised hacks—such as those carried out by LulzSec and Anonymous—that we should be concerned about.

With computers increasingly interfacing with every part of our lives, it is the undetected and subtle ways in which hackers can take control of these interfaces that is of most concern.

And as recent global events[40] have highlighted, it is possibly not just the teen-age hackers we should be worried about but the governments who are employing them.

As Thompson might have put it: "When the going gets weird, the weird turn pro."

2.4   Are Anonymous Hackers Really on Trial, or Is FBI Payback Misdirected?

5 September 2011

It's a scene reminiscent of a thousand police dramas: the FBI arrived[41] at the door of 20-year-old journalism student Mercedes Haefer,[42] guns drawn, at 6 a.m. one morning last July.

She was still in her pyjamas, getting ready for work.

Haefer is one of 14 individuals who last week pleaded not-guilty in San Jose for waging cyber-attacks against e-commerce giant PayPal.[43]

The warrant for Haefer stated federal officers were looking for anything associated with hacking, infiltrating or Distributed Denial of Service (DDoS) attacks.[44]

---

[39] Branch, Philip, LulzSec takes down CIA website in the name of fun, fun, fun, Accessed online 1 July 2013.

[40] Wright, Craig S, World's biggest-ever cyber attacks uncovered – and it's only the beginning, http://theconversation.com/worlds-biggest-ever-cyber-attacks-uncovered-and-its-only-the-beginning-2677, Accessed online 1 July 2013.

[41] An Interview With a Target of the FBI's Anonymous Probe, http://gawker.com/5757995/an-interview-with-a-target-of-the-fbis-anonymous-probe, Accessed on 5 September 2011.

[42] FBI Exposes The Terrifying Face Of "Anonymous", http://www.thesmokinggun.com/documents/internet/fbi-exposes-terrifying-face-anonymous-748293, Accessed on 5 September 2011.

[43] PayPal, https://www.paypal.com/au/webapps/mpp/home, Accessed on 5 September 2011.

[44] Zombie computers, cyber security, phishing … what you need to know, http://theconversation.edu.au/zombie-computers-cyber-security-phishing-what-you-need-to-know-1671, Accessed on 5 September 2011.

Oh, and they were looking for a Guy Fawkes mask—evidence that would link Mercedes with the hacker group Anonymous (who have claimed such masks as their own) and, specifically, Operation Payback.[45]

2.4.1   Payback

Operation Payback saw DDoS attacks on a number of companies, in particular Paypal. Anonymous claimed the attacks were retribution for decisions by executives at these companies to withdraw payment facilities from Wikileaks.[46]

The FBI knew Haefer was associated with Anonymous because of her involvement on the group's IRC[47] channels, where she was known as "NO".

But she denied[48] having taken part directly in any of the DDoS attacks on PayPal.

Haefer was indicted[49] along with 13 others on two charges of causing damage against PayPal's computers. They carry a maximum penalty of 15 years in jail and a fine of $500,000. Two other people were charged separately.

Haefer is enrolled in a journalism and media pre-major course at the University of Nevada and Las Vegas.[50]

Commenting on the charges against Haefer, the director of the Hank Greenspun School of Journalism and Media,[51] Professor Daniel Stout said, "We don't condone unethical behavior that results in the harm of the audience."

He also said that if Haefer had continued her studies she would have taken courses that ultimately produce journalists with a strong sense of ethics (Haefer is still enrolled at UNLV and Professor Stout has since moderated his comments[52]).

Despite a superficial understanding of what a DDoS attack comprises (and despite the fact Haefer had not been tried when he made his statement), he was ready to brand both the act and Haefer as criminal and unethical.

---

[45]Operation Payback: WikiLeaks Avenged by Hacktivists, http://www.pcworld.com/article/212701/operation_payback_wikileaks_avenged_by_hactivists.html, Accessed on 5 September 2011.

[46]WikiLeaks Supporter 'Operation Payback' Targets PayPal, Amazon, http://www.pcmag.com/article2/0,2817,2374090,00.asp, Accessed on 5 September 2011.

[47]Internet Relay Chat, http://en.wikipedia.org/wiki/Internet_Relay_Chat, Accessed on 5 September 2011.

[48]An Interview With a Target of the FBI's Anonymous Probe, http://gawker.com/5757995/an-interview-with-a-target-of-the-fbis-anonymous-probe, Accessed on 5 September 2011.

[49]Consumer credit cashing, http://freemercedes.org/, Accessed on 5 September 2011.

[50]UNLV student arrested by FBI for hacking in support of Wikileaks, http://www.unlvrebelyell.com/2011/07/25/unlv-student-arrested-by-fbi-for-hacking-in-support-of-wikileaks/, Accessed on 5 September 2011.

[51]Jessica Zimmerman JMS's Outstanding Graduate Student for November, http://journalism.unlv.edu/, Accessed on 5 September 2011.

[52]Haefer asserts innocence, http://www.unlvrebelyell.com/2011/08/08/haefer-asserts-innocence/, Accessed on 5 September 2011.

In an examination of the ethics of DDoS attacks[53] Gabriella Coleman,[54] a socio-cultural anthropologist at New York University, makes a distinction between criminal acts such as hacking and non-violent political acts such as sit-ins.

In doing so, she raises the possibility of regarding DDoS as the digital equivalent of an occupation.

That said, in the case of a sit-in, the aim may include being arrested to draw more attention to a cause—and it's not clear that any of the alleged members of Anonymous were anticipating being arrested.

The indictment used for the so-called Anonymous 16 includes the charge of intentional damage to a computer.

2.4.2 DDoS

A DDoS works by sending repeated requests to a website very quickly, exhausting resources and blocking access to regular users.

In the grand scheme of hacks, DDoS is a nuisance but not a major threat to a company, unlike, say, losing the details of user accounts and passwords.

This was a view shared by Deputy Assistant FBI Director Steven Chabinski.[55]

"There has not been a large-scale trend toward using hacking to actually destroy websites, [but] that could be appealing to both criminals or terrorists," Chabinsky told radio station NPR[56] in July.

"That's where the 'hacktivism,' even if currently viewed by some as a nuisance, shows the potential to be destabilizing."

Ethics

Leaving aside considerations as to whether DDoS attacks are themselves ethical, the charge that the Anons lack a sense of ethics, as suggested by Professor Stout and others, seems even less certain.

If anything, it's the Anons' sense of righting the wrongs of corporations and governments that underpins most of their activities.

Haefer said she became interested in the activities of Anonymous in part because of a sense of injustice at the inappropriate punishment for a woman accused of distributing 24 songs.

She was referring to the US$2 million fine imposed on Jammie Thomas-Rasset for sharing music, a fine which was later reduced to a US$54,000.

---

[53] The ethics of digital direct action, http://www.aljazeera.com/indepth/opinion/2011/08/20118308455825769.html, Accessed on 5 September 2011.

[54] Gabriella Coleman, http://steinhardt.nyu.edu/faculty_bios/view/Gabriella_Coleman, Accessed on 5 September 2011.

[55] FBI Tries To Send Message With Hacker Arrests, http://www.npr.org/2011/07/20/138555799/fbi-arrests-alleged-anonymous-hackers, Accessed on 5 September 2011.

[56] FBI Tries To Send Message With Hacker Arrests, http://www.npr.org/2011/07/20/138555799/fbi-arrests-alleged-anonymous-hackers, Accessed on 5 September 2011.

Haefer's case can be contrasted by that of a 16-year-old woman from France who claimed the hack of San Fransisco's Bay Area Rapid Transport Police Officers Association last month.

The young hacker had released the personal details of 100 officers. Going by the handle "Lamaline_5mg", she claimed this was her first hack, and that she had little experience and had picked up enough information to hack the site in less than 4 h.

Whereas Haefer claimed no previous technical knowledge, Lamaline was technically savvy enough to use techniques to cover her tracks, making her protestations of technical naivety slightly suspect.

Interestingly, Lamaline had not associated herself with Anonymous—in fact, some people on an Anonymous chat room condemned the attack as irresponsible.

2.4.3 Kicking an Open Door

One confounding factor in the actions of Anons is the relatively low barrier to entry for participation.

A simple search online will provide links to downloadable software to enable the participation in a DDoS.

Software such as the LOIC is simple to use and requires no technical expertise. There are readily accessible videos that demonstrate their use.

Anyone can go on to the Anonymous IRC channel and listen in. You can follow the activities of Anonymous and others on Twitter.

Accompanying this ease of access is the separation of actions and consequence— a separation encapsulated by using DDoS software.

Unsophisticated users would potentially struggle to understand how traceable their actions are.

The fact the FBI had little trouble in rounding up the 14 suspects being tried together in the DDoS attacks is more a testament to the ease of tracing individuals than a reflection of the technical abilities of the FBI.

Their single unifying feature of those[57] arrested in connection with Operation Payback is their young age, given most of those charged are in their twenties.

The reaction against Anonymous from the general public, lawmakers and security specialists comes across almost as a generational conflict.

This is epitomised by Haefer having to leave her father's home because he supposedly viewed his daughter (in Haefer's words) as "a terrorist".

And Haefer? She still believes[58] in the positive things Anonymous is doing and is looking forward to making that known, without a mask, at her day in court.

---

[57]FBI Exposes The Terrifying Face Of "Anonymous", http://www.thesmokinggun.com/file/paypal-service-attack?page=0, Accessed on 5 September 2011.

[58]Haefer asserts innocence, http://www.unlvrebelyell.com/2011/08/08/haefer-asserts-innocence/, Accessed on 5 September 2011.

2.5   Comodo Hacker, TurkGuvenligi…Out for Lulz
   or Breaking the Internet?

12 September 2011

Two recent hacking incidents have highlighted the increasing fragility of the internet's core infrastructure. They serve as a stark reminder that online security is somewhat illusory.

The weaknesses have been known for some time but the move to implement solutions has lacked momentum.

But events in the past few months may have pushed internet providers to a tipping point.

2.5.1   Comodo Hacker Breaks SSL

The more serious of the two incidents was carried out by a hacker called the Comodo Hacker,[59] or Ich Sun[60] as his Twitter account was known.

In March, he hacked[61] a company called Comodo,[62] which is responsible for issuing certificates[63] that underpin the secure internet protocol SSL,[64] or Secure Sockets Layer—a cryptographic protocol that provides communication security.

These certificates are highly visible: you can see them when the padlock icon appears on a browser URL when you are connected to a secure site—for example, your bank.

Essentially, the hacker was able to use Comodo to create fake certificates for sites such as google.com and long.yahoo.com.[65]

This hack was detected and disclosed early and its consequences were limited.

At the time, the hacker was identified as a 21-year-old Iranian national from information that he released.[66]

---

[59] Hacker claims he can exploit Windows Update, http://www.computerworld.com/s/article/9219876/Hacker_claims_he_can_exploit_Windows_Update?taxonomyId=89, Accessed on 12 September 2011.

[60] Ich Sun Rising – The Story Of How SSL Certificate Authorities Died, http://diceylee.blogspot.com.au/2011/09/ich-sun-rising-story-of-how-ssl.html, Accessed on 12 September 2011.

[61] Google, Yahoo, Skype targeted in attack linked to Iran, http://news.cnet.com/8301-31921_3-20046340-281.html?tag=mncol;txt, Accessed on 12 September 2011.

[62] Comodo, http://www.comodo.com/, Accessed on 12 September 2011.

[63] What is SSL and what are Certificates? http://tldp.org/HOWTO/SSL-Certificates-HOWTO/x64.html, Accessed on 12 September 2011.

[64] Transport Layer Security, http://en.wikipedia.org/wiki/Secure_Sockets_Layer, Accessed on 12 September 2011.

[65] Iranian hackers obtain fraudulent HTTPS certificates: How close to a Web security meltdown did we get? https://www.eff.org/deeplinks/2011/03/iranian-hackers-obtain-fraudulent-https, Accessed on 12 September 2011.

[66] ComodoHacker's Pastebin, http://pastebin.com/u/ComodoHacker, Accessed on 12 September 2011.

The hacker wanted to impress the world with his skill, and sought to justify the hack as retaliation against what he perceived as actions by the US and Israel, in particular, in their role in the Stuxnet virus attack[67] against an Iranian nuclear facility.

He insisted he was working alone and not, as allegations had claimed, that the attack was organised by the Iranian Government.[68]

2.5.2   Comodo Hacker Reprised

The Comodo hacker promised more to come, and was true to his word. Last month, the Dutch security company Fox-IT[69] was asked to investigate the appearance of a rogue certificate for google.com online.

Although the certificate had been identified and revoked (effectively cancelled) on August 29, the hacker had compromised DigiNotar,[70] the company responsible for issuing the certificate, during the period from June 27 to July 22.

There is evidence[71] the google.com certificate had been used in Iran to fool users into thinking they were connecting securely to Google sites when, in fact, they were probably logging into sites controlled by the Iranian Government.

All communication, emails, usernames and passwords would have been available in unencrypted form.

The fact the certificates were being used to spy on the Iranian people was bad enough, but the problems didn't stop there.

It turned out that DigiNotar, based in the Netherlands, was also responsible for issuing certificates for the Netherlands Government,[72] among many other companies and organisations.

The hacker had issued 531 certificates from DigiNotar. This caused the browser manufacturers, Google, Mozilla (Firefox), Microsoft and eventually Apple to

---

[67] A Declaration of Cyber-War, http://www.vanityfair.com/culture/features/2011/04/stuxnet-201104, Accessed on 12 September 2011.

[68] Comodo Report of Incident - Comodo detected and thwarted an intrusion on 26-MAR-2011, https://www.comodo.com/Comodo-Fraud-Incident-2011-03-23.html, Accessed on 12 September 2011.

[69] Fox-IT, http://www.rijksoverheid.nl/bestanden/documenten-en-publicaties/rapporten/2011/09/05/diginotar-public-report-version-1/rapport-fox-it-operation-black-tulip-v1-0.pdf, Accessed on 12 September 2011.

[70] Link no longer goes to specified page, http://www.diginotar.com/, Accessed on 12 September 2011.

[71] Google users in Iran targeted in certificate scam, http://www.google.com/hostednews/afp/article/ALeqM5g4RgXPBowpoyZnscQ8o7-L4AlOpQ?docId=CNG.9e34c99182f5659a398b6521776 6ca17.21, Accessed on 12 September 2011.

[72] Dutch Government Struggles to Deal With DigiNotar Hack, http://www.pcworld.com/article/239639/dutch_government_struggles_to_deal_with_diginotar_hack.html, Accessed on 12 September 2011.

remove DigiNotar from their list of trusted Certificate Authorities[73] (CAs) and issue patches[74] to their software.

The Dutch Government and other DigiNotar customers will need to replace all of their DigiNotar certificates with certificates from another CA.

2.5.3   TurkGuvenligi Breaks DNS

Another hacker (group) was, in the meantime, subverting a different piece of the internet. This hack was by someone calling himself TurkGuvenligi (The Legend)[75] and basically involved a technique of DNS Hijacking.[76]

The Domain Name System (DNS) is the way names such as http://www.google.com are translated into numbers, allowing programs to communicate with each other over the internet.

DNS Hijacking involves substituting the real address for another one.

So in the case of the TurkGuvenligi hack, sites such as Vodafone, The Register, The Telegraph and National Geographic were pointed to a website with the TurkGuvenligi name and a statement celebrating "World Hackers Day".

The importance of the TurkGuvenligi hack is that, combined with fake SSL certificates, it means a person would have no idea they were not at the real site.

In the past, security professionals[77] have claimed a spoofed DNS would not matter so much because, if you used a secure SSL connection, the browser would alert you to the fact that the certificate wasn't correct.

By combining the Comodo Hacker's exploit with that of TurkGuvenligi's DNS attack you have a situation whereby literally anyone could fool a very large number of people into thinking there was nothing wrong.

2.5.4   The Internet Is Broken

Society has increasingly come to rely on the internet for almost every aspect of life, from commerce through to health, personal expression and political dissent.

---

[73] Certificate authority, http://en.wikipedia.org/wiki/Certificate_authority, Accessed on 12 September 2011.

[74] What is a software patch? http://www.oss-watch.ac.uk/resources/softwarepatch, Accessed on 12 September 2011.

[75] Theregister.co.uk, Vodafone, Telegraph, Acer, National Geographic got hacked by Turkguvenligi, http://thehackernews.com/2011/09/theregistercouk-biggest-news-site-got.html#_, Accessed on 12 September 2011.

[76] DNS hijacking, http://en.wikipedia.org/wiki/DNS_hijacking, Accessed on 12 September 2011.

[77] How to protect from man-in-the-middle attacks, http://www.net-security.org/secworld.php?id=7087, Accessed on 12 September 2011.

A great deal of this activity relies on being able to operate securely when needed.

When you are using your bank account, buying something online or organising a demonstration against a policy you don't agree with, you need a secure connection to a legitimate site.

The events of the past few months have highlighted that we cannot rely on the current infrastructure to provide any sort of guarantee of a secure environment.

2.5.5 Solutions to Fix the Internet?

So, are there any alternatives to the current infrastructure that would be better?

On the SSL side, the Perspectives Project[78] from Carnegie Mellon University has released a solution called "Convergence".

In this scheme, instead of having a list of Certificate Authorities dictated by the browser, you can nominate people you trust (such as your local university) to validate a site that you are visiting.

The benefit of this is that you can change the list and have as many or as few "notaries" validate the site for you.

Another alternative to DNS that also helps with the SSL problem, but does not completely solve it, is DNSSEC,[79] or Domain Name System Security Extensions, a suite specifications for securing certain kinds of information provided by DNS.

This provides security extensions to DNS and attempts to resolve the underlying problems[80] with DNS hijacking.

Unlike Convergence, DNSSEC requires governments and internet providers to implement the fix. Coordination is only beginning to happen.[81]

Whatever the full extent of the motives of these hackers, a clear outcome is that the internet is vulnerable to exploitation by governments, terrorists, criminals, activists and lulz-seekers.

Staying safe online can certainly be helped by awareness and good security practice, but greater truths are emerging.

Your internet security increasingly comes down to the fact you weren't in the wrong place at the wrong time.

---

[78]What is Perspectives? http://perspectives-project.org/, Accessed on 12 September 2011.

[79]Domain Name System Security Extensions, http://en.wikipedia.org/wiki/Domain_Name_System_Security_Extensions, Accessed on 12 September 2011.

[80]DigiNotar SSL Breach, http://isc.sans.edu/diary/DigiNotar+SSL+Breach/11479, Accessed on 12 September 2011.

[81]DNSSEC Takes Off in Wake of Root Zone Signing, http://www.circleid.com/posts/20110830_dnssec_takes_off_in_wake_of_root_zone_signing/, Accessed on 12 September 2011.

2.6 Betrayed? LulzSec Arrest Over Sony Hack Reveals Trust Issues

5 October 2011

On September 22, 23-year-old college student Cody Kretsinger was arrested by the FBI[82] for his part in the hack of Sony Pictures Entertainment by the high-profile hacking group LulzSec.[83]

The hack resulted in the exposed information of more than 37,500 people who had registered for online promotions.[84] The hack itself and the reasons behind it have become secondary, but it was part of a campaign against Sony[85] by the hacking groups Anonymous[86] and LulzSec after the company pursued Sony PlayStation three games hackers and in particular George Holt, or "GeoHot".

2.6.1 Betrayal

What made this arrest notable is that the FBI tracked Kretsinger, or "recursion" as he was also known, by obtaining logs of his activity from a proxy service provider called Hide My Ass (HMA).[87]

HMA was aware LulzSec members had been using their services from chat logs publicised by The Guardian newspaper[88] but had chosen not to do anything about it. This changed when they were allegedly served with a court order in the UK.[89]

There is now some expectation that a second LulzSec hacker, "Neuron", who had also admitted to using the HMA service, might be tracked down.[90]

---

[82] Member of Hacking Group LulzSec Arrested for June 2011 Intrusion of Sony Pictures Computer Systems, http://www.fbi.gov/losangeles/press-releases/2011/member-of-hacking-group-lulzsec-arrested-for-June-2011-intrusion-of-sony-pictures-computer-systems, Accessed on 5 October 2011.

[83] LulzSec takes down CIA website in the name of fun, fun, fun, http://theconversation.edu.au/lulzsec-takes-down-cia-website-in-the-name-of-fun-fun-fun-1858, Accessed on 5 October 2011.

[84] Cody Kretsinger, Arizona College Student, Charged In Sony Hacking Case, http://www.huffingtonpost.com/2011/09/23/cody-kretsinger-arizona-c_n_977490.html, Accessed on 5 October 2011.

[85] Operation Payback brings you #OpSony, http://www.anonnews.org/?p=press&a=item&i=787, Accessed on 5 October 2011.

[86] Are Anonymous hackers really on trial, or is FBI payback misdirected? http://theconversation.edu.au/are-anonymous-hackers-really-on-trial-or-is-fbi-payback-misdirected-3205, Accessed on 5 October 2011.

[87] Hide My Ass! Free Proxy and Privacy Tools, http://hidemyass.com/, Accessed on 5 October 2011.

[88] LulzSec IRC leak: the full record, http://www.guardian.co.uk/technology/2011/jun/24/lulzsec-irc-leak-the-full-record, Accessed on 5 October 2011.

[89] Lulzsec fiasco, http://blog.hidemyass.com/2011/09/23/lulzsec-fiasco/, Accessed on 5 October 2011.

[90] Second LulzSec hacker 'Neuron' could be tracked down via UK VPN, http://www.guardian.co.uk/technology/2011/sep/26/lulzsec-second-hacker?INTCMP=ILCNETTXT3487, Accessed on 5 October 2011.

2.6.2 Just Business, Right?

The actions of HMA in handing over logs to the FBI has been a rude awakening for many and has sparked condemnation from commentators on Twitter.[91]

It illustrates that many in the hacker community have strong principles that they expect others of like mind to hold—it's just who happens to be in the group of "like minds" at any one time that's the issue.

HMA is a commercial company that markets its services by exploiting the idea it's supportive of the hacker's cause—even somewhat cynically exploiting its role[92] in aiding Egyptian protesters in circumventing government censorship to access Twitter.

To many in the West, including in government and security circles, there's nothing wrong with helping an Egyptian resident to break a law in a country whose government had effectively lost support. The issue is not a moral one, but simply a practical one, given it's less likely the Egyptian Government would be able to obtain a UK court order to persuade a service such as HMA to hand over logs.

Representatives of other virtual private network[93] (VPL) service providers such as AirVPN[94] (which allow users to appear as if they are on a different network) have come out to condemn HMA's actions and question statements issued by the company that "all VPN providers keep logs".

AirVPN does not keep logs and accepts anonymous payment by online currency provider Bitcoin.[95] Privacy International[96] has also questioned the actions of a provider that sells itself on the ability to keep your online activity anonymous and untraceable.

2.6.3 Staying Hidden on the Internet

In the chatroom logs[97] of several LulzSec hackers there's some discussion about how to stay secure and, in particular, how to use VPN technology to remain unidentified.

---

[91] Get instant updates on #hidemyass, https://twitter.com/search/realtime/%23hidemyass, Accessed on 5 October 2011.

[92] Lulzsec fiasco, http://blog.hidemyass.com/2011/09/23/lulzsec-fiasco/, Accessed on 5 October 2011.

[93] Virtual private network, http://en.wikipedia.org/wiki/Virtual_Private_Network, Accessed on 5 October 2011.

[94] Important notice about security, https://airvpn.org/index.php?option=com_kunena&func=view&catid=2&id=891&Itemid=142#891, Accessed on 5 October 2011.

[95] Bitcoin: a pirate's booty or the new global currency? http://theconversation.edu.au/bitcoin-a-pirates-booty-or-the-new-global-currency-3130, Accessed on 5 October 2011.

[96] Enjoy internet freedom and anonymity, https://www.privacyinternational.org/blog/enjoy-internet-freedom-and-anonymity-terms-and-conditions-apply, Accessed on 5 October 2011.

[97] LulzSec private log, http://pastebin.com/QZXBCBYt, Accessed on 5 October 2011.

VPN service providers establish servers in multiple countries and allow users to connect to these.

The most common use for this would be to appear as if you are a user in the US, for example, to bypass any restrictions imposed by your local internet service provider or government.

The uses of this technology range from Chinese residents wanting to access blocked sites such as Facebook to residents outside the US wanting to watch streaming video that is only available to US residents.

goblinbox (queen of the ad hoc bento).

The issue with VPN services is that, as the HMA/LulzSec episode has highlighted, the HMA has no obligation to keep private the details of the communication through their services.

Although HMA representatives claimed in this case they were served a court order, there's no evidence the company received anything other than a request from the FBI.

As the company is UK-based, it seems unlikely the FBI would have been able to obtain a UK court order for an activity that occurred in the US.

Rather, people at HMA may have been concerned their business would have been affected and servers in the US shut down.

There is also another possibility: services such as HMA are sometimes (whether rightly or wrongly) referred to as "Honeypots"—sites set up by authorities to masquerade as independent commercial operations.

2.6.4   Tor: A Better Path to Anonymity?

Given HMA is a commercial organisation, it was curious that the LulzSec hackers would have used it and others like it. An alternative to the commercial services is a service called Tor.[98]

Tor was originally developed as a project of the US Naval Research Laboratory[99] and received further support from the Electronic Frontier Foundation EFF[100] and other donors.

It works by encrypting traffic from a user's computer and sending it through a number of Tor Servers that are run by volunteers.

The message is encrypted and re-encrypted: each time it passes through a server, a layer of encryption is removed. Eventually, the message exits but, when combined with secure communication, it's not possible for an external observer to tell which path the communication took and where it originated.

---

[98] Tor Project: Anonymity Online https://www.torproject.org/, Accessed on 5 October 2011.

[99] U.S. Naval Research Laboratory, http://www.nrl.navy.mil/, Accessed on 5 October 2011.

[100] Electronic Frontier Foundation - Defending your rights in the digital world, https://www.eff.org/, Accessed on 5 October 2011.

Tor suffers from some weaknesses[101] but, combined with special browser software, it can allow users to remain largely anonymous.

Normal download speeds can be ten times slower whilst using Tor—so it's conceivable LulzSec hackers didn't use it for this reason.

In the chatroom logs, a user by the name of "lol" (also known as "kayla" and who has possibly also been subsequently arrested comments on how slow Tor is. In hindsight, the extra time would have been worth the effort.

The VPN providers AirVPN advise users to always use their VPN services over Tor.

2.6.5   Who Can You Trust?

The arrest of Cody Kretsinger has served as an object lesson to the hacker community about the difficulties iof remaining anonymous and untraceable online.

More to the point is the fact a considerable amount of background information was actually leaked to the press in the first place by former LulzSec group member "m_nerva", later identified as Marshal Webb from Ohio.[102]

The lesson the hackers learned the hard way is also a salutary one for all dissidents, whistle-blowers and activists: in situations where much is at stake, no precaution is too great.

General awareness of tools such as Tor and others such as Freenet[103] will become as fundamental as knowing how to use a browser. In all of this, commercial companies and networks will always act in their own interests.

Unfortunately, it comes down to one simple fact: it's hard to trust anyone when your life depends on it.

2.7   Anonymous Versus Los Zetas Drug Cartel…A Merry Mexican Dance

8 November 2011

In recent weeks, the fractured nature of Anonymous,[104] the hacktivist collective, has come to the fore after it declared war on Los Zetas, a Mexican drug cartel.

---

[101] Tor (anonymity network), http://en.wikipedia.org/wiki/Tor_%28anonymity_network%29, Accessed on 5 October 2011.

[102] Snitches getting various stitches, http://pastebin.com/MBEsm5XQ, Accessed on 5 October 2011.

[103] Freenet, https://freenetproject.org/, Accessed on 5 October 2011.

[104] Anonymous: The secret group's 5 biggest hacks, http://theweek.com/article/index/212846/anonymous-the-secret-groups-5-biggest-hacks, Accessed on 8 November 2011.

Dubbed "Operation Cartel", it was announced[105] by Anonymous Veracruz, ostensibly in response to an Anonymous member being "kidnapped" while handing out leaflets during Operation Paperstorm.[106]

Nobody doubts the desperate situation in Mexico, with a drug war that has claimed the lives of[107] (at least) 40,000 people in the past 5 years. Border towns such as Juarez have played host to 8,000 deaths[108] in the past 3 years alone and the violence has spread to previously safe cities such as Veracruz.[109]

The pervasiveness of death has been accompanied by a vicious cycle of ambiguous, unreliable information and fear.

Commenting on the Anonymous announcement, Deborah Bonello, a Mexican reporter wrote in The Guardian[110]:

"The ability to distribute information that is unvetted, unverified and often from unnamed sources across a plethora of platforms is both a blessing and a curse. A blessing because information is harder to suppress and control, but a curse because of the opportunity it creates for propaganda and misinformation that is then reported by the media and acted upon by the public as fact."

She was talking about the drug cartels, but the quote could have been applied equally to Anonymous. After the announcement, Stratfor analyst Ben West[111] released a video report stating any attempts by Anonymous to expose the Zetas could be met with a "risk of abduction, injury and death".

The rather tenuous link West made between evidence of the use of "computer scientists" by the cartels to engage in cybercrime, to track Anonymous attackers, and then to follow up with assassinations was ignored by all later reports.[112]

The Anonymous story then became even more confused as the operation—scheduled for November 5—was called off.[113] The kidnapped Anonymous member

---

[105] Link no longer goes to specified page, http://www.youtube.com/watch?v=bJORGO1Q2VY&feature=youtu.be, Accessed on 8 November 2011.

[106] Operation: Paperstorm, http://oppaperstorm.wordpress.com/, Accessed on 8 November 2011.

[107] AFP: Mexicans honor drug war victims on Day of the Dead, http://www.mexicoreporter.com/2011/11/02/afp-mexicans-honor-drug-war-victims-on-day-of-the-dead/, Accessed on 8 November 2011.

[108] Mexico: Impunity and profits - Josh Rushing travels to the city dubbed the murder capital of the world. http://www.aljazeera.com/programmes/faultlines/2011/06/201161493451742709.html, Accessed on 8 November 2011.

[109] Mexico drugs war: Inside Veracruz as conflict spreads deeper, http://www.bbc.co.uk/news/world-latin-america-15372946, Accessed on 8 November 2011.

[110] Anonymous acts are a key feature of Mexico's drug wars, http://www.guardian.co.uk/commentisfree/2011/nov/01/anonymity-mexico-drug-wars?INTCMP=ILCNETTXT3487, Accessed on 8 November 2011.

[111] Dispatch: Anonymous' Online Tactics Against Mexican Cartels, http://www.stratfor.com/analysis/20111101-dispatch-implications-online-tactics-against-mexican-cartels, Accessed on 8 November 2011.

[112] Is Mexican cartel the next 'Anonymous' target? http://edition.cnn.com/2011/10/31/world/americas/mexico-anonymous-threat/?hpt=wo_c2, Accessed on 8 November 2011.

[113] Mexico: Fear, Uncertainty and Doubt over Anonymous' #OpCartel, http://globalvoicesonline.org/2011/10/31/mexico-fear-uncertainty-and-doubt-over-anonymous-opcartel/, Accessed on 8 November 2011.

was apparently returned[114] along with a threat that the Zetas would kill ten people for every name of a Zeta associate released by Anonymous.

There has been no evidence produced that there was a kidnap in the first place, nor of the subsequent release of names or the threat of follow-up deaths.

But this is not the end. Barrett Brown, a former member of Anonymous, declared last week that OpCartel was still on.[115] Brown further claimed to be in possession of emails linking US officials and others with the Zetas. Barrett Brown is writing a book[116] about Anonymous, but is viewed with scepticism by others in Anonymous and on Twitter.[117]

Other than releasing names (Dox) of individuals likely to be involved with the Zetas, it was never clear what Anonymous would be able to do. But, like all other businesses, drug cartels are increasingly using technology as the basis for their operations.

It is this dependence on computers and networks that makes them potentially vulnerable to groups such as Anonymous (and of course governments that are fighting them legitimately).

The Stratfor analysis claimed the drug cartels were using hackers of their own to engage in cybercrime. They are using sophisticated electronics and communications networks,[118] and using social media to track victims.[119]

The use of social media especially has escalated recently with cartel members misdirecting the police by reporting a shootout on Twitter and then carrying out an operation elsewhere.

The rapidity of news spreading on Twitter also caused panic when two Veracruz residents tweeted that gunmen were kidnapping children from schools. It later turned out to be a false alarm and the two residents were arrested and charged with terrorism and sabotage.

They were later released after protests from internet-freedom and human-rights activists.

Given moves by the drug cartels to control media, including social media, it's possible the Zetas and other drug cartels would be concerned about possible attention paid by groups such as Anonymous.

---

[114] Anonymous calls off outing of cartel after release of kidnapped member, http://arstechnica.com/tech-policy/2011/11/anonymous-calls-off-outing-of-narco-cartel-after-release-of-kidnapped-member/, Accessed on 8 November 2011.

[115] OpCartel, a Name Emerges [Update], http://www.forbes.com/sites/seanlawson/2011/11/05/opcartel-a-name-emerges/, Accessed on 8 November 2011.

[116] It Pays to Be the Face of Anonymous, http://gawker.com/5856604/it-pays-to-be-the-face-of-anonymous, Accessed on 8 November 2011.

[117] Get instant updates on #OpCartel, https://twitter.com/search?q=%23OpCartel, Accessed on 8 November 2011.

[118] Marines dismantle Los Zeta communications network in Veracruz, http://www.borderlandbeat.com/2011/09/marines-dismantle-los-zeta.html, Accessed on 8 November 2011.

[119] Mexican Drug Cartels Now Menace Social Media, http://www.npr.org/2011/09/23/140745739/mexican-drug-cartels-now-menace-social-media, Accessed on 8 November 2011.

The "Anonymous brand" brings with it media and public attention. The web defacements and DDoS attacks[120] are little more than inconvenience for the targets but serve to publicise significant societal issues. This is something Anonymous itself recognises.

Another campaign that never materialised was #OpFacebook.[121] The initial suggestion was that Facebook would be brought down or attacked on November 5. Anonymous denied this later,[122] saying on Twitter that the group would not "kill" the messenger.

Anonymous thrives on pushing its message over whatever media it can, including, as in the case of Operation Paperstorm,[123] paper.

The difficulty with all Anonymous campaigns is sustainability. Having brought the Mexican situation to the public's attention, the meme just as rapidly dissipates as newer events take centre stage. But there are plenty of reasons why the Americans should care about this.

If you believe Fox News,[124] it would appear the human misery brought about by drug cartels is causing tens of thousands of Mexicans to flee across the border.

More importantly, the drugs that are being fought over in Mexico are largely destined for the USA and will continue to bring untold ruin in their wake.

2.8 Hackers Hit Steam: Is It Time to Open the Valve on e-Commerce Regulation?

15 November 2011

One of the world's largest online video gaming networks, Steam,[125] has been hacked and its 35 million users may have had their accounts "compromised". And yes, "compromised" means their (encrypted) credit card details may have been stolen.

At the risk of asking the obvious, have we finally reached the moment for stricter regulation of e-commerce, the buying and selling of products online? In Australia,

---

[120]Zombie computers, cyber security, phishing … what you need to know, http://theconversation. edu.au/zombie-computers-cyber-security-phishing-what-you-need-to-know-1671, Accessed on 8 November 2011.

[121]OpFaceBook, http://pastebin.com/nzaNLWfF, Accessed on 8 November 2011.

[122]AnonymousFacebookAttack:RealorFake?http://www.pcmag.com/article2/0,2817,2390805,00. asp, Accessed on 8 November 2011.

[123]Operation Paperstorm starting Saturday December 18, 2010, http://www.operationprotest.com/ operation-paperstorm-starting-dec-18-2010, Accessed on 8 November 2011.

[124]Report: 230,000 Displaced by Mexico Drug War, http://www.foxnews.com/world/2011/03/25/ report-230000-displaced-mexico-drug-war-1121351146/, Accessed on 8 November 2011.

[125]Steam, http://store.steampowered.com/, Accessed online 15 November 2011.

the amount of cash spent in this way now sits at around AU$30 billion a year[126]; globally online spending is projected to reach[127] US$1.24 trillion a year by 2015.

Staff at the game company Valve,[128] which owns and operates Steam, uncovered an intrusion into a user database while investigating a security breach of its discussion forums earlier this month. At first the firm said the discussion groups were offline for maintenance.

But a message posted[129] on Steam by Valve co-founder Gabe Newell last week revealed the sites were shut down because of defacement—and that the breach may have gone beyond the company's discussion forums.

2.8.1   The Worst of Times

The Steam hack comes in an already bad year for internet companies and their reputations for data management—not least the Sony Playstation Network, which saw 77 million accounts[130] compromised by hackers in May.

E-commerce sites[131] have become something of a staple for hackers. Even security firms[132] offering security devices that are meant to protect customers by providing second level[133] log-in security have been hacked.

The hackers, in the case of Steam, gained access to "information including user names, hashed and salted passwords, game purchases, email addresses, billing addresses and encrypted credit card information".

Newell stated that he was "truly sorry", and tried to assure users that, "We don't have evidence of credit card misuse at this time. Nonetheless you should watch your credit card activity and statements closely".

Yet another company closing the stable door after the horse has bolted.

The big question I'd be asking myself as a user is: will Valve take responsibility for any losses incurred by me? No information has been issued on this as yet.

---

[126] Australian online commerce to hit $37billion by 2013, eCommerce Report, http://www.ecommercereport.com.au/?p=1952, Accessed online 15 November 2011.

[127] Cisco: Global e-commerce to hit $1.4 trillion by 2015, Power Retail, http://www.powerretail.com.au/news/cisco-global-e-commerce-to-hit-1-4-trillion-by-2015/, Accessed online 15 November 2011.

[128] Valve, http://www.valvesoftware.com/, Accessed online 15 November 2011.

[129] Gabe Newell, Steam, http://forums.steampowered.com/forums/announcement.php?f=14, Accessed online 15 November 2011.

[130] Credibility at risk in Sony hacking scandal, The Conversation, http://theconversation.edu.au/credibility-at-risk-in-sony-hacking-scandal-1038, Accessed online 15 November 2011.

[131] Millions of e-commerce Sites Hacked to Serve Malware, PC Magazine, http://www.pcmag.com/article2/0,2817,2390677,00.asp#fbid=UMuHudFsSLB, Accessed online 15 November 2011.

[132] Hacked security firm leaves Aussies vulnerable, Fairfax, http://www.smh.com.au/technology/security/hacked-security-firm-leaves-aussies-vulnerable-20110321-1c2i4.html, Accessed online 15 November 2011.

[133] Second-level ISP, http://en.wikipedia.org/wiki/Second-level_ISP, Accessed online 15 November 2011.

Newell recommended Steam and forum account passwords be changed, but was not going to "force" users to do this.

Steam account passwords can be different to the forum passwords, which is why he added: "if you have used your Steam forum password on other accounts you should change those passwords as well".

One golden rule should be instilled, very clearly, in everyone's mind: you should never, under any circumstances, use the same password for more than one site on which you use your credit card.

There are solutions, provided there is will—and it's getting hard to argue against doing something urgently.

Credit card companies should force large and medium e-commerce sites to utilise secondary security such as tokens or SMS confirmation when users log in. Some of the Australian banks now offer secondary security and this should be replicated throughout e-commerce more generally.

Further regulation of online e-commerce providers is necessary—internet crime is growing and governments need to act now to reverse this trend.

2.9 Anonymous, WikiLeaks and Email Dumps: The Ultimate Weapon?

15 February 2012

Of all the tactics used by hacker collective Anonymous[134] in any of its "operations", the release of their victims' emails has been one that potentially could cause the most damage.

Previous releases have claimed the job of Aaron Barr—former CEO of security firm HBGary[135]—and unveiled the covert operations[136] of intelligence analysis firm Strategic Forecasting Inc. (STRATFOR).

Most recently, media sites have claimed the hacking and release of emails[137] of military law firm Puckett & Faraj by Anonymous would effectively destroy the company.

---

[134] Anonymous (group), http://en.wikipedia.org/wiki/Anonymous_%28group, Accessed on 15 February 2012.

[135] Anonymous speaks: the inside story of the HBGary hack, http://arstechnica.com/tech-policy/2011/02/anonymous-speaks-the-inside-story-of-the-hbgary-hack/, Accessed on 15 February 2012.

[136] Link no longer goes to specified page, http://occupythe99percent.com/2012/02/stratfor-intelligence-leaked-by-anonymous-reveals-spying-on-occupy-movement-and-deep-green-resistance/, Accessed on 15 February 2012.

[137] Anonymous May Have Completely Destroyed Military Law Firm, http://www.gizmodo.com.au/2012/02/anonymous-may-have-completely-destroyed-military-law-firm/#more-512210, Accessed on 15 February 2012.

By comparison, other hacktivist tactics (such as the release of usernames, passwords or credit card information) are annoying and inconvenient, but essentially transient in their impact. Passwords can be changed, credit cards can be replaced and money refunded.

Intuitively, you would expect the release of internal communications of a company to be potentially devastating. There is the likelihood of revealing unknown secrets to the public and interested parties. At the very least, the truth of what lies behind the corporate image portrayed to the public is laid bare.

2.9.1 What WikiLeaks Taught Us

In recent times, the world has witnessed the impact of the release[138] of about 250,000 US diplomatic cables on WikiLeaks.[139]

But despite the potential and the perception, does the release of this sort of communication really do that much damage? Commentators have long been dismissing the actual impact of the release of the cables on WikiLeaks.

As Anatol Lieven, professor in the War Studies Department of King's College London commented at the time[140]: "it was hardly news that US officials privately despise Hamid Karzai and believe that his family are deeply involved in the heroin trade".

Others[141] have also questioned the impact, if any, of the cables' release. Some[142] have even argued that the cables' release actually helped the US by debunking conspiracy theories about its foreign policy.

Would-be leakers face several challenges when trying to capitalise on the information they have obtained. The biggest is actually sifting through millions of emails or internal documents for significant and interesting content.

It is a massive task and one that takes time, resources and money. The other problem is to get anyone to actually act on the information. This is made all the harder if you are attacking organisations that have close links to the agencies that would normally prosecute any perceived wrongdoing.

In the case of the high-profile hacks by Anonymous, were the outcomes as damaging as the victims and the media claimed?

---

[138] Bradley Manning, http://en.wikipedia.org/wiki/Bradley_Manning, Accessed on 15 February 2012.

[139] WikiLeaks, http://en.wikipedia.org/wiki/Wikileaks, Accessed on 15 February 2012.

[140] Analysis: Impact of Wikileaks' US cable publications, http://www.bbc.co.uk/news/world-us-canada-11918573, Accessed on 15 February 2012.

[141] WikiLeaks' 16th minute, http://blogs.reuters.com/jackshafer/2012/01/18/wikileaks-16th-minute/, Accessed on 15 February 2012.

[142] America should give Assange a medal, http://www.ft.com/cms/s/61f8fab0-06f3-11e0-8c29-00 144feabdc0,Authorised=false.html?_i_location=http%3A%2F%2Fwww.ft.com%2Fcms %2Fs%2F0%2F61f8fab0-06f3-11e0-8c29-00144feabdc0.html&_i_referer=#axzz1m8IDUqqC, Accessed on 15 February 2012.

2.9.2   Aaron Barr: Death of a CEO

Anonymous's initial success with the release of corporate emails was in February 2011 with the hack and making-public[143] of emails from security firm HBGary Federal and HBGary Inc.

The hack was prompted by a report[144] in the Financial Times in which Aaron Barr, CEO of HBGary Federal, claimed he was about to identify leaders of Anonymous.

After the publication of the emails and the highlighting of its varied revelations, Barr resigned.[145]

The full revelations[146] of the HBGary emails brought to light a "dirty tricks campaign" aimed at WikiLeaks involving not only HBGary Federal but other firms, potentially at the behest of the Bank of America.

HBGary Inc appears[147] to have come out of the episode largely unscathed. The company quickly distanced[148] itself from HBGary Federal and claimed the actions were entirely the doings of Aaron Barr.

Rather than losing customers, HBGary claimed[149] to have "ended up getting additional business".

In fact, Anonymous may have also ended up doing HBGary an additional favour in helping the company divest itself of Aaron Barr, who was increasingly being described as "embattled".[150]

---

[143] Anonymous speaks: the inside story of the HBGary hack, http://arstechnica.com/tech-policy/2011/02/anonymous-speaks-the-inside-story-of-the-hbgary-hack/, Accessed on 15 February 2012.

[144] Cyberactivists warned of arrest, http://www.ft.com/intl/cms/s/87dc140e-3099-11e0-9de3-00144feabdc0,Authorised=false.html?_i_location=http%3A%2F%2Fwww.ft.com%2Fcms%2Fs%2F0%2F87dc140e-3099-11e0-9de3-00144feabdc0.html&_i_referer=#axzz1m8IDUqqC, Accessed on 15 February 2012.

[145] HBGary Federal CEO Aaron Barr Steps Down, http://threatpost.com/en_us/blogs/hbgary-federal-ceo-aaron-barr-steps-down-022811, Accessed on 15 February 2012.

[146] HBGary, http://en.wikipedia.org/wiki/Hb_gary, Accessed on 15 February 2012.

[147] Anonymous attack on HBGary Federal didn't ruin us, says HBGary CEO, http://www.networkworld.com/news/2011/120911-hbgary-anonymous-253924.html, Accessed on 15 February 2012.

[148] HBGary's Open Letter to Customers and the Defense Marketplace, http://www.infosecisland.com/blogview/13062-HBGarys-Open-Letter-to-Customers-and-the-Defense-Marketplace.html, Accessed on 15 February 2012.

[149] Anonymous attack on HBGary Federal didn't ruin us, says HBGary CEO, http://www.networkworld.com/news/2011/120911-hbgary-anonymous-253924.html, Accessed on 15 February 2012.

[150] HBGary Federal CEO Aaron Barr Steps Down, http://threatpost.com/en_us/blogs/hbgary-federal-ceo-aaron-barr-steps-down-022811, Accessed on 15 February 2012.

2.9.3   STRATFOR: Uncovering an Intelligence Conspiracy?

Christmas definitely did not arrive for STRATFOR. The company's site[151] was hacked by Anonymous on Christmas Eve, its website defaced, more than 2 GB of emails removed, and the STRATFOR private subscriber list and details of 90,000 credit cards from subscribers taken. The stolen credit card details were allegedly used to make donations to various charities.[152]

There have been claims the STRATFOR emails would reveal the company was carrying out more specific and possibly covert intelligence-gathering than it had publicly admitted.

This was denied by[153] George Friedman, STRATFOR's founder and CEO who said: "as they search our emails for signs of a vast conspiracy, they will be disappointed".

STRATFOR is now facing a class-action lawsuit[154] demanding US$50m in damages for failing to secure its computer systems and encrypt credit card information.

As for the impact on the company, there has been the cost of offering all of its subscribers[155] identity theft protection.

Apart from that, interestingly, the firm has earned some respect for the way in which it dealt with the hack, and actually sympathy[156] from the public for its victim status.

2.9.4   Puckett & Faraj: Semper Fidelis (Always Faithful)

Puckett & Faraj is the law firm that defended[157] Frank Wuterich for his role in the Haditha massacre[158] in which 24 unarmed Iraqi men, women and children were killed by US Marines.

---

[151] Stratfor, http://www.stratfor.com/, Accessed on 15 February 2012.

[152] http://imgur.com/QalSt, Accessed on 15 February 2012.

[153] Hackers Will Be Disappointed in Stolen Emails, Says Stratfor CEO, http://www.msnbc.msn.com/id/45963111/ns/technology_and_science-security/t/hackers-will-be-disappointed-stolen-emails-says-stratfor-ceo/#.UL7apdd_U25, Accessed on 15 February 2012.

[154] Stratfor Faces Lawsuit for Failing to Secure Customer Data, http://news.softpedia.com/news/Stratfor-Faces-Lawsuit-for-Failing-to-Secure-Customer-Data-251459.shtml, Accessed on 15 February 2012.

[155] Stratfor Offers Customers Identity Theft Protection After Hack, http://www.forbes.com/sites/alexknapp/2011/12/30/stratfor-offers-customers-identity-theft-protection-after-hack/, Accessed on 15 February 2012.

[156] Stratfor - Austin, TX - Publisher - Facebook, https://www.facebook.com/stratfor, Accessed on 15 February 2012.

[157] Anonymous Leaks US Marine Corps Massacre Case, http://www.gizmodo.com.au/2012/02/anonymous-leaks-us-marine-corps-massacre-case/, Accessed on 15 February 2012.

[158] Haditha killings, http://en.wikipedia.org/wiki/Haditha_killings, Accessed on 15 February 2012.

Wuterich, accused of negligent homicide in the deaths of two women and five children, escaped with a demotion to private and was only charged with dereliction of duty.

Anonymous became incensed[159] by the iniquity of a justice system that failed to prosecute a US marine who admitted his role in killing civilians while Bradley Manning,[160] the soldier at the heart of the WikiLeaks prosecution, faced life imprisonment. Anonymous hacked the website[161] of Puckett & Faraj and released 2.6 GB of emails and documents.

Some of the emails[162] have shown the extent to which the firm, run by former marines, lobbied influential military personnel and congressmen to assist in "making this whole case go away".

Although there were initial suggestions[163] the hack and release of emails could destroy the firm, the website at least[164] is back up, albeit showing content that is out-of-date.

As with the view that WikiLeaks may have actually helped the US with the release of diplomatic cables, the exposure by Anonymous of underhand dealings of a law firm may have also perversely served to promote the company.

In the system of US military justice that appears to have already foregone an ethical basis and is already comfortable with backroom deals, the revelations will come as no surprise and certainly would not put off potential customers seeking to escape prosecution. In fact, it would likely do quite the reverse.

2.9.5　Did It Make a Difference?

In all three of the Anonymous hacks, the companies not only survived but actually seemed to benefit from the potentially catastrophic events. That's not to say they all came out of the process with their integrity intact.

HBGary Federal was uncovered for attempting to run a dirty tricks campaign against WikiLeaks. STRATFOR was shown up for its cavalier handling of

---

[159] Anonymous reveals Haditha massacre emails, http://rt.com/usa/news/anonymous-time-wuterich-attorneys-463/, Accessed on 15 February 2012.

[160] Bradley Manning, http://www.bradleymanning.org/learn-more/bradley-manning, Accessed on 15 February 2012.

[161] Anonymous Leaks US Marine Corps Massacre Case, http://www.gizmodo.com.au/2012/02/anonymous-leaks-us-marine-corps-massacre-case/, Accessed on 15 February 2012.

[162] Link no longer goes to specified page, http://cryptome.org/2012/01/wuterich/wuterich-politics.pdf, Accessed on 15 February 2012.

[163] Anonymous May Have Completely Destroyed Military Law Firm, http://www.gizmodo.com.au/2012/02/anonymous-may-have-completely-destroyed-military-law-firm/#more-512210, Accessed on 15 February 2012.

[164] Link no longer goes to specified page, http://theconversation.edu.au/www.puckettfaraj.com/, Accessed on 15 February 2012.

customers' credit cards. The hack of Puckett & Faraj highlighted the case of Haditha and the US Marines' involvement in the deaths of 24 unarmed Iraqi civilians.

Another highlighted aspect is that, in a world where the personal is increasingly public, the impact of revealing another's private life is rapidly diminishing.

In the same way we remember little of what WikiLeaks released, the targets of Anonymous will continue to thrive, possibly having implemented more secure systems and, of course, thinking twice about what they put in writing.

2.10   A Tale of 'Betrayal': What Anonymous Can Teach Us About Online Relationships

13 March 2012

Whenever the press covers a story about hackers, a great deal of the discussion concerns the nature of online identity, the cohesiveness of hacking groups,[165] and the individuals that identify with these groups. This is particularly the case with discussion of hackers that consider themselves part of the hacktivist group Anonymous.[166]

This is due, in part, to the apparently co-operative manner in which Anonymous operates, and the oft-quoted Anonymous mantra ("we are Anonymous, we are legion[167]") that de-emphasises the individual and promotes the idea of the "group".

This lack of emphasis on the individual is slightly ironic given most of the news about Anonymous in the past year—including the most notable hacks of 2011—centred on individual hackers whose identities are known.

But issues of identity and group dynamics have been brought to a head by recent stories about the unmasking by US authorities[168] of FBI informant Hector Xavier Monsegur. Monsegur is also known online as Sabu, and is purportedly the leader of LulzSec[169] (an offshoot of Anonymous).

---

[165] Anonymous hackers arrested across world, http://www.theaustralian.com.au/news/world/anonymous-hackers-arrested-across-world/story-e6frg6so-1226285008481, Accessed on 13 March 2012.

[166] Anonymous, https://theconversation.edu.au/pages/anonymous, Accessed on 13 March 2012.

[167] We Are Anonymous, We Are Legion, http://www.yalelawtech.org/anonymity-online-identity/we-are-anonymous-we-are-legion/, Accessed on 13 March 2012.

[168] LulzSec Leader Sabu Unmasked, Aids FBI Hacker Sweep, http://www.informationweek.com/security/attacks/lulzsec-leader-sabu-unmasked-aids-fbi-ha/232602103, Accessed on 13 March 2012.

[169] LulzSec, https://theconversation.edu.au/pages/lulzsec, Accessed on 13 March 2012.

According to court reports unsealed last week, Monsegur had been helping the FBI build cases[170] against fellow hackers soon after he was arrested and released on bail[171] back in June 2011.

Sabu's story says a lot about what we actually know about people with whom we only interact online. In the case of Sabu, it turns out, we didn't know very much. His online persona was very different from his real-life self.

This perhaps shouldn't be very surprising given people generally have multiple and varied personas online—which often, if not always, differ from their real-life personas.

The psychiatrist Carl Jung[172] described the persona[173] as the mask that people wear to hide their true selves from society. On the internet, the effect of a persona is more pronounced because we lose other cues—such as how people talk, where they work and how they interact with others—that could potentially reveal how close the persona is to someone's "true self".

Much of the coverage of Sabu's unmasking focused on the nature of his online persona. The discussion ranged from his role within Anonymous and LulzSec, to his dominating and opinionated presence on Twitter.[174] Other commentators have even claimed[175] he was just a second- or third-tier hacker within Anonymous, even though he was involved with[176] most of the prominent hacking activity that took place under the Anonymous name last year.

Sabu himself gave interviews with private internet relay chat (IRC)[177] sessions and more detailed question-and-answer sessions on Reddit.[178]

[170] Hacker Sabu Worked Nonstop As Government Informer, http://www.informationweek.com/security/vulnerabilities/hacker-sabu-worked-nonstop-as-government/232602334, Accessed on 13 March 2012.

[171] EXCLUSIVE: Unmasking the world's most wanted hacker, http://www.foxnews.com/tech/2012/03/06/exclusive-unmasking-worlds-most-wanted-hacker/?intcmp=related, Accessed on 13 March 2012.

[172] Carl Jung, http://en.wikipedia.org/wiki/Carl_Jung, Accessed on 13 March 2012.

[173] Masked Self: The Persona in Jungian Theory, http://directory.leadmaverick.com/Helping-Psychology/DallasFort-WorthArlington/TX/10/11154/index.aspx, Accessed on 13 March 2012.

[174] Anonymousabu, https://twitter.com/search/anonymousabu, Accessed on 13 March 2012.

[175] LulzSec arrests will do limited damage to hacktivist movement, https://theconversation.edu.au/lulzsec-arrests-will-do-limited-damage-to-hacktivist-movement-5753, Accessed on 13 March 2012.

[176] Court documents shed light on extent of Anonymous and LulzSec activity, http://www.v3.co.uk/v3-uk/news/2157516/court-documents-shed-light-extent-anonymous-lulzsec-activity, Accessed on 13 March 2012.

[177] Internet Relay Chat, http://en.wikipedia.org/wiki/Internet_Relay_Chat, Accessed on 13 March 2012.

[178] AMA Request Sabu from LuLSec this would be amazing, http://www.reddit.com/r/IAmA/comments/kpfsp/ama_request_sabu_from_lulsec_this_would_be_amazing/, Accessed on 13 March 2012.

It took the unmasking of Sabu to reveal something approaching the truth about Monsegur as a person. The New York Times featured a story[179] describing 28-year-old Hector Monsegur as a Puerto Rican "party boy of the projects", who cared for his sister's two children. Monsegur was also revealed as a petty criminal and general neighbourhood nuisance, but someone who actually did care about the social issues he believed he was fighting for.[180]

As mentioned, the unmasking of Sabu makes it clear that it's very difficult to know the truth about someone from the persona they present online. This is especially true when that persona is being pieced together from fragments of tweets or even chat logs.

Commentary on individuals, relationships and organisational structures within Anonymous is also almost impossible. One should ultimately be wary of anyone making claims on these subjects without appropriate disclaimers.

But it's the reactions to Sabu's "betrayal"[181] of his fellow hackers that's potentially the most interesting aspect of this whole story. Other members of Anonymous were apparently left "emotionally devastated[182]" and "shocked" by the news Monsegur was an FBI informant.

It seems strange anyone would be surprised that Sabu's first loyalty was to himself and his family. It speaks volumes about the unrealistic view that people have of online relationships.

Our online ties are influenced by how well we know people in real life. If we don't know the person in real life, or have met them only casually, it can be argued that our ties with them online could only ever be weak.

This is, in part, because of the principle discussed earlier—it is difficult to really know anything about people online because their personas will differ from their real-life selves. You can never be sure who you are interacting with.

This means loyalty between members of a group who only associate with each other online is, by necessity, going to be fragile. Or to put it another way, most, if not all, online social ties are weak.

The responses to Sabu's "betrayal" are even more curious given the turning of hackers into informants is actually quite common. This phenomenon is described well in Kevin Poulsen's book Kingpin[183] about credit card fraudsters who regularly turned on each other to save themselves.

---

[179] Hacker, Informant and Party Boy of the Projects, http://www.nytimes.com/2012/03/09/technology/hacker-informant-and-party-boy-of-the-projects.html?_r=1&, Accessed on 13 March 2012.

[180] UNOFFICIAL ZERT PATCH CAUSES NYC PLANECRASH, http://seclists.org/fulldisclosure/2006/Oct/253, Accessed on 13 March 2012.

[181] LulzSec Leader Was Snitch Who Helped Snag Fellow Hackers, http://www.wired.com/threatlevel/2012/03/lulzsec-snitch/, Accessed on 13 March 2012.

[182] Anonymous Rocked by News That Top Hacker Snitched to Feds, http://www.wired.com/threatlevel/2012/03/anonymous-sabu-reaction/, Accessed on 13 March 2012.

[183] Kingpin: How One Hacker Took Over the Billion-Dollar Cybercrime Underground, http://www.amazon.com/Kingpin-Hacker-Billion-Dollar-Cybercrime-Underground/dp/0307588688, Accessed on 13 March 2012.

The story of Sabu is probably not over yet. He has gone into hiding but it seems unlikely we've heard the last from him. Perhaps the most prescient comment on this whole saga to date was made by Sabu himself during his Reddit Q&A[184]:

"Stick to yourselves. If you are in a crew—keep your opsec[185] up 24/7. Friends will try to take you down if they have to."

2.11 Why Is Anonymous Hacking Australia?

31 July 2012

Hacktivists are campaigning against the Australian government's proposed changes to privacy laws. *Source*: **Ben Fredericson**[186]

---

[184] AMA Request Sabu from LuLSec this would be amazing, http://www.reddit.com/r/IAmA/comments/kpfsp/ama_request_sabu_from_lulsec_this_would_be_amazing/, Accessed on 13 March 2012.

[185] Operations security, http://en.wikipedia.org/wiki/OPSEC, Accessed on 13 March 2012.

[186] Fredericson B., Flickr, http://www.flickr.com/photos/xjrlokix/3932488768/, Accessed online 21 December 2012.

A few days ago, Anonymous[187] activists hacked into AAPT,[188] stole 40 GB of data[189] including customer information and forced offline ten Australian government websites.[190]

Anonymous members stated in an online internet relay chat (IRC)[191] interview[192] with the ABC that the hacking attacks were part of an ongoing campaign against the government's proposed changes to privacy laws.[193]

2.11.1   Privacy Changes

One of the proposed changes being discussed by the Parliamentary Joint Committee on Intelligence and Security (PJCIS)[194] in an inquiry into potential reforms of national security legislation[195] is a requirement for internet service providers (ISPs) to store user online activity for 2 years.

This means that everything you do, from social networking, emails, web browsing, chat sessions, Skype[196] sessions and so on would be monitored, stored and made available to government intelligence agencies as and when needed.

Last week, it was reported on the website Slashdot[197] that Microsoft had made Skype easier to monitor.[198] Lauren Weinstein, co-founder of People for Internet

---

[187] Anonymous, http://anonnews.org/, Accessed online 31 July 2012.

[188] AAPT, http://www.aapt.com.au/, Accessed online 31 July 2012.

[189] Connelley C., Anonymous hackers claim ISP user data stolen from AAPT, News Limited, 26 July 2012, http://www.news.com.au/technology/hacked-anonymous-steals-user-data-from-aussie-isp/story-e6frfro0-1226435629217, Accessed online 31 July 2012.

[190] Connelley C., Anonymous hackers cripple Aussie government websites, News Limited, 25 July 2012, http://www.news.com.au/technology/anonymous-hackers-cripples-aussie-government-websites/story-e6frfro0-1226433788501, Accessed online 31 July 2012.

[191] Internet Relay Chat, http://www.irc.org/, Accessed online 31 July 2012.

[192] Ross N. and Main L., The ABC interviews Anonymous regarding AAPT hack, Australian Broadcasting Corporation, 26 July 2012, http://www.abc.net.au/technology/articles/2012/07/26/3554598.htm, Accessed online 31 July 2012.

[193] Govt defends need to snoop on online and phone records, AAP, 12 July 2012, http://www.news.com.au/technology/govt-defends-need-to-keep-internet-data/story-e6frfro0-1226424390925, Accessed online 31 July 2012.

[194] Parliamentary Joint Committee on Intelligence and Security, Australian Government, http://www.aph.gov.au/Parliamentary_Business/Committees/House_of_Representatives_Committees?url=pjcis/index.htm, Accessed online 31 July 2012.

[195] Inquiry into potential reforms of National Security Legislation, Parliamentary Joint Committee on Intelligence and Security, Australian Government, http://www.aph.gov.au/Parliamentary_Business/Committees/House_of_Representatives_Committees?url=pjcis/nsl2012/index.htm, Accessed online 31 July 2012.

[196] Skype, Microsoft, http://www.skype.com/, Accessed online 31 July 2012.

[197] Slashdot, http://slashdot.org/, Accessed online 31 July 2012.

[198] Microsoft makes Skype easier to monitor, Slashdot, 26 July 2012, http://yro.slashdot.org/story/12/07/26/2243206/microsoft-makes-skype-easier-to-monitor, Accessed online 31 July 2012.

Responsibility,[199] a privacy advocacy group, was quoted[200] in The Washington Post as saying:

> The issue is, to what extent are our communications being purpose-built to make surveillance easy?
> When you make it easy to do, law enforcement is going to want to use it more and more. If you build it, they will come.

During the ABC IRQ interview, Anonymous representatives made the following statement against increased government surveillance of the online world:

> Whilst our own rights to privacy dwindle, corporate rights to commercial confidentiality and intellectual property skyrocket. Whilst we no longer know about many of the activities of our governments, our governments have the means to accumulate unprecedented vast banks of data about us [...]
> The attacks are a way to draw attention to the msg we wish to deliver to the ppl of au.

The hacking attacks by Anonymous on government websites and AAPT were designed to highlight to the Australian public the difficulty of keeping stored data private. By carrying out hacking attacks and then making public pronouncements Anonymous hopes to convince Australians not to support changes to the current privacy laws.

Source: **scragz**[201]

---

[199] People for Internet responsibility, http://www.pfir.org/, Accessed online 31 July 2012.

[200] Timberg C. and Nakashima E., Skype makes chats and user data more available to police, Washington Post, 26 July 2012, http://www.washingtonpost.com/business/economy/skype-makes-chats-and-user-data-more-available-to-police/2012/07/25/gJQAobI39W_story.html?hpid=z1, Accessed online 31 July 2012.

[201] Scragz, Flickr, http://www.flickr.com/photos/scragz/2340505105/, Accessed online 21 December 2012.

Data retention[202] policies vary around the world. The European Union has had a data retention directive[203] since 2006 that specifies types of data that are to be retained for periods of between 6 months and 2 years.

In recent weeks, the United Kingdom government has begun debating a draft Communications Data Bill[204] that includes compulsory data retention for a wide range of information, such as websites visited, for a period of 1 year.

2.11.2   Spy Games

So why are governments around the world increasing internet surveillance? Four reasons spring to mind:

1) Terrorism. The threat of terrorists using the internet to plan, support and carry out terrorist acts has prompted the Attorney-General's Department[205] to discuss the need to increase the powers of organisations such as the Australian Security Intelligence Organisation (ASIO),[206] the Australian Secret Intelligence Service (ASIS)[207] and the Defence Signals Directorate (DSD).[208]
2) Cyber warfare.[209] On July 19, in the first public address[210] by a head of ASIS, Nick Warner, identified cyber warfare as a major threat:

> The field of cyber operations is one of the most rapidly evolving and potentially serious threats to our national security in the coming decade.
> Government departments and agencies, together with corporate Australia, have been subject to concerted efforts by external actors seeking to infiltrate sensitive computer networks.

---

[202] Telecommunications data retention, Wikipedia, http://en.wikipedia.org/wiki/Telecommunications_data_retention, Accessed online 31 July 2012.

[203] Directive 2006/24/EC of the European Parliament and of the Council, European Union, 15 March 2006, http://eur-lex.europa.eu/LexUriServ/LexUriServ.do?uri=OJ:L:2006:105:0054:0063:EN:PDF, Accessed online 31 July 2012.

[204] Draft Communications Data Bill, UK Government, http://www.official-documents.gov.uk/document/cm83/8359/8359.pdf, Accessed online 31 July 2012.

[205] Attorney General's Department, Australian Government, http://www.ag.gov.au/Pages/default.aspx, Accessed online 31 July 2012.

[206] Australian Security Intelligence Organisation, http://www.asio.gov.au/, Accessed online 31 July 2012.

[207] Australian Secret Intelligence Service, Australian Government, http://www.asis.gov.au/, Accessed online 31 July 2012.

[208] Defence Signals Directorate, Australian Government, http://www.dsd.gov.au/, Accessed online 31 July 2012.

[209] Phair N., Last online of defence: why is ANZUS prepping for a cyber war?, The Conversation, 20 September 2011, https://theconversation.edu.au/last-online-of-defence-why-is-anzus-prepping-for-a-cyber-war-3418, Accessed online 31 July 2012.

[210] Cullen S., Spy chief concerned by threat of cyber warfare, Australian Broadcasting Corporation, 19 July 2012, http://www.abc.net.au/news/2012-07-19/spy-service-reaches-pivotal-point/4141622, Accessed online 31 July 2012.

Developments in cyber are a two-edged sword for an agency like ASIS.

They offer new ways of collecting information, but the digital fingerprints and
footprints which we all now leave behind complicate the task of operating
covertly.

3) Cybercrime.[211] Criminals use the internet for their everyday activities much as
any modern business does. In 2011 Symantec,[212] a provider of internet security
software, estimated the cost of cybercrime to Australians had reached about
A$4.6 billion annually.

4) Hacking. Copyright and intellectual property theft over the internet has become
endemic. Much of the hacking remains unreported and business has become
decidedly worried about the effects of competitors gaining access to intellectual
property.[213]

2.11.3   Control

Governments around the world are slowly regulating the internet. Failure to do so
will come at an unbearable cost to the nation, business and to individuals.

There is nothing Anonymous can do to stop this inevitable process—so why
can't they get on board? The group could highlight weaknesses in the internet, websites
and business systems so that appropriate action can be taken.

To put it simply, there's no need for Anonymous to steal data from a company
and then post this data on a public website. This action is counterproductive and
strengthens the government's argument for greater regulation.

But the point Anonymous is trying to make, that Australian companies and the
government cannot be trusted to securely implement a data retention scheme, is
probably very true.

In the past 2 years, many large Australian companies have been hacked and
customer information stolen including credit card details. The penalties to companies for a data breach are minor and therefore very little effort is expended by business
to adequately protect customer information.

Governments around the world are stumbling forward with data retention policies
without adequate plans for how the data is to be secured, how the data retention
process is to be audited and by whom, and what the penalties will be for failure to
ensure the data remains secure.

---

[211]Cybercrime, Australian Federal Police, http://www.afp.gov.au/policing/cybercrime.aspx,
Accessed online 31 July 2012.

[212]Symantec, http://www.symantec.com/, Accessed online 31 July 2012.

[213]Riley M. and Vance A., Inside the Chinese Boom in Corporate Espionage, Bloomberg, 15
March 2012, http://www.businessweek.com/articles/2012-03-14/inside-the-chinese-boom-in-
corporate-espionage, Accessed online 31 July 2012.

We are in a new phase online where the blind are leading the blind, trying to find a path towards a more secure and regulated internet that enshrines our right to privacy.

Further Reading

- SCAMwatch—a helping hand against online scammers[214]
- The internet is insecure—Let's build a better one, fast[215]
- Zombie computers, cyber security, phishing … what you need to know[216]

2.12   Anonymous' Operation Australia: Can the Federal Police Stop Them?

10 August 2012

What's being done about the latest spate of Anonymous attacks? *Source*: ottawanonymous[217]

[214]Gregory M.A., SCAMwatch – a helping hand against online scammers, The Conversation, http://theconversation.edu.au/scamwatch-a-helping-hand-against-online-scammers-6842, 4 July 2012.

[215]Gregory M.A., The internet is insecure – let's build a better one, fast, The Conversation, http://theconversation.edu.au/the-internet-is-insecure-lets-build-a-better-one-fast-3977, 26 October 2011.

[216]de Neef M., Zombie computers, cyber security, phishing … what you need to know, The Conversation, 3 June 2011, https://theconversation.edu.au/zombie-computers-cyber-security-phishing-what-you-need-to-know-1671, Accessed online 31 July 2012.

[217]Ottawanonymous, Flickr, http://www.flickr.com/photos/24709063@N02/2435792032/, Accessed online 21 December 2012.

About 10 a.m. this morning, Anonymous used Twitter to announce an attack on the Australian Security Intelligence Organisation (ASIO)[218] website. Anonymous claimed the ASIO website would be unavailable for the rest of the day.

The ASIO website was down for about 30 min after the attack and is now operating slowly or not at all. It appears the attack may be ongoing, but ASIO's technical staff are recovering the situation.

Anonymous has been claiming attacks would occur on ASIO and on the Defence Signals Directorate[219] (DSD) website via the Anonymous Operation Australia Twitter account.[220]

The Anonymous attacks are part of an ongoing campaign[221] against the government proposal[222] to introduce a data retention scheme that would require carriers and ISPs to store the web history of every Australian for 1–2 years.

Anonymous has been using distributed denial of service[223] (DDoS) attacks for some time now as part of this campaign. Late last month Anonymous used DDoS or website defacing attacks on ten government websites.[224]

The question that every Australian should be asking the government and the Australian Federal Police[225] (AFP) is what are they doing about the Anonymous attacks?

Anonymous has now launched attacks on a range of government websites, broken into an AAPT server and stolen customer data which was recently partially released on the web.[226]

When is the AFP going to declare the Anonymous attacks a major crime and dedicate resources to finding the perpetrators? Can the AFP stop the Anonymous attacks?

The answer is "no" if today's events are any indicator. What makes the situation even worse is that Anonymous gave the AFP and ASIO plenty of warning—yet the attack succeeded.

---

[218] Australian Security Intelligence Organisation, Australian Government, http://www.asio.gov.au/, Accessed online 10 August 2012.

[219] Defence Signals Directorate, Australian Government, http://www.dsd.gov.au/, Accessed online 10 August 2012.

[220] OperationAustralia, Anonymous, https://twitter.com/Op_Australia/status/233718148367536128, Accessed online 10 August 2012.

[221] Gregory M.A., Why is Anonymous hacking Australia?, The Conversation, 31 July 2012, https://theconversation.edu.au/why-is-anonymous-hacking-australia-8480, Accessed online 10 August 2012.

[222] Inquiry into potential reforms of National Security Legislation, Joint Parliamentary Committee on Intelligence and Security, Australian Government, http://www.aph.gov.au/Parliamentary_Business/Committees/House_of_Representatives_Committees?url=pjcis/nsl2012/index.htm, Accessed online 10 August 2012.

[223] Denial of Service attack, Wikipedia, http://en.wikipedia.org/wiki/Denial-of-service_attack, Accessed online 10 August 2012.

[224] Connelly C., Anonymous hackers cripple Aussie government websites, News Limited, 25 July 2012, http://www.news.com.au/technology/anonymous-hackers-cripples-aussie-government-websites/story-e6frfro0-1226433788501, Accessed online 10 August 2012.

[225] Australian Federal Police, http://www.afp.gov.au, Accessed online 10 August 2012.

[226] Barwick H., Anonymous releases some AAPT data, CIO, 30 July 2012, http://www.cio.com.au/article/432044/anonymous_releases_some_aapt_data_/, Accessed online 10 August 2012.

Is Anonymous correct in its assertion the government proposal to implement a 2-year data retention scheme will put all Australians at risk of far worse outcomes than the current Anonymous campaign?

It is time for the AFP to demonstrate to all Australian's that their internet history can be protected by government authorities.

What hope have the companies that would be forced to implement the data retention scheme got of combating internet criminals if the government and AFP are powerless to stop Anonymous?

A good way for the AFP to demonstrate their capability to stop internet crime would be to identify and arrest the members of Anonymous who are participating in Operation Australia.

Another possible approach similar, to that employed by US authorities,[227] would be for the AFP to offer the Anonymous members jobs?

Electronic Frontiers Australia[228] (EFA) stated on July 13 that:

> EFA is deeply concerned about the proposed changes to National Security legislation foreshadowed in the discussion paper issued this week by the Attorney-General's Department.
> These proposed changes, if implemented in their entirety, would appear to amount to a massive expansion of surveillance activity across the entire community, accompanied by a corresponding reduction in accountability for that surveillance activity, and are therefore a potentially significant threat to the civil liberties and privacy of all Australians.

In the USA earlier this month a bill that would establish security standards to prevent cyberattacks on the US critical infrastructure failed to pass the Senate.[229] Clearly, the US government is struggling to regulate the internet and to protect their vital infrastructure.

Key reasons for the failure of the US bill were the financial burden that would be placed on private companies, a view that government intervention was not necessary, and the provision for sharing cyberthreat data between government and industry. The data retention and sharing worried many people about potential privacy and security breaches.

A recommended first step for the Australian government is to invest in research that would enhanced privacy and security and provide real outcomes that can be implemented here.

For me a litmus test of the government's intentions is whether or not it will mandate the use of Secure Socket Layer[230] (SSL) certificates for email. In my view SSL should be mandatory from the customer's device to the Simple Mail Transfer Protocol[231] (SMTP) server and between SMTP servers. This simple step would greatly improve privacy and security.

---

[227] Johnson K., 'I want you': Uncle Sam hiring criminal hackers, American Free Press, 4 July 2012, http://americanfreepress.net/?p=4863, Accessed online 10 August 2012.

[228] Electronic Frontiers Australia, https://www.efa.org.au/, Accessed online 10 August 2012.

[229] O'Keefe E. and Nakashima E., Cybersecurity bill fails in Senate, The Washington Post, 3 August 2012, http://www.washingtonpost.com/world/national-security/cybersecurity-bill-fails-in-senate/2012/08/02/gJQADNOOSX_story.html, Accessed online 10 August 2012.

[230] Transport Layer Security, Wikipedia, http://en.wikipedia.org/wiki/Secure_Sockets_Layer, Accessed online 10 August 2012.

[231] Simple Mail Transfer Protocol, Wikipedia, http://en.wikipedia.org/wiki/Simple_Mail_Transfer_Protocol, Accessed online 10 August 2012.

The internet is a critical piece of infrastructure that is being used in ways beyond its original design. Authorities should not try to use the internet in ways that will jeopardise the security and privacy of Australians.

They should be able to provide people with a guarantee their security and privacy will be protected.

Further Reading
- Why is Anonymous hacking Australia?[232]
- Anonymous, child porn and the wild, wild web[233]
- The internet is insecure—let's build a better one, fast[234]

2.13 'You've Been Hacked': Why Data-Breach Reporting Should Be Mandatory

19 October 2012

If someone got access to your personal information, wouldn't you want to know? *Source:* **subcircle[235]**

---

[232] Gregory M.A., Why is Anonymous hacking Australia?, The Conversation, 31 July 2012, https://theconversation.edu.au/why-is-anonymous-hacking-australia-8480, Accessed online 10 August 2012.

[233] Gregory M.A., Anonymous, child porn and the wild, wild web, The Conversation, 28 October 2011, http://theconversation.edu.au/anonymous-child-porn-and-the-wild-wild-web-4005, Accessed online 10 August 2012.

[234] Gregory M.A., The internet is insecure – let's build a better one, fast, The Conversation, 26 October 2011, http://theconversation.edu.au/the-internet-is-insecure-lets-build-a-better-one-fast-3977, Accessed online on 10 August 2012.

[235] Subcircle, Flickr, http://www.flickr.com/photos/subcircle/500995147/, Accessed online 21 December 2012.

In an age of Facebook, eBay and online banking, data privacy is becoming more important than ever before. The majority of Australians have personal information stored online with a range of organisations and companies—information we'd rather the whole world didn't have access to.

A discussion paper[236] released by federal Attorney-General Nicola Roxon on Wednesday could be a step forward in the fight to keep private data, well, private.

Entitled "Australian Privacy Breach Notification", the discussion paper asks whether companies and other organisations should be required to report any breaches that occur to personal data they are storing.

2.13.1　You're Getting Mail

Only a day after Ms Roxon released the discussion paper we saw a great example of why mandatory data-breach notification is required.

On Thursday Australia Post shut down[237] its electronic parcel tracking service after a computer malfunction exposed the personal details of thousands of customers who were sent parcels. Mandatory data-breach reporting would have required Australia Post to tell customers of the breach immediately, rather than having the message delivered through the media the following day.

Of course, Australia Post is not alone—many large Australian companies and organisations—including Telstra,[238] Defence[239] and Medvet[240]—have suffered data breaches in the recent past.

---

[236] Australian Privacy Breach Notification, Australian Government, http://www.ag.gov.au/Consultationsreformsandreviews/Pages/Australian-Privacy-Breach-Notification.aspx, Accessed online on 19 October 2012.

[237] Bita N., Australia Post in online privacy breach, News Limited, 19 October 2012, http://www.news.com.au/business/companies/australia-post-in-online-privacy-breach/story-fndalbsz-1226498834454?sv=1684ecf6a51b387578fce1b3187fa84c&buffer_share=5b32d&utm_source=buffer, Accessed online on 19 October 2012.

[238] Moses A., Telstra's 734,000 account privacy blunder breached multiple laws: regulators, Fairfax Media, 29 June 2012, http://www.smh.com.au/it-pro/security-it/telstras-734000-account-privacy-blunder-breached-multiple-laws-regulators-20120629-2165z.html, Accessed online on 19 October 2012.

[239] Cooper H., Defence under investigation over privacy breach, Australian Broadcasting Corporation, 6 March 2012, http://www.abc.net.au/news/2012-03-05/defence-under-investigation-over-privacy-breach/3870002, Accessed online on 19 October 2012.

[240] Moses A., Paternity and drug test details leak online in privacy breach, Fairfax Media, 18 July 2011, http://www.smh.com.au/technology/security/paternity-and-drug-test-details-leak-online-in-privacy-breach-20110718-1hkyn.html, Accessed online on 19 October 2012.

2.13.2   Time to Take Privacy Seriously

In a press release on Wednesday explaining the motivations behind the new discussion paper, Ms Roxon said[241]:

Australians who transact online rightfully expect their personal information will be protected.

What Ms Roxon didn't say was the majority of companies don't seem to take customer privacy very seriously.

Currently, if an Australia company suffers a data or security breach, they are encouraged (but not required)[242] to disclose the details to the Privacy Commissioner.

But the reality is very few companies report data-breach notifications, and the number of reports is dropping.[243] These facts are corroborated by a review of data breaches reported online[244] by customers and in the media.[245]

And, as former hacker Kevin Mitnick told Fairfax[246] on August 9, there's little motivation for a company to admit they've been hacked and had data stolen:

Think about it: if you were running a multi-million dollar company and your database of customer information was stolen would you want to tell your clients? No.

Most [US] companies did not until the laws required them to. It's in the best interest of organisations—when they're attacked and information is stolen—to tell nobody.

---

[241] New privacy protection on the cards, Attorney-General Department, Australian Government, 17 October 2012, http://www.attorneygeneral.gov.au/Media-releases/Pages/2012/Fourth%20 Quarter/17October2012-Newprivacyprotectiononthecards.aspx, Accessed online on 19 October 2012.

[242] Data breach notification, Office of the Australian Information Commissioner, Australian Government, April 2012, http://www.oaic.gov.au/publications/guidelines/privacy_guidance/data_ breach_notification_guide_april2012.html, Accessed online on 19 October 2012.

[243] Media release: Privacy Commissioner supports the release of mandatory data breach notification discussion paper, Office of the Australian Information Commissioner, Australian Government, 17 October 2012, http://www.oaic.gov.au/news/media_releases/media_release_121017_mdbn_paper. html, Accessed online on 19 October 2012.

[244] Moses A., Thousands of privacy breaches going unreported, Fairfax Media, 27 July 2012, http:// www.theage.com.au/technology/technology-news/thousands-of-privacy-breaches-going- unreported-20110727-1hzes.html, Accessed online on 19 October 2012.

[245] Harrison D. and Grubb B., Roxon proposes compulsory reporting of online privacy breaches, Fairfax Media, 17 October 2012, http://www.smh.com.au/it-pro/security-it/roxon-proposes-com- pulsory-reporting-of-online-privacy-breaches-20121017-27qf0.html, Accessed online on 19 October 2012.

[246] Grubb B., Infamous hacker's grim warning for Australia, Fairfax Media, 9 August 2012, http:// www.smh.com.au/it-pro/security-it/infamous-hackers-grim-warning-for-australia-20120801- 23efy.html, Accessed online on 19 October 2012.

2.13.3   Consumer Confidence

Not everyone is a fan of the proposed mandatory data-breach reporting. The Australian Banking Association (ABA) acting chief, Tony Burke said today[247] that mandatory data breach reporting would lead to:

> an unwarranted loss of confidence in Australia's payment systems to the detriment of all.

> Attempting to notify individuals potentially affected could lead to significant levels of community concern, disproportionate to the actual level of risk, which could well be zero.

What Mr Burke does not appear to acknowledge is the fundamental right of every Australian to know if their personal data has been compromised. Australians should be able to select a bank based upon the bank's record of keeping personal data secure.

2.13.4   Protecting the People

So how would mandatory data-breach reporting help the average consumer?

As Australian Privacy Commissioner Timothy Pilgrim said[248] in a press release on Wednesday:

> Where personal information has been compromised, notification can be essential in helping individuals to regain control of that information. For example, an individual can ... change passwords or account numbers if they know a data breach has occurred.

If nothing else, it will force companies to let consumers know directly if their information has been compromised—surely better than reading about it in the newspaper the next day or finding out when a criminal uses the information to commit fraud.

2.13.5   What Companies Will Have to Do

The possibility of mandatory data-breach notification laws raises the question of impact on Australian organisations. For some the new requirements would have a minimal effect, but for many others there would be need for change.

---

[247]Colley A., Banks seek to hide privacy breaches from customers, News Limited, 19 October 2012, http://www.theaustralian.com.au/australian-it/government/banks-seek-to-hide-privacy-breaches-from-customers/story-fn4htb9o-1226498999294, Accessed online on 19 October 2012.

[248]Media release: Privacy Commissioner supports the release of mandatory data breach notification discussion paper, Office of the Australian Information Commissioner, Australian Government, 17 October 2012, http://www.oaic.gov.au/news/media_releases/media_release_121017_mdbn_paper. html, Accessed online on 19 October 2012.

The first question every Australian company will need to be able to answer is: "If there is a data breach will we recognise that the breach has occurred?"

For many organisations this will not be an easy question to answer. Most Australian companies are connected to the internet using low-cost security devices that are typically set up using default settings.

Professionals are not contracted to monitor the company's connection to the internet and systems that provide products or services to customers over the internet.

What this means is Australian companies will need to audit every system that interfaces with the internet to ensure security breaches can be identified. Security systems will also need to be able to collect information that can be provided to the authorities if a security breach leads to a data breach.

One approach that should be adopted by Australian companies is to utilise Intrusion Detection Systems (IDS)[249] which are set up, maintained and monitored by appropriately trained network engineers.

Companies will need to adopt a culture that will raise the focus on security and privacy to a level previously not seen in Australia.

The Attorney-General should consider introducing a mandatory annual network and system security audit for all companies or organisations that may be subject to a data breach.

2.13.6   The Overseas Angle

Most US states now have data-breach notification laws and the US federal government is considering introducing uniform national laws.

Europe is in a similar situation. The existing laws don't cover all organisations subjected to potential data breaches and only electronic communication providers (carriers) are required to notify regulators and customers of data breaches.

The European Union is also considering laws that would cover all organisations that may be subject to data breaches.

The timing of Ms Roxon's announcement, considering the aforementioned moves in the US and Europe, may lead to a belief that Australia is acting in concert with legislative changes overseas.

Australia must be prepared to get out in front of other nations because privacy and security reform is long overdue.

---

[249]Intrusion detection system, Wikipedia, http://en.wikipedia.org/wiki/Intrusion_detection_system, Accessed online on 19 October 2012.

2.13.7   Early Days

Ms Roxon's announcement and the release of the discussion paper should be applauded because Australians are being subjected to privacy attacks from all angles.

Examples that we should remember include the Sony PlayStation data breach[250] in which 1.5 million Australian accounts were exposed, and the Google Wi-Fi[251] data harvest.

Of course the discussion paper is just the first step down the path of mandatory data-breach reporting in Australia and many questions remain. Including:

- who should be notified in the case of a data breach?
- should penalties apply when an organisation fails to comply?

But as we move forward in this era of online transactions and social media—an era that will feature the NBN and its many opportunities and applications—there's a need for security and privacy legislation to keep pace.

Most importantly, there's a need for Australians to feel confident that their personal information is being kept safe by those we entrust it to.

The federal government is seeking submissions following the release of their discussion paper. To have your say, visit the *Attorney-General's website*[252] for details. Submissions close November 23.

---

[250] Moses A., PlayStation hack: 1.5M Aussie accounts exposed, Fairfax Media, 2 May 2011, http://www.smh.com.au/digital-life/games/playstation-hack-15m-aussie-accounts-exposed-20110502-1e3pc.html, Accessed online on 19 October 2012.

[251] Hearn L., Privacy watchdog probes Google's Wi-Fi data harvest, Fairfax Media, 19 May 2010, http://www.smh.com.au/technology/technology-news/privacy-watchdog-probes-googles-wifi-data-harvest-20100519-vckv.html, Accessed online on 19 October 2012.

[252] Australian Privacy Breach Notification, Attorney-General Department, Australian Government, http://www.ag.gov.au/Consultationsreformsandreviews/Pages/Australian-Privacy-Breach-Notification.aspx, Accessed online on 19 October 2012.

Chapter 3
Cyber Crime, Cyber Security and Cyber Warfare

The digital world has become a battleground for the forces of good and evil. There is an ever increasing awareness that the digital world provides an unlimited opportunity to further one's goals.

Newly constituted police cyber squads battle organized crime groups online in what has become a never ending conflict due to the ability of organized crime to operate remotely through untraceable accounts and an endless supply of compromised computers. Scarce police resources are being redirected to the fight against online crime gangs. The paucity of arrests highlights just how difficult it is to find and bring international criminal gangs that operate on the Internet to justice.

Nation states are constantly battling online to gain a military advantage and to portray opponents as evil hackers in an effort to gain an advantage for their cause in international public perception. Traditional soldiers with guns and bullets have been supplemented by bright young geeks with computers and a tool chest with the latest viruses, worms and malware.

For many people the battle rages around them and they continue their online activities blissfully unaware of the darker side to the Internet. When this dark side crosses over into the lives of ordinary people the effect can be devastating. Protection from online criminal organisations should be a high priority that prompts regular reviews of security and privacy measures.

3.1 You've Got Mail: How to Stop Spam and Reduce Cyber Crime

29 June 2011

M.A. Gregory and D. Glance, *Security and the Networked Society*,
DOI 10.1007/978-3-319-02390-8_3, © Springer International Publishing Switzerland 2013

Imagine a world where spam didn't exist. It isn't hard to do. *Source*: **David Hegarty[1]**

We've all received them: emails offering special prices on Viagra, offering fortunes we didn't know we had, offering links to fantastic websites we simply *must* visit right away.

Annoying as! But the technology to stop spam and other undesirable emails not only exists, it's been around for years.

With cyber crime costing Australia more than a billion dollars a year[2], it's well and truly time we did something to improve our defences. And what better way to start than by securing email: a piece of technology that most of us use every day.

3.1.1   Cyber-Crime for Dummies

One of the easiest methods for carrying out cyber-crime is to send an unsolicited or spam email which contains: a virus; an attempt to acquire an individual's sensitive information (known as "phishing"[3]); or some other mechanism for perpetrating internet crime.

---

[1]Hegarty D., Computer email spam, Flickr, with permission 15 January 2013, http://www.flickr. com/photos/hegarty_david/2255499619/, Accessed online 21 December 2012.

[2] Your system might be at risk—Australia's cyber security, http://www.aspi.org.au/publications/ publication_details.aspx?ContentID=296&pubtype=9, Accessed online 29 June 2011.

[3]Requests for your account information ('phishing' scams), http://www.scamwatch.gov.au/content/ index.phtml/tag/RequestsForYourAccountInformation, Accessed online 29 June 2011.

The current worldwide email system is based on a standard called the Simple Mail Transport Protocol (SMTP)[4] which was created in 1982 and last updated in 2008.

The system has served us well for decades, but it also allows fake emails to be sent and received with no way of tracing them to their point of origin.

In the last 30 years there have been a number of updates to SMTP, including two methods that can be used to improve security and fight spam.

3.1.2 Sign-In to Send

The first update, released in 1995, was an extension of SMTP called SMTP-AUTH[5]. This was introduced to allow authentication of email clients.

Say your email system at work uses SMTP-AUTH. Whenever your email client (such as Microsoft Outlook or Apple Mail) communicates with the server that stores, receives and sends your emails, the server would ask the client for a password.

In this way, all email traffic sent through an email server is authenticated and can be traced in the case of fake or malicious emails.

While SMTP-AUTH is a great idea in theory, it hasn't been adopted in practice because many organisations use email systems that either don't implement SMTP-AUTH correctly or don't specify that it should be turned on.

Worryingly, it's also possible to fake the credentials required by the SMTP-AUTH rules in an email message and to make matters worse mail servers may be setup on hijacked computers solely for the purpose of sending fake or malicious emails.

As a result, SMTP-AUTH is practically useless if used alone.

SPAM song by Monty Python[6] Spam…not always what the discerning customer wants.

3.1.3 Lockdown

The second extension to SMTP that can be used to fight spam—Secure SMTP (also known as SMTPS)—was introduced in 1997. SMTPS has the benefit of using the encrypted Secure Sockets Layer (SSL)[7] communication protocol, an approach used to secure e-commerce and online banking services today.

---

[4]Simple Mail Transfer Protocol, http://www.ietf.org/rfc/rfc2821.txt, Accessed on 29 June 2011.

[5]SMTP Authentication, http://www.fehcom.de/qmail/smtpauth.html, Accessed online 29 June 2011.

[6]SPAM Song Monty Python, http://www.youtube.com/watch?v=g8huXkSaL7o, Accessed online 29 June 2011.

[7]Introduction to SSL, https://www.symantec.com/page.jsp?id=how-ssl-works, Accessed online 29 June 2011.

If your workplace wanted to utilise SMTPS, it would need to:

- Choose one of the many SSL certificate providers (such as VeriSign[8])
- Complete a verification process to prove the identity of the business
- Pay the price for the SSL certificate (around $50 a year)
- Install the SSL certificate on the company's email server

With the SSL certificate installed on the email server, all communication between the server and the client (and with other mail servers) would be both authenticated and encrypted.

3.1.4   Tracing Spam and Other Nasties

With SMTPS implemented, spam and malicious emails can then be tracked back to the source email server.

If an email server is found to be the source of spam or other email-related criminal activities, the authorities could issue a notice to the company that owns the email server.

The notice would contain details of the infraction and identify actions to be taken to prevent the problem happening again.

If an email server is found to be a constant source of problem emails, the authorities could act to: fine the company that owns the email server or revoke the SSL certificate issued for the email server domain, thereby removing the email server from service.

Cyber crime is now a significant worldwide problem and every effort must be made to reduce or stop the problem: people's lives are being negatively affected and the economy is being harmed.

The Australian Government must act to reduce internet crime. Implementing the mandatory use of SMTPS would be a good start.

The Australian Government could go one step further and send delegates to the United Nations—which controls the standards used for the internet—and lobby for the immediate introduction of SMTPS worldwide.

One step at a time though…

3.2   Ein Spy: Is the German Government Using a Trojan to Watch Its Citizens?

11 October 2011

---

[8]Buy SSL Certificates, https://www.verisign.com.au/ssl/buy-ssl-certificates/index.html, Accessed online 29 June 2011.

On October 8, Berlin's hacking collective the Chaos Computer Club[9] (CCC) announced it had analysed a piece of software[10] it believed had been written by the German Government.

Once installed on a computer, the software could quietly listen to conversations on Skype[11], log keystrokes and switch on the computer's web-cam. It would then report this data back to servers, two of which were identified[12]—one in the US and the other in Germany.

The program could also be remotely updated and potentially used to install and run other programs. The security company F-Secure's Mikko Hypponen reported[13] its own findings on the malware[14] (malicious software) and confirmed the CCC's analysis.

It dubbed the trojan[15] "R2D2", from the text "CRPO-r2d2-POE" used by the software to initiate data transfer.

Regarding the German government's involvement in the R2D2 trojan, Mikko wrote:

> "We have no reason to suspect CCC's findings, but we can't confirm that this trojan was written by the German government. As far as we see, the only party that could confirm that would be the German government itself."

But the CCC believed it had found an example of a "Bundestrojaner" (Government trojan) which, from 2007, was being used to conduct online searches of suspects by law enforcement agencies without much restriction. In 2008, a ruling by a German Constitutional Court[16] restricted use to cases in which human lives or state property were in danger, and only after permission had been granted by a judge.

The CCC maintains the German government used a different term for the spy software o get around the restrictions on online searches: "Quellen-TKÜ". That means "source wiretapping", listening to conversations on sources such as Skype, for example, in order to prevent a person from encrypting the conversation.

But the capabilities of the R2D2 trojan allowed for much more than this.

The trojan itself was poorly written and potentially allowed for others to take control of the software once installed. The concern here is that someone could take over the malware and capture information themselves or plant false evidence.

---

[9]Chaos Computer Club, http://www.ccc.de/, Accessed on 11 October 2011.

[10]Chaos Computer Club analyzes government malware, http://www.ccc.de/en/updates/2011/staatstrojaner, Accessed on 11 October 2011.

[11]Rebuilding the damaged brain: can stem cells be used as repair kits? http://theconversation.edu.au/rebuilding-the-damaged-brain-can-stem-cells-be-used-as-repair-kits-3557, Accessed on 11 October 2011.

[12]Possible Governmental Backdoor Found ("Case R2D2"), http://www.f-secure.com/weblog/archives/00002249.html, Accessed on 11 October 2011.

[13]Possible Governmental Backdoor Found ("Case R2D2"), http://www.f-secure.com/weblog/archives/00002249.html, Accessed on 11 October 2011.

[14]Defining Malware: FAQ, http://technet.microsoft.com/en-us/library/dd632948.aspx, Accessed on 11 October 2011.

[15]Defining Malware: FAQ, http://technet.microsoft.com/en-us/library/dd632948.aspx, Accessed on 11 October 2011.

[16]Germany's Highest Court Restricts Internet Surveillance, http://www.dw.de/germanys-highest-court-restricts-internet-surveillance/a-3152627-1, Accessed on 11 October 2011.

3.2.1   Government Use of Malware

The use of backdoor trojan[17] software by law enforcement agencies came to the fore
in 2001 when the NSA[18] or FBI were rumoured to have produced software known
as Magic Lantern[19].

This software emerged as part of a Freedom of Information request filed by the
Electronic Privacy Information Center that revealed documents[20] concerning a project
called "Carnivore".

That project allowed for full online surveillance of a particular internet address.
It was used in conjunction with a Magic Lantern backdoor trojan specifically
targeted at capturing encryption passwords. This, in turn, would allow the FBI to
unencrypt captured communication.

At the time, anti-virus software companies were faced with the dilemma of
whether to remove known government backdoor trojans. In 2001, various anti-virus
software vendors made declarations[21] about whether their software would remove a
suspected FBI backdoor trojan.

Companies such as F-Secure stated categorically[22] they would never knowingly
leave detected malware on a computer. Representatives of security software company Sophos agreed but Eric Chien, chief researcher at Symantec[23] at the time stated
the company would not detect Government malware[24].

The assumption was that the software would have enough protective mechanisms in place to prevent the wrong people gaining control of it. As has been demonstrated by the case of the R2D2 trojan, this is quite clearly not the case.

The software has very few protective mechanisms and was open to hijacking, as
the CCC demonstrated[25].

---

[17] What is a backdoor trojan? http://www.geekstogo.com/190/what-is-a-backdoor-trojan/, Accessed on 11 October 2011.

[18] Welcome to the National Security Agency - NSA/CSS, http://www.nsa.gov/, Accessed on 11 October 2011.

[19] Magic Lantern (software), http://en.wikipedia.org/wiki/Magic_Lantern_%28software%29, Accessed on 11 October 2011.

[20] Error 404, http://epic.org/privacy/carnivore/foia_documents.html%5D, Accessed on 11 October 2011.

[21] Antivirus vendors are wary of FBI's Magic Lantern, http://gcn.com/articles/2001/12/06/antivirus-vendors-are-wary-of-fbis-magic-lantern.aspx, Accessed on 11 October 2011.

[22] Policy on Detecting Government Spy Programs, http://www.f-secure.com/en/web/labs_global/policies, Accessed on 11 October 2011.

[23] Norton from Symantec: You Need The Speed, http://www.symantec.com/norton/ps/2up_de_de_nis360t3.html?om_sem_cid=hho_sem_ic:au:ggl:en:e|kw0000006084, Accessed on 11 October 2011.

[24] AV Vendors Split Over FBI Trojan, http://www.securityfocus.com/news/292, Accessed on 11 October 2011.

[25] Chaos Computer Club analyzes government malware, http://www.ccc.de/en/updates/2011/staat-strojaner, Accessed on 11 October 2011.

As more human activity migrates to the internet, including criminal and terrorist activities, governments (and law enforcement agencies in particular) will be turning to every available technique to intercept and collect information.

Germany's BND (foreign intelligence service), it was alleged by Der Spiegel[26], used spyware to monitor the Ministry of Commerce and Industry in Afghanistan and obtain confidential documents, passwords and email.

Surveillance trojans have also been used by the Swiss, and the Austrian Police[27].

3.2.2   An Open Barrel

The CCC has made a number of allegations[28] about the origins and potential ramifications of the R2D2 trojan. The group firstly assumed this was a "Bundestrojaner light" because it was sent the software from someone who presumably had cause to believe they were being subjected to a source wiretapping.

Also, according to senior technology consultant Graham Cluley[29] of Sophos[30], there were comments in the code that were suggestive of a link with German authorities, including the phrase "Ozapftis"—a Bavarian phrase meaning the "Barrel is open", invoked when the first barrel is opened at Oktoberfest.

Why this is indicative of a German government hacker rather than an independent German hacker who likes beer is open to debate.

Even if the trojan is one the Government has deployed, it is again an assumption to believe they would utilise the extra capabilities without first seeking a judge's permission, which, since the 2008 ruling, they are entitled to do in certain limited circumstances.

Although, as has been seen in the US, laws that cover protection against terrorism, such as the Patriot Act[31] are more commonly being used for a range of other purposes, including drug trafficking which made up 73.7 % of Patriot Act "sneak-and-peak" searches in 2009[32].

---

[26] German Spies Put Afghan Ministry under Surveillance, http://www.spiegel.de/international/germany/bnd-affairs-broadens-german-spies-put-afghan-ministry-under-surveillance-a-549894.html, Accessed on 11 October 2011.

[27] Austrian Police to use crime-busting Trojans, http://news.techworld.com/security/10446/austrian-police-to-use-crime-busting-trojans/, Accessed on 11 October 2011.

[28] Chaos Computer Club analyzes government malware, http://www.ccc.de/en/updates/2011/staatstrojaner, Accessed on 11 October 2011.

[29] 'Government' backdoor R2D2 Trojan discovered by Chaos Computer Club, http://nakedsecurity.sophos.com/2011/10/09/government-backdoor-trojan-chaos/?utm_source=twitter&utm_medium=gcluley&utm_campaign=naked%2Bsecurity, Accessed on 11 October 2011.

[30] Sophos UTM, http://www.sophos.com/en-us/, Accessed on 11 October 2011.

[31] USA PATRIOT Act (H.R. 3162), http://epic.org/privacy/terrorism/hr3162.html, Accessed on 11 October 2011.

[32] Use of Patriot Act Sneak-And-Peek Powers for Drug War Further Eclipsed Terrorism Uses in 2009, http://irregulartimes.com/index.php/archives/2011/02/04/use-of-patriot-act-power-for-drug-war-skyrockets/, Accessed on 11 October 2011.

There are a number of observations that can be made from the CCC's announcement:

First, anti-spyware software from any company that would even contemplate not detecting malware, irrespective of its origins, would have to be treated with caution. Companies that have declared their approach to detecting all malware should be favoured.

Second, it brings into question the use of government sponsored anti-virus initiatives unless they give free choice of vendors to the public. Why would you trust a government sponsored anti-virus software package if they are also producing malware for general use?

Finally, it's interesting to note the R2D2 trojan would only work if the person being targeted was using a PC with Windows. So perhaps the easiest solution for anxious German citizens at present is to use Linux, an Apple Mac OSX computer or a smart phone?

3.3 Spying, Flying and Delivering Tacos: With Drones, the Sky's the Limit

28 March 2012

The Federal Government is considering allowing[33] the US to base military surveillance drones on the Cocos Islands[34]—an Australian territory located in the Indian Ocean between Australia and Sri Lanka.

The news comes 4 months after the US and Australia agreed to a closer military alliance[35] during Barack Obama's visit to Australia last year.

Aerial drones (otherwise known as unmanned aerial vehicles[36]) are now a fixture of the modern skyline and the Cocos Island discussion is only the most recent mention of drones in the media.

The rise of drone technology is due largely to their flexibility—a drone need only be constructed to carry a camera for surveillance or a weapon. Not having to accommodate a pilot makes a huge difference to the design and, more importantly, the costs of building and running the machine.

While convenience and utility is driving the use of drones, important questions are being raised about their use for surveillance of civilian populations and in unmanned missions to target enemy combatants.

---

[33] Government won't rule out Aussie base for US drones, http://www.abc.net.au/news/2012-03-28/gillard-tight-lipped-on-us-drones-claim/3916460, Accessed on 28 March 2012.

[34] Cocos (Keeling) Islands, http://en.wikipedia.org/wiki/Cocos_%28Keeling%29_Islands, Accessed on 28 March 2012.

[35] Obama and Gillard boost US-Australia military ties, http://www.guardian.co.uk/world/video/2011/nov/16/obama-gillard-us-australia-military-video, Accessed on 28 March 2012.

[36] Unmanned aerial vehicle, http://en.wikipedia.org/wiki/Unmanned_aerial_vehicle, Accessed on 28 March 2012.

Drones come in many shapes, sizes and capabilities. An Israeli-made Eitan drone (see video above) for instance, is the size of a Boeing 737 (with a wingspan of 26 m), can stay in the air for 20 h and reach an altitude of 40,000 ft (roughly 12,000 m).

At the other extreme, the Nano Hummingbird[37] (see video below) is constructed to look like a real hummingbird, has a 6.5-in. (roughly 17 cm) wingspan and can fly for 8 min using the power of an AA battery.

US Predator B drones[38] have wingspans of 66 ft (roughly 20 m), can reach an altitude of 50,000 ft (roughly 15,000 m) and stay in flight for 30 h.

These are drones that have been regularly used[39] in Afghanistan and Pakistan for targeted assassinations by the CIA. In the past 8 years, the CIA's drone program has been responsible for the assassinations of 2,223 alleged Taliban, al-Qaeda and other militants in 289 strikes.

The US police, and other countries' police forces are using drones for surveillance operations with suggestions it is only a matter of time[40] before they are equipped with non-lethal and lethal weapons.

Drones have also found their way into civilian use. In the US, a federal law[41] allows the Federal Aviation Administration[42] to use drones for commercial uses, include selling real-estate, monitoring oil spills, dusting crops and filming movies.

But possibly the most original drone applications include their use to play musical instruments [43] and to deliver fast food[44].

San Francisco-based (where else?) start-up Tacocopter[45] has set up a business in which orders for Mexican fast food made on a smartphone are delivered to the customer, wherever they are, by drone.

Unfortunately for the company, the use of drones for delivering fast food has not received FAA approval. This is perhaps unsurprising, given the difficulties involved in delivering a food package without maiming or killing the recipient.

---

[37] Nano Hummingbird, http://www.avinc.com/nano, Accessed on 28 March 2012.

[38] General Atomics MQ-9 Reaper, http://en.wikipedia.org/wiki/General_Atomics_MQ-9_Reaper, Accessed on 28 March 2012.

[39] U.S. and Pakistan bargain over CIA drones, http://www.ctvnews.ca/u-s-and-pakistan-bargain-over-cia-drones-1.787129, Accessed on 28 March 2012.

[40] Police drones to be equipped with non-lethal weapons?, http://rt.com/usa/news/drone-surveillance-montgomery-weapon-507/, Accessed on 28 March 2012.

[41] Drones Set Sights on U.S. Skies, http://www.nytimes.com/2012/02/18/technology/drones-with-an-eye-on-the-public-cleared-to-fly.html?pagewanted=all, Accessed on 28 March 2012.

[42] Federal Aviation Administration, http://www.faa.gov/, Accessed on 28 March 2012.

[43] Robot Quadrotors Perform James Bond Theme, http://www.youtube.com/watch?v=_sUeGC-8dyk&feature=youtu.be, Accessed on 28 March 2012.

[44] Tacocopter Aims To Deliver Tacos Using Unmanned Drone Helicopters, http://www.huffingtonpost.com/2012/03/23/tacocopter-startup-delivers-tacos-by-unmanned-drone-helicopter_n_1375842.html?1332538432, Accessed on 28 March 2012.

[45] Tacocopter, http://tacocopter.com/, Accessed on 28 March 2012.

But it isn't the just the military and small businesses that are employing drone technology. You or I can head to our local store and purchase, say, the popular Parrot AR. Drone[46] for around US$300.

This 380-g "quadrotor" can be flown[47] using an iPhone or iPad controller that displays pictures from on-board cameras. Although flying the drone still takes some skill, it has on-board electronics including an ultrasound device that enables it to hover when the controls are released.

It is not clear what the average person would use a drone for other than for spying on their neighbours or terrorising their dog. But in Poland, a drone was recently used to film police[48] tackling rioters in Warsaw. CNN has even used consumer-level drones[49] to film a town that suffered extensive storm damage.

Despite the obvious benefits of drone technology for a range of uses, there are some considerable drawbacks.

Although drones are uninhabited and some can even fly missions without control from the ground, one of the problems[50] faced by the US Air Force has been, ironically, the lack of trained staff to fly them.

Another, more serious threat is the use of malware[51] (or malicious software), such as the virus that infected US drone-control systems[52].

And then there's the possibility someone could capture your drone, as was the case of Iran's capture[53] of a US RQ-170 stealth drone[54], possibly by fooling[55] its GPS system.

As well as the technical and operational concerns about drone technology, there are also significant privacy concerns that need to be addressed. To concerned citizens, drones pose a danger of increased surveillance.

---

[46]Parrot AR.Drone, http://ardrone.parrotshopping.com/us/p_ardrone_main.aspx, Accessed on 28 March 2012.

[47]Parrot AR.Drone iPad Controlled Remote Control Aircraft Test Flight Demo Linus Tech Tips, http://www.youtube.com/watch?feature=endscreen&NR=1&v=bkKeijmgXW0, Accessed on 28 March 2012.

[48]WATCH!!!!! 2/2 drone launched by protesters at Warsaw, Poland, http://www.youtube.com/watch?v=FmhV-ymivJk, Accessed on 28 March 2012.

[49]CNN uses a small drone to shoot aerial footage of storm and tornado damage (05/07/2011), http://www.youtube.com/watch?v=SmpwTVvS67Y, Accessed on 28 March 2012.

[50]Air Force Buys Fewer Drones—But Ups Drone Flights, http://www.wired.com/dangerroom/2012/02/air-force-drones/, Accessed on 28 March 2012.

[51]Malware, http://en.wikipedia.org/wiki/Malware, Accessed on 28 March 2012.

[52]Exclusive: Computer Virus Hits U.S. Drone Fleet, http://www.wired.com/dangerroom/2011/10/virus-hits-drone-fleet/, Accessed on 28 March 2012.

[53]Why Iran's capture of US drone will shake CIA, http://www.bbc.co.uk/news/world-us-canada-16095823, Accessed on 28 March 2012.

[54]Lockheed Martin RQ-170 Sentinel, http://en.wikipedia.org/wiki/Lockheed_Martin_RQ-170_Sentinel, Accessed on 28 March 2012.

[55]Link no longer goes to specified page, http://news.yahoo.com/blogs/technology-blog/iran-may-captured-u-stealth-drone-hacking-gps-030447469.html, Accessed on 28 March 2012.

In a society that is already monitored[56] by fixed closed-circuit cameras, the ability to increase that surveillance to any area is seen by some as yet another encroachment on the privacy of the individual[57].

But it would seem drone-related privacy concerns are being taken seriously in some circles. The Electronic Frontier Foundation (EFF[58]) in the US has filed a Freedom of Information Act request[59] to gain access to records from the FAA detailing who is currently using drones.

In a similar vein, the American Civil Liberties Union (ACLU)[60] has published a report[61] looking at the privacy issues around the use of drones and recommending courts impose limits on the use of drones for surveillance.

Defence Minister Stephen Smith has described the Cocos Island drone base as "very much a long-term prospect". It's clear we'll be hearing about this technology for some time yet.

Further Reading

- History repeating: Australian military power in the Cocos Islands[62]—Liam McHugh
- The Drone as Privacy Catalyst[63]—Ryan Calo
- Protecting Privacy From Aerial Surveillance: Recommendations for Government Use of Drone Aircraft[64]—American Civil Liberties Union

3.4 Flame. A Weapon of the US-Led Cyberwar or Corporate Spyware?

2 June 2012

---

[56]Closed-circuit television, http://en.wikipedia.org/wiki/Closed-circuit_television, Accessed on 28 March 2012.

[57]What privacy do you have left to lose? Beware the drone, http://www.networkworld.com/columnists/2012/031212-backspin.html, Accessed on 28 March 2012.

[58]Electronic Frontier Foundation, https://www.eff.org/, Accessed on 28 March 2012.

[59]Drone Flights in the U.S, https://www.eff.org/foia/faa-drone-authorizations, Accessed on 28 March 2012.

[60]American Civil Liberties Union, http://www.aclu.org/, Accessed on 28 March 2012.

[61]Report: "Protecting Privacy From Aerial Surveillance: Recommendations for Government Use of Drone Aircraft", http://www.aclu.org/technology-and-liberty/report-protecting-privacy-aerial-surveillance-recommendations-government-use, Accessed on 28 March 2012.

[62]History repeating: Australian military power in the Cocos Islands, https://theconversation.edu.au/history-repeating-australian-military-power-in-the-cocos-islands-4484, Accessed on 28 March 2012.

[63]The Drone as Privacy Catalyst, http://www.stanfordlawreview.org/online/drone-privacy-catalyst, Accessed on 28 March 2012.

[64]Link no longer goes to specified page, https://www.aclu.org/files/assets/protectingprivacyfromaerialsurveillance.pdf, Accessed on 28 March 2012.

Owni, Wikileaks and others' site on surveillance software http://spyfiles.org

Iran it seems has been the target of another novel form of malware christened "Flame"[65]. Much has been made of this new threat because of novel characteristics that set it apart from traditional malware. It is much larger in size that normal malware (20 MB vs a more traditional 1 MB) and consists of a modular architecture with components that have more in common with normal corporate software than with "regular" viruses and worms.

It is Flame's use of normal business technologies that made the malware look like regular corporate software and possibly helped it escape detection for so long. Mikko Hypponen, CEO of security firm F-Secure, has commented[66] that Flame basically "hid in plain sight" making itself indistinguishable from all other software running on the infected PCs. However, security companies also failed to detect the possibly related malware Stuxnet and Duqu and they were very different from everyday software. Illustrating perhaps, the general limitations of commercial grade anti-virus software in detecting highly specialised malware.

Because of the countries targeted by Flame (Iran and its Middle East neighbours), suspicion has fallen on the US and Israel as Flame's creators. It now seems that

---

[65] Virus News, Kaspersky Lab and ITU Research Reveals New Advanced Cyber Threat, http://www.kaspersky.com/about/news/virus/2012/Kaspersky_Lab_and_ITU_Research_Reveals_New_Advanced_Cyber_Threat, Accessed online 1 July 2013.
[66] Hypponen, Mikko, Why Antivirus Companies Like Mine Failed to Catch Flame and Stuxnet, http://www.wired.com/threatlevel/2012/06/internet-security-fail/, Accessed online 1 July 2013.

Stuxnet may have been part of an official US operation[67] called "Olympic Games", specifically targeting enemy countries' critical infrastructure. It has been alleged that Flame was not part of this program. Stuxnet specifically targeted and aimed to damage nuclear facilities whilst Flame appears to be a more general espionage tool, recording conversations, keystrokes, screenshots and other information from its infected hosts.

In this respect, Flame has more in common with the German Trojan software R2D2 that was used by the German authorities to spy[68] on its own citizens.

It is somewhat surprising that no commentators have made the connection between Flame and the dozens of commercially available spyware[69]. The levels of sophistication between Flame and commercially available surveillance software are similar—the only difference being that Flame has the ability to replicate and infect other machines whereas surveillance software's installation is normally targeted.

In fact, there is nothing to say that Flame was not actually installed or being used by the Governments of the countries involved to spy on their own citizens. The belief that Stuxnet was of Israeli or US origin was held on the basis that the programming skills required and funding for the development would have only been found in these countries. But as has been detailed on the Spyfiles site[70], the more general surveillance software is relatively inexpensive and can be bought "off-the-shelf". So anyone could have been the originator, even private corporations.

The origins and objectives of Flame will probably never be known. It reaffirms however, that cyber threats are increasingly common and real and that protecting ourselves and our infrastructure against them increasingly difficult.

3.5   SCAMwatch: A Helping Hand Against Online Scammers

4 July 2012

---

[67] Sanger, David E. Obama Order Sped Up Wave of Cyberattacks Against Iran, http://www.nytimes.com/2012/06/01/world/middleeast/obama-ordered-wave-of-cyberattacks-against-iran.html?pagewanted=1&_r=1&_r=0, Accessed online 1 July 2013.

[68] Glance, David, Ein spy: is the German government using a trojan to watch its citizens? https://theconversation.com/ein-spy-is-the-german-government-using-a-trojan-to-watch-its-citizens-3765, Accessed online 1 July 2013.

[69] Link no longer goes to specified page, http://spyfiles.org/, Accessed online 1 July 2013.

[70] Link no longer goes to specified page, http://spyfiles.org/, Accessed online 1 July 2013.

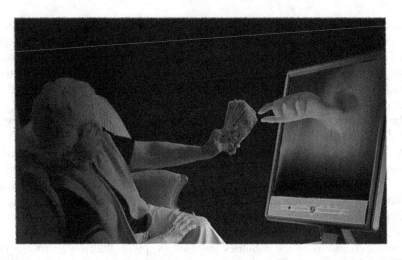

Thinking you know every trick in the book doesn't mean you really do. Don Hankins CC0[71]

Crimes of confidence, known as scams, are on the rise. You probably know the basics. The way the most common type of scam works involves you being presented with an offer, product or service for which you pay and then don't receive anything.

Scams have always been big business and perpetrators have adapted quickly to new technology. Telephone, mail and now the internet have provided an ever-growing platform for large-scale, and coordinated, scam attacks.

Why should we be worried? What's the real scale of the problem?

Well, the Director General of Britain's MI5, Jonathan Evans last week warned[72] that:

Vulnerabilities in the internet are being exploited aggressively not just by criminals but also by states," and "the extent of what is going on is astonishing—with industrial-scale processes involving many thousands of people lying behind both State sponsored cyber espionage and organised cyber crime.

Multinationals offering services online, with customer's banking details logged on their servers, continue to get hacked at an ever increasing pace, and some more than once.

---

[71] Hankins D., Flickr, http://www.flickr.com/photos/23905174@N00/2524306151/in/photostream, Accessed online 21 December 2012.

[72] Whitehead T., Cyber crime a global threat, MI5 head warns, The Telegraph, 26 Jun 2012, http://www.telegraph.co.uk/news/uknews/terrorism-in-the-uk/9354373/Cyber-crime-a-global-threat-MI5-head-warns.html, Accessed online 4 July 2012.

Many people will know the Apple iTunes and app store accounts[73] were hacked recently. Such hacks go on all the time, but without the attendant publicity generated by a story involving a company of Apple's stature.

A study[74] by the Carnegie Mellon University's Cylab[75] found that only 13 % of companies had a privacy officer—someone whose job it would be to police online security.

According to Jody Westby, CEO of security firm Global Cyber Risk[76] and adjunct distinguished follow at Carnegie Mellon:

It's no wonder there are so many breaches. Privacy, security and cybercrime are three legs of the same stool.

The responsibility for the rise in organised crime does not solely lie with corporations and the government. Everyone needs to take the time necessary to become aware of how organised criminals are going to try to effect a scam.

One important first step towards learning how to deal with scams is to visit the SCAMwatch[77] website launched recently by the Australian Competition and Consumer Commission (ACCC)[78].

SCAMwatch provides information to consumers and small business about how to recognise, avoid and report scams[79].

What becomes immediately apparent at SCAMwatch is the large number of active scams found today. Scams are designed to target every aspect of our daily lives and focus on finding some weakness, need or desire that can be taken advantage of.

---

[73] Cooper M., Hack warning on iTunes accounts, Fairfax, 19 June 2012, http://www.smh.com.au/digital-life/consumer-security/hack-warning-on-itunes-accounts-20120619-20lps.html, Accessed online 4 July 2012.

[74] Westby J.R., How Boards & Senior Executives are Managing Cyber Risks, CyLab, Carnegie Mellon University, 16 May 2012, http://www.rsa.com/innovation/docs/CMU-GOVERNANCE-RPT-2012-FINAL.pdf, Accessed online 4 July 2012.

[75] CyLab, Carnegie Mellon University, http://www.cylab.cmu.edu/, Accessed online 4 July 2012.

[76] Global cyber risk LLC, http://globalcyberrisk.com/, Accessed online 4 July 2012.

[77] SCAMwatch, Australian Competition and Consumer Commission, http://www.scamwatch.gov.au/, Accessed online 4 July 2012

[78] Australian Competition and Consumer Commission, http://www.accc.gov.au/, Accessed online 4 July 2012

[79] Report a scam, SCAMwatch, https://www.scamwatch.gov.au/content/index.phtml/itemId/694011, Accessed online 4 July 2012.

Source: **jepoirrier**[80]

By definition, scammers create scams to look genuine. By convincing you that the scam is real you become more likely to carry out the actions necessary for the scam to succeed.

SCAMwatch is an important education tool that provides examples of scams, descriptions of how the scammers will try to entice you and recent scam victim stories[81] that are provided to encourage Australians to learn from their experiences.

There have already been criticisms of the service. If you use the SCAMwatch scam report form[82] the information you provide is sent to the ACCC and not to the Australian federal or state police. A better solution—many argue, and I tend to agree— would be for the scam report to be sent to all of the appropriate Australian authorities.

A list of other organisations that you should contact to report a scam can be found here[83].

But, for any of its faults, SCAMwatch is an impressive educational tool that includes simple and easy-to-understand descriptions of common scams with excellent advice on how we can better protect ourselves, including:

- SCAMwatch email alerts[84]. These provide warnings when a sharp increase in the execution of a particular scam is identified. Companies that do not have a person

---

[80]Poirrier J.M., Flickr, http://www.flickr.com/photos/jepoirrier/2046188221/, Accessed online 21 December 2012.

[81]Victim stories and latest news, SCAMwatch, http://www.scamwatch.gov.au/content/index. phtml/itemId/693979, Accessed online 4 July 2012.

[82]Report a scam, SCAMwatch, https://www.scamwatch.gov.au/content/index.phtml/ itemId/694011, Accessed online 4 July 2012.

[83]Report a scam to another organisation, SCAMwatch, http://www.scamwatch.gov.au/content/ index.phtml/itemId/854913, Accessed online 4 July 2012.

[84]Register for free: SCAMwatch email alerts, SCAMwatch, https://www.scamwatch.gov.au/con-tent/index.phtml/tag/ScamWatchEmailAlerts/, Accessed online 4 July 2012.

responsible for security and privacy should nominate someone to receive the SCAMwatch email alerts.

- The little black book of scams[85] is excellent reading. Ask for the printer version to be sent to you or download the PDF version to read on your computer, Kindle or iPad.
- See-a-scam[86] samples provide details on a range of real scams and examples of how the scammers will try to trick you.
- The scam awareness videos[87] are a light-hearted series of videos that take you through various scams.

So that we get a reality check about the serious nature of the material presented on SCAMwatch, the site includes recent scam victim stories[88].

Personally, I don't need to see the stories on SCAMwatch to know how heart-rendering the after-effects of being scammed can be. Members of my family, as with many other families, have been scammed and lost considerable sums of money.

Source: **B. Rosen**[89]

---

[85] The little black book of scams, Australian Competition and Consumer Commission, http://www.accc.gov.au/content/index.phtml/tag/littleblackbookofscams, Accessed online 4 July 2012.

[86] See-a-scam,   SCAMwatch,   http://www.scamwatch.gov.au/content/index.phtml/tag/SeeaScamSamples, Accessed online 4 July 2012.

[87] Scam awareness videos, SCAMwatch, http://www.scamwatch.gov.au/content/index.phtml/tag/scamawarenessvideos, Accessed online 4 July 2012.

[88] Victim stories and latest news, SCAMwatch, http://www.scamwatch.gov.au/content/index.phtml/tag/victimstories, Accessed online 4 July 2012.

[89] Rosen, B., http://www.flickr.com/photos/rosengrant/3545047810/, Accessed online 4 July 2012.

The collective disgust of society towards scammers will not stop them because today scammers often hide, operate and disappear again exclusively in cyberspace. Trying to slam a door in their face just won't work.

Take the time, visit SCAMwatch, learn and empower yourself and your organisation in the fight against scams.

3.6   Obama's Not Dead, But Does Twitter Need #Better #Security?

13 July 2011

On July 4, a hacker took control of one of the Twitter accounts of US broadcaster FoxNews.com and sent out several tweets announcing President Obama had been shot[90].

Because it was a national holiday and nobody was available at Twitter to help, Fox News only regained control of the account some hours later and by that time the original tweets had spread around the world.

Even though the original posts were eventually removed, the hashtag[91] #ObamaDead continued, with people still resending the original message 6 days later.

This act was followed by another Twitter account being hacked in the UK when someone took over the account of PayPal UK and posted offensive tweets[92] aimed at embarrassing the company.

Identity theft is increasingly common, but the hacking of a news organisation and the tastelessness of the messages sent has brought into question the perceived lack of security of Twitter. This has led several security analysts[93] to suggest Twitter is lagging behind other services in robust security options.

3.6.1   Stepping It Up

They have also argued that Twitter should make all access to the website secure by default and should also implement what is called two-step verification.

Secure connections are the easy part: you simply replace "http" with "https" in the address. Twitter doesn't make this the default, but you can personally change this in your settings.

---

[90]Robbins, Liz & Stelter, Brian, Hackers Commandeer a Fox News Twitter Account, http://www.nytimes.com/2011/07/05/business/media/05fox.html?hp, Accessed online 1 July 2013.

[91]Parr, Ben, HOW TO: Get the Most Out of Twitter #Hashtags, http://mashable.com/2009/05/17/twitter-hashtags/, Accessed online 1 July 2013.

[92]Bennett, Shea, Paypal UK Twitter Profile Hacked By Angry Customer, http://www.mediabistro.com/alltwitter/paypal-uk-hacked-twitter_b11109, Accessed online 1 July 2013.

[93]Finkle, Jim & Strom, Roy, Twitter security lags some other sites: experts, http://www.reuters.com/article/2011/07/08/us-twitter-idUSTRE7667EL20110708, Accessed online 1 July 2013.

Two-step verification is more sophisticated. It involves logging into a service using a password and a temporary number that is provided as a phone text message or from an application running on your phone. So even if a hacker got hold of the password, it would not be possible for them to get access to the number.

Or would it?

Nobody really knows how the hackers got access to the accounts of Fox News or PayPal UK. The most likely explanation is a lack of process in handling the accounts and their passwords at both Fox News and PayPal UK, making it relatively easy to get the password details through phishing[94].

In 2002, the famous hacker Kevin Mitnick[95] revealed his techniques in a book called The Art of Deception. He recounted how most of his hacks were carried out by using passwords and codes obtained through "social engineering".

In some cases this was just by phoning a user and asking them what their password was!

Phishing is an extension of social engineering and simply involves getting users who know the password to reveal it. By pretending that you need to update account details and asking the user to fill out their security information on a fake web site, for example.

Bruce Schneier, a well-known security expert, blogged in 2005[96] about the limitations of two-step verification as a means of protecting access on the internet. Although more secure than a single password, two-step verification is not immune to phishing.

It would be possible to fake a login page for Twitter and get the details of both the password and the temporary number. Schneier also described another weakness, from a so-called "Trojan-attack"—installing software on a user's PC that is able to intercept usernames and passwords.

3.6.2   People Are Insecure

The main point that Schneier made, though, is that no security mechanism is completely secure, as people always remain the weak point in any security scheme. There is also a balance between ease-of-use and the level of security.

Google, for example, will allow a computer to remember the verification code for 30 days because of the inconvenience of having to enter the code each time you log in. Obviously this weakens the overall security offered by two-step verification.

---

[94]De Neef, Matt, Zombie computers, cyber security, phishing ... what you need to know, http://theconversation.com/zombie-computers-cyber-security-phishing-what-you-need-to-know-1671, Accessed online 1 July 2013.

[95]Wright, Robert, Brave New World Dept: HACKWORK, http://www.newyorker.com/archive/1996/01/29/1996_01_29_032_TNY_CARDS_000374975, Accessed online 1 July 2013.

[96]Schneier, Bruce, Two-Factor Authentication: Too Little, Too Late, http://www.schneier.com/essay-083.html, Accessed online 1 July 2013.

In any organisation where an account is shared, two-step verification may be seen as too restrictive as multiple people will need to share the mechanism that generates the verification number.

Security is as much about the perception of being secure as it is about the reality of being secure. What security analysts are asking Twitter to do is to fit an alarm system, put bars on their windows and a deadlock on their door.

They are ignoring the fact that hackers can still find the front door keys under the mat.

While services such as Twitter can find ways of improving the range of security mechanisms they offer, the most effective security strategy is always going to be about how individuals deal with their personal information, including passwords.

There are basic security principles that everyone should always adopt (antivirus software, strong passwords, secure connections, etc.). But the single most important thing is to not reveal your password to anyone—nobody needs to know it—even the company whose service you are using.

3.7   Hiring James Bond 00.7…'Illegal' Hackers Need Not Apply

6 December 2011

It's unlikely James Bond would have been recruited this way. The perks of this job do not include driving an Aston Martin, sipping martinis in exotic locations or saving the UK by shooting the cat-stroking villain.

Nowadays, a secret service job involves a computer, possibly located in a basement, and the only thing you are going to be intimate with is low-level computer programming code.

But recruitment to a secret service job was the intention of a mystery challenge that appeared at (http://www.canyoucrackit.co.uk)[97] last week.

Specifically, it was to work as a cybersecurity programmer for GCHQ[98]. GCHQ—the Government Communications Headquarters—is one of the three UK Intelligence and Security Agencies, the other two being MI5 and MI6.

Once canyoucrackit was launched, word circulated[99] on Twitter and solutions to the three stages of the challenge started appearing[100] on the net.

---

[97] Can you crack it - behind the code, http://www.canyoucrackit.co.uk/, Accessed on 6 December 2011.

[98] GCHQ - About us, http://www.gchq.gov.uk/AboutUs/Pages/index.aspx, Accessed on 6 December 2011.

[99] Get instant updates on canyoucrackit, https://twitter.com/search/realtime?q=canyoucrackit, Accessed on 6 December 2011.

[100] Can you crack it? Stage 2 Solution, http://www.silly-science.co.uk/2011/12/02/can-you-crack-it-stage-2-solution/, Accessed on 6 December 2011.

The site had some shortcomings, however, and enthusiasts found it was possible to circumvent the need to enter a code at all by entering the web address (http://www.canyoucrackit.co.uk/soyoudidit.asp)[101]. That's when it was realised the challenge was part of a recruitment drive for GCHQ[102].

Comments quickly circulated about the fact the starting salary for a "cyber security specialist" at GCHQ was about £25,000—a fraction of what a good security programmer could earn in industry.

The idea that solutions to the challenge would be posted and circulated was always part of the plan. TMP Worldwide[103]. the agency behind the challenge, had issued a press release[104] detailing that the rationale of the challenge was to "seed a message into social media channels" and that the desired result of the campaign was to reach people with a particular mindset and to encourage them to find out about GCHQ. The ultimate aim was to foster interest in GCHQ as an employer.

The other thing to note was that GCHQ would not accept anyone who had hacked illegally. Presumably this meant you couldn't include hacking as part of your skill set on your CV?

What was absolutely clear, though, was that while the challenge itself succeeded in captivating interest, the people who were generating the solutions were not interested in the prospect of a job. The resulting media focus[105] has also been on how GCHQ is engaging with programmers in terms of their programming interests rather than their desire for national security.

The job required a good university degree, which contained a certain irony: it is unlikely many computer science graduates would have been able to solve the challenge from what they had been taught at university. Very few universities now teach Assembler[106] or generic problem solving skills.

This type of campaign has been run before. As far back as 1941, crossword puzzle competitions were being used as a means of selecting people to work[107] at the secret code breaker unit at Bletchley Park in the UK

---

[101] Can you crack it? http://www.canyoucrackit.co.uk/soyoudidit.asp, Accessed on 6 December 2011.

[102] GCHQ, http://www.gchq.gov.uk/Pages/homepage.aspx, Accessed on 6 December 2011.

[103] TMP Worldwide, http://www.tmpw.co.uk/, Accessed on 6 December 2011.

[104] Link no longer goes to specified page, http://www.tmpw.co.uk/About-TMP/News/GCHQ-targets-code-breakers-to-support-national-cyber-security-/, Accessed on 6 December 2011.

[105] GCHQ aims to recruit computer hackers with code-cracking website, http://www.guardian.co.uk/media/2011/dec/01/gchq-computer-hackers-ad, Accessed on 6 December 2011.

[106] What is assembler? http://searchdatacenter.techtarget.com/definition/assembler, Accessed on 6 December 2011.

[107] The Spy Who Spent the War in Bed: And Other Bizarre Tales from World War II, http://books.google.com.au/books?id=Hp8roGUGki8C&pg=PP20&lpg=PP20&dq=recruiting+crossword+for+bletchley+park&source=bl&ots=YwhZnb7U86&sig=bwllJ3TZYVLRP0g1aUAFEwESkYI&hl=en&ei=b4bbTt2bA-eciAfmr8DmDQ&sa=X&oi=book_result&ct=result&resnum=4&ved=0CDUQ6AEwAw#v=onepage&q=recruiting%20crossword%20for%20bletchley%20park&f=false, Accessed on 6 December 2011.

More recently, the Australian equivalent of GCHQ, the DSD (Defence Signals Directorate[108] ran an ad that contained cryptic text. Although this was supposed to pique interest, there was no explicit need to solve the puzzle. But the text was similar to the canyoucrackit challenge in that it translated into low level programming code[109] that eventually resulted in a web address to a hidden page[110].

Unlike the canyoucrackit challenge, the DSD ads generated very little discussion anywhere.

The US Cyber Challenge[111] organisation has been set up to try to stimulate interest in cyber security and to recruit individuals by running online competitions and cyber security camps.

Security agencies globally are facing increasing challenges[112] against escalating cyber threats. In the cyber arms race, western countries in particular are struggling [113] to attract enough smart people to work in these agencies.

This has led people such as Misha Glenny, author of "DarkMarket[114]" to suggest security agencies should be hiring the hackers[115], as countries including Russia and China are allegedly doing.

The hiring of hackers is obviously a contentious issue but something the NSA in the US was at least publicly[116] willing to consider.

Increasingly, private companies are moving into providing tools and expertise in the cyber security space. Like all software, this is becoming commoditised and available for purchase legally or otherwise.

As was revealed recently[117], the German company DigiTask has sold trojan software for communications interception on laptops.

---

[108] DSD Defence Signals Directorate: Australian Government signals intelligence and information security agency, http://www.dsd.gov.au/, Accessed on 6 December 2011.

[109] An Unusual DSD Job Ad, http://www.tucuxi.org/unusual-ad/, Accessed on 6 December 2011.

[110] Decoded: DSD Defence Signals Directorate, http://www.dsd.gov.au/decoded.html, Accessed on 6 December 2011.

[111] Link no longer goes to specified page, https://www.nbise.org/uscc/index.cfm, Accessed on 6 December 2011.

[112] Cyber security and the online arms race: the battle has just begun, http://theconversation. edu.au/cyber-security-and-the-online-arms-race-the-battle-has-just-begun-1495, Accessed on 6 December 2011.

[113] US recruiting cyber security warriors, http://www.abc.net.au/news/2010-07-22/us-recruiting-cyber-security-warriors/916052, Accessed on 6 December 2011.

[114] DarkMarket by Misha Glenny, http://www.randomhouse.com/book/201064/darkmarket-by-misha-glenny, Accessed on 6 December 2011.

[115] Misha Glenny: Hire the hackers! http://www.ted.com/talks/misha_glenny_hire_the_hackers. html, Accessed on 6 December 2011.

[116] U.S. government hankers for hackers, http://www.reuters.com/article/2011/08/02/idUS-N1E7701KK20110802, Accessed on 6 December 2011.

[117] Ein spy: is the German government using a trojan to watch its citizens? http://theconversation. edu.au/ein-spy-is-the-german-government-using-a-trojan-to-watch-its-citizens-3765, Accessed on 6 December 2011.

The private spy software industry covers everything from viruses to botnets[118] that can control thousands of mobile phones and is worth $5 billion a year. Last week saw the publication[119] by Wikileaks of 287 documents about this industry.

A companion site, called the Spy Files[120], developed by French media company Owni has an interactive map detailing the countries where systems have been sold. Nobody should be particularly surprised about the pervasiveness of this technology, nor the fact it has mysteriously turned up in the hands of regimes which should not have had access because of national bans on dealing with rogue states.

National security agencies are increasingly using these off-the-shelf systems in their surveillance of both internal and external threats and for protective and combative purposes.

US agencies at least have another advantage: they can get access to underlying software systems that underpin the everyday use of the internet, such as Google, Facebook and Twitter.

From this perspective the necessity for US-based agencies to recruit and develop programmers of their own is not as critical.

One can't help feeling, however, that if they threw in the offer of exploding pens or a company car equipped with missiles they'd have a much greater chance of success.

3.8   Telstra BigPond Failure Exposes More Than Just Customer Details

12 December 2011

At approximately 1 p.m. on Friday, a customer of Telstra BigPond—Australia's largest internet service provider—posted[121] on a forum that:

> "If you do a Google search for that number [the number for Telstra's 'Bundles' department, 1800 008 851], you get a very interesting result. Um, Telstra, that's customer information just sitting out on the open Web…That page also seems to suggest that he shouldn't have given me the number, but should have put me through."

The customer had been trying to get a discount on a special "bundle[122]" of services. Customers who had opted for the bundled services were the ones being managed within the software system, a customer relationship management program, that was exposed on the Internet.

---

[118]botnet (zombie army), http://searchsecurity.techtarget.com/definition/botnet, Accessed on 6 December 2011.

[119]WikiLeaks: The Spy Files, http://wikileaks.org/the-spyfiles.html, Accessed on 6 December 2011.

[120]Link no longer goes to specified page, http://www.spyfiles.org/, Accessed on 6 December 2011.

[121]Our best ever Cable Broadband deal, http://forums.whirlpool.net.au/forum-replies.cfm?t=1801978&p=27& #r533, Accessed on 12 December 2011.

[122]Telstra - T-Bundle Home Bundles Pricing & Plans, https://onlineshop.telstra.com.au/bundles/?&red=/bundle-save/index.cfm&red=/bundle_save/home-bundles.html&red=/bundle_save/home-bundles.html&tc=G|E|D|TP|tbunls|HomeBundleDealPackageCombinedServiceTerms&s_kwcid=TC|15760|telstra%20BigPond%20bundles||S|e|9110461684, Accessed on 12 December 2011.

The forum conversation quickly turned to an exploration of what details were accessible: usernames, passwords, full names, home and mobile numbers and addresses. It appeared the passwords may have been[123] the initial ones issued to customers when their account was set up.

A user sent a complaint to Telstra and it was presumably then that staff at the company realised what had happened.

By 5:20 p.m., one forum user noted the site had been taken down. By then, access was also blocked to services such as email and account information. BigPond services remained blocked for most users for another 24 h and when access returned, approximately 60,000 users' passwords had been reset[124] (including mine).

Telstra users were not notified and would only have found out about the outage if they contacted the help desk or through articles appearing in the Sydney Morning Herald[125] or The Australian.[126]

Resetting a password involved a lengthy wait on the telephone. As of Sunday evening, this was at least 45 min and so it appeared Telstra had not deployed any extra staff to handle the consequences of the breach. Whoever was manning the @telstra account on Twitter[127] tried to empathise with customers without being able to do anything meaningful.

Telstra staff were apparently investigating[128] how the site was exposed to the public and would notify the Privacy Commissioner[129]. The fact the system was not password-protected and relied only on the expectation that nobody would discover the web address stretches credulity somewhat.

This is not the first time Telstra has breached customer privacy. In 2010, the company posted[130] 220,000 letters containing account information belonging to customers.

With all incidents such as these, the best a company can hope for it that its customers are understanding. This, to some degree, depends on the company acting quickly to resolve the problem, informing everyone of the details and then moving rapidly to get customers' issues resolved.

None of which Telstra managed to achieve—it took 24 h to get services such as email back online.

---

[123] Our best ever Cable Broadband deal, http://forums.whirlpool.net.au/archive/1801978#r32205950, Accessed on 12 December 2011.

[124] Telstra Leaves BigPond User Details Exposed, http://www.gizmodo.com.au/2011/12/telstra-leaves-bigpond-user-details-exposed/, Accessed on 12 December 2011.

[125] BigPond plugs privacy leak, http://www.smh.com.au/it-pro/security-it/bigpond-plugs-privacy-leak-20111210-1oox7.html, Accessed on 12 December 2011.

[126] Private details exposed on web, http://www.theaustralian.com.au/australian-it/private-details-exposed-on-web/story-e6frgakx-1226218584262, Accessed on 12 December 2011.

[127] Telstra (Telstra) on Twitter, https://twitter.com/telstra, Accessed on 12 December 2011.

[128] BigPond plugs privacy leak, http://www.smh.com.au/it-pro/security-it/bigpond-plugs-privacy-leak-20111210-1oox7.html, Accessed on 12 December 2011.

[129] Australian Government – Office of the Australian Information Commissioner, http://www.privacy.gov.au/, Accessed on 12 December 2011.

[130] Telstra botched mail-out exposes 220,000 customers, http://www.smh.com.au/technology/security/telstra-botched-mailout-exposes-220000-customers-20101027-173du.html, Accessed on 12 December 2011.

Customers are being told they will be contacted within 2–3 days. As one those customers, I received this message on Twitter:

"Really sorry if your details were released. We will be contacting affected customers within the next couple of days to discuss."

Telstra is seemingly not mobilising extra staff to handle support calls or password resets.

It has not been a good 4 weeks for large Australian corporations after the Qantas fleet grounding and associated PR gaffes[131]. Telstra has managed to—almost—follow suit in alienating its customers.

The only thing missing in this instance is a Downfall parody[132].

3.9 We're Watching You: Why the Government Should Focus on Cybersecurity, Not Surveillance

16 August 2012

Time and money spent spying on Australians could be better spent on protecting them.
Source: **Thibault Martin-Lagadette[133]**

---

[131] #QantasLuxury: a Qantas social media disaster in pyjamas, http://theconversation.edu.au/qantasluxury-a-qantas-social-media-disaster-in-pyjamas-4421, Accessed on 12 December 2011.

[132] qantas-twitter_downfall.wmv, http://www.youtube.com/watch?feature=player_embedded&v=QTCwPlWzZnQ, Accessed on 12 December 2011.

[133] Martin-Lagardette, T., Flickr, http://www.flickr.com/photos/naixn/2447827016/, Accessed online 21 December 2012.

Earlier this week Greens Senator Scott Ludlam asked[134] the Federal Government to reveal whether the TrapWire[135] video surveillance system is being used in Australia or if it has been used in the past.

Senator Ludlam's request follows an article on the website of Fairfax papers (an article which has since been removed) suggesting TrapWire is in operation in Australia. If such technology *is* in use, it raises genuine concerns about the government-backed surveillance of the Australian people.

TrapWire is described by the vendor as a video surveillance system with capabilities that will assist in preventing terrorist attacks prior to the event. The system is designed to collect video and, by using specialised data mining and video analysis techniques, can identify suspicious people and actions (such as leaving a bag unattended) that might represent a pre-cursor to a terrorist or criminal act.

Concern[136] about the use of TrapWire has gone global[137] after Wikileaks suggested the US government is using TrapWire to spy on everyone[138].

TrapWire does not operate in isolation but uses facial recognition to identify everyone that is filmed. What this means is that everyone is being identified, tracked and having their information stored in databases that are under the control of a private security company.

Of course, surveillance is not new—many cities and companies around the world utilise CCTV surveillance systems[139]. What *is* new is the ability of TrapWire to analyse the video, identify everyone that appears in the video and to then store this information in a database.

Senator Ludlam has voiced the concerns that many Australians will have about the introduction of systems such as TrapWire.

Indeed, there are many questions that need to be answered:

- Are foreign companies operating intelligent surveillance systems within Australia?
- Where is the data stored?
- What information is leaving Australia?

---

[134]Ludlam S., Greens question use of 'Trapwire' surveillance system in Australia, Australian Greens, http://scott-ludlam.greensmps.org.au/content/media-releases/greens-question-use-%E2%80%98trapwire%E2%80%99-surveillance-system-australia, Accessed online 16 August 2012.

[135]Trapwire Inc., http://www.trapwire.com/, Accessed online 16 August 2012.

[136]Whittaker Z., Wikileaks uncovers TrapWire surveillance: FAQ, ZDNet, 14 August 2012, http://www.zdnet.com/wikileaks-uncovers-trapwire-surveillance-faq-7000002513/, Accessed online 16 August 2012.

[137]Wagenseil P., Is TrapWire surveillance really spying on Americans?, NBC News, 13 August 2012, http://www.nbcnews.com/technology/technolog/trapwire-surveillance-really-spying-americans-939948, Accessed online 16 August 2012.

[138]Shane S., WikiLeaks Stirs Global Fears on Antiterrorist Software, The New York Times, News Limited, 13 August 2012, http://www.nytimes.com/2012/08/14/us/trapwire-antiterrorist-software-leaks-set-off-web-furor.html?_r=1&, Accessed online 16 August 2012.

[139]Closed-circuit television, Wikipedia, http://en.wikipedia.org/wiki/Closed-circuit_television, Accessed online 16 August 2012.

- What privacy and security provisions have been made to protect Australians from the incorrect use of the data?
- Is this information being made available by the operator to other companies, government departments or the police?
- Who is responsible for auditing data retention and for ensuring data remains safe, secure and is not traded at a later date?

The use of TrapWire has angered citizens around the world. *Source*: **Frederic Bisson**[140]

The increased concern about intelligent data mining systems such as TrapWire comes just days after the Attorney-General Nicola Roxon shelved plans[141] to implement a policy that would have seen the web history of all Australian internet users retained for 2 years.

The government's capitulation on this issue is at odds with statements made by a senior national security official to Fairfax Media[142] on August 10 2012:

Ms Roxon's decision to refer the proposals to the parliamentary joint committee for intelligence and security was symptomatic of "the risk adverse character of the government"

"These reforms are urgently needed to deal with a rapidly evolving security environment, but there isn't much appetite within the government for anything that attracts controversy."

---

[140]Bisson F., Flickr, http://www.flickr.com/photos/zigazou76/7670892420/, Accessed online 21 December 2012.

[141]Saarinen J., Roxon reportedly pushes back data retention law, ITNews, 10 August 2012, http://www.itnews.com.au/News/311506,roxon-reportedly-pushes-back-data-retention-law.aspx, Accessed online 16 August 2012.

[142]Dorling P., Roxon puts web surveillance plans on ice, Fairfax Media, 10 August 2012, http://www.theage.com.au/technology/technology-news/roxon-puts-web-surveillance-plans-on-ice-20120809-23x9l.html, Accessed online 16 August 2012.

While the intelligence and security community may want increased surveillance to protect the national interest there are good reasons to put a freeze on increased surveillance and data retention schemes. For a start, we need to wait until technology has been implemented that will improve the capability for government and companies to adequately protect data.

Australians should be very worried about increased data retention and the introduction of new intelligent surveillance systems by stealth.

Now that the Attorney-General has taken the step to put the controversial data retention scheme on the backburner, she should announce what the government is going to do to improve privacy and security for Australians on the net.

One suggestion is a national committee to review privacy and security and to report on the introduction of technologies that would improve the secure operation of the digital network within Australia. The committee should be broadly based and include members from academia, government, industry and civil liberties organisations such as Electronic Frontiers Australia[143].

The committee should consider:

- the immediate mandatory introduction of Internet Protocol version 6[144]
- the immediate mandatory introduction of Secure Socket Layer encryption[145] for all websites and traffic over the Australian digital network
- mandatory use of two-factor authentication[146] for all electronic commerce and other electronic systems that store customer information
- best-practice requirements for securing electronic systems
- triple-factor authentication for access to any electronic system deemed to be national infrastructure
- a mandatory requirement for all government departments and companies to carry out annual security audits of electronic systems and report the audit to a newly established federal security agency
- a mandatory requirement for all electronic system security breaches and hacking attempts to be reported to the newly established federal security agency.

Australia must not wait for the rest of the world to act to implement a more secure digital network. Instead we should take a lead role in doing so.

Furthermore, until the government can guarantee the privacy and security of Australians on the net there should be a moratorium on the introduction of intelligent networked surveillance systems such as TrapWire.

---

[143] Electronic Frontiers Australia, https://www.efa.org.au/, Accessed online 16 August 2012.

[144] IPv6, Wikipedia, http://en.wikipedia.org/wiki/IPv6, Accessed online 16 August 2012.

[145] Transport Layer Security, Wikipedia, http://en.wikipedia.org/wiki/Secure_Sockets_Layer, Accessed online 16 August 2012.

[146] Two-factor authentication, Wikipedia, http://en.wikipedia.org/wiki/Two-factor_authentication, Accessed online 16 August 2012.

Further Reading

- Anonymous' Operation Australia—can the federal police stop them?—Mark Gregory, The Conversation[147]

3.10   Cybercrime Bill Makes It Through: But What Does That Mean for You?

23 August 2012

Australia's place in the online world is changing, with significant consequences. *Source*: **Vlad**[148]

Yesterday afternoon the Australian Senate passed the Cybercrime Legislation Amendment Bill 2011[149] following amendments[150] suggested by the Labor Party.

---

[147]Gregory M.A., Anonymous' Operation Australia – can the federal police stop them?, The Conversation, 10 August 2012, http://theconversation.edu.au/anonymous-operation-australia-can-the-federal-police-stop-them-8778, Accessed online on 16 August 2012.

[148]Vlad, Flickr, http://www.flickr.com/photos/vladus/1933814881/, Accessed online 21 December 2012.

[149]Cybercrime Legislation Amendment Bill 2011, Australian Government, 22 August 2012, http://parlinfo.aph.gov.au/parlInfo/search/display/display.w3p;query=Id:%22legislation/billhome/r4575%22, Accessed online 23 August 2012.

[150]Amendments, Cybercrime Legislation Amendment Bill 2011, Australian Government, http://parlinfo.aph.gov.au/parlInfo/search/display/display.w3p;query=Id:%22legislation/amend/r4575_amend_6c550c60-3a7a-4582-b978-30c4b9cb28e0%22, Accessed online 23 August 2012.

It's been more than a year[151] since the bill was first introduced to the lower house and in that time it's faced opposition both inside[152] and outside[153] parliament.

The purpose of the bill is to align Australia with the Council of Europe Convention on Cybercrime[154], to which 34 other countries—including the US, Germany and most European nations—are already signatories.

3.10.1   Special Effects

The bill effects changes in the Telecommunications Act 1997[155] and Telecommunications (Interception and Access) Act 1979[156] and will force carriers and internet service providers (ISPs) to preserve stored communications, when requested by certain domestic authorities (such as the Australian Federal Police), or when requested by those authorities acting on behalf of nominated foreign countries.

This means a warrant will be needed before the police or security agencies can force carriers or ISPs to monitor, capture and store website use, data transmissions, voice and multimedia calls, and all other forms of communication over the digital network.

But, as mentioned, the introduction of this bill has attracted significant criticism.

Writing for Crikey[157] in August 2011, Bernard Keane highlighted a number of concerns about the bill, including the fact there are no restrictions on the use of information requested by foreign countries. A foreign country could call upon Australia to assist in an investigation that may lead to the death penalty.

Criticism also came from non-profit online rights organisation Electronic Frontiers Australia[158] (EFA). In its submission last year to the Federal Government's

---

[151] Cybercrime Legislation Amendment Bill 2011, Australian Government, http://www.aph.gov.au/ Parliamentary_Business/Bills_Legislation/Bills_Search_Results/Result?bId=r4575, Accessed online 23 August 2012.

[152] Flawed Cybercrime bill dodges national security inquiry, The Greens, 20 August 2012 http:// wa.greens.org.au/content/flawed-cybercrime-bill-dodges-national-security-inquiry, Accessed online 23 August 2012.

[153] Keane B., And softly went our privacy into the night, Crikey, 23 August 2012, http://www. crikey.com.au/2012/08/23/and-softly-went-our-privacy-into-the-night/, Accessed online 23 August 2012.

[154] Convention on Cybercrime, Wikipedia, http://en.wikipedia.org/wiki/Convention_on_Cybercrime, Accessed online 23 August 2012

[155] Telecommunications Act 1997, Australian Government, http://www.austlii.edu.au/au/legis/cth/ consol_act/ta1997214/, Accessed online 23 August 2012.

[156] Telecommunications (Interception and Access) Act 1979, Australian Government, http://www. austlii.edu.au/au/legis/cth/consol_act/taaa1979410/, Accessed online 23 August 2012.

[157] Keane B., Flawed cybercrime bill begs for attention, Crikey, 16 August 2011, http://www.crikey. com.au/2011/08/16/cybercrime-legislation-australia/, Accessed online 23 August 2.

[158] Electronic Frontiers Australia, https://www.efa.org.au, Accessed online 23 August 2012.

Joint Select Committee on Cyber-safety Inquiry[159] (which made recommendations[160] that led to amendments to the bill) the EFA wrote:

> EFA is very concerned with amendments to the computer crime offences in the Criminal Code, and believe these parts of the current legislation are both deeply problematic, and unnecessary for adherence to the Convention.

> EFA is concerned that some aspects of this legislation can potentially enable arbitrary interference with privacy and correspondence. We believe it should treated with great caution.

> But worse, we believe the Criminal Code changes would apply serious criminal penalties, up to ten years' imprisonment, on a very broad range of actions, well beyond what is required for the Convention, and for this reason the legislation should be rejected in its current form.

3.10.2 Toeing the Line

So why did the government, with opposition support, proceed with the bill in the face of criticism[161] by industry and civil liberties advocates such as EFA?

It could be argued that the Cybercrime Legislation Amendment Bill 2011 is a much-needed update of existing legislation and that it brings Australia in line with Europe. And there's no doubt that the digital network is being used ever increasingly for crime, espionage and terrorism.

Indeed, following the passing of the Bill, Attorney-General Nicola Roxon stated:

> This is good news for fighting crime, and will help make it easier for police to track down cybercriminals around the world.

> This will help combat criminal offences relating to forgery, fraud, child pornography and infringement of copyright and intellectual property.

3.10.3 Where We're At

The introduction of the new bill comes at an interesting time. On August 10 Nicola Roxon decided to defer plans[162] to increase web surveillance—a plan which would have affected all Australians by introducing a 2-year data-retention plan for ISPs.

---

[159] Joint Select Committee on Cyber-Safety, Australian Government, http://www.aph.gov.au/ Parliamentary_Business/Committees/House_of_Representatives_Committees?url=jscc/index. htm, Accessed online 23 August 2012.

[160] Lee M., Cybercrime Bill passes Senate, set to become law, ZDNet, 22 August 2012, http://www. zdnet.com/au/cybercrime-bill-passes-senate-set-to-become-law-7000002971/, Accessed online 23 August 2012.

[161] Inquiry into Cybercrime Legislation Amendment Bill 2011, Australian Government, http:// www.aph.gov.au/Parliamentary_Business/Committees/House_of_Representatives_ Committees?url=jscc/cybercrime_bill/subs.htm, Accessed online 23 August 2012.

[162] Dorling P., Roxon puts web surveillance plans on ice, Fairfax Media, 10 August 2012, http:// www.theage.com.au/technology/technology-news/roxon-puts-web-surveillance-plans-on-ice-20120809-23x9l.html, Accessed online 23 August 2012.

In essence, if that plan ever comes to fruition, everything you do online—every keystroke, website visited, video watched—would be monitored and stored for 2 years.

3.10.4   Unanswered Questions

So the bill's been passed. But the underlying issues remain, and do nothing to address the following critical questions:

- What is the government doing to build a more secure network?
- What is it doing to develop best-practice guides for individuals and companies operating on the network?
- Should Australia really be implementing laws that allow foreign governments to access its information?
- Will Australian carriers and ISPs now be required to hand over to the US everything that exists on the network, including private personal information for people such as Julian Assange of Wikileaks[163]?
- What about emails and phone calls that Julian Assange makes to his parents and family in Australia from the Ecuadorian embassy in London?

The Australian government needs to step back and look at how to address some of the concerns being voiced within Australia.

The Cybercrime Legislation Amendment Bill 2011 will assist law enforcement agencies but failure to address the underlying problems that exist with technology used in the network will mean law enforcement will simply be treading water.

The bill will now return to the lower house for approval and will likely become law before the end of 2012.

Further Reading

- Why is Anonymous hacking Australia?—Mark Gregory, The Conversation[164]
- Anonymous' Operation Australia—can the federal police stop them?—Mark Gregory, The Conversation[165]

---

[163] WikiLeaks, http://www.wikileaks.org/, Accessed online 23 August 2012.

[164] Gregory M.A., Why is Anonymous hacking Australia?, The Conversation, 31 July 2012, https://theconversation.edu.au/why-is-anonymous-hacking-australia-8480, Accessed online 23 August 2012.

[165] Gregory M.A., Anonymous' Operation Australia – can the federal police stop them?, The Conversation, 10 August 2012, http://theconversation.edu.au/anonymous-operation-australia-can-the-federal-police-stop-them-8778, Accessed online on 23 August 2012.

- We're watching you: why the government should focus on cybersecurity, not surveillance—Mark Gregory, The Conversation[166]
- And softly went our privacy into the night—Bernard Keane, Crikey[167]

3.11   Why Data Retention Laws Won't Work

12 September 2012

Attorney-General Nicola Roxon took an unusual step yesterday, launching a **video on YouTube**[168] to put a new position on the proposed cyber-security and cyber-crime laws.

In the past week Roxon made statements that appeared to pre-empt the report being prepared by the Parliamentary Joint Committee on Intelligence and Security on proposed reforms to Australia's data retention laws.

The proposed reform would see telcos store their customer's internet usage data for up to 2 years. Over the course of the video, Roxon put forward the case that these laws would help catch cyber-criminals and paedophiles. She also clarified that the government would wait until the Joint Committee's report before making any final decision around the reforms.

Yet, despite these clarifications it is little wonder why advocacy groups such as GetUp! and Electronic Frontiers Australia are concerned about the government's position.

Roxon has again failed to address one key concern: the fact that her comments seem to hint at a pre-ordained outcome to the Parliamentary Joint Committee on Intelligence and Security's review and an inevitable change in our cyber-security legislation.

Aside from the **ethical debate**[169] relating to this reform, there are two questions that are pivotal to these cyber-security changes:

Do we need the proposed data collection and retention regime? And should the government's proposed data collection and retention regime be implemented now?

---

[166]Gregory M.A., We're watching you: why the government should focus on cybersecurity, not surveillance, The Conversation, 16 August 2012, http://theconversation.edu.au/were-watching-you-why-the-government-should-focus-on-cybersecurity-not-surveillance-8846, Accessed online on 23 August 2012.

[167]Keane B., And softly went our privacy into the night, Crikey, 23 August 2012, http://www.crikey.com.au/2012/08/23/and-softly-went-our-privacy-into-the-night/, Accessed online 23 August 2012.

[168]Polites H., Roxon turns to YouTube to argue data retention reforms, Technology Spectator, 11 September 2012, http://www.technologyspectator.com.au/roxon-turns-youtube-argue-data-retention-reforms, Accessed online 12 September 2012.

[169]Gregory M.A., Giving 'Big Brother' a black eye, Technology Spectator, 17 August 2012, http://www.technologyspectator.com.au/giving-big-brother-black-eye, Accessed online 12 September 2012.

To answer the first question: there is clear justification that an improved data collection and retention regime is needed to combat crime, terrorism and cyber warfare.

But as for the second, in my opinion there is no reason why the government needs to introduce such legislation. Let me explain why.

3.11.1 It's About the Systems, Not the Legislation

The digital network is being used in ways for which it was not designed. Privacy and security are almost non-existent in the digital world and this should be a concern for all Australians. Small steps have been taken to improve the underlying infrastructure, systems and protocols, however, much larger steps are needed before the digital network is ready for the proposed data collection and retention regime and changes to cyber-crime laws.

Failing to update the infrastructure, systems and protocols being used on the digital network will negate the effectiveness of any changes to Australian law. The criminals and terrorists will still be able to act with impunity by using secure VPNs, TOR and the darknet. Cyber-warfare and criminal hacking with the intent to steal national secrets and intellectual property will continue unabated. Foreign efforts to discover weaknesses in national digital infrastructure and carry out preparatory attacks on business, government and infrastructure will occur more frequently.

In Europe an extended data retention policy has been adopted and a **recent report**[170] has highlighted the lessons learnt in Europe during the implementation of the new laws. In Sweden, carriers and ISPs were given 2 months to comply with the new laws. In response, Nils Weidstam—a public policy expert for the Swedish firm IT&Telekomforetagen said, "Telia, the operator [Swedish telecommunications company], will likely need up to 2 years to implement these systems".

In the article, Mark Newton, a network engineer from a large Australian ISP hinted at a similar scenario:

> "The Australian government similarly does not appear to grasp the complexity of storing data in a manner suitable for evidence. There seems to be a view within government that retaining data can be accomplished by simply telling telcos to stop deleting it. There needs to be an auditable chain of evidence, security requirements to mitigate the risk of tampering, high reliability requirements so that evidence doesn't simply disappear due to hardware failure, requirements for staff to have security clearances to process law-enforcement access requests; expensive storage in expensive data centres with expensive backup strategies maintained by expensive staff."

---

[170]Tung L., Lessons learnt in data retention law, Fairfax Media, 11 September 2012, http://www.smh.com.au/it-pro/business-it/lessons-learnt-in-data-retention-law-20120910-25oap.html, Accessed online 12 September 2012.

3.11.2   Australia Shouldn't Follow America's Lead

In the USA it was **reported earlier this week**[171] that Debora Plunkett, of the secretive National Security Agency—whose responsibilities include protecting US government computer networks—predicted that Congress would pass long-stalled cyber-security legislation within the next year. Ms Plunkett's comments reflect a growing concern within US officials, lawmakers and security agency heads about the country's cyber security.

The push in the US to get cyber security laws through Congress has also failed to address the technical requirements of implementing the new laws and to address the underlying problems with privacy and security in the digital network.

In Europe, Australia and the US lawmakers are attempting to paint a lemon (the digital network) as an orange. And they appear to be keen on convincing everyone that because it is an orange now an it's all OK. But, a lemon is still a lemon no matter what.

Australia should not follow the US and Europe without first carrying out a study on how to improve privacy and security on the digital network and the first step along this path is to make substantial changes to the network. A committee of technical experts should review the digital network, prioritise technical changes and report on when the digital network will have the capability to provide adequate privacy and security for all Australians and at this point the proposed changes to cyber-crime and cyber security laws should be revisited.

3.12   The Dark Side to Data Retention

4 October 2012

The government review into cyber-security has turned into a free for all by government agencies demanding access to data that would be collected under the proposed 2 year data retention regime.

Proposed changes to the national legislation covering telecommunications and the digital network are being seen by government agencies as a once in a generation opportunity to get access to the online usage history of all Australians.

The Australian Securities and Investment Commission (ASIC) has gone further[172] and asked for telecommunication intercept capability. If the government is not careful the review could become a farce—if we have not already reached that point. The push for enhanced powers not only raises question marks about how the process

---

[171] Reuters, US cyber security legislation set to pass next year: NSA, Technology Spectator, 10 September 2012, http://www.technologyspectator.com.au/us-cyber-security-legislation-set-pass-next-year-nsa, Accessed online 12 September 2012.

[172] Adhikari S., ASIC seeks beefed up data interception powers, Technology Spectator, 28 September 2012, Accessed online 4 October 2012.

will be managed, but also the prospect of consumers jumping on to the darknet to protect their privacy.

The end result of this could well be that ISPs end up with a whole stack of useless information.

3.12.1   Swamping the ISPs

Under future legislation that meets the agency wish list carriers and Internet Service Providers (ISP) could be swamped with telecommunication intercept and retained data access notices. However, there is precious little information on how the entire exercise will be managed.

How would a carrier or ISP guarantee that data is not tampered with, hacked into, leaked or that agencies don't trip over each other with concurrent investigations?

The same questions apply to telecommunication intercepts. These are important issues that merit careful consideration and it's crucial that no changes are set in motion before the state of the digital network is reviewed extensively[173].

3.12.2   TOR and the Darknet

One possible outcome if any changes are indeed made to the Telecommunications (Interception and Access) Act 1979[174], the Telecommunications Act 1997[175], the Australian Security Intelligence Organisation Act 1979[176] and the Intelligence Services Act 2001[177] is the prompt development of an industry that will train Australian in how to use TOR[178] and the darknet.

The darknet is a network of servers that are not accessible over the Internet but can be accessed by using secure virtual private network (VPN) connections to darknet

[173] Gregory M.A., Why data retention laws won't work, Technology Spectator, 12 September 2012, http://www.technologyspectator.com.au/why-data-retention-laws-won-t-work, Accessed online 4 October 2012.

[174] Telecommunications (Interception and Access) Act 1979, Australian Government, http://www.comlaw.gov.au/series/c2004a02124, Accessed online 4 October 2012.

[175] Telecommunications Act 1997, Australian Government, http://www.comlaw.gov.au/series/c2004a05145, Accessed online 4 October 2012.

[176] Australian Security Intelligence Organisation Act 1979, Australian Government, http://www.comlaw.gov.au/series/c2004a02123, Accessed online 4 October 2012.

[177] Intelligence Services Act 2001, Australian Government, http://www.comlaw.gov.au/series/c2004a00928, Accessed online 4 October 2012.

[178] Tor, Tor Project, https://www.torproject.org/, Accessed online 4 October 2012.

node servers. TOR is a software application that provides secure VPN connections to darknet nodes.

When TOR is used people can access darknet servers or by using anonymisers people can access servers on the internet. An anonymiser makes tracking the person using the internet almost impossible to find. Well, technically you could find the user but the process is so hard that it is almost not worth the effort.

What this means is that the data collected under the proposed data retention scheme could be of little or no value. All that will be collected is an indication that a person has commenced a secure VPN connection to a server that is likely to be outside Australia and therefore outside Australian control.

As the traffic over the secure VPN is encrypted there would be in effect nothing to monitor, collect and store for 2 years. The carriers and ISPs could have whole data centres full of useless encrypted information. This would be a scene reminiscent of Yes Minister where an efficiency award went to a hospital with no patients.

I wonder if the review or the government has considered this possibility?

3.12.3   Viable Alternatives

Rather than a half-baked policing option perhaps the government should look for viable alternatives that reinforce the digital network, which is not secure and must be rebuilt urgently to improve privacy and security.

It appears a small step may occur soon in the UK where Nominet, the non-profit body responsible for overseeing all net addresses ending in UK, is proposing an important change.

Under Nominet's proposal companies would be able to use domain names shortened to http://www.domain.uk and by making this change agree to several conditions. The conditions include the mandatory use of Domain Name System Security Extensions (DNSSEC) and have a proven company presence in the UK.

DNSSEC is a security protocol that utilises a digital signature to ensure that the domain is valid when accessed, for example when browsing to http://www.mydomain.uk. This reduces the likelihood of domain hijacking and other attacks on domains and websites.

The Nominet proposal is a small step forward that should be immediately implemented in Australia.

We can also add to this the compulsory use of secure HTTP (HTTPS), secure connections between email servers (SMTPSEC), secure connections between email servers and client applications (SMTPS) and the immediate introduction of Internet Protocol (IP) version 6 (with IP version 4 turned off).

If the government is serious about boosting Australia's credentials then implementing the aforementioned technical changes to the digital network would be a good start. The security and privacy benefits for all Australians will be a natural by-product of that process.

3.13   The Privacy Perils of Biometric Security

11 October 2012

It may sound like something straight out of a James Bond movie, but believe it or not, Australia's major banks are moving to embrace biometric security systems.

There are two main reasons why the banks are moving in this direction; both of which revolve around customer experience. The first is to improve their customer's experience whilst utilising ATMs and Eftpos machines and terminals. The second is to remove the need for customers to carry around a wallet or purse full of plastic cards.

But the move is a bit of a gamble, as it's still uncertain as to how consumers will respond to this new technology.

3.13.1   The Case for a Biometric Security System

Biometric security systems utilise some aspect of a person's physiology to verify identity. Law enforcement agencies have been using biometrics including fingerprints and DNA to solve crimes for decades.

But are biometric security systems practical for anything other than law enforcement?

Banks aim to introduce biometric security systems to reduce the incidence of fraud. There's also the fact that ATMs and Eftpos are time consuming, require customers to have a plastic card that stores account details and to remember a Personal Identification Number (PIN).

By using biometric security there would not be a need for customers to have the plastic card nor to remember a PIN.

Customers would press a thumb against a scanner or have their eye scanned and then be able to complete the transaction.

ATM and Eftpos security could be enhanced by using a combination of biometric security and a near field communications (NFC) capable smartphone that has a bank provided security application installed. A customer would have their thumb or eyes scanned and then wave their phone near the ATM or Eftpos terminal to complete a financial transaction.

There is no doubt that a combination of biometric security and NFC would improve customer experience when using ATM or Eftpos and remove the need for customers to carry plastic.

Introducing the biometric into banking would overcome the bank's customer service challenges, but there are still lingering issue around the technology.

3.13.2 Hollywood Leads the Way in Circumventing Biometric Security

Movies have embraced biometric security—not because biometric security is a futuristic concept that moviegoers will find entertaining but because movie makers have found moviegoers are captivated by portrayals of how to overcome biometric security systems—many of which are gruesome.

With a new James Bond film on the way it may be a good time to revisit how biometric security systems were portrayed in previous Bond films. In *Die Another Day*, James Bond cut off the arm of a dead bad guy so that he can press the hand against a door security scanner to open a door. In *Never Say Never Again* one of the bad guys had an eye transplant to fool a retinal scanner protecting nuclear weapons.

Many films have now been released that highlight how to circumvent biometric security systems. This is an unfortunate situation where movies have generally portrayed biometric security in a bad light but possibly for all the right reasons—biometric security systems are not perfect.

But perfect or not biometric security systems do have practical use. In the US biometric security based gun safes have been available for many years and have been found to reduce the incidence of a child finding the key to a gun safe, accessing the guns inside and killing themselves in a gun related accident.

3.13.3 Can We Trust the Banks with Our Biometrics?

Another issue could be privacy concern by customers that they do not want to utilise biometric security systems. There is concern that companies that utilise biometric security systems will trade or sell biometric data collected from their customers.

In 2003 at a Security in Government Conference Malcolm Crompton the Federal Privacy Commissioner highlighted the use of new biometric technologies as being either Privacy Invasive Technologies (PIT) or Privacy Enhancing Technologies (PET) depending on implementation and use.

Add to this a point made by Roger Clarke[179] a visiting professor at the Australian National University.

"Biometrics are among the most threatening of all surveillance technologies, and herald the severe curtailment of freedoms, and the repression of 'different thinkers', public interest advocates and 'troublemakers'" he said.

---

[179] Clarke R., Biometrics and Privacy, Xamax Consultancy, 2001, http://www.rogerclarke.com/DV/Biometrics.html, Accessed online 11 October 2012.

3.13.4 An Inevitable Move to Biometric Security

Philip Chronican CEO of ANZ Australia recently indicated that a Newspoll survey commissioned by the ANZ found that 67 % "would be comfortable" using an eye scanner. The bank now plans to slowly introduce biometrics into ATM machines commencing in 2013 and initially permit deposits to be made using biometric security.

Be assured that our future will include the use of biometric security. In 5 years biometric security will be incorporated into many aspects of our lives. There will be benefits including not having to carry plastic cards for financial transactions, magnetic cards to access swipe card activated doors or keys to start your car.

But what is the cost? An Australian's right to privacy will be compromised unless the government bans the trade or sale of biometric data and sets an appropriately high jail term for directors of companies that fail to comply.

3.14   The Next Generation of Digital Assaults

22 November 2012

Imagine trying to connect to the network and finding that you cannot. It's a frightening scenario that could play out sooner than you think given the technologies being developed and deployed today.

These technologies can be used to attack and paralyse part or all of the digital network and internet and there is ample evidence of nation states taking a keen interest in developing offensive and defensive capabilities to disrupt networks.

Today the network is critical for everyday activities like banking, social media, email and many other activities. At the current rate of technical progress one can only imagine just how entrenched this dependence will be.

So how likely is the prospect of a cyber-war? In the past couple of weeks we have seen a cyber-war take place between Israel and Hamas[180] in the Middle East. We also have ongoing lower intensity cyber-wars between a number of countries including Iran, Israel, China, USA, Japan, Europe and North Korea.

The reason so many countries are getting their hands dirty is because it's in their best interest to have a cohesive strategy to wage cyber-war, even if the ultimate goal for many is to simply possess an active deterrent. The digital network is strategic national infrastructure and future disagreements between countries are likely to include cyber-attacks even if the disagreement does not spill over to a shooting war.

By 2022 most nations will have developed some form of cyber-warfare capability. Rich nations will expend more money and be able to develop sophisticated tools for

---

[180]Ackerman G. and Ramadan S. A., Israel Wages Cyber War with Hamas as Civilians Take Up Computers, Bloomberg News, 19 November 2012, http://www.businessweek.com/news/2012-11-19/israel-wages-cyber-war-with-hamas-as-civilians-take-up-computers, Accessed online 22 November 2012.

offensive and defensive operations. Poorer nations will look to cheaper tools but may still be effective participants in any future cyber-war.

3.14.1   Cost to Paralyse

So how much money does it take to paralyse a network?

Earlier this month, a report[181] highlighted the efforts of the wireless research group[182] at Virginia Tech who had developed a simple jamming system that could disable access to a 4G Long Term Evolution (LTE) base station. The cost of the jamming system was $650.

In Australia there are about 10,000 base stations and access points to the wireless cellular network for the three carriers. If you miniaturise and mass produce the jamming device then the cost might be about $100 per unit. So for about $10 million dollars you could produce enough devices to jam the entire Australian mobile phone network.

To put this into context, let's consider the Afghanistan war where the US is spending about US $3.6 billion a month. The cost of implementing a jamming system is cheap by comparison. Build into the devices the capability to operate remotely and you could pre-position the devices months or years before they're needed.

Satellites are already quite vulnerable to attack and are expected to be one of the first casualties in any future major conflict. In 2007 and 2010 China destroyed satellites[183] using missiles. It is to be expected that over the next decade the US and Europe will further develop systems to protect satellites in the event of missile attack though the effectiveness of any space based defensive system is likely to be limited.

In a limited cyber-war there are two ways that satellites can be attacked. The first is to jam signals to and from satellite base stations and the second is to attack the traffic going to and from the satellite base station. Let us consider our National Broadband Network (NBN). There will be about 10 satellite base stations for three satellites. One simple but crude approach would be to dig up the fibre cables leading to the base stations and splice into the cables. This would be a slow process, but one that we see already happening over the past 50 years with nations using submarines to splice into[184] undersea telecommunication cables.

---

[181]Talbot D., One Simple Trick Could Disable a City's 4G Phone Network, MIT Technology Review, 14 November 2012, http://www.technologyreview.com/news/507381/one-simple-trick-could-disable-a-citys-4g-phone-network/, Accessed online 22 November 2012.

[182]Wireless Research Group, Virginia Tech, http://wireless.vt.edu/, Accessed online 22 November 2012.

[183]Xiaokun L., US report claims China shoots down its own satellite, China Daily, 19 July 2010, http://www.chinadaily.com.cn/world/2010-07/19/content_10121179.htm, Accessed online 22 November 2012.

[184]Neil Jr., Spy agency taps into undersea cable, ZDNet, 23 May 2001, http://www.zdnet.com/news/spy-agency-taps-into-undersea-cable/115877, Accessed online 22 November 2012.

By 2022, fully developed techniques to attack national optical networks will be available. Again a crude but simple approach would be to dig up and tap into fibres at key locations around a network—this is known as fusion splicing[185]. Once a fibre has been spliced into this connection can be used to disrupt the traffic flowing down the fibre or as a means to inject viruses and worms into the network.

More sophisticated approaches include the introduction of dormant malware into thousands of home and office computers that can be woken up when needed to carry out mass attacks on key infrastructure such as the Domain Name System (DNS)[186].

Techniques will be in place to attack national infrastructure connected to the digital network. Possibilities include overloading power substations, opening dams, turning all of the traffic lights red, damaging machinery in factories by turning it on and off repeatedly.

3.14.2   Kill Switch on the Ready

This may be sound like Hollywood fodder but the evidence suggests otherwise. Israel and the US have been accused[187] of attacking Iran's nuclear reactors by using a computer virus that turned the centrifuges, that create the nuclear material, on and off until they broke.

Nations will need to ensure that there are manual kill switches on key infrastructure that will disconnect the infrastructure from the digital network in the event of a cyber-attack, however, by the time a person gets to the kill switch the damage may already be done.

Compounding the existing problem is the presence of organised crime and their ongoing attempts to develop sophisticated tools to attack banks and financial transaction systems connected to the digital network. By 2022, we should expect organised crime to be a major player in any disruptions to the network.

The evolving arms-race will see nations implement security assurance testing regimes, which means that equipment connected to the network will be tested using a security assurance framework. This regime will include live testing of the network to discover if the network has been tampered with. More sophisticated approaches will need to be developed to discover devices like the 4G jammer. Currently, this cyber-warfare capability is in its infancy and Australia is now looking to develop this capability.

---

[185]Fusion splicing, Wikipedia, http://en.wikipedia.org/wiki/Fusion_splicing, Accessed online 22 November 2012.

[186]Domain Name System, Wikipedia, http://en.wikipedia.org/wiki/Domain_Name_System, Accessed online 22 November 2012.

[187]Sanger D.E., Obama Order Sped Up Wave of Cyberattacks Against Iran, The New York Times, 1 June 2012, http://www.nytimes.com/2012/06/01/world/middleeast/obama-ordered-wave-of-cyberattacks-against-iran.html?pagewanted=all&_r=1&, Accessed online 22 November 2012.

Most of us remain unaware of the constant battles taking place on the network between nations and between law enforcement and organised crime. The network in 2022 will be the most important battle ground the world has ever seen.

3.15 ADFA Hack Alarm Bells

12 December 2012

The University of New South Wales (UNSW) Canberra College was hacked into on 15 November 2012 by a hacker known as Darwinaire who is associated with the Anonymous group. The incident has seen private details of thousands of staff and students at the Australian Defence Force Academy (ADFA) pilfered in what is tantamount to a national security failure.

The relative ease with which the hacker was able to break in should set alarm bells ringing at ADFA. Equally alarming is the anaemic response of those charged with keeping the information secure in the first place.

Darwinaire's **candid comments to Fairfax**[188] not only highlight the weakness of the security protocols in place but also raise serious questions about accountability.

The hacker told Fairfax that he was shocked by the lack of online security at the UNSW Canberra College

"I know right, very surprised I didn't get kicked out. So simple, took like three minutes."

He also told Fairfax he carried out the hack attack because he was bored and did it for fun.

UNSW has stated that it took action to reduce the possibility of further hacking when the hack attack was identified. However, the **email sent to students and staff**[189] a day after the hack are quite an amazing read.

3.15.1 Too Much Spin, Too Little Action

The university makes two remarkable claims in the email

"We believe that the impact on you will be minimal but you should still carefully read the information below."

---

[188]Mannheim M., Military personnel data hacked for 'fun', Fairfax, 11 December 2012, http://www.theage.com.au/it-pro/security-it/military-personnel-data-hacked-for-fun-20121211-2b6yp.html, Accessed online 12 December 2012.

[189]Creagh S., UNSW email to staff and students following ADFA hack, The Conversation, 11 December 2012, https://theconversation.edu.au/unsw-email-to-staff-and-students-following-adfa-hack-11289, Accessed online 12 December 2012.

"Student [staff] name and birthday information may be used for attempts at identity theft and again this requires additional vigilance."

The university makes an unjustified claim that the impact on individuals will be minimal and then moves on to place the onus onto the 10,000 staff and students affected to remain "vigilant" in case the stolen information is used in the future for identity theft.

The future for most of the students attending the college may be 60 or more years. Why should they remain vigilant for the rest of their lives simply because an organisation which owes them a duty of care was lax? Not only is UNSW running with ridiculous spin on this matter but appears to have forgotten who the people are that attend the UNSW Canberra College.

3.15.2 A Forensic Examination

Given that ADFA is the testing ground of our current and future military leaders the data breach should be treated as a national security incident and warrants a thorough forensic examination.

The loss of any personal information that may be used to build a profile on military officers or to impersonate a military officer must be taken seriously by the Minister for Defence Stephen Smith and he should immediately call an inquiry into the matter. The ability to impersonate military leaders using digital means is a key weapon that will be employed in future warfare.

It is for this reason that my advice to Stephen Smith and to Defence is that all military members, especially commissioned officers should be required to become invisible on the internet at the point they enter the military until such time as they retire—yes that means no social media, no online games, no Apple iTunes or Google accounts and so on.

Defence must take action now and send specialists to investigate network and information security at the UNSW Canberra College. A report should be prepared within 30 days and recommendations made regarding how to ensure a similar data breach never occurs again at the UNSW Canberra College. The UNSW Canberra College should be forced to act on the outcome of the investigation.

3.15.3 Making Accountability Paramount

This event occurred more than 2 weeks ago and has only recently been made public. Has UNSW submitted a **data breach report**[190] to the Office of the Australian Information Commissioner (OAIC)?

---

[190] Gregory M.A., 'You've been hacked': why data-breach reporting should be mandatory, The Conversation, 19 October 2012, https://theconversation.edu.au/youve-been-hacked-why-data-breach-reporting-should-be-mandatory-10220, Accessed online 12 December 2012.

If not, why not? As this is my alma mater I was dismayed to hear that my personal information may have been placed on the web. While it appears that my personal information has not been compromised (there were only a couple of computers on the campus when I attended) I found the matter a cause for concern. Government, companies and organisations need to understand that people are concerned about their personal information and it is not sufficient to make statements like "We believe that the impact on you will be minimal". Failure to secure customer information is not something that should be shrugged off.

The UNSW should identify who was responsible for the data breach. Should someone lose their job for a data breach of this magnitude? Absolutely.

Should UNSW be held accountable by the people affected by the data breach? Yes. What is wrong about this situation is that week after week Australians are told of yet another major hacking event. Government, companies and organisations are not required to report data breaches to the OAIC and the penalty for lax information security is a dose of bad press.

It appears the only way that action will be taken to force better security of personal private information will be a class action law suit against a large organisation that has compromised customer details. It may actually be in our best interest that this happen sooner rather than later. It's time for the government to take action to prevent major data breaches rather than wax lyrical about a 2 year data retention law to identify the villains in this story.

Chapter 4
Internet

Internet use has grown as new devices, technologies and systems become available. The Internet has facilitated change in possibly more ways than any other technology based system in history.

Bitcoin, a new currency, exists only on the Internet and can now be used to purchase products and services. The idea of an online currency that is out of the control of any nation or bank would have been implausible without the Internet.

New systems are being deployed to connect customers at every increasing speeds and to provide greater bandwidth for improved television, video, games, education and health systems. The Australian National Broadband Network aims to provide optical fibre connections to every house in Australia and this comes at a time when the rest of the world is waking to the need to implement next generation networks that will satisfy the ever increasing desire for more bandwidth and higher transmission speeds.

How we use the Internet is also changing and the move to the "cloud" highlights the always on nature of the Internet.

The rush to cloud computing promises to provide access to information and applications "anywhere at any time", however the increasing amount of user data flowing across the Internet adds a technical dimension and cost to cloud computing that has not been completely overcome.

Increased data flows have been facilitated by a move away from copper transmission systems to optical fibre transmission systems. Increased available bandwidth has brought about a steady reduction in the cost of data transmission. As long as the price of data continues to decrease the shift to the cloud will increase in momentum.

M.A. Gregory and D. Glance, *Security and the Networked Society*,
DOI 10.1007/978-3-319-02390-8_4, © Springer International Publishing Switzerland 2013

4.1 Music Pirates Won't Rush to iCloud for.forgiveness

15 June 2011

Some people, including on this site[1], have suggested there's a loophole in Apple's new iCloud that will allow people who illegally download music to somehow "launder" their dirty music files, getting a nice clean, and legal, license to the music stored on iCloud. This argument is flawed for two main reasons.

The first has to do with how the laws of copyright work and the second is to do with why people share or download music (and movies) in the first place.

4.1.1 The Law

Unlike existing cloud services offered by Amazon[2] and Google[3], Apple will search your hard disk looking for music; for any track it recognises, it will give you access to download a legitimate version of that track from the iCloud.

In Australia, copyright law allows the public to "format-shift" their music. If you have a CD, you're allowed to "rip" it into another format so that you can listen to the music on another device such as an iPod or phone.

You can even share this music with other members of your household, but not with anyone outside. Importantly, you have to keep the original copy of the music. If you give that original away, or sell it, you have to get rid of all copies you've made of the music.

iTunes Match[4], which, at a cost of $24.99, matches a user's existing music library against the 18 million tracks held in iTunes store, will work on the basis of assuming that you have a legal version of the music on your disk.

It will have to do this to stay in keeping with the copyright laws in the US which are similar to that in Australia. So if you were acting illegally before you used Apple's iCloud, you will still be deemed illegal afterwards.

---

[1]Sussex, Roland & Cody, Alan, Long John iCloud Silver: has Steve Jobs cleared the decks for pirates? http://theconversation.com/long-john-icloud-silver-has-steve-jobs-cleared-the-decks-for-pirates-1742, Accessed on 1 July 2013.

[2]Amazon Cloud Drive: Learn More, http://www.amazon.com/gp/feature.html?ie=UTF8&docId=1 000796931&ref_=cd_lm_rd_fp, Accessed on 1 July 2013.

[3]Google Play, https://play.google.com/about/, Accessed on 1 July 2013.

[4]AppleInsider Staff, Apple announces iTunes Match music service for $24.99 per year, http://appleinsider.com/articles/11/06/06/apple_announces_itunes_match_music_streaming_for_24_99_per_year.html, Accessed on 1 July 2013.

4.1.2   Dancing in the Dark

The second and probably more relevant issue is this: why you would anyone bother to "launder" their pirated music? Some 60 % of 18 to 24 year olds surveyed[5] in the UK in 2009 admitted to using peer-to-peer[6] networks to download music.

They had, on average, 8,000 music files in their collection—a staggering 17 days' worth of tunes. The main reasons cited for downloading illegally were to do with cost (it was free), accessing hard-to-get music and simply trying new music out.

The other key findings of this survey were that the majority of the young people were more bothered by the moral aspect of piracy (the fact musicians are losing money) than the legal one.

They were not particularly interested in streaming the music, as offered by a number of services currently. Physical ownership of the files was important because it meant they could transfer them to other devices, as was the fact they could listen to music offline (in the car or on the bus, for example).

4.1.3   Teenage Kicks

Picture this: I am a 16 year old with 8,000 music files and I only feel mildly guilty that I downloaded them or got them from my friends.

I listen to the music mostly on my computer and then on my iPod, which I synchronise with my computer after having carefully constructed my favourite playlists.

Why would I feel motivated to pay $25 a year to download this exact same music again?

It certainly won't be, as some have been arguing, so I can claim to be the legal owner of the music—even if I cared about this, I clearly wouldn't be the legal owner.

4.1.4   Live and Let Die

Downloading music and movies gives people access to things they would not be able to access any other way, either because it would cost too much or because it's simply not available for sale.

Competing against "free-and-now" is hard to do, but there are signs that the music industry at least is starting to do exactly that.

It used to be the case that live music was the promotional, loss-making part of the business to drive recorded music sales.

Increasingly, the music industry is seeing that the money can be made from live music, concerts and music festivals, while the recorded music could be used as a give-away to promote these social events.

---

[5]Bahanovich, David & Collopy, Dennis, Music Experience and Behaviour in Young People, http://www.ukmusic.org/assets/media/uk_music_uni_of_herts_09.pdf, Accessed on 1 July 2013.
[6]P2P, http://www.techterms.com/definition/p2p, Accessed on 1 July 2013.

Live is the only thing that can't be replicated: everything else—with or without the iCloud—is up for grabs.

4.2   Ten Reasons Why Google+ Will Never Be Facebook

30 June 2011

Google is hoping that the saying "if at first you don't succeed, try, try, again" will work out for them with Google+[7].

Launched as a private beta version on Tuesday, Google+ is the search giant's latest attempt at a version of Facebook. The company has tried this before with products such as Orkut, Google Wave and Buzz.

Google+ brings together four applications: "Photos" allows users to upload photos; "Hangouts" is a videoconferencing type application; "Sparks" provides a news feed; and "Circles", which is the bit that allows "Googlers" to organise friends into different groups and share things with them.

The problem Facebook poses for Google is real. Both the current and former Google CEOs, Larry Page and Eric Schmidt have admitted they didn't take the threat of Facebook seriously. Facebook users are already looking at more pages on the web than Google users (including YouTube) and spending longer doing it[8].

Advertising money will follow the users—and given this is Google's main source of income—this poses a significant threat to its bottom line.

4.2.1   So Why Will Google+ Never Be a Threat to Facebook?

1) The name. Google has always been tarred with the brush that it is run by engineers who by-and-large are not the world's experts when it comes to social interactions. Proof of this comes in the choice of a technical-sounding name for a social service.

   Why make a social site you want teenagers to hang out on sound like a computer language?

2) What if you threw a party and nobody came? Social networks, by definition, only succeed if there is a network of people to be social with.

   Google will face a significant challenge in building up enough users on Google+ to allow for individual social networks to form. A typical teenager may have 700 friends on Facebook that has taken years to build up.

   Unless Facebook decides to allow users to export all of their friends to Google+, rebuilding this network on a new site would be a task very few people would be willing to do.

---

[7]Cain Miller, Claire, Another Try by Google to Take On Facebook, http://www.nytimes.com/2011/06/29/technology/29google.html, Accessed on 1 July 2013.

[8]Rao, Leena, comScore: Facebook Keeps Gobbling People's Time, http://techcrunch.com/2011/02/07/comscore-facebook-keeps-gobbling-peoples-time/, Accessed on 1 July 2013.

3) You are a business colleague, not a friend. One of Google+'s selling points is the ability to group people into different categories and share with that group. Facebook allows this but it isn't the main way of communicating with friends.

    Although this feature allows users to be selective about what they share with whom, it makes the system harder to use. People don't fit into neat categories; work colleagues can be friends too.

    What people are interested in is not determined just by the fact they are a friend, work colleague, member of a club, etc.

4) I like it here. If people are unwilling to have multiple similar social network environments, the reasons for moving would be that you are either unhappy about Facebook or that Google+ offers you something Facebook doesn't.

    From the announced features, Google has not discovered the killer app in this space—there is nothing compelling enough to make someone move, along with the 700 friends they might have on Facebook.

    It is also clear that Facebook is not going to sit by and watch Google+ take its market—any radically popular features introduced in Google+ would find their way into Facebook.

5) Here today, gone tomorrow. Google has a history of introducing and then killing apps that aren't working out for them. The company recently announced[9] that Google Health and Google PowerMeter are being discontinued.

    Google Wave was killed off only a few months after its public launch. Given this history, people are going to worry that the same fate awaits Google+ if it doesn't prove as popular as Google hoped.

6) The sum of the parts is greater than the whole. Google+ is a collection of what are essentially four separate applications. Facebook is a single application. Putting a launch pad interface on separate applications doesn't bring cohesion to the separate parts.

    This is where Google still doesn't understand that just because applications involve a social interaction, this doesn't make them all equally relevant in social networks.

7) I've already said too much. Google is already regarded with suspicion when it comes to how much information they gather about their users and the uses they put that information to. There will be a general reluctance to share even more personal information with Google.

    Admittedly, Facebook faces a similar perception, but the range of things people rely on with Google is different.

8) Who will tend the farm? Another feature of Facebook that Google+ won't have is social games. FarmVille[10] on Facebook has 38 million active users creating and tending for virtual farms.

    Social gaming is another reason Facebook is so popular. It does not appear that playing games is a Google+ feature.

---

[9]Brown, Aaron & Weihl, Bill, An update on Google Health and Google PowerMeter, http://google-blog.blogspot.com.au/2011/06/update-on-google-health-and-google.html, Accessed on 1 July 2013.

[10]FarmVille (requires Facebook login), http://www.farmville.com/, Accessed on 1 July 2013.

9) There is an app for that. Other than Facebook already doing what Circles does, videoconferencing is already covered by Skype and other applications, as are photo uploading and news feeds.
10) Google+, the movie. It's never going to happen.

4.3 Bitcoin: A Pirate's Booty or the New Global Currency?

31 August 2011

On July 19, Doctor Nefario, founder of the Global Bitcoin Stock Exchange, arrived at Seattle airport[11] and was asked if he had enough money to cover his stay in the US.

He replied that he did, but that it was in Bitcoin[12], an electronic cryptographic currency.

Unfortunately, not only did the Customs and Border Protection Authority not know what Bitcoin was, they didn't accept it as a valid currency and so refused him entry.

This ignorance of Bitcoin is shared by many, even though there is currently aroundUS$63.6 million of Bitcoin in circulation[13] (versus approximately US$950 billion in hard cash).

4.3.1 What is Bitcoin?

Bitcoin is a "cryptographic currency" that was first proposed[14] in 2008 by a programmer using the supposed alias Satoshi Nakamoto[15].

In early 2009, Nakamoto released software[16] that would implement the creation, sending and receiving Bitcoins over a peer-to-peer network.

His main motivation[17] was to avoid the need for "financial institutions serving as trusted third parties to process electronic payments" such as a bank or PayPal.

The scheme allowed the receiver to be sure the Bitcoin received was genuine and hadn't been sent elsewhere.

Nakamoto also thought Bitcoins would be largely anonymous.

---

[11] No Electronic devices, http://blog.glbse.com/no-electronic-devices, Accessed on 31 August 2011.

[12] Bitcoin - P2P digital currency, http://bitcoin.org/, Accessed on 31 August 2011.

[13] Bitcoin Watch, http://bitcoinwatch.com/, Accessed on 31 August 2011.

[14] Bitcoin P2P e-cash paper, http://www.mail-archive.com/cryptography@metzdowd.com/msg09959.html, Accessed on 31 August 2011.

[15] Satoshi Nakamoto, https://en.bitcoin.it/wiki/Satoshi_Nakamoto, Accessed on 31 August 2011.

[16] Bitcoin - P2P digital currency, http://bitcoin.org/, Accessed on 31 August 2011.

[17] Link no longer goes to specified page, http://bitcoin.org/bitcoin.pdf, Accessed on 31 August 2011.

Although theoretically possible, the exact nature of this anonymity is still being debated[18] and it's clear that, to achieve it, users need to take a series of precautions.

4.3.2   Other Side of the Coin

It was the anonymity of Bitcoin and its relation to an illicit online market place called Silk Road[19] that really brought Bitcoins to the public's and US Government's attention.

Silk Road can be used, among other things, to buy and sell drugs and other contraband.

This led two US Senators to demand Silk Road be shut down[20] and Bitcoin investigated.

Further concern was expressed that Bitcoins could be used for money-laundering (although, given the relatively illiquid nature of the currency, this would be on a relatively small scale).

The fact Bitcoin was adopted by organisations such as Wikileaks[21] and LulzSec[22] would not have surprised anyone.

While the US authorities could bring pressure to bear[23] on financial institutions such as Visa, Mastercard or PayPal to stop payments going to Wikileaks, there is no central authority in charge of Bitcoin, making it very much more difficult to control.

Having said that, it's not clear how much funding Wikileaks receives in the form of Bitcoins.

4.3.3   Using Bitcoins

You can get Bitcoins in two ways. The first, and most difficult, is through what is called Bitcoin mining[24].

---

[18] An Analysis of Anonymity in the Bitcoin System, http://anonymity-in-bitcoin.blogspot.com.au/2011/07/bitcoin-is-not-anonymous.html, Accessed on 31 August 2011.

[19] The Underground Website Where You Can Buy Any Drug Imaginable, http://gawker.com/5805928/the-underground-website-where-you-can-buy-any-drug-imaginable, Accessed on 31 August 2011.

[20] Silk Road (marketplace), http://en.wikipedia.org/wiki/Silk_Road_%28bitcoin%29, Accessed on 31 August 2011.

[21] Wikileaks, http://wikileaks.org/, Accessed on 31 August 2011.

[22] LulzSec, http://en.wikipedia.org/wiki/LulzSec, Accessed on 31 August 2011.

[23] PayPal says cut WikiLeaks account because of US position, http://www.google.com/hostednews/afp/article/ALeqM5iD3QvVjHsBxDqcimhweNxVxZblA, Accessed on 31 August 2011.

[24] Bitcoin, http://en.wikipedia.org/wiki/Bitcoin#.22Mining.22, Accessed on 31 August 2011.

This involves using computers to perform some of the cryptographic operations involved in making the Bitcoin network work. If you are the first to solve the calculations, you are rewarded with a certain number of Bitcoins.

A simpler way of getting Bitcoins is to buy them through one of the many Bitcoin exchanges.

One such exchange is Mt Gox[25], which allows you to buy Bitcoins using funds transfers of ordinary cash and e-Cash.

Once you've added funds to your account, buying Bitcoins is like buying shares: you can place an order to buy at the market rate or at a preferred rate.

Once you have the Bitcoins, you can leave them in your account on the exchange. You can also transfer them to a digital wallet on your computer or to an online e-wallet service.

You can then use your Bitcoins to buy goods and services[26] ranging from books to website development to legal services.

It seems clear the majority of Bitcoin is being bought and sold for investment purposes. This is another underlying cause for some of the fluctuation in rates that have beset the currency, which has seen its value go from US$1 to US $30 USD at its peak. It is currently around US $10.

4.3.4   Safety Concerns

The underlying system of transferring Bitcoin may be secure enough, but Bitcoin suffers from a number of vulnerabilities that have led to widely-publicised problems in the Bitcoin universe.

One of the first Bitcoin incidents occurred in June 2011 when Mt Gox was hacked and the user database of 61,000 users was taken.

The hackers used those usernames and passwords to transfer 25,000 Bitcoins— approximately US$225,000—to an account.

From there, they then tried to sell them on, but succeeded in only removing about $1,000-worth because of the daily limit imposed by Mt Gox.

As a consequence of the hack, the exchange rate for Bitcoin on Mt Gox plummeted before climbing back to the pre-hack level.

The second event was when another Bitcoin service, MyBitcoin.com, was hacked resulting in the site closing down along with all of the account holders' Bitcoins.

Approximately US$2 million of Bitcoin (valuation at the time) was lost, with one account holder who helped promote the site to family and friends losing about $250,000.

And then there was Bitomat, another Bitcoin site.

---

[25] Mt Gox – Bitcoin Exchange, https://mtgox.com/, Accessed on 31 August 2011.
[26] Trade, https://en.bitcoin.it/wiki/Trade, Accessed on 31 August 2011.

Based in Poland, a technical error on the part of the operator caused the server to crash, losing access to the Bitcoins in the process.

Mt Gox has recently taken over the accounts of Bitomat and offered to refund the lost coins to those users to help ensure the continuation of Bitcoin.

4.3.5   Future of Bitcoin

The "idea" of Bitcoin clearly has resonance with certain groups of people.

An electronic currency free from mediation and interference of governments and corporations, and which can be anonymous, is ideal for groups operating on the fringes of society—activists (cyber or otherwise), libertarians and, yes, criminals.

4.4   The Internet Is Insecure: Let's Build a Better One, Fast

26 October 2011

How many versions of the internet do we need? At least two, for the sake of security. *Source:* **pixabay CC0**[27]

A few days ago, senior FBI official Shawn Henry[28] called for the creation of a new and secure "alternative internet"[29] to secure key infrastructure and financial systems.

---

[27] Pixabay, http://pixabay.com/en/system-network-news-personal-71228/, Accessed online 21 December 2012.

[28] Shawn Henry FBI, http://www.fbi.gov/about-us/executives/Henry, Accessed online 26 October 2011.

[29] Top FBI man wants secure, alternate web, http://www.cio.com.au/article/404896/top_fbi_man_wants_secure_alternate_web/#closeme, Accessed online 26 October 2011

He assessed the process of connecting systems of national significance to the internet as a recipe for disaster, and he was right: the internet is insecure. And yet we use it today for everything from social media, shopping and banking through to education and, in the near future, eHealth[30].

The last of these, edging towards becoming reality[31] in Australia, simply should not proceed within the current system.

The rate of cyber-crime[32] on defence, government, business and residential systems is increasing and little can be done to stop it. Why? Because the digital network was not designed with security in mind.

The Australian government recently announced[33] the 2009 review of government security and infrastructure will be implemented and the current 124 individual internet gateways[34] (the place where multiple networks interconnect to exchange traffic) will be reduced to eight—the minimum number needed for operational efficiency and reliability.

The idea is to concentrate spending on a reduced number of gateways with the aim of improving security and, with new equipment, improve operations.

The government's actions are a step forward, but they don't tackle the root cause of the security problem—the insecure internet. And what about all the other users of the internet, business and residential customers included?

Most cannot afford the many multiple millions of dollars government is now spending on new gateways[35]—gateways that ultimately cannot and should not be relied upon to secure systems and infrastructure of national importance.

General Keith Alexander[36], director of the US National Security Agency and head of the US Pentagon's Cyber Command, recently used a speech in Baltimore to call[37] for the Pentagon and intelligence agencies to step up efforts to secure networks and systems.

---

[30]What is eHealth, http://www.ehealthinfo.gov.au/, Accessed online 26 October 2011.

[31]New body to manage risk in e-health record system, http://www.theaustralian.com.au/australian-it/new-body-to-manage-risk-in-e-health-record-system/story-e6frgakx-1226175593129. Accessed online 26 October 2011.

[32]Zombie computers, cyber security, phishing … what you need to know, http://theconversation.edu.au/zombie-computers-cyber-security-phishing-what-you-need-to-know-1671,   Accessed online 26 October 2011.

[33]Government agencies seek better cyber protection, http://www.theage.com.au/it-pro/government-it/government-agencies-seek-better-cyber-protection-20111020-1m921.html, Accessed online 26 October 2011.

[34]Internet gateway, http://itlaw.wikia.com/wiki/Internet_gateway, Accessed online 26 October 2011.

[35]Internet Gateway Reduction Program, http://www.intermedium.com.au/category/tag/internet-gateway-reduction-program, Accessed online 26 October 2011.

[36]Keith Alexander NSA, http://www.nsa.gov/about/leadership/bio_alexander.shtml, Accessed online 26 October 2011.

[37]NSA Chief Plays Offense on Cloud, Cybersecurity, http://www.informationweek.com/news/government/security/231901327, Accessed online 26 October 2011.

General Alexander also called for more government coordination with private companies to improve public network security.

In a key observation, he said that when a computer network is infected someone should be able to disconnect it.

4.4.1   The Internet as a Runaway Vehicle

The current situation cannot be allowed to continue. Internet crime, intellectual property and identity theft is growing[38]. Countries have begun to prepare for cyber warfare[39].

Criminal organisations have already made billions and appear to be re-investing to develop new and more sophisticated scams.

Another way of looking at the internet is to consider the analogy of the car in the twentieth century.

There can be no doubt the twentieth century was the century of the car. We all wanted one, speed was encouraged and by 1970 there were 3,600 road deaths annually[40] in Australia.

The number of permanent and disabling injuries associated with road trauma had reached a peak.

Government had to act and did so. Seat belts and lower speed limits were introduced and car companies were forced to redesign with safety as a priority.

The same point in history is now upon us for the internet. The government must act to reduce cyber-crime and to secure the key systems and infrastructure.

As already mentioned, the Australian government must not launch its eHealth systems until security can be guaranteed. If necessary, eHealth should only be utilised on a separate network—the start of a secure network for key national systems and infrastructure, as described by Shawn Henry.

One of the most important services on the internet today is still one of the most insecure: email. The fastest way for a criminal organisation to breach security is through the use of email.

It is fundamental that SMTPSec (the use of SSL certificates[41] for SMTP server to SMTP server communications) and SMTPS[42] (the use of SSL certificates for SMTP server to client communications) be implemented immediately.

---

[38] Cyber crime hits 431 million adults in 24 countries, http://www.odt.co.nz/news/technology/180572/cyber-crime-hits-431-million-adults-24-countries, Accessed online 26 October 2011.

[39] Cyber security and the online arms race: the battle has just begun, http://theconversation.edu.au/cyber-security-and-the-online-arms-race-the-battle-has-just-begun-1495, Accessed online 26 October 2011.

[40] Road fatalities and fatality rates - 1925 to 2003, http://www.abs.gov.au/ausstats/abs@.nsf/Previousproducts/1301.0Feature%20Article302005?opendocument&tabname=Summary&prodno=1301.0&issue=2005&num=&view=, Accessed online 26 October 2011.

[41] Secure Socket Layer, http://www.webopedia.com/TERM/S/SSL.html, Accessed online 26 October 2011.

[42] SMTP Secure, http://en.wikipedia.org/wiki/SMTPS, Accessed online 26 October 2011.

New legislation is needed that sets out a path towards Australia having two separate networks. One would remain the public internet and the other would be a secure network for key national systems and infrastructure.

Authority to disconnect parts of the network and to disconnect countries from the Australian network should be detailed. Protocols need to be put in place for these actions to occur and it must be decided who will carry out the actions.

Legislation should set out a timeline and framework whereby equipment and systems suppliers will be required to improve their products with safety and security in mind.

Certain well-known security flaws in the way computers are made and sold must be identified in the legislation and made illegal. One example is that operating systems can be sold without adequate integrated anti-virus and anti-malware capability. To return to our analogy, that would be like selling a car without seat belts today.

All computers connected to the internet should be registered and the computer operating system should report the computers state including the health of the anti-virus and anti-malware checks.

Do you see the parallel with cars? Car registration is now mandatory for any vehicle utilising public roads. Car roadworthy checks are carried out annually or in some states randomly and whenever a vehicle is sold.

Australia is taking a positive lead by working with other nations to identify and try to solve some of the issues with the internet. But the pace of this world-wide effort is glacial and more needs to be done.

4.5   UK Court Ruling on ISP Filtering: Copyright Victory or Download Defeat?

31 October 2011

A fully regulated internet may have come another step closer. *Source*: **Horia Varian CC0**[43]

---

[43]Copyright, Horia Varlan, Flickr, http://www.flickr.com/photos/horiavarlan/4839454263/sizes/l/in/photostream/, Accessed online 21 December 2012.

Last week, the English High Court ordered[44] British Telecom (BT) to block access to a members-only website that offers links to pirated films.

NewzBin2, the site in question, offers links to pirated films on what's been described as a "grand scale".

The ruling—which gives BT just 14 days to act—follows legal action by the Motion Picture Association[45] (MPA) earlier this year.

It's the first copyright infringement case of its kind, legally requiring an internet service provider (ISPs) to deal with the thorny issue of illegal downloads.

The High Court outcome is already being hailed as a major win for movie studio bosses in their ongoing copyright protection battles.

Chris Marchich, managing director of the Motion Picture Association in Europe stated[46]: "Securing the intervention of the ISPs was the only way to put the commercial pirates out of reach for the majority of consumers.

"This move means we can invest more in our own digital offerings delivering higher quality and more variety of products to the consumer."

BT, which has for some years employed an internet filtering system called Cleanfeed[47] to block access to child pornography, welcomed the High Court outcome.

That same system—created in 2003 and live since June 2004—will now be used to filter NewzBin2.

---

[44]England and Wales High Court (Chancery Division) Decisions, Case No. HC10C04385, http://www.bailii.org/cgi-bin/markup.cgi?doc=/ew/cases/EWHC/Ch/2011/2714.html&query=Newzbin&method=Boolean, Accessed online 31 October 2011.

[45]Motion Picture Association of America, http://www.mpaa.org/, Accessed online 31 October 2011.

[46]BT given two weeks to block piracy site, http://www.techradar.com/news/internet/bt-given-two-weeks-to-block-piracy-site-1036760, Accessed online 31 October 2011.

[47]Cleanfeed (content blocking system), Wikipedia, http://en.wikipedia.org/wiki/Cleanfeed_(content_blocking_system), Accessed online 31 October 2011.

Source: **Newzbin**[48]

A spokesperson for BT said it was "helpful to have the order now and the clarity that it brings".

The ruling may also give the company an avenue for dealing with an anticipated backlash from rights groups and groups sponsoring freedom online: BT, the company can rightly claim, has been forced to implement filtering, and has no choice in the matter.

The MPA has already stated it will likely request other ISPs to block NewzBin2. With or without that, the judgement is likely to have an impact elsewhere in the world, including Australia.

In 2008, the Australian Federation Against Copyright Theft[49] (AFACT) took action against iiNet—a prominent ISP—claiming that iiNet had allowed its users to illegally download copyrighted movies.

The Australian Federal Court ruled[50] in February this year that iiNet did not authorise the acts of infringement that occurred on its internet service.

---

[48]Newzbin, https://c479107.ssl.cf2.rackcdn.com/files/4972/width668/Newzbin.jpg, Accessed online 31 October 2011.

[49]Australian Federation Against Copyright Theft, http://www.afact.org.au/, Accessed online 31 October 2011.

[50]Roadshow Films Pty Limited v iiNet Limited [2011] FCAFC 23, Federal Court of Australia – Full Court, http://www.austlii.edu.au/au/cases/cth/FCAFC/2011/23.html, Accessed online 31 October 2011.

The Australian High Court granted AFACT special leave to appeal the Full Court of the Federal Court in August and it's likely the matter will return[51] to the High Court later this year.

It's perfectly possible the Australian High Court will take notice of the latest international developments relating to this matter.

In the US, the six largest ISPs have agreed to a voluntary "six strikes"[52] system of copyright notices and mitigation measures, including offender download speed reductions, mandatory copyright education and an appeals process.

In New Zealand, a copyright protection system has been in place[53] since 1998, which includes warnings, detection and enforcement notices that ultimately may lead to offenders being fined up to NZ$15,000.

In the UK a similar system[54] was announced last year—it includes detection, infringement notices, a frequent offender register and an appeals body.

The English High Court has effectively added to the copyright protection available to movie studios by requiring ISPs to block access to identified websites that permit customers to download copyright material.

Internet filters were introduced[55] in Australia this year by major ISPs including Telstra, Optus and several smaller ISPs. The providers announced they would voluntarily block more than 500 websites.

This step has drawn criticism from groups such as Electronic Frontiers Australia[56] and other groups supporting online freedom and no censorship[57] of the internet.

Should we be worried or relieved? That comes down to opinion and personal choice.

It's only a matter of time before the internet is fully regulated in Australia. The English High Court decision brings this reality one step closer.

---

[51] iiNet v AFACT: What's going to happen in the High Court?, ARN, http://www.arnnet.com.au/article/403399/iinet_v_afact_what_going_happen_high_court_/?fp=4&fpid=56736#closeme, Accessed online 31 October 2011.

[52] Major ISPs agree to "six strikes" copyright enforcement plan, ARS Technica, http://arstechnica.com/tech-policy/news/2011/07/major-isps-agree-to-six-strikes-copyright-enforcement-plan.ars, Accessed online 31 October 2011.

[53] Copyright protection in New Zealand, http://www.med.govt.nz/business/intellectual-property/copyright/copyright-protection-in-new-zealand, Accessed online 31 October 2011.

[54] UK Digital Economy Act 2010, Wikipedia, http://en.wikipedia.org/wiki/Digital_Economy_Act_2010, Accessed online 31 October 2011.

[55] Telstra, Optus to start censoring the web next month, News.com.au, http://www.news.com.au/technology/internet-filter/telstra-optus-to-begin-censoring-web-next-month/story-fn5j66db-1226079954138#ixzz1Q1W8lmsl, Accessed online 31 October 2011

[56] Electronic Frontiers Australia, http://www.efa.org.au/, Accessed online 31 October 2011.

[57] No Clean Feed – Stop Internet Censorship in Australia, http://nocleanfeed.com/, Accessed online on 31 October 2011.

4.6   Stop Online Piracy Act Draws Battle Lines for 'Control' of the Internet

21 November 2011

Is tighter online regulation a cause for despair or jubilation? *Source*: **William Clifford CC0[58]**

Battle lines have been drawn in the US between proponents of the Stop Online Piracy Act[59] (SOPA), currently being debated, and those who oppose any regulation of the internet.

On one side are organisations that will benefit by copyright being applied to the internet, including the Motion Picture Association of America, the American Federation of Musicians, the Directors Guild of America, the Screen Actors Guild and other copyright holders. They are joined by drug companies keen to block online pharmacies from utilising copyright material without permission as a means of generating cheap online sales from outside the US.

On the other side are a broad range of organisations including leading internet companies—Google, AOL, eBay, Facebook, Twitter and many others. An open letter[60] was sent to Congress last week outlining their concerns with SOPA.

---

[58] Clifford W., Flickr, http://www.flickr.com/photos/williac/993220684/, Accessed online 21 December 2012.

[59] Stop Online Piracy Act, H.R. 3261, 112th Congress, 2011-12, http://www.govtrack.us/congress/bill.xpd?bill=h112-3261, Accessed online 21 November 2011.

[60] Open letter opposing Protect IP and SOPA, http://www.protectinnovation.com/downloads/letter.pdf, Accessed online 21 November 2011.

Also in support of the anti-SOPA stance are civil liberties groups—and others such as the Electronic Frontiers Foundation, which posted an overview of SOPA[61].

Earlier this year, Australian internet service providers (ISPs)—including Telstra, Optus and Primus Telecom—implemented internet filters to block Interpol's list[62] of child-abuse websites.

In England, the High Court ordered[63] British Telecom to block access to a members-only website called NewzBin2 that offers links to pirated films.

Critics of SOPA employ a common image—SOPA as a "bull in a china shop"— and emphasise their preferred approach is a voluntary code of conduct that includes identification of copyright breaches and voluntary removal of the copyright material upon receipt of a copyright breach notification.

This is similar to the argument used in Australia against the proposed mandatory internet filter[64] to be used to block child-abuse websites. In Australia many organisations argued a mandatory internet filter would lead to government censorship of the internet.

It has been suggested, by opponents, that SOPA would have worldwide consequences because US consumers using websites while physically outside the US would bring that website within US jurisdiction. But this concern is of little consequence as there is already international jurisdictional precedence.

In 2000, Joseph Gutnick successfully sued[65] Dow Jones and Company in the Supreme Court of Victoria. This court case was of considerable note because the offending article was placed on a Dow Jones website.

In defence, Dow Jones claimed the article was published in the US and therefore any defamation action should take place in the US.

The Supreme Court of Victoria did not agree with the Defence, deciding the internet is an online publishing network and under common law defamatory matter is published in each place in which it is read, seen or heard.

In 2002, the Australian High Court upheld the decision after an appeal by Dow Jones.

Arguing the internet should be treated differently to other forms of media is not sustainable in the long term.

---

[61] SOPA: Hollywood Finally Gets A Chance to Break the Internet, Electronic Frontier Foundation, https://www.eff.org/deeplinks/2011/10/sopa-hollywood-finally-gets-chance-break-internet, Accessed online 21 November 2011.

[62] Worst of List, Interpol, http://www.interpol.int/Crime-areas/Crimes-against-children/Access-blocking/Criteria_for_inclusion_in_the_Worst_of_list, Accessed online 21 November 2011.

[63] UK court ruling on ISP filtering: copyright victory or download defeat?, The Conversation, http://theconversation.edu.au/uk-court-ruling-on-isp-filtering-copyright-victory-or-download-defeat-4040. Accessed online 21 November 2011.

[64] Internet censorship in Australia, Wikipedia, http://en.wikipedia.org/wiki/Internet_censorship_in_Australia#Proposed_future_legislation_.28mandatory_filtering.29,   Accessed   online   21 November 2011.

[65] Dow Jones & Co. Inv. V Gutnick, http://en.wikipedia.org/wiki/Dow_Jones_%26_Co._Inc._v_Gutnick, Accessed online 21 November 2011.

Google claims to be in favour of a watered down version of SOPA. Yet Google has a poor track record that will count against any arguments put by the company. In August, Google agreed to pay[66] US$500 million to settle a US Department of Justice case because it let online pharmacies in Canada use Google's Adwords[67] system to advertise prescription drugs to US consumers.

It is also argued SOPA would force many organisations to move websites and cloud computing facilities outside the US in an attempt to limit any effect SOPA would have on their worldwide operations.

Censorship is a common claim which is strongly denied by the lead sponsor of SOPA, Lamar Smith, a Texas Republican. Smith wrote[68]: "The First Amendment is not a cover for engaging in criminal activity".

"The infringing websites in question have ample opportunity to participate in judicial proceedings, if they choose to do so. The bill's actions are directed toward websites that are trafficking in illegal goods or copyrighted material".

Change is needed.

The internet has become a haven[69] for international crime organisations. Scams, SPAM, viruses, malware, hacking, intellectual property loss and identity theft are now common occurrences online. Innocent people are having their lives ruined and governments must act.

A growth in internet-related legislation to protect copyright holders is likely in the next 5 years. Governments will bring legislation into line with recent court cases where copyright holders have successfully argued copyright protection extends to the internet.

The future of entertainment is likely to depend on government legislation reducing rampant online copyright breaches.

Copyright holders have for several years taken court action against individuals who download copyright material without permission.

Better regulation of the internet will reduce the need for copyright holders to take legal action against individual consumers, allowing websites containing illegal copyright material to be targeted, wherever they are hosted in the world.

The internet is not special, and should not receive special treatment.

---

[66] Google Forfeits $500 Million Generated by Online Ads & Prescription Drug Sales by Canadian Online Pharmacies, US Department of Justice, http://www.justice.gov/opa/pr/2011/August/11-dag-1078.html, Accessed online 21 November 2011.

[67] AdWords, Google, https://accounts.google.com/ServiceLogin?service=adwords&cd=AU&hl=en_AU&ltmpl=adwords&passive=false&ifr=false&alwf=true&continue=,   https://adwords.google.com.au/um/gaiaauth?apt%3DNone%26ltmpl%3Dadwords&error=newacct&sacu=1, Accessed online 21 November 2011.

[68] H.R. 3261 Manager's Amendment Summary, US Congress, http://judiciary.house.gov/issues/Rouge%20Websites/Stop%20Online%20Piracy%20Act%20Fact%20Sheet.pdf, Accessed online. 21 November 2011, new link to amended document, http://judiciary.house.gov/issues/Rogue%20Websites/Summary%20Manager's%20Amendment.pdf .

[69] Zombie computers, cyber security, phishing ... what you need to know, The Conversation, http://theconversation.edu.au/zombie-computers-cyber-security-phishing-what-you-need-to-know-1671, Accessed online 21 November 2011.

4.7 Beyond.com…An Online World Where Anything.goes?

12 January 2012

I ♥ INTERNET

Is a custom domain name worthy of your attention and love? *Source*: **Codice Internet CC0**[70]

At 11 o'clock this morning (Melbourne time), the Internet Corporation for Assigned Names and Numbers (ICANN)[71] started accepting applications[72] for custom top-level domain (TLD)[73] names.

Simply put, this means web addresses will no longer have to end with suffixes such as .com, .net or .org. It will now be possible to purchase domain names such as .food, .beer, .sydney or, well, anything you like really.

The introduction of new internet address suffixes will allow industries, businesses, and individuals to register unique web addresses to reflect their brand or values. Importantly, it will also allow applicants to register TLDs in any language[74], not just English.

But there's a catch.

It costs US$185,000 to apply for a custom TLD, with an ongoing fee of US$25,000 per year for a minimum of 10 years. ICANN has been criticised for these costs and rightly so—the internet is fully automated (meaning very little work for ICANN at all) and these costs are little more than exploitation.

It's not clear what ICANN will do with this additional income, but they have indicated that US$2 million has been set aside[75] to assist needy applicants—applicants from developing countries, for example.

---

[70]Codice Internet, Flickr, http://www.flickr.com/photos/codiceinternet/2929723344/, Accessed online 21 December 2012.

[71]Internet Corporation for Assigned Names and Numbers, http://www.icann.org/, Accessed online 12 January 2012.

[72]New gTLDs Update: Applications Accepted Today; New Guidebook Posted; Financial Assistance for Qualifying Applicants, ICANN, http://www.icann.org/en/announcements/announcement-11jan12-en.htm, Accessed online 12 January 2012.

[73]Top Level Domains (gTLDs), ICANN, http://www.icann.org/en/tlds/, Accessed online 12 January 2012.

[74]Bored by .org and .com? The world is your.oyster, The Conversation, https://theconversation.edu.au/bored-by-org-and-com-the-world-is-your-oyster-1940, Accessed online 12 January 2012.

[75]New gTLDs Update: Applications Accepted Today; New Guidebook Posted; Financial Assistance for Qualifying Applicants, ICANN, http://www.icann.org/en/announcements/announcement-11jan12-en.htm, Accessed online 12 January 2012.

But let's put this into perspective: with needy applicants receiving a discount of US$138,000 on their application cost (US$47,000 vs. US$185,000), the seed fund will support less than 15 needy custom TLD applicants across the entire world.

So how popular will custom TLDs be?

Well, some experts are predicting[76] we could see more than 1,000 TLDs being introduced every year.

I'm inclined to think that the initial take-up will be slow, with the costs being prohibitively expensive for all but the largest organisations. Smaller companies will probably wait for the costs to drop before applying for their own TLD.

Over time, businesses will probably start making room for TLDs in their marketing budgets. With a TLD, an organisation could implement internet addresses in a logical structure that fits the organisation or a product range. For instance, car manufacturer Holden could purchase the .holden TLD and create the commodore.holden and cruze.holden addresses.

But it's search engines that are likely to see the greatest benefit from the introduction of custom TLDs.

Say I'm looking to buy a new car and I want to check out Holden's range. Do I go to holden.com or cars.holden? The simple solution is to use a search engine as my home page and type "holden cars" into the search box.

Of course, this is what happens already, but search engines will see the introduction of new TLDs as an opportunity to start charging for TLD ranking.

The algorithms that underpin search engines such as Google or Bing are weighted, based on criteria such as payments for keywords or ranking priority. To ensure a new TLD is ranked above .com, .net or the TLD of a rival company, businesses will need to factor in an additional annual payment.

Assuming the costs drop as time passes, the introduction of custom TLDs is likely to be a big step forward for the internet, for online business, and for how we interact with internet-connected devices in the future.

Imagine a future where speech-enabled, internet-connected devices are more commonplace and further developed. Rather than having to type "http://www.holden.com.au" into my device, I will be able to simply say "Holden" and, given that Holden would then own the .holden TLD, my speech-enabled device would take me straight to their site based on my voice command.

But that vision is still a little while off and the first custom TLDs won't be in use until 2013. Until then, it will be interesting to see just how many organisations are willing to pay the hefty US$185,000 price tag for their own customised slice of the web.

---

[76] Web Braces for 1,000 New Top Level Domains a Year, The Wall Street Journal, http://blogs.wsj.com/tech-europe/2011/11/22/web-braced-for-1000-new-top-level-domains-a-year/, Accessed online 12 January 2012.

4.8   Wardriving and Surviving: Who Else is Using Your Wi-Fi?

4 April 2012

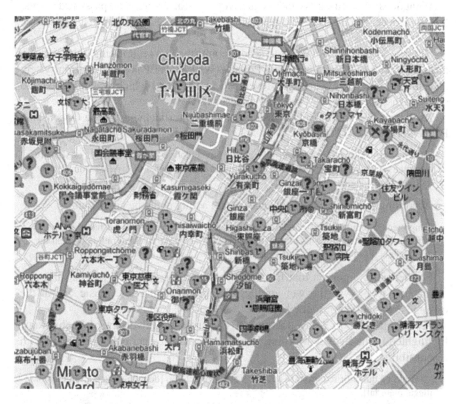

Open and poorly secured Wi-Fi networks are vulnerable to exploitation by others. *Source:* **David Pursehouse: Central Tokyo Wi-Fi**[77]

Late last month the Queensland Police started a new project[78] to highlight the urgent need for secure wireless internet connections[79].

The "wardriving" project involves police driving the streets of Queensland, searching for unsecured Wi-Fi coming from houses and businesses.

---

[77] Pursehouse D., Flickr, http://www.flickr.com/photos/mdid/3219551589/, Accessed online 21 December 2012.

[78] War Driving Project to help prevent identity theft, Queensland Police, http://qpsmedia.govspace. gov.au/2012/03/22/war-driving-project-to-help-prevent-identity-theft/, Accessed online 4 April 2012.

[79] Secure your wireless network at home., Queensland Police, http://www.police.qld.gov.au/ programs/cscp/eCrime/wireless.htm, Accessed online 4 April 2012.

(Given Wi-Fi signals can have a range of up to 100 m, a family's Wi-Fi connection can be accessible from well outside the home.)

When an open or poorly secured Wi-Fi access point is found, it is logged by Queensland Police, who will later send a letter with information on how to secure Wi-Fi access points (such as routers).

What does "unsecured Wi-Fi" mean? Well, it means there is no password set and that open access to the Wi-Fi access point is available to anyone with a compatible device.

"Poorly secured" Wi-Fi refers to access points that are set up using older security measures, such as Wired Equivalent Privacy (WEP)[80]. WEP is an encryption system that utilises a security technique developed in 1999 and which was outdated and replaced in 2003 by Wi-Fi Protected Access (WPA)[81].

As Detective Superintendent Brian Hay said in a statement for the Queensland Police Service News[82]:

> "Having WEP encryption is like using a closed screen door as your sole means of security at home. The WPA or WPA2 security encryption is certainly what we would recommend as it offers a high degree of protection."

According to Hay, the consequences of not acting could be significant:

> "Unprotected or unsecured wireless networks are easy to infiltrate and hack," he said. "Criminals can then either take over the connection and commit fraud online or steal the personal details of the owner. This is definitely the next step in identity fraud."

Furthermore, a person that has access to open residential Wi-Fi can use this connection to browse the web or illegally download movies, music or—at the extreme end—child pornography.

As Nicolas Suzor, a law lecturer at Queensland University of Technology, highlighted in the Sydney Morning Herald[83], the homeowner could be landed with responsibility:

> "It could be quite difficult to prove that it wasn't in fact you [downloading copyrighted or illegal material]."

This is potentially a major problem for residential Wi-Fi users and one that the Queensland Police has decided to reduce by committing resources from the Fraud and Corporate Crime Group[84].

---

[80] Wired Equivalent Privacy, Wikipedia, http://en.wikipedia.org/wiki/Wired_Equivalent_Privacy, Accessed online 4 April 2012.

[81] Wi-Fi Protected Access, Wikipedia, http://en.wikipedia.org/wiki/Wi-Fi_Protected_Access, Accessed online 4 April 2012.

[82] War Driving Project to help prevent identity theft, Queensland Police, http://qpsmedia.govspace. gov.au/2012/03/22/war-driving-project-to-help-prevent-identity-theft/, Accessed online 4 April 2012.

[83] Wi-Fi hijackers cause download of trouble, Fairfax, http://www.smh.com.au/technology/secu-rity/wifi-hijackers-cause-download-of-trouble-20110715-1hhrm.html, Accessed online 4 April 2012.

[84] Fraud investigation training, Queensland Police, http://www.police.qld.gov.au/News+and+Alerts/campaigns/synergy/profile.htm, Accessed online 4 April 2012.

Another concern is that Wi-Fi users often have mobile devices and computers connected to the one broadband connection. As a result, when someone gains access to their open Wi-Fi they can access all of the devices and computers on that home network.

4.8.1 A Long Drive

The Queensland Police wardriving effort is certainly not the first of its kind. In fact, wardriving has been occurring since the inception of Wi-Fi in the 1990s.

In 2010, Google Australia was found to be collecting Wi-Fi information[85] by cars sent out to record street views. At the time, Communications Minister Stephen Conroy claimed[86] Google's actions constituted "the largest privacy breach in the history of Western democracies".

The Queensland Police have commenced the project and to ensure they do not commit a breach of privacy have configured their systems to collect only limited information; just enough to be able to identify open or poorly secured Wi-Fi so the owner can be notified.

And when you look at the statistics, it seems there are a lot of homeowners that need to be notified.

In a test done across Sydney in July 2011, the Sydney Morning Herald[87] identified "unsecured Wi-Fi networks in ten out of 20 residential locations…In total, 328 networks were detected with 2.6 % operating without password protection."

Needless to say, the problem of unsecured Wi-Fi is not an exclusively Australian problem.

In December 2004, students worked to map Wi-Fi in Seattle[88] over a few weeks and found 5,225 Wi-Fi access points, of which 44 % were secured with WEP encryption, 52 % were open, and 3 % were pay-for-access.

The wardriving by students in Seattle was legal, but several issues[89]—such as privacy, security and people downloading pornography—were identified.

---

[85] Privacy watchdog probes Google's Wi-Fi data harvest, Fairfax, http://www.smh.com.au/technology/technology-news/privacy-watchdog-probes-googles-wifi-data-harvest-20100519-vckv.html,Accessed online 4 April 2012.

[86] 'Put your money where your mouth is,' Conroy told, Fairfax, http://www.smh.com.au/technology/technology-news/put-your-money-where-your-mouth-is-conroy-told-20100526-wd22.html, Accessed online 4 April 2012.

[87] Wi-Fi hijackers cause download of trouble, Fairfax, http://www.smh.com.au/technology/security/wifi-hijackers-cause-download-of-trouble-20110715-1hhrm.html, Accessed online 4 April 2012.

[88] Seattle Wi-Fi Map Project, University of Washington, http://depts.washington.edu/wifimap/, Accessed online 4 April 2012.

[89] Seattle's packed with Wi-Fi spots, The Seattle Times, http://seattletimes.nwsource.com/html/businesstechnology/2002183464_wifimap18.html, Accessed online 4 April 2012.

The information collected by students identified that in areas with large numbers of overlapping Wi-Fi access points, signals can cause interference and open wireless networks can cause security risks. Students found some of the Wi-Fi access points had names "Open to share, no porn please" and "Free access, be nice".

4.8.2 Tools of the Trade

Over the years, many tools have been developed to assist in the capture of Wi-Fi details during a wardrive. One classic wardriving tool is NetStumbler[90]. Other, more modern, tools can be found at wardrive.net[91].

After Wi-Fi access point information is collected using one of the above tools, the data can be uploaded to an online map, such as those featured on wigle.net[92].

A map of Wi-Fi connections in Melbourne from wigle.net *Source*: **wigle.net[93]**

The results from Queensland Police's wardriving efforts are yet to be seen but in the meantime, it would be wise to make sure your Wi-Fi is being used by you, and no-one else.

---

[90] Netstumber software, http://www.netstumbler.com/downloads/, Accessed online 4 April 2012.

[91] Wardriving tools, http://www.wardrive.net/wardriving/tools, Accessed online 4 April 2012.

[92] Wireless Geographic Logging Engine, Wigle, http://wigle.net/, Accessed online 4 April 2012.

[93] Wiggle.net, http://www.wigle.net/, Accessed online 4 April 2012.

For more information on the War Driving Project or tips on how to secure your connection, visit the Queensland Police Service website[94].

4.9   The NBN, Service Providers and You…What Could Go Wrong?

23 May 2012

How can consumers get what they want on an NBN-enabled Australia without getting wires crossed? *Source*: **Copyright © 2013 NBN Co Limited. All rights reserved[95]**

Unless you've been boycotting all forms of media in the past 5 years, you'll be aware that the National Broadband Network (NBN)[96] is well and truly on its way.

For some of us[97] the NBN is already here, and for others it will hopefully arrive in a year or two. But for most Australians, the NBN will not arrive for 5–10 years.

---

[94]Secure your wireless network at home, Queensland Police, http://www.police.qld.gov.au/safewifi, Accessed online 4 April 2012.

[95]Optic fibre cable, NBNCo, http://medianet.multimediarelease.com.au/bundles/8f3c311a-2311-428c-a19a-5cfa481a9a22, Accessed online 21 December 2012.

[96]Explainer: the National Broadband Network (NBN), The Conversation, https://theconversation.edu.au/explainer-the-national-broadband-network-nbn-207, Accessed online 23 May 2012.

[97]Communities in the rollout, NBN Co, http://www.nbnco.com.au/rollout/about-the-rollout/communities-in-the-rollout.html?icid=pub:rollout:1yr:bod:all-towns-maps, Accessed online 23 May 2012.

The NBN rollout map (see below) provides an estimated guide to where and when the NBN will be rolled out.

The coming of the NBN provides significant opportunities to address consumers' concerns about the conduct of internet and phone providers but it also presents a range of significant challenges.

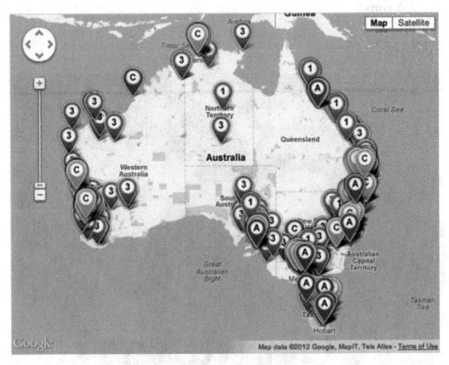

Click for full functionality. *Source*: **Copyright © 2013 NBN Co Limited. All rights reserved**[98]

Let me start by discussing what happens if there's a change in government during the NBN rollout—not unlikely given recent polls[99] suggesting this will happen in the next 18 months.

The Coalition has been scathing of the Fibre to the Home (FTTH)[100] solution for the cabled portion of the NBN.

---

[98] NBN rollout map, NBN Co, http://www.nbnco.com.au/rollout/rollout-map.html?icid=pub:rollou t:1yr:bod:map-lp, Accessed online 23 May 2012.

[99] Newspoll May 2012, http://polling.newspoll.com.au/image_uploads/120701%20Federal%20 Voting%20Intention%20&%20Leaders%20Ratings.pdf, Accessed online 23 May 2012.

[100] Internode's new Bibre to the Home plans match NBN, impress media, http://www.impress.com. au/press-releases-mainmenu-1/internode-mainmenu-48/1360-internodes-new-fibre-to-the-home-plans-match-nbn-.html, Accessed online 23 May 2012.

In his recent Budget reply speech[101] the Leader of the Opposition, Tony Abbott, said: "Why spend A\$50bn[102] on a National Broadband Network so customers can subsequently spend almost three times their current monthly fee for speeds they might not need?".

He gave a clear indication of the preferred Coalition option when he stated: "Why dig up every street when fibre to the node (FTTN) could more swiftly and more affordably deliver twenty-first century broadband?".

Simply put, a fibre to the node approach would see fibre optic cable routed to "neighbourhood cabinets"[103] with the final stretch, from neighbourhood cabinets to homes and businesses, being covered by existing copper cable.

If the Coalition forms a government at the next election (late next year) and changes direction with the NBN rollout, it's possible that built-up areas, already delayed into the later stage of the current NBN rollout plans, will not be serviced by FTTH.

It's possible the current goal of providing FTTH to 93 % of Australians will change to include a mix of FTTH and FTTN for about 80 % of Australians and the other 13 % will be moved on to the NBN wireless network.

Optic fibre being installed underground. *Source*: **Copyright © 2013 NBN Co Limited. All rights reserved**[104]

---

[101] Tony Abbott's Budget Reply Speech, AustralianPolitics.com, http://australianpolitics. com/2012/05/10/abbott-budget-reply-speech.html, Accessed online 23 May 2012.

[102] The top 10 NBN myths debunked, NBN Myths, http://nbnmyths.wordpress.com/2010/09/26/12/, Accessed online 23 May 2012.

[103] Fibre to the node: Turnbull to meet with Quigley, Delimiter, http://delimiter.com.au/2011/10/24/ fibre-to-the-node-turnbull-to-meet-with-quigley/, Accessed online 23 May 2012.

[104] NBNCo, http://www.nbnco.com/, Accessed online 21 December 2012.

One of the potential opportunities provided by the NBN rollout will be a chance to improve consumer experience of phone and internet providers.

In 2009/10 167,955 complaints[105] were made to the telecommunications ombudsman and 197,682 complaints[106] in 2010/11.

A complaint I hear during discussions about service providers is the lack of transparency that customers find for nearly every aspect of their interaction with service providers, their use of services and network performance.

Transparency related to the network performance and the customer's interaction with service providers can be introduced using technology available today.

The status of individual network connections including all backhaul links[107]) (the connections from the exchanges or points where customers enter the network to the carrier core networks) should be made available in real-time through the internet.

This would allow internet users to check whether their service provider's networks are down or whether they've encountered a localised problem or other performance issue.

Also, the capacity of all aggregation (the bundling of customer traffic onto larger capacity links) and backhaul links should be made available so that customers can see in real-time what the performance is.

Included in this need for transparency is the real-time performance of the international links through which most of Australia's online content is delivered.

---

[105] Telecommunications Ombudsman receives 167,955 complaints about phone, internet companies, News Limited, http://www.news.com.au/breaking-news/telecommunications-ombudsman-receives-167955-complaints-about-phone-internet-companies/story-e6frfku0-1225965111952, Accessed online 23 May 2012.

[106] Mobile phone issues drive record number of consumer complaints to the TIO, Telecommunications Industry Ombudsman, http://www.tio.com.au/publications/media/mobile-phone-issues-drive-record-number-of-consumer-complaints-to-the-tio, Accessed online 23 May 2012.

[107] Backhaul (telecommunications), Wikipedia, http://en.wikipedia.org/wiki/Backhaul_(telecommunications), Accessed online 23 May 2012.

Optic fibre installation underground. *Source*: **Copyright © 2013 NBN Co Limited. All rights reserved**[108]

Customer service requests, including adding services, moving services and changing services, should be possible online and with greater transparency and tracking capability.

After a customer service request has been made the customer should be able to use the service provider reference number to see the service request on the internet and to track the steps taken to satisfy the service request. This is not done currently.

Why is this important? This gem[109] by Fairfax writer, Adam Turner, might give you a bit of an idea. His piece highlights the frustration of dealing with the Telstras and Optuses of this world.

Thousands of similar stories are available online and chances are you or someone close to you has had a similar experience.

Recently I moved home and tried to move my Telstra landline and Business ADSL on the day of the move.

I have services on the ADSL that must remain online 24/7 so this was a critical part of my move to a new home and I thought it was all ready to go.

---

[108] NBNCo, http://www.nbnco.com/, Accessed online 21 December 2012.

[109] Telstra v Optus – battle of the incompetents, Fairfax, http://blogs.smh.com.au/digital-life/gadgetsonthego/2008/08/18/telstravoptus.html, Accessed online 23 May 2012, new link http://blogs.smh.com.au/gadgetsonthego/archives/2008/08/ or http://techtalkradio.com.au/adamturner-view-from-the-couch-2008.php

Unfortunately, when I first spoke with Telstra about the move, I was told that it would take up to 10 days to move the ADSL after the Telstra landline was moved.

I explained how important it was for the phone and ADSL to move at the same time, and was told that it could be done within 4 h if a technician was available at the exchange.

Several days later, after initially accepting this explanation and putting in the service request, I had second thoughts and arranged for a new landline service to be connected at my new home so that the old landline could remain connected until the ADSL was moved to the new home.

Sure enough, on the night before the move my landline at the old place was disconnected thus also disconnecting the Telstra Business ADSL.

I called Telstra immediately (at midnight) to see if the landline had been connected at my new home and that the ADSL would be moved that morning and was promptly told it would take up to 10 days for the ADSL to be connected, even though it was a business service and that no guarantees should have been given.

I explained that the old landline should not have been disconnected until the ADSL had been moved and that an earlier service request to move the landline and ADSL from the old home to the new home had been processed.

When I mentioned this service request had been cancelled and I had placed a new service request for a new landline at the new home and for the ADSL to be moved whilst both landlines were to remain operational the Telstra representative looked at the records and said: "it appears a mistake has occurred at our end".

Panic set in and I then spent about 8 h on my mobile to Telstra, talking to about 20 different people while they worked out what went wrong.

After this, I finally got connected to a very kind and helpful Telstra Business ADSL service representative who reconnected the landline and ADSL at my old home.

I was a nervous and tired wreck by the end of the day.

My Telstra Business ADSL was moved to my new home about 7 days later.

Customers currently make service requests on the phone and many service providers do not provide written confirmation of the service request. Instead the customer is give a reference number, leaving them in the dark about what the service provider is actually going to do.

A clear issue is the lead times for service requests to occur. Most service providers only commit to carrying out a service request at some point in the future—say 5–10 days—or at some time in the future dependent on a wholesale service provider, such as Telstra Wholesale.[110].

A wholesale provider owns the infrastructure (e.g. the copper cable from exchanges to your home) and service providers lease access to the infrastructure to provide services such as fixed telephony or ADSL.

Service providers[111] have recently made moves to reduce the time taken for consumers to get access to their services.

[110]Telstra Wholesale, http://www.telstrawholesale.com.au/, Accessed online 23 May 2012.

[111]iiNet launches faster ADSL transfer process, Delimiter, http://delimiter.com.au/2012/03/20/iinet-launches-faster-adsl-transfer-process/, Accessed online 23 May 2012.

ABC Mobile Studio. *Source*: **ABC CC BY-SA**[112]

A major step forward with the NBN will be the capability to gain access to more than one service provider at the same time.

Initially customers will be able to access one data service provider and two voice service providers (though one is required to be the same as the data service provider).

If the customer utilises a service wholesaler[113] then it will be possible to get access to services from more than one service provider.

You might ask: "How will I ever get the service providers to move their services on the same day if I move to a new home?"

Chaos right?

This upcoming multi-service-provider feature[114] of the NBN needs to be explained and a new industry code of practice needs to be introduced to ensure service providers improve service management practices.

Failure to address how service providers offering services over the NBN are coordinated will see complaints to the ombudsman grow to new heights.

The NBN will provide Australians with a raft of exciting new opportunities. For services providers, it will provide a much-needed chance to improve their customer relations and procedures.

And who wouldn't welcome that?

---

[112] ABC Mobile Studio, ABC, https://commons.wikimedia.org/wiki/File:ABC_Mobile_Studio_ Caravan.jpg, Accessed online 21 December 2012.

[113] Optus to offer NBN wholesale services, ZDNet, http://www.zdnet.com/optus-to-offer-nbn-wholesale-services-1339312211/, Accessed online 23 May 2012.

[114] Multi-Service-Provider, NBN Explained, http://nbnexplained.org/wordpress/what-will-it-deliver/product-overview/#footnote_6_694, Accessed online 23 May 2012.

4.10   Cheaper Hardware, Software and Digital Downloads? Here's How

30 July 2012

Consumers have options if they want to avoid the feeling of being out of tune with world prices.
Source: **LaserGuided**[115]

Australians are paying about twice as much as they should for a range of tech products including computers, software and digital downloads.

It's time for the government to act to bring this shameful situation to an end, to stop foreign multinationals from ripping us off. But until then, people should take steps to lower the cost of buying tech products. How? Read on.

4.10.1   Choice Report into High IT Prices

The Australian consumer watchdog Choice[116] made a submission[117] to the Parliamentary Inquiry into IT Pricing[118] last week. It found the cost of IT products to Australian consumers could not be justified and that price discrimination was a systemic problem.

[115]LaserGuided, Flickr, http://www.flickr.com/photos/pilax/57002123/, Accessed online 21 December 2012.

[116]Choice, http://www.choice.com.au/, Accessed online 30 July 2012.

[117]Carwright M., The digital price divide, Choice, 18 July 2012, http://www.choice.com.au/media-and-news/consumer-news/news/choice-lodges-submission-on-it-price-discrimination.aspx, Accessed online 30 July 2012.

[118]Inquiry into IT Pricing, House Standing Committee on Infrastructure and Communications, Australian Government, http://www.aph.gov.au/Parliamentary_Business/Committees/House_of_Representatives_Committees?url=ic/itpricing/tor.htm, Accessed online 30 July 2012.

The Choice report highlights that the high cost of IT products disadvantages all consumers and prevents Australian companies from competing in the digital economy. The flow-on effect was higher prices for everyone in Australia.

Choice reported that for one product—Microsoft's Visual Studio 2010 Ultimate with MSDN[119] (New Subscription)—it would be cheaper to fly an employee to the US and back twice, and for this employee to purchase the product while overseas. The product's retail monetary price difference is US$8,665.29 between Australia and the US.

4.10.2   Excuses Made for High Prices

Multinationals have argued that rental, labour and transportation costs, and the associated GST, cause the disparity. Another gem of a reason was the argument by foreign companies that Australia was a small market and therefore the cost of selling products here would be higher due to marketing costs.

The excuses are flimsy and transparently false. The Choice report states that these cumulative costs do not account for the doubling in prices for IT hardware and software. Digital downloads from some foreign multinationals are sold to Australians more than 50 % higher than to US consumers.

Choice spokesman Matt Levey said:

> "Global companies [are] pricing these products at a point where they think people are going to buy it, regardless if that's at parity with other countries.
>
> They use a number of technological barriers to actually prevent Australians from accessing these products from parallel importing them and direct importing them from cheaper markets."

4.10.3   How to Purchase Directly from the USA

Many large US based online stores such as Lands End[120] and L.L. Bean[121] offer similar products to those available in Australia at quite amazing prices and provide international shipping.

But some companies utilise a range of practices to prevent international customers from purchasing directly from the USA. The company might reject the purchase based on the shipping address, the type of credit card used or because your computer is located in Australia.

---

[119] Visual Studio 2010 Ultimate with MSDN, Microsoft, http://www.microsoftstore.com/store/msaus/en_AU/pdp/productID.250026800, Accessed online 30 July 2012.

[120] Lands' End, http://www.landsend.com/, Accessed online 30 July 2012.

[121] L.L. Bean, http://www.llbean.com/, Accessed online 30 July 2012.

Other factors you need to check on before making an international purchase are whether the product will work here and if the warranty will be supported.

To purchase directly from the USA it's important to only use reputable mail forwarding companies and to read the fine print before any purchase. Mail forwarding has become a very competitive market so check competitor prices often.

To purchase directly from the USA follow these steps:

- Register with a company that provides a USA address and mail forwarding. Examples are Shipito[122], MyUS[123], ForwardIt[124], and the Australian-based PriceUSA[125].
- Register with an international payment provider that provides purchase insurance, such as PayPal[126].
- If you wish to purchase on a site such as Ebay USA[127], set the USA address you have been provided with by the shipping company as your registered PayPal address and current shipping address.

Another hurdle to overcome is the use of geo blocking[128] by websites such as Apple iTunes[129]. Geo blocking is a recent move by global online stores to segment the world into markets and control access to products and pricing.

A recent article[130] by Dan Warne on Australian Business Traveller provides a step by step guide on how to create a US iTunes account in Australia. Unfortunately if you also have an Australian iTunes account or sync over multiple devices, you may need to log out of one account and in to the other when carrying out updates or making purchases.

Another approach is to purchase US iTunes gift cards and have them shipped to you from the USA. You cannot use Australian iTunes gift cards (available from stores such as Coles and Woolworths) on the US iTunes website.

---

[122] Shipito, http://www.shipito.com/, Accessed online 30 July 2012.

[123] MyUS.com, http://www.myus.com/, Accessed online 30 July 2012.

[124] ForwardIt, http://www.forwardit.us/, Accessed online 30 July 2012.

[125] PriceUSA, http://www.priceusa.com.au/, Accessed online 30 July 2012.

[126] PayPal, http://www.paypal.com/, Accessed online 30 July 2012.

[127] Ebay USA, http://www.ebay.com/, Accessed online 30 July 2012.

[128] Geo-blocked,   PCMag.com,   http://www.pcmag.com/encyclopedia_term/0,1237,t=geo-blocked&i=61864,00.asp, Accessed online 30 July 2012.

[129] iTunes, Apple, http://www.apple.com/itunes/, Accessed online 30 July 2012.

[130] Warne D., How to get a US iTunes account in Australia, Australian Business Traveller, 20 July 2012, http://www.ausbt.com.au/how-to-get-a-us-itunes-account-in-australia, Accessed online 30 July 2012.

4.10.4   Why the Australian Government Has to Act

I have written in the past about the mobile phone data plan rip-off [131] and the international roaming rip-off[132]. The common theme here is that international multinationals consider Australia to be affluent and therefore a target for overpricing.

The Australian political mantra that free trade and low tariffs will be to the Australian consumer's benefit is obviously not working.

Choice's three recommendations to combat international price discrimination are:

1. Educate consumers through government initiatives so people know their rights when shopping online—particularly in relation to returns and refunds, accessing legitimate parallel imports from foreign markets, as well as privacy and security.
2. Investigation by the Federal Government into whether technological measures enabling suppliers to discriminate against Australian consumers, such as region-coding or identifying IP addresses, should continue to be allowed.
3. Keep the low-value threshold (LVT)[133] exemption for GST and duty on imported goods unchanged at A$1,000.

It seems Choice has advocated a softly-softly approach to solving the problem of high IT prices in the hope that the Australian government may take baby steps toward solving this problem. I fully support what Choice is advocating, but Australians need to demand more urgent and immediate steps to stop multinationals from price gouging.

Further Reading

- Verizon Wireless vs Telstra: the great mobile rip-off continues[134]
- Are Australian international roaming charges the greatest rip-off in history?[135]

---

[131] Gregory M.A., Verizon Wireless vs Telstra: the great mobile rip-off continues, The Conversation, 12 July 2012, https://theconversation.edu.au/verizon-wireless-vs-telstra-the-great-mobile-rip-off-continues-8132, Accessed online 30 July 2012.

[132] Gregory M.A., Are Australian international roaming charges the greatest rip-off in history?, The Conversation, 30 November 2011, https://theconversation.edu.au/are-australian-international-roaming-charges-the-greatest-rip-off-in-history-4340, Accessed online 30 July 2012.

[133] Low Value Parcel Processing Taskforce, Australian Customs and Border Protection Service, http://www.customs.gov.au/site/low-value-threshold.asp, Accessed online 30 July 2012.

[134] Gregory M.A., Verizon Wireless vs Telstra: the great mobile rip-off continues, The Conversation, 12 July 2012, https://theconversation.edu.au/verizon-wireless-vs-telstra-the-great-mobile-rip-off-continues-8132, Accessed online 30 July 2012.

[135] Gregory M.A., Are Australian international roaming charges the greatest rip-off in history?, The Conversation, 30 November 2011, https://theconversation.edu.au/are-australian-international-roaming-charges-the-greatest-rip-off-in-history-4340, Accessed online 30 July 2012.

4.11   Who Owns Your Digital Content?

7 September 2012

The story so far has Bruce Willis at loggerheads with Apple over the right to pass on his vast digital music collection when Bruce takes on an action hero role in heaven.

The epic has gone viral and appears to have been a rumour that got out of control.

Charles Arthur writing on **The Guardian**[136] goes so far as to suggest

- *So now let the search begin for the origin of this. There's an article from Marketwatch[137] which bears an odd resemblance—but it has no mention of legal challenge. It's all talk about Estates and Wills.*
- *Which brings us to a horrible pause: might it be that someone saw a mention of "Estates and Wills" and thought it was "estates and Willis"?*
- *The origin of this story may be lost on the web, but the story has spectacularly highlighted a key problem with how companies are "selling" digital media over the network.*

In the Marketwatch article Evan Carroll, co-author of "Your Digital Afterlife" states

- *I find it hard to imagine a situation where a family would be OK with losing a collection of 10,000 books and songs*
- *Legally dividing one account among several heirs would also be extremely difficult*

4.11.1   The Truth

The average person may be shocked to learn that you pay companies like Apple and Amazon.com to license digital content—you do not get to own the digital files.

What this means is that you pay to use the digital media files and do not own the right to transfer the files to another person, even as an inheritance.

Amazon's quite clear with this point in its terms of use. It states "you do not acquire any ownership rights in the software or music content".

---

[136] Arthur C., No, Bruce Willis isn't suing Apple over iTunes rights, The Guardian, 3 September 2012, http://www.guardian.co.uk/technology/blog/2012/sep/03/no-apple-bruce-willis, Accessed online 7 September 2012.

[137] Fottrell Q., Who inherits your iTunes library?, Marketwatch, The Wall Street Journal, News Limited, 23 August 2012, http://articles.marketwatch.com/2012-08-23/finance/33336852_1_digital-content-digital-files-apple-and-amazon, Accessed online 7 September 2012.

4.11.2   Apple's Legal Loophole

Apple's terms of use for digital media is limited to Apple devices that are used by the account holder.

Definitions of what constitutes an 'account holder' are vague at best and aren't really explained by either Amazon and Apple. At best guess, the 'account holder' is the person that can currently login to the account.

Does this mean that if someone hacks into the account and take it over, they become the account holder and the previous owner loses the right to access the account? It could take some time and involve substantial cost to prove ownership of an account that is setup with vague details.

What about inheritance or the transfer of an account through the sale of its details?

Online suppliers of digital media limit access to content and restrict the trade in digital media to maximise the profits through its sale. This means that if a family wants to listen to one song on all of their devices, they will all have to but it separately.

4.11.3   An Argument Against Digital Media

Until companies that provide digital media can justify the practice of restricting transfer of ownership and transfer for use onto multiple devices, there's still an argument for sticking with physical media such as DVDs, CDs and books.

However, this argument ignores the practicality and widespread adoption of digital media.

Take for instance the e-book. The introduction of the Kindle and iPad have brought about an explosion in e-book sales and has also reduced the sales of physical books.

As with most things digital today, it is recommended that consumers look for digital media suppliers that have flexible policies and utilise generic digital media formats like the mp3 music file format so that transferring the digital media is not impossible without resorting to breaking a licensing agreement.

As for Bruce Willis, he shall be remembered as the action hero that inadvertently reminded us that he may not Die Hard but when he does why should his digital media die with him.

4.12   Telstra's Post-NBN Future

18 October 2012

Australia's telecoms landscape is undergoing a significant change as the fibre revolution swings into action but what will Australia's premier ICT provider Telstra look like in 2020?

Some might hope that Telstra will be a smaller company than it is now; a few might even hope that Telstra no longer exists. It's likely that both groups will be disappointed when 2020 rolls around to find Telstra still holding on to the number one spot. However, for that to happen the telco will have to negotiate a few bumps in the road along the way, caused not by competition but by some of the underlying internal structural issues that Telstra has yet to resolve.

By the end of this decade the information revolution will be at a higher plateau and the rapid rate of change in the ICT marketplace would still be underway. There will be industry winners and losers and it is likely that there will be one high profile casualty in Australia—Vodafone, in part because of Vodafone's poor performance which has hurt the Vodafone brand but also because of Vodafone's failure to move beyond being principally a mobile cellular provider.

4.12.1   Telstra in 2020

By 2020, Telstra will have completed an upgrade of its mobile network to the "Next 4G" network (LTE-Advanced) which would be fully ITU-T IMT-Advanced compliant. Customers will be experiencing download speeds of just over 100 Mbps and the range of services available over the Telstra mobile network continue to dwarf alternate mobile offerings.

There will also be a couple of other advancements along the way. Here's one possible scenario.

In 2016, Telstra releases the Telstra "Car-T-Box" which integrates the customer's car into the Telstra network using either Wi-Fi or the Next G network and provides customers with triple play (movies, telephone and Internet) as they drive around within the Telstra network footprint. The Car-T-Box will be software upgradeable to ensure it is compliant with the introduction of the Telstra integrated Wi-Fi capability. It will automatically connect to the Telstra T-Box when in Wi-Fi range or over the Next G network and permit customers to download movies and music to their cars.

The ITU-T IMT-Advanced feature set promises Wi-Fi integration and facilitates seamless mobile handover to Telstra integrated Wi-Fi networks. By this time Telstra has entered into Wi-Fi infrastructure agreements with fast food outlets, shopping centres, airports, sporting facilities and so on.

By 2017, Telstra has rolled out 50,000 IMT-Advanced compliant Wi-Fi access points at approximately 6,500 venues around Australia.

By 2018, over four million cars are fitted with the Telstra Car-T-Box and in early 2020 four out of five vehicles on Australian roads were fitted with the Telstra Car-T-Box making it Telstra's third most successful product of all time.

This is just one of many possible pathways that Telstra can take to maintain its market dominance.

4.12.2 Leaving the Silos Behind

By 2020, Telstra will have moved from a silo based organisation, where every product is managed and operated separately, to a customer focused organisation.

Customers will be able to view and manage every aspect of their interaction with Telstra through the customer portals. They will also be able to add, change and remove services through the portal and then view the internal Telstra processes of making the service changes in real-time. A call to Telstra will be to a person who has access to all of Telstra's products and services and can carry out every aspect of customer support without having to forward the customer to another call centre.

As things stand now, Telstra is still on a long road to identifying and rectifying the many anomalies brought about by being a silo based organisation. Current gems include:

- Telstra Business ADSL customers do not have access to Telstra Bigpond yet residential customers connected to the same DSLAM pay the same amount as the business customer, get more downloads and have access to Telstra Bigpond.
- Telstra business mobile customers can have data share plans yet Telstra business mobile customers cannot share data with their family members who also have mobiles and tablets on the Telstra network.

That's two in a long list of anomalies that will most likely be reported in 2020 by an interested historian to have been longer than a ball of string.

4.12.3 NBN Delivery a Big Hit

By 2020, Telstra will report that the delivery of service offerings through the NBN has been a major success story. This success will be anchored by an aggressive campaign to grow the number of services available to customers over the NBN, a process that should start next year.

This process will also be instrumental in ensuring that Telstra Bigpond's dominance prior to the NBN is not affected as the network is rolled out—in fact Telstra will hope that Bigpond's subsequent growth will reduce the influence of smaller ISPs.

The separation of Telstra's wholesale and retail arms has been one of the driving forces behind the NBN and the future of the telco's wholesale arm could be dictated by a move away from reselling fixed, backhaul, international and other infrastructure access to include wholesale service provision.

This new direction will be based on realising the growth potential of the surge in specialised service providers entering the market and wishing to gain access to customers by piggybacking onto Telstra's bundled products.

It's likely that Telstra will negotiate exclusive license agreements with specialised service providers and begin offering the services to Telstra and non-Telstra customers through the wholesale division.

Another potential growth area for Telstra's wholesale division will be the growth of customer choice products. As part of Telstra's new customer focus mantra, customers will be permitted to request services offered by Telstra's competitors and vice versa. Customers will have the ability to request access to services offered by companies within Australia or overseas. Some potential scenarios may include, Telstra offering AFL football coverage to non-Telstra customer's mobile devices or permitting customers to request access to the Optus library of old movies—secured by Optus under license from Google.

The separation of Telstra's wholesale and retail arms will change the landscape, improve competition (partly due to the NBN effect) and ultimately contribute to Telstra becoming Australia's premier ICT customer focused organisation.

So what will Telstra look like in 2020? Well, it will still be the biggest player in town but the overall size of the ICT market will easily be three times the size it is now. Most importantly, customers will have more choice from a larger number of service providers, greater satisfaction and the benefits of the fibre revolution will be there for all to see.

4.13   Teleworking's Hidden Risks

2 November 2012

For many, the word 'teleworking' brings to mind a picture of a person sitting on a beach with a notebook. The reality is a little less encouraging.

Teleworking or telecommuting as it is also known has not become a feature of everyday life and <10 % of Australians have a telework agreement with their employer.

Which leads to the question why? The reasons might surprise and at the same time cause some concern.

4.13.1   Where We Currently Sit with Teleworking

A study by the Australian Bureau of Statistics (ABS) in June 2000 found that 430,000 people engaged in some form of teleworking. This figure had increased by 370 % by 2006 when another study by the ABS found that 1,595,500 Australians teleworked at least some of the time. This amounts to about 17 % of the workforce.

While the amount of employees in teleworking seems to be increasing, the number of employers offering teleworking arrangements remains low.

In August 2011, the Minister for Broadband, Communications and the Digital Economy, Senator Stephen Conroy offered insight into where Australia stands in terms of teleworking.

> "According to the ABS, just six per cent of employees from Australia have reported having any kind of telework arrangement with their employer."

He went on to contrast our efforts to that of other countries.

"In the US, 10 per cent of US employees telework at least one day a month and eight European Union countries reported that more than 10 per cent of workers involved in telework a quarter of the time or more and that was in 2005," he said.

One of the government's goals as part of its Digital Economy initiative[138] is to double teleworking agreements in Australia to more than 12 %. It's attempting to push the National Broadband Network as an enabler of this goal and is holding a National Teleworking week[139] from November 12 to November 16 to promote awareness of the trend. In light of this, the government's NBN website includes the following reasons for more Australians to work from home:

- Improve workforce participation opportunities
- Boost enterprise productivity
- Reduce urban congestion on roads and public transport, especially at peak times
- Reduce air pollution, greenhouse gas emissions and fuel consumption associated with commuting
- Improve the economic and cultural vitality of local areas as the workforce decentralises
- Provide time and cost savings for employees

4.13.2 The Downside to Teleworking

The government paints the move to teleworking as being quite a rosy endeavour, however there are some less talked about downsides to this tech trend.

While employers benefit from having to provide less office space—and therefore pay less on rent and utilities for an office—employees need to make sure they aren't receiving a dud deal with their teleworking agreement.

Employees must ensure that their teleworking agreement includes allowances to cover the additional costs faced when working from home. Some of these costs include telephone, electricity, internet access and provision of a suitable computer or notebook.

Of course, if your company is paying these costs then they may want to ensure that you are using these resources for your work. With teleworking eliminating the ability for managers to directly supervise work, companies may turn to technology such as video VoIP[140] and monitoring systems to ensure that their employees keep on task.

---

[138] Telework, Department of Broadband, Communications and the Digital Economy, http://www.dbcde. gov.au/digital_economy/programs_and_initiatives/telework, Accessed online 2 November 2012.

[139] 61 new telework partners sign on as NBN takes off, Media Release, Senator Stephen Conroy, 11 May 2012, http://www.minister.dbcde.gov.au/media/media_releases/2012/066, Accessed online 2 November 2012.

[140] VoIP, Technology Spectator, http://www.technologyspectator.com.au/tech-speak/term/voip, Accessed online 2 November 2012.

On one extreme, an organisation may even go so far as to install an invasive monitoring application on the teleworker's computer that monitors time spent working and utilises a camera to take photos at regular intervals. It's also possible for someone at the company office to take control of the teleworker's computer camera to see if the teleworker is at the computer.

4.13.3 Taking Teleworking to the Extreme

Jumping on the teleworking bandwagon may also give companies a taste of another tech trend, outsourcing.

There may come a point where an organisation decides that if an employee doesn't need to be in the office, it may be cheaper to replace them with lower cost overseas workers. Many companies already utilise this approach with customer call centres, information technology support and software or system development.

The internet has already created a large pool of skilled teleworking enabled labour that companies can harness at a lower cost. vWorker[141] is just one example of a site that provides companies with skilled professionals that can work for them on a job-by-job basis.

The reality is that unless you provide a specialised service it is likely that there will be people from emerging economies who will do most tasks for much less.

4.13.4 Consider the Risks Before You Leap Onto the Trend

The gloss of the teleworking trend seems to overshadow the risks. Technology may now enable greater teleworking possibilities, but it's also given a boost to employers potential to spy on their staff and outsource labour.

Employees wanting a teleworking policy need to ensure that they are not being blindsided by employers with the prospect of added workplace freedom.

Sure, the prospect of working from home—or from a tropical beach—may seem tempting, but it won't mean much if your receiving a rawer deal from your workplace to do it.

4.14 Is Remote and Rural Australia Being Dudded by the NBN?

5 November 2012

---

[141] vWorker, http://www.vworker.com/, Accessed online 2 November 2012.

Are the people that live in remote areas any less important than those in urban areas? *Source:* **Steve Jurvetson**[142]

The National Broadband Network (NBN)[143] is an important nation-building project that's being implemented at a time of fundamental change in the way we utilise services over the digital network.

For most Australians—those of us in big cities—the NBN will be a big improvement over the existing access network, thanks to fibre connections[144].

But for the 7 % of Australians in regional and remote areas, the NBN will take the form of either fixed wireless[145] or satellite services.

These services will provide customers with download speeds of 12 MB/s compared[146] to the 100 MB/s fibre customers will enjoy. The disparity in upload speeds is even greater[147].

So are these wireless and satellite services really good enough? Are Australians in rural areas being dudded of appropriate infrastructure?

And should there be flexibility in the NBN roll-out plan to allow remote shires to contribute to bringing fibre to their communities?

---

[142] Jurvetson S., Flickr, http://www.flickr.com/photos/jurvetson/1223730777/, Accessed online 21 December 2012.

[143] National Broadband Network, Department of Broadband, Communications and the Digital Economy, http://www.nbn.gov.au/, Accessed online 5 November 2012.

[144] Fibre, fixed wireless and satellite, NBN Co, http://www.nbnco.com.au/rollout/about-the-nbn/fibre-wireless-satellite.html, Accessed online on 5 November 2012.

[145] What is fixed wireless broadband?, Department of Broadband, Communications and the Digital Economy, http://www.nbn.gov.au/2012/04/27/what-is-fixed-wireless-broadband/, Accessed online on 5 November 2012.

[146] Top 10 frequently asked questions about the NBN, NBN Co, http://www.nbnco.com.au/faq.html, Accessed online on 5 November 2012.

[147] Top 10 frequently asked questions about the NBN, NBN Co, http://www.nbnco.com.au/faq.html, Accessed online on 5 November 2012.

4.14.1   Remote Control

The remote Barcoo Shire[148] in western Queensland is a pertinent example of a region that will miss out on the best of the NBN.

Bruce Scott, former mayor of Barcoo Shire told ABC Radio's AM[149] in late September:

> The national information superhighway is so critically important and if we've got a second-rate service coming into these communities what reason is there for people to stay?

Scott said that while satellite services planned for Barcoo are a great solution for domestic broadband, they won't support communities that need real-time, high-bandwidth services services such as health care, education and government services.

> Satellites will not provide video links for hospital clinics, for access to school curriculums—it won't provide what is needed for these towns to function.

Current Barcoo Shire mayor Julie Groves and Geoffrey Morton, mayor of Diamantina Shire[150]—to the west of Barcoo Shire—proposed earlier this year[151] that 700 km of optic fibre, costing A\$22 million, should be laid to connect five towns in their shires to the NBN.

Julie Groves told AAP and Suzanne Tindal[152] in July:

> We also need our residents and visitors to be able to access mobile communication for safety, business and social media.

> Our younger generation will not stay if they are not connected.

In Western Australia, South Australia and the Northern Territory remote towns and communities are sure to have similar concerns to those voiced in the Barcoo and Diamantina Shires.

[148] Shire of Barcoo, Wikipedia, http://en.wikipedia.org/wiki/Barcoo_Shire, Accessed online on 5 November 2012.

[149] Small S., Outback Qld goes it alone for high-speed internet, Australian Broadcasting Corporation, 29 September 2012, http://www.abc.net.au/news/2012-09-29/outback-qld-goes-it-alone-for-high-speed-internet/4287308?goback=%2Egde_107152_member_169965194, Accessed online on 5 November 2012.

[150] Shire of Diamantina, Wikipedia, http://en.wikipedia.org/wiki/Shire_of_Diamantina, Accessed online on 5 November 2012.

[151] Tindal S., Qld councils struggle to make fibre NBN a reality, ZDNet, 25 July 2012, http://www.zdnet.com/qld-councils-struggle-to-make-fibre-nbn-a-reality-7000001524/, Accessed online on 5 November 2012.

[152] Tindal S., Qld councils struggle to make fibre NBN a reality, ZDNet, 25 July 2012, http://www.zdnet.com/qld-councils-struggle-to-make-fibre-nbn-a-reality-7000001524/, Accessed online on 5 November 2012.

4.14.2   Design Flaw

As well as dudding residents of rural Australian towns, the current NBN design fails to take into account the more than two million Australians and international tourists that take to the roads every year during winter and journey into the outback[153].

In 2011 outback Queensland had an estimated[154] 381,000 international and domestic visitors who stayed for more than two million nights.

As mentioned, the NBN makes provision for fixed wireless and satellite services yet caravans and motor homes are often moved into remote Australia and reside in one or more locations for months on end.

The NBN will not cater for caravans and motor homes and so for many tourists, WiFi is the only low-cost option.

Unfortunately, for many regional and remote towns—such as those in the Barcoo and Diamantina shires—WiFi hot-spots are not available. Nor are they likely to become available if business is forced to use the NBN fixed wireless and satellite services.

We have already reached the point where travellers need and expect to have internet access. This, in turn, means WiFi is a fundamental service that travellers demand.

Fibre is needed to help support businesses such as caravan parks, hotels and motels so they can provide WiFi to their customers.

Mobile cellular services are also very limited in rural areas. At the Birdsville horse races[155] held every September, only Telstra and Optus provide (limited) mobile service and there is only limited cellular data available[156].

As a result, holiday-makers in rural areas have little or no opportunity to utilise the digital network on their journeys.

Quite simply, without fibre connections to regional towns and communities, rural and remote Australia will be left behind.

---

[153] Snapshots 2012, Caravan or Camping in Australia, Tourism Research Australia, http://www.ret. gov.au/tourism/Documents/tra/Snapshots%20and%20Factsheets/2012/CC_Snapshot_2012.pdf, Accessed online on 5 November 2012.

[154] Queensland invites Aussies for an Outback Queensland spring Eventure, Tourism Queensland, 30 March 2012, http://www.tq.com.au/news-room/corporate-media-news/corporate-media-news_ home.cfm?pageType=storyView&obj_uuid=E284005C-BD8B-CCFD-FE88- 12D7E79DCFEB&appendPageTitle=Queensland%20invites%20Aussies%20for%20an%20 Outback%20Queensland%20spring%20Eventure, Accessed online on 5 November 2012.

[155] Birdsville races, Birdsville Race Club, http://www.birdsvilleraces.com/home.html, Accessed online on 5 November 2012.

[156] Birdsville races, Birdsville Race Club, http://www.birdsvilleraces.com/Races2008/ FAQ#Mobile%20reception, Accessed online on 5 November 2012.

4.14.3   Funding

As is ever the problem with large infrastructure projects, cost is one of the driving factors. While it would be unfeasible to lay enough fibre to connect all Australians to the NBN, it would certainly be possible to increase fibre coverage.

Barcoo and Diamantina shires have committed A\$5.5 million to extending fibre coverage into their jurisdictions, calling for state and federal funding to make the plans a reality.

The new Queensland government is in cost-cutting mode[157] and is therefore unlikely to be keen to participate until the budget is an improved position.

But the previous Queensland state government[158] had committed A\$2.8 million and indicated it would consider dollar-for-dollar matching.

While the federal government has provided more than A\$350 million to fund regional broadband-related projects—including the Digital Regions Initiative[159], Clever Networks[160], Indigenous Communications Program[161] and the Regional Backbone Blackspots Program[162]—it is yet to respond to the Barcoo and Diamantina proposal.

It is unlikely the federal government will want to contribute to a fibre network in one area of remote Australia, given the risk of other remote shires calling for similar funding.

Furthermore, efforts to increase fibre roll-out in rural areas are likely to undermine the NBN Co. business case and invite concern about whether or not the NBN satellites[163] are needed.

---

[157]Williams P., Politically sharp Queensland budget might cut both ways for Newman, The Conversation, 12 September 2012, https://theconversation.edu.au/politically-sharp-queensland-budget-might-cut-both-ways-for-newman-9480, Accessed online on 5 November 2012.

[158]Tindal S., Qld councils struggle to make fibre NBN a reality, ZDNet, 25 July 2012, http://www.zdnet.com/qld-councils-struggle-to-make-fibre-nbn-a-reality-7000001524/, Accessed online on 5 November 2012.

[159]Digital Regions Initiative, Department of Broadband, Communications and the Digital Economy, http://www.dbcde.gov.au/funding_and_programs/digital_regions_initiative, Accessed online on 5 November 2012.

[160]Clever Networks, Department of Broadband, Communications and the Digital Economy, http://www.dbcde.gov.au/digital_economy/programs_and_initiatives/clever_networks, Accessed online on 5 November 2012.

[161]Indigenous Communications Program, http://www.dbcde.gov.au/funding_and_programs/indigenous_communications_program, Accessed online 5 November 2012.

[162]Regional Backbone Blackspots Program, Department of Broadband, Communications and the Digital Economy, http://www.dbcde.gov.au/funding_and_programs/national_broadband_network/national_broadband_network_Regional_Backbone_Blackspots_Program, Accessed online 5 November 2012.

[163]Biddington B., Australia will soon have a national space policy – no giggling, please, The Conversation, 15 October 2012, https://theconversation.edu.au/australia-will-soon-have-a-national-space-policy-no-giggling-please-9917, Accessed online 5 November 2012.

4.14.4   Is There Room for Flexibility?

Regional and remote Australia fulfils an important and valuable role in many aspects of Australian business, society and culture.

As Australians we need to ask ourselves the question: are the people that live in remote areas any less important than those that live in urban areas?

Should the government and NBN Co be flexible with the proposed NBN roll-out? More specifically, should remote shires be able to contribute towards fibre network connections if there is demand and a willingness among the community?

The answer should be a resounding yes.

The federal government needs to positively respond to the Barcoo and Diamantina proposal so the project can move ahead. Other regional and remote councils are likely to follow the Barcoo and Diamantina shires with their own proposals and those too should be supported.

The need for flexibility with the NBN roll-out should not be a political football: it should be an opportunity for all Australians to participate equally in the digital revolution, irrespective of where they live or travel around this nation.

4.15   Redefining Defamation in the Online Age

16 November 2012

Google found itself in hot water this month, after a Melbourne Supreme Court jury found the search giant guilty of defaming[164] Melbourne resident Milorad Trkulja through its search engine.

The ruling is set to forever change the meaning of defamation in Australia. The law, once reserved for incendiary media commentary, is now seemingly relevant to all internet technologies.

In awarding Trkulja $200,000 in damages, the court has reinforced the dictum that even some of the world's largest companies can no longer use emergent technologies as an excuse against enduring laws.

Internet search engines technologies created and maintained by engineers working in some of the world's largest multi-nationals. It's always been accepted that companies are responsible for what their engineers create and society anticipates that engineered systems work for societies benefit and "do no harm". Defective products and services are required to be fixed when a problem has been identified and internet technologies are no different from any other.

---

[164]Polites H., Melbourne man successively sues Google, seeks $339,000 in defamation damages, Technology Spectator, 1 November 2012, http://www.technologyspectator.com.au/melbourne-man-successively-sues-google-seeks-339000-defamation-damages, Accessed online 16 November 2012.

However, Google begged to differ when they refused to take down Trkulja's picture from their search engine.

They continued to publish this defamatory material between October and December 2009, despite receiving a letter from Trkulja's lawyers asking for its removal.

Trkulja's ended up taking the search giant to the Supreme Court ad his persistence now stands vindicated.

In determining the company's penalty, Justice David Beach identified that Google's search engine published the defamatory material because it was designed to do so and therefore "Google Inc is like the newsagent that sells a newspaper containing a defamatory article. While there might be no specific intention to publish defamatory material, there is a relevant intention by the newsagent to publish the newspaper for the purposes of the law of defamation."

It's a surprise that Google didn't see such an outcome coming. This wasn't the first time Trkulja had sued—and won—against a search engine.

Earlier this year Yahoo!7 Inc was found guilty of defaming Mr Trkulja because the Yahoo!7 search engine returned with his picture when the search phrase 'Melbourne Crime' was used. Yahoo!7 was ordered to pay Mr Trkulja $225,000 in damages.

Both of these court cases are important because their outcomes are likely to set a precedent that will be adopted internationally.

Australian courts have a history of not accepting arguments put by large international companies about their responsibilities for what appears on internet websites. Both the judge and jury saw through Yahoo and Google's arguments that they should be treated differently to other organisations that publish material on the internet.

After all, search engine query results could surely be considered as some form of publication.

Perhaps the giants would have suffered less if they had paid attention to a landmark Australian defamation ruling in 2002.

In 2000, Joseph Gutnick, another Melbourne resident, successfully sued Dow Jones & Co in the Supreme Court of Victoria. This court case was of considerable note because the offending article was placed on a Dow Jones website and that the server hosting the website was located in the US.

In defence, Dow Jones claimed the article was published in the US and therefore any defamation action should take place in the US.

The Supreme Court of Victoria did not agree with the defence, deciding the internet is an online publishing network and under common law defamatory matter is published in each place in which it is read, seen or heard.

In 2002, the Australian High Court upheld the decision after an appeal by Dow Jones.

The outcome from the Dow Jones case set an international precedent: it identified there is no defence in arguing that the internet should be treated differently to other forms of media. The Google and Yahoo!7 cases have now added to the Gutnick outcome by including search engine query output as published material and therefore subject to defamatory laws applied to other forms of media.

What is interesting is that Google and Yahoo!7 decided to fight the matter in court having earlier ignored Mr Trkulja's written requests for relief from what he considered was a defamatory situation. Large internet organisations won't win friends by forcing David and Goliath court cases.

Society expects companies to have a process to deal with customer complaints and to act in good faith when a customer identifies a problem. Should large multinationals operating on the internet be treated any differently to any other international company operating in Australia? Should technology be used as an excuse not to comply with Australian law?

We should expect Australian courts to provide clear and unequivocal guidance that international companies operating on the internet must adhere to Australian law and technology should not be used as an excuse. Regulation of the internet is happening; slowly but surely.

4.16   Unlimited Government and Police Control of the Internet? There's No Filter for That

21 November 2012

A pandora's box may have been opened, without a clear idea of how best to proceed. *Source*: **Ian Smith**[165]

---

[165]Smith I., Flickr, http://www.flickr.com/photos/86964759@N00/4087681008, Accessed online 21 December 2012.

Good news. A decision made earlier this month by Australia's Minister for Broadband, Communications and the Digital Economy Senator Stephen Conroy may have inadvertently opened the door for unlimited government and police control of the internet.

On November 9, Senator Stephen Conroy said[166]:

> Australia's largest ISPs [internet service providers] have been issued with notices [by the Australian Federal Police] requiring them to block illegal [child pornography] sites in accordance with their obligations under the Telecommunications Act 1997[167].

Conroy's decision to scrap a much publicised internet filter[168], a commitment made by Labor ahead of the 2007 election, was seen by many as a victory for common sense and by others as a missed opportunity to crack down on criminal activity in cyberspace.

But an unexpected result appears to be unlimited government and police control of the internet.

To understand how this has happened we need to look at Section 313 of the Telecommunications Act 1997[169] and how it can be used to compel carriers and ISPs to implement just about anything, including internet filters.

4.16.1 Section 313 Explained

Section 313, with seven subsections, covers the obligations of carriers and carriage service providers. The first two subsections are:

(1) A carrier or carriage service provider must, in connection with:

  (a). the operation by the carrier or provider of telecommunications networks or facilities; or
  (b). the supply by the carrier or provider of carriage services;
     do the carrier's best or the provider's best to prevent telecommunications networks and facilities from being used in, or in relation to, the commission of offences against the laws of the Commonwealth or of the States and Territories.

---

[166]Media Release, Child abuse material blocked online, removing need for legislation, Minister for Broadband, Communications and the Digital Economy Stephen Conroy, 9 November 2012, http://www.minister.dbcde.gov.au/media/media_releases/2012/180, Accessed online 21 November 2012.

[167]Telecommunications Act 1997, Australian Government, http://www.austlii.edu.au/au/legis/cth/consol_act/ta1997214/, Accessed online 21 November 2012.

[168]Coorey P., Conroy backs away from internet filter, Fairfax Media, 9 November 2012, http://www.smh.com.au/technology/technology-news/conroy-backs-away-from-internet-filter-20121108-290ym.html, Accessed online 21 November 2012.

[169]Section 313, Telecommunications Act 1997, Australian Government, http://www.austlii.edu.au/au/legis/cth/consol_act/ta1997214/s313.html, Accessed online 21 November 2012.

(2) A carriage service intermediary must do the intermediary's best to prevent telecommunications networks and facilities from being used in, or in relation to, the commission of offences against the laws of the Commonwealth or of the States and Territories.

The government's announcement on November 9 appears to indicate an interpretation of Section 313 that subsection (1) and (2) stand alone and provide broader powers than may be understood if all of the subsections were read together.

This interpretation was challenged on November 9 by Simon Breheny[170] from the Institute of Public Affairs who stated[171]:

> The use of an obscure provision of the legislation raises serious legal issues—it is highly doubtful whether the law can be used to compel ISPs to block websites at the Minister's behest.

> If the Minister always had the power to impose an internet filter without the need for new legislation section 313 would have been used from the beginning.

Surely, the questions highlighted below now need to be addressed:

1) **Why has it taken the AFP so long to act?**

The Australian Federal Police (AFP)[172] is responsible for enforcing Commonwealth criminal law[173].

The Telecommunications Act 1997 has been around for 15 years so why has it taken the AFP—an organisation with access to the best lawyers in Australia—this long to "discover" that Section 313 of the Telecommunications Act 1997[174] can be used to compel carriers, carriage service providers[175] and ISPs to implement internet filters to block webpages listed on the Interpol's "worst of" list[176].

By finally using Section 313 of the Telecommunications Act 1997 the AFP has "crossed the Rubicon"[177]—the point of no return.

---

[170] Breheny S., Director, Legal Rights Project, Institute of Public Affairs, http://ipa.org.au/people/simon-breheny, Accessed online 21 November 2012.

[171] Breheny S., Gillard government's new censorship regime worse than internet filter, Institute of Public Affairs, http://www.ipa.org.au/publications/2114/gillard-government's-new-censorship-regime-worse-than-internet-filter, Accessed online 21 November 2012.

[172] Australian Federal Police, Australian Government, http://www.afp.gov.au/, Accessed online 21 November 2012.

[173] Criminal Law, Australian Government, http://www.comlaw.gov.au/, Accessed online 21 November 2012.

[174] Section 313, Telecommunications Act 1997, Australian Government, http://www.austlii.edu.au/au/legis/cth/consol_act/ta1997214/s313.html, Accessed online 21 November 2012.

[175] Carriage service providers, Sect 87, Telecommunications Act 1997, Australian Government, http://www.austlii.edu.au/au/legis/cth/consol_act/ta1997214/s87.html, Accessed online 21 November 2012.

[176] Access blocking, Interpol, http://www.interpol.int/Crime-areas/Crimes-against-children/Access-blocking/The-INTERPOL-%22Worst-of%22-list, Accessed online 21 November 2012.

[177] Rubicon, Wikipedia, http://en.wikipedia.org/wiki/Rubicon, Accessed online 21 November 2012.

2) **Will the AFP only act when told to do so by a minister?**

Commissioner Tony Negus[178], the head of the AFP, needs to publicly clarify whether the AFP intends to use Section 313 in the fight against internet-based organised crime and, if not, why not.

Will the AFP only act when a minister tells the AFP to do so?

3) **Will the AFP cherry-pick the crimes it tackles online?**

Is the AFP going to judiciously select which crimes should be tackled using Section 313?

Australians are being hammered daily by organised criminals who use the internet to carry out an ever-expanding list of sophisticated crimes such as scams[179] which target individuals and businesses.

On September 6, Norton's cybercrime report 2012[180] suggested that, over the past 12 months, cybercrime cost Australians A\$1.65 billion and that more than 5.4 million Australians have been affected by cybercrime in the past year.

Australians expect the AFP to use every reasonable tool at its disposal to fight cybercrime[181] and to enforce all duly passed criminal laws[182].

Will the AFP now use Section 313 to block access to Apple's iTunes[183] and Google's Android App Store[184] because they are the repository for apps[185] that steal personal information found on smart phones and tablets[186]?

Will the AFP now use Section 313 to block internet access to and from China which is suspected of carrying out state-sponsored hacking[187] of government[188],

---

[178] AFP Commissioner Tony Negus APM, Australian Federal Police, http://www.afp.gov.au/about-the-afp/executive-structure/negus-tony.aspx, Accessed online 21 November 2012.

[179] SCAMwatch, Australian Competition and Consumer Commission, http://www.scamwatch.gov.au/content/index.phtml/itemId/693900, Accessed online 21 November 2012.

[180] 2012 Norton Cybercrime Report, Symantec, http://now-static.norton.com/now/en/pu/images/Promotions/2012/cybercrimeReport/2012_Norton_Cybercrime_Report_Master_FINAL_050912.pdf, Accessed online 21 November 2012.

[181] Cyber Crime, Australian Crime Commission, http://www.crimecommission.gov.au/publications/crime-profile-series-fact-sheet/cyber-crime, Accessed online 21 November 2012.

[182] Criminal Law, Australian Government, http://www.comlaw.gov.au/, Accessed online 21 November 2012.

[183] iTunes, Apple, https://www.apple.com/au/itunes/, Accessed online 21 November 2012.

[184] Play, Google, https://play.google.com/store/apps, Accessed online 21 November 2012.

[185] Constantin L., Many Free iPhone and Android Apps Steal Personal Information, Softpedia, 29 July 2010, http://news.softpedia.com/news/Many-Free-iPhone-and-Android-Apps-Steal-Personal-Information-149651.shtml, Accessed online 21 November 2012.

[186] Patterson S., Android Apps Found Stealing Personal Information, WebProNews, 16 April 2012, http://www.webpronews.com/android-apps-found-stealing-personal-information-2012-04, Accessed online 21 November 2012.

[187] Riley M. and Lawrence D., Hackers Linked to China's Army Seen From EU to D.C., Bloomberg, 27 July 2012, http://www.bloomberg.com/news/2012-07-26/china-hackers-hit-eu-point-man-and-d-c-with-byzantine-candor.html, Accessed online 21 November 2012.

[188] Cooper H., Hackers targeting Australia's electronic secrets, Australian Broadcasting Corporation, 25 September 2012, http://www.abc.net.au/news/2012-09-25/hackers-target-australias-electronic-secrets/4280104, Accessed online 21 November 2012.

national institutions[189], national infrastructure[190], business[191] and other organisations?

Lets remember that on March 24 this year, the government banned Huawei[192] from tendering for the National Broadband Network on national security grounds.

Should Section 313 be used to force carriers and ISPs to implement a 2-year data retention scheme[193] if the AFP and other security agencies identify that by doing so this action will assist in the fight against cyber criminals, terrorists and enemy states?

Crimes[194] carried out online are global and among the worst crimes affecting Australians[195].

4) **What can the AFP now do?**

It may not be immediately obvious but by using Section 313 the AFP might decide to force carriers and ISPs to implement important technology changes to the internet that would assist in crime fighting.

Email has long been a vehicle for cybercrime so the AFP could use Section 313 to require carriers and ISPs to implement the mandatory use of SMTPS[196] and SMTPSec[197].

SMTPS is the use of secure authentication and communication between a customer and an email provider and SMTPSec is the use of secure communication between email providers.

---

[189] Keneally M., Chinese government 'hacks into White House office in charge of the nuclear launch codes', Mail Online, 1 October 2012, http://www.dailymail.co.uk/news/article-2211230/Chinese-government-hacks-White-House-office-charge-nuclear-launch-codes.html, Accessed online 21 November 2012.

[190] Maley P. and Bingemann M., Spies feared China was hacking the NBN, News Limited, 28 March 2012, http://www.theaustralian.com.au/national-affairs/defence/spies-feared-china-was-hacking-the-nbn/story-e6frg8yo-1226311796483, Accessed online 21 November 2012.

[191] Latimer C., Chinese hack Australian miners' emails, Australian Mining, 15 April 2011, http://www.miningaustralia.com.au/news/chinese-hack-australian-miners-emails, Accessed online 21 November 2012.

[192] Barker G., China's Huawei banned from NBN, Financial Review, 24 March 2012, http://www.afr.com/p/technology/china_giant_banned_from_nbn_9U9zi1oc3FXBF3BZdRD9mJ, Accessed online 21 November 2012.

[193] Gregory M.A., The dark side to data retention, Technology Spectator, 4 October 2012, http://www.technologyspectator.com.au/dark-side-data-retention?utm_source=exact&utm_medium=email&utm_content=112963&utm_campaign=kgb&modapt=commentary, Accessed online 21 November 2012.

[194] Crime Profile Series, Australian Crime Commission, http://www.crimecommission.gov.au/publications/crime-profile-series-fact-sheet, Accessed online 21 November 2012.

[195] Organised Crime in Australia 2011, Australian Crime Commission, http://www.crimecommission.gov.au/sites/default/files/files/OCA/2011/oca2011.pdf, Accessed online 21 November 2012.

[196] SMTPS, Wikipedia, http://en.wikipedia.org/wiki/SMTPS, Accessed online 21 November 2012.

[197] Gregory M.A., The dark side to data retention, Technology Spectator, 4 October 2012, http://www.technologyspectator.com.au/dark-side-data-retention?utm_source=exact&utm_medium=email&utm_content=112963&utm_campaign=kgb&modapt=commentary, Accessed online 21 November 2012.

Section 313 could be used to force the immediate implementation and mandatory use of Internet Protocol v6[198], the Domain Name System Security Extensions (DNSSec)[199] and Hypertext Transfer Protocol Secure (HTTPS)[200].

The lack of government action to force much-needed and readily available technology upgrades to the internet may now result in draconian outcomes[201] that have a significantly detrimental impact on the privacy of all Australians and the operation of the internet.

5) **What** should **the AFP do now?**

Now that Section 313 has been used in the fight against online child pornography, the AFP could be expected to broaden the fight against cybercrime.

So should Section 313 have been used by the AFP—or has a Pandora's box been opened, without any clear idea of how best to proceed?

A quote from Rudolph "Rudy" Giuliani III in Time Magazine[202] on October 15, 1984 remains strikingly relevant today:

> It's about time law enforcement got as organised as organised crime.

4.17   The UN's Internet Gabfest

30 November 2012

How do you fix a big problem? Well, one thing you don't do is call the United Nations and then ask that August body to do something that it has never done before.

Yet, this is exactly what appears to be happening when the United Nations' International Telecommunication Union (ITU) meets at the World Conference on International Telecommunications (WCIT-12)[203] in Dubai next week.

---

[198] Fry M., The end of the internet? IPv4 versus IPv6, The Conversation, 4 April 2011, http://the-conversation.edu.au/the-end-of-the-internet-ipv4-versus-ipv6-145, Accessed online 21 November 2012.

[199] Domain Name System Security Extensions, Wikipedia, http://en.wikipedia.org/wiki/Domain_Name_System_Security_Extensions, Accessed online 21 November 2012.

[200] HTTP Secure, Wikipedia, http://en.wikipedia.org/wiki/HTTP_Secure, Accessed online 21 November 2012.

[201] Gregory M.A., The dark side to data retention, Technology Spectator, 4 October 2012, http://www.technologyspectator.com.au/dark-side-data-retention?utm_source=exact&utm_medium=email&utm_content=112963&utm_campaign=kgb&modapt=commentary, Accessed online 21 November 2012.

[202] Organized Crime, Time Magazine, 1984, http://topics.time.com/organized-crime/articles/5/, Accessed online 21 November 2012.

[203] World Conference on International Telecommunications (WCIT-12), International Telecommunications Union, Dubai, United Arab Emirates, 3-14 December 2012, http://www.itu.int/en/wcit-12/Pages/default.aspx, Accessed online 30 November 2012.

The ITU (International Telecommunication Union) is the United Nations specialised agency for information and communication technologies. The ITU allocates global radio spectrum and satellite orbits, develops the technical standards that ensure networks and technologies seamlessly interconnect, and strives to improve access to ICTs to underserved communities worldwide.

However, the ITU does not—and never has—regulated the internet beyond ensuring technologies used can talk to each other. So this should make for a rather facinating event.

4.17.1 The Process

Various countries and international organisations have formed groups that will put forward different wish lists for discussion at the meetings next week. Some of the proposals are jaw droppers that would effectively kill the internet as we know it today.

This meeting has been long planned and Australia, along with the other 192 countries that will be represented at WCIT, will be well prepared to work towards positive outcomes. Australia will be sending the our communications minister senator Stephen Conroy and a considerable slew of aids and members of his department.

WCIT will be an opportunity for international agreement on changes to the management of telecommunications and the internet. Some of the items that appear almost daily in the media and therefore likely to be high on the agenda. They include:

1. International roaming charges—excessive unjustifiable rorting by carriers on a global scale.
2. Technology changes—the list of new technologies and updates to be adopted never diminishes
3. Cyber-crime—huge growing crime problem that is now beyond any individual nation's control.
4. Cyber-warfare—growing daily and ready to explode at a moment's notice.
5. Cyber-terrorism—how nations will defend themselves from organised digital attacks.
6. Privacy and security—privacy and security of personal information.
7. Freedom of speech—including political censorship on the net.
8. Individual rights—The rights to be protected from defamation, bullying, harassment, hate crimes
9. Tax minimisation—Should large internet based multi-nationals be permitted to tax minimise and rip-off nations like Australia?
10. ICT price gouging—should large internet based multi-nationals be permitted to price gouge in nations like Australia using techniques such as geolocation[204]?

---

[204]Geolocation, Wikipedia, http://en.wikipedia.org/wiki/Geolocation, Accessed online 30 November 2012.

4.17.2   Is a Consensus Even Possible?

What is interesting about this list is that each nation that participates in WCIT will have a different perspective on how to solve each problem and countries that can agree on most things are likely to disagree on some points.

Proposals put forward in a discussion paper called "Trends in Telecommunication Reform 2012: Smart Regulation in a Broadband World[205]" have already been met with scepticism and outright denial. For the ITU to be suggesting that it get involved in regulating the internet is a recipe for a bigger disaster than the one we have now.

One thing is for certain; the debate at WCIT will be lively. Nations, multi-national vendors and carriers, and international organisations such as unions will all be singing their own tunes as loudly as possible.

What can we expect from this meeting? First of all there is no consensus on what the problems are with international telecommunications and the internet today, so there is no hope of any substantive solutions being adopted. It is certain that the US will insist that there will be no changes adopted that affect US based companies (and this includes their ability to rip-off Australians) and freedom of speech. China and Russia will argue for regulation that opposes any position put by the US and Europe.

But there is a glimmer of light.

At WCIT there is likely to be consensus about one thing—the need to force international roaming charges down. Even the US is likely, reluctantly, to agree that there is a need to force the carriers to significantly reduce international roaming charges[206].

Beyond this what happens is anyone's guess.

4.18   Ready for a NBN Emergency?

7 December 2012

Telstra is expected to fully restore its services in south-west Victoria by the end of this week with the telco's boss David Thodey promising a thorough investigation into the fire that took out the Warrnambool exchange in late November.

A suitably contrite Thodey was at pains this week to point out[207] that he and his team understood the gravity of the situation and the restoration of services was of paramount importance.

---

[205]Trends in Telecommunication Reform 2012: Smart regulation for a broadband world, International Telecommunication Union, http://www.itu.int/ITU-D/treg/publications/trends12.html, Accessed online 30 November 2012.

[206]Gregory M.A., International roaming charges rip-off: the ITU gets involved …, The Conversation, 20 September 2012, https://theconversation.edu.au/international-roaming-charges-rip-off-the-itu-gets-involved-9663, Accessed online 30 November 2012.

[207]Thodey D., My visit to Warrnambool today, Telstra News, 4 December 2012, http://exchange.telstra.com.au/2012/12/04/my-visit-to-warrnambool-today/, Accessed online 7 December 2012.

"In fact, it would normally take 2 years to build an exchange and our incredible team are aiming to have completely restored the exchange in 2 weeks," Thodey said.

Thodey's compliment to the Telstra team is fully warranted given the nature of what is being attempted. Restoration of any of the Telstra exchanges, many of which are more than 50 years old and contain a myriad of old interconnected systems including many kilometres of copper cable, in such a short time is an excellent outcome.

The Warrnambool episode clearly illustrates the importance of robust continuity plans and given that the NBN will be backbone of our digital future, NBN Co's response to the incident warrants a closer look.

The NBN is critical national infrastructure and it must be treated as such. Can business, industry, schools and hospitals survive a 2 week outage of the network as they become more and more dependent on broadband applications?

In the week after the fire a NBN Co spokesperson told[208] *Technology Spectator* that it had a contingency plan for such a scenario. However, the statement doesn't, and shouldn't, instil the necessary confidence.

"We have put in place extensive practices and processes to handle a network outage of this type, and to recover services as quickly as possible. As you know these are very rare events, but contingencies are planned."

The last part of this statement is the easiest to dispel so it will be analysed first.

The fire in the Telstra Warrnambool exchange was not caused by a natural disaster so Telstra cannot claim a force majeure situation. Fires can and do occur in large network installations and for this reason anti-fire systems[209] are commonplace in data centres that house critical information systems for government, business and organisations.

Will key NBN locations be protected by anti-fire systems? I certainly hope so but we have nothing official to base this presumption on.

4.18.1   Not So Rare After All

The statement by the NBN Co spokesperson that "these are very rare events" relies upon our short collective memories to provide a subtly misleading impression of the facts.

---

[208]Wallbank P., Counting the cost of a Telstra outage, Technology Spectator, 28 November 2012, http://www.technologyspectator.com.au/counting-cost-telstra-outage, Accessed online 7 December 2012.

[209]Olzak T., The mystical world of data center fire suppression, TechRepublic, 27 July 2010, http://www.techrepublic.com/blog/security/the-mystical-world-of-data-center-fire-suppression/4113, Accessed online 7 December 2012.

Melbournians will remember the chaos on the roads when CityLink's network failed preventing control of critical infrastructure within the tunnels forcing CityLink to close[210] the Burnley and Domain tunnels.

A quick Google search for Telstra ADSL outages returns 228,000 results. A quick review of some of the results should remind us that these "rare events" are in fact not rare at all.

In 2001 a Telstra ADSL outage caused by an authentication server failure[211] caused a national ADSL failure for 7 h. Comments on the SLUG email list were not complimentary and a comment by "Alister" is just as relevant today as it was then when he said "It's not the 1 dollar but the lost business from having NO internet connection for a good part of Thursday. No chance of a refund on that."

In 2004 a Telstra software upgrade that went wrong caused a national ADSL outage that lasted for almost a day. The event caused outrage that was reflected by posts on *Whirlpool*[212].

In 2006 a Telstra ADSL outage[213] occurred that caused NSW customers to lose access to ADSL for almost a day.

In 2010 a Telsta Bigpond server failure[214] caused a 4 day Bigpond outage that "affected dial-up, cable, ADSL, satellite and Next G wireless services across the east coast and e-mail nationally".

Network outages due to pests like ants and rats have occurred regularly over the years and Telstra has a webpage listing some of the more interesting unexpected encounters in the field[215]. Network outages caused by pests can be expected and actions taken to minimise possible outages.

Will the NBN be deployed utilising anti-pest techniques learnt as a result of Telstra's vast pest experience? Again, we don't know.

On June 9, 2012 it was reported[216] that the company responsible for the NBN roll-out in the Darling Downs region failed to lay rodent-proof cables in a bid to cut costs. The Federal Member for Groom Ian Macfarlane said "This just fits in with the whole shemozzle of the NBN".

[210]Harris A. and Gillet C., Burnley and Domain tunnels reopened but drivers still face long road home, Herald Sun, News Limited, 3 October 2012, http://www.heraldsun.com.au/news/burnley-and-domain-tunnels-reopened-but-drivers-still-face-long-road-home/story-e6frf7jo-1226486984920, Accessed online 7 December 2012.

[211]Alister, [SLUG] Telstra Outage, http://www.progsoc.uts.edu.au/lists/slug/2001/June/msg01131.html, Accessed online 7 December 2012.

[212]Sweeney P., Nationwide ADSL outage, Whirlpool, 12 August 2004, http://whirlpool.net.au/news/?id=1295, Accessed online 7 December 2012.

[213]Quintans D., ADSL outage over NSW, 16 December 2006, http://www.desiquintans.com/permalink.php?PostID=102, Accessed online 7 December 2012.

[214]Cochrane N., Bigpond emails still await delivery to some, itnews, 22 September 2010, http://www.itnews.com.au/News/232931,bigpond-emails-still-await-delivery-to-some.aspx, Accessed online 7 December 2012.

[215]Unexpected encounters in the field Part 4, Telstra, 15 October 2012, http://exchange.telstra.com.au/2012/10/15/unexpected-encounters-in-the-field-part-4/, Accessed online 7 December 2012.

[216]Calcino C., Rats put bite on NBN roll-out, The Chronicle, 9 June 2012, http://www.thechronicle.com.au/news/rats-put-bite-on-nbn-roll-out/1410950/, Accessed online 7 December 2012.

4.18.2   Practices and Processes

The first part of the NBN Co spokesperson's statement "We have put in place extensive practices and processes to handle a network outage of this type, and to recover services as quickly as possible" begs the question "What practices and processes"?

NBN Co should support their spokesperson's statement by immediately handing a copy of the NBN Co "failure event practices and processes" to the Australian Communications and Media Authority or to the Department of Broadband, Communications and the Digital Economy which is conducting an inquiry[217].

The 2 week outage suffered by business around Warrnambool is economically unsustainable and unacceptable in the twenty-first century. Building the NBN with a cavalier attitude to failure events must be avoided at all costs.

NBN Co should develop a section of the company website that addresses how it intends to provide improved service levels to the Australian public and complete details of how it intends to deal with failure events and anticipated outage times for different types of failure events.

The Communications Minister Stephen Conroy should call NBN Co chief Mike Quigley and instruct NBN Co to carry out a failure event planning exercise in mid-2013. The exercise should include the sudden demise of a major point of interconnect (PoI) in Melbourne or Sydney. NBN Co should then exercise the "failure event practices and processes" that we have been assured have been prepared and restore service utilising backup infrastructure brought to the location during the exercise. The results of the exercise should be reported fully. Perhaps it's also worth pondering whether NBN Co should get assistance from Defence and other national agencies in the event of a major failure event.

The NBN is vital for Australia's future and it is therefore important that Australian's be fully informed regarding every aspect of the network. The Warrnambool exchange fire must serve as a timely motivator for NBN Co to provide more information about the resiliency of the network and how long it would take to restore service in the event of a failure, big or small.

4.19   Qantas Drops In-flight Wi-Fi: The NBN to the Rescue?

12 December 2012

---

[217] AAP, Conroy announces inquiry into Warrnambool Telstra blackout, Technology Spectator, 29 November 2012, http://www.technologyspectator.com.au/conroy-announces-inquiry-warrnambool-telstra-blackout, Accessed online 7 December 2012.

If we assume that demand for in-flight internet is going to increase, it's time we did something about it. *Source*: **Kentaro Lemoto**[218]

The trial of in-flight Wi-Fi[219] on six Qantas Airbus A380s flying between Melbourne, Los Angeles and London has ended, following an announcement[220] by the carrier last week.

So why does this matter? And could the National Broadband Network (NBN)[221] come to the rescue, at least in Australia? Well, hypothetically, but before we get there …

If you've been through an Australian airport recently you would have seen the large number of Qantas billboards publicising the Wi-Fi service, a service that was offered free to first- and business-class passengers who have a Wi-Fi-enabled device.

Premium economy passengers could also access the Wi-Fi service but needed to purchase data packs during the flight.

Qantas launched the Wi-Fi trial in March utilising a system provided by OnAir[222], an IT services company, and the Inmarsat "SwiftBroadband[223]" service. This service

[218]Lemoto K., Flickr, http://www.flickr.com/photos/kentaroiemoto/4841025516/, Accessed online 21 December 2012.

[219]Brain M. and Wilson T.V., How Wi-Fi works, How stuff works, http://www.howstuffworks.com/wireless-network.htm, Accessed online 12 December 2012.

[220]Creedy S., Qantas pulls plug on in-flight Wi-Fi, News Limited, 4 December 2012, http://www.theaustralian.com.au/australian-it/it-business/qantas-pulls-plug-on-in-flight-wifi/story-e6fr-ganx-1226529268338, Accessed online 12 December 2012.

[221]Oppermann I., Explainer: the National Broadband Network (NBN), The Conversation, 30 March 2011, https://theconversation.edu.au/explainer-the-national-broadband-network-nbn-207, Accessed online 12 December 2012.

[222]OnAir, http://www.onair.aero/, Accessed online 12 December 2012.

[223]Inmarsat, Swiftbroadband, Satcom, https://www.satcomdirect.com/main/aviation/swiftbroad-band-swift-broadband-sbb/default.aspx, Accessed online 12 December 2012.

connects the aircraft to a satellite[224] which relays data to and from the internet via a ground station.

So, what went wrong?

4.19.1 Cost

One important factor was the high cost of the Wi-Fi service. The cost for data varied between $12.90 and $39.90 for data packs of up to 35 MB.

According to Vodafone[225] the $39.90, 35 MB data pack used on a smartphone would let you watch a 15-min YouTube[226] video, send or receive roughly 1,000 emails (without attachments), or browse 150 webpages.

A $35 Optus[227] mobile phone plan provides 200 MB of included data, $200 included mobile calls and unlimited national SMS.

By contrast, an in-home ADSL2+ service offered by TPG[228] or iiNet[229] provides about 100GB for $39.95. That's roughly 3,000 times the amount of data, for the same price as Qantas' Wi-Fi offering.

4.19.2 Time of Flight

A Qantas spokesperson was last week quoted as saying[230]:

> most of our A380 services operate at night and so another dampener on demand was the fact people preferred to sleep than surf the web.

Qantas long-haul flights that operate at night are geared towards customers being encouraged to sleep for a large portion of the flight.

---

[224] Kaleem Z., How does airplane Wi-Fi work?, WLAN Book, 21 December 2009, http://wlanbook.com/how-does-airplane-wifi-work/, Accessed online 12 December 2012.

[225] How much data will I use, Vodafone, http://www.vodafone.ie/internet-broadband/internet-on-your-mobile/usage/, Accessed online 12 December 2012.

[226] YouTube, Google, http://www.youtube.com/, Accessed online 12 December 2012.

[227] Optus Mobile, https://www.optus.com.au/, Accessed online 12 December 2012.

[228] TPG, http://www.tpg.com.au/, Accessed online 12 December 2012.

[229] iiNet, http://www.iinet.net.au/, Accessed online 12 December 2012.

[230] Creedy S., Qantas pulls plug on in-flight Wi-Fi, News Limited, 4 December 2012, http://www.theaustralian.com.au/australian-it/it-business/qantas-pulls-plug-on-in-flight-wifi/story-e6fr-ganx-1226529268338, Accessed online 12 December 2012.

The editor of Australian Business Traveller[231], David Flynn last week reviewed[232] Qantas's Wi-Fi and reported that customers used the data allowance very quickly. Flynn queried the value of the Wi-Fi service when he said:

> They've just introduced refinements such as doonas into international business class. What the free Wi-Fi trial shows is that business travellers would prefer a better sleep than being connected in-flight.

4.19.3   Competitors

Two airlines that offer Wi-Fi services on long-haul flights to and from Australia are Singapore Airlines and Emirates.

The Emirates Wi-Fi service on its Airbus A380s is provided with a charge of US$15 (A$14.10) for 25 MB or US$25 (A$23.90) for 100 MB using a notebook or US$7.50 (A$7.20) for 5 MB for mobile phones.

Singapore Airlines's Wi-Fi service is available on selected flights with pricing ranging from US$25 (A$23.90) for 30 MB and US$10 (A$9.50) for 10 MB.

Emirates' research is reported[233] to have found three-quarters of all in-flight net use is during the "awake" hours of the flight.

So what about airline Wi-Fi services within Australia?

Providing Wi-Fi services on planes operating domestic routes is just as problematic as for the long-haul international routes. The availability of satellites that can be used for domestic airline Wi-Fi services is limited and the cost would be similar to that for international flights.

If we can assume—the arguments about whether people would rather be sleeping notwithstanding—Wi-Fi access on domestic routes will increasingly seen as desirable, there is a solution standing right in front of us.

4.19.4   NBN Satellite-connected Wi-Fi Services

NBN Co is launching two satellites[234] in 2015 to support remote customer connections to the National Broadband Network (NBN)[235].

---

[231]Flynn D., Qantas scrubs plans for inflight internet, Australian Business Traveller, 3 December 2012, http://www.ausbt.com.au/qantas-scrubs-plans-for-inflight-internet, Accessed online 12 December 2012.

[232]Flynn D., Hands-on review: Qantas' A380 in-flight wifi internet trials, Australian Business Traveller, 17 March 2012, http://www.ausbt.com.au/hands-on-review-qantas-airbus-a380-in-flight-wifi-internet-trials, Accessed online 12 December 2012.

[233]Gliddon J., Qantas axes in-flight Wi-Fi, CRN, 4 December 2012, http://www.crn.com.au/News/325155,qantas-axes-in-flight-wi-fi.aspx, Accessed online 12 December 2012.

[234]The three NBN technologies, NBN Co, http://www.nbnco.com.au/for-schools/fact-sheets/the-three-nbn-technologies.html, Accessed online 12 December 2012.

[235]Oppermann I., Explainer: the National Broadband Network (NBN), The Conversation, 30 March 2011, https://theconversation.edu.au/explainer-the-national-broadband-network-nbn-207, Accessed online 12 December 2012.

A criticism I made of the NBN in an earlier article[236] on The Conversation is the decision not to cater for moving vehicles such as planes, trains and buses—all part of important national transport systems.

The NBN satellites could be used to provide low-cost reliable Wi-Fi services to domestic planes and interstate trains and buses.

When the NBN legislation[237] was drawn up in 2011 there seemed to have been a decision made to limit the NBN and ensure mobile operators were the only providers available for broadband connections to cars, trucks, caravans, mobile homes, planes, trains and buses.

In my opinion, the government and the opposition need to revisit this decision and agree to change the legislation so that the NBN satellites can be used to provide Wi-Fi services on domestic planes and interstate trains and buses.

There is a strong economic justification for doing this as it will ensure the satellites are an economic success and it will provide a social dividend to the travelling public who will have domestic access to Wi-Fi on interstate or long-distance domestic routes.

But if we want this to happen we need to act fast. Why?

Satellites[238] provide coverage to large areas by using many antennae that focus on slightly overlapping regions of varying size.

Each region is allocated data capacity and the total capacity of the satellite is equivalent to the sum of the capacity allocated to the regions.

When the satellite design is completed and the satellite launched the antenna region coverage and capacity cannot be varied.

For this reason, it's time to act now.

[236] Gregory M.A., Is remote and rural Australia being dudded by the NBN?, The Conversation, 5 November 2012, https://theconversation.edu.au/is-remote-and-rural-australia-being-dudded-by-the-nbn-10251, Accessed online 12 December 2012.

[237] Regulation and legislation, NBN Co, http://www.nbnco.com.au/about-us/corporate-nbn-responsibility/regulation-legislation.html, Accessed online 12 December 2012.

[238] Braue D., Coalition hasn't checked its satellite facts. Here they are …, Australian Broadcasting Corporation, 16 February 2012, http://www.abc.net.au/technology/articles/2012/02/16/3432368. htm, Accessed online 12 December 2012.

Chapter 5
Smart Phones

The smart phone represents the greatest Internet related technology advance over the past decade. The smart phone has become, in the space of 5 years, a must have device and the number of smart phones in service is growing rapidly. In time there will be more smart phones than people and this reality highlights the ubiquitous nature of the smart phone.

For telecommunication companies the smart phone has become a cash cow and customers are being charged extortionate prices for connections and data. International roaming charges for telephone calls and data are a scandalous rip-off and it is only through government intervention that this problem is being addressed. For most countries government intervention has yet to occur but for those, such as the European Union (EU), where government has stepped in to prevent the rip-off from continuing, customers enjoy the mobility benefits that smart phones provide even when they travel to other EU countries.

Smart phones continue to evolve and there is now a range of shapes and sizes available. The rapid rise of smart phone sales saw the tablet computer re-enter the market after a failed attempt more than a decade ago. Customers are faced with a daunting task today to identify what smart phone is right for them and it is often only through trial and error that customers settle upon a smart phone.

5.1 Are Australian International Roaming Charges the Greatest Rip-Off in History?

30 November 2011

M.A. Gregory and D. Glance, *Security and the Networked Society*,
DOI 10.1007/978-3-319-02390-8_5, © Springer International Publishing Switzerland 2013

The mark-up on data charges can be as much as 200 times the actual cost. *Source*: LGEPR CC0[1]

What's the greatest rip-off going? Maybe so many come to mind that you're reaching for a pen.

Your list might look something like this:

- bottled water[2]
- sports drinks[3]
- petrol price rises[4] just before a long weekend or public holiday
- credit card interest rates and surcharges.[5]

And let's not forget international companies that prevent Australians from buying products directly from their US website, forcing them to purchase goods through a local website where products are much more expensive.

Apple's iTunes is a good current example[6] of the online price discrimination practices facing Australian consumers.

---

[1]LGEPR, Flickr, http://www.flickr.com/photos/lge/3626821949/, Accessed online 21 December 2012.

[2]Bottled water, Clean Up Australia, http://www.cleanup.org.au/au/Whatelsewesupport/bottled-water.html, Accessed online 30 November 2011.

[3]Sports drinks review and compare, Choice, http://www.choice.com.au/reviews-and-tests/food-and-health/food-and-drink/beverages/sports-drinks-review-and-compare.aspx, Accessed online 30 November 2011.

[4]RACQ blasts petrol retailers' school holiday 'rip off', Fairfax, http://www.brisbanetimes.com.au/queensland/racq-blasts-petrol-retailers-school-holiday-rip-off-20110916-1kckl.html, Accessed online 30 November 2011.

[5]Retailers 'ripping off' customers on credit card surcharges, Yahoo!7, http://au.finance.yahoo.com/news/Retailers-ripping-customers-yahoo7finance-3258920710.html, Accessed online 30 November 2011.

[6]How iTunes buyers are ripped off, News Limited, http://www.adelaidenow.com.au/ipad/how-itunes-buyers-are-ripped-off/story-fn6bqphm-1225981956267, Accessed online 30 November 2011.

Of course, this discrimination is not limited to goods purchased online.

An OECD report[7] published in May this year states that Australia is the third most expensive country in 34 OECD countries studied.

But back to our list.

If you have made a trip overseas recently your tally of rip-offs may include international data roaming charges. And for good reason.

Forgetting to turn off the data connection to your phone before you hop on a plane can mean your next mobile phone bill will contain a nasty, and very expensive, shock.[8]

In May this year, the Australian and New Zealand governments announced they would investigate the high cost of using a mobile phone when travelling across the Tasman.

A review[9] by The Australian Business Traveller highlighted a problem which—rightly—is causing outrage.

Source: Mark Skipper[10]

---

[7]International Mobile Data Roaming, Organisation for Economic Co-operation and Development Report, http://www.oecd.org/dataoecd/57/62/48127892.pdf, Accessed online 30 November 2011.

[8]Roam around to avoid bill shock, Choice, http://www.choice.com.au/blog/2011/may/data-roaming-bill-shock.aspx, Accessed online 30 November 2011.

[9]Australia/New Zealand governments to investigate global roaming rip-off, Australian Business Traveller, http://www.ausbt.com.au/au-nz-govts-to-discuss-global-roaming-rip-off, Accessed online 30 November 2011.

[10]Skipper M., Flickr, http://www.flickr.com/photos/bitterjug/1491759856/, Accessed online 21 December 2012.

Depending on which network your phone belongs to, the cost can be as much as $AUD20/MB for international data roaming and $AUD4.40 per minute to call home to Australia from New Zealand.

Is this good value? To put it in perspective, the cost of transferring data over the internet is now available at $AUD0.10/MB or less.

5.1.1   Take, Take, Take

So is international data roaming the greatest rip-off in history? Possibly not, but it must be near the top given the mark-up on data charges is sitting at around 200 times the actual cost.

Representatives from Australian telecommunication companies will argue they have costs associated with providing their service, contract charges with the partnering telecommunication companies overseas; they'll also point to the high cost of undersea cables to Australia.

But there are strong incentives for governments to look at ways of reducing unwanted costs and barriers.

Successive Australian governments have been tardy in dealing with this matter. There is a strong and compelling argument for the Australian Consumer and Competition Commission[11] (ACCC) to be given greater powers to force Australian telecommunication companies to significantly reduce international roaming charges.

Australians are encouraged to travel and do business overseas, yet the issue of excessive international data roaming charges persists.

Over the past decade, government committees have looked at this issue many times and produced numerous reports—the 2009 House of Representatives Standing Committee investigation[12] being a case in point.

Sadly, the outcome of this review—a recommendation that travellers be made aware of alternatives to mobile roaming—was of little consequence.

---

[11] Australian Competition and Consumer Commission, http://www.accc.gov.au/, Accessed online 30 November 2011.

[12] Mobile roaming, http://www.aph.gov.au/house/news/news_stories/news_Comms_Mar09.htm, Accessed online 30 November 2011, new link http://www.dbcde.gov.au/mobile_services/mobile_roaming.

Source: Gail Hamilton CC0[13]

Sadly, the outcome of this review—a recommendation that travellers be made aware of alternatives to mobile roaming—was of little consequence.

As a starting point, the Australian and New Zealand governments should immediately regulate to force down the cost of international mobile phone and data roaming between both countries. There doesn't appear to be technical or economic reasons why this can't occur.

The cost of using an Australian mobile phone for calls or data while in Wellington, New Zealand, should be no more expensive than the cost of using an Australian mobile phone for calls or data while in Hobart.

What should we do in the short term?

Australians travelling overseas need to ensure they turn their mobile phone's data connection off before leaving. The best solution is still to purchase a cheap pre-paid mobile phone and SIM card on landing and to use this for data connections.

Is this ideal? No, it's not. Do we have a choice? Sadly, no, unless we want to continue being charged through the nose at literally hundreds of times the going rate for data transfer.

5.2   Apple's iPhone 4S Is a Game Changer…Siri-ously

17 October 2011

The recent release of the Apple iPhone 4S was met with some disappointment[14] because it wasn't the iPhone 5.

---

[13] Hamilton G., Flickr, http://www.flickr.com/photos/29881930@N00/2086641268/, Accessed online 21 December 2012.

[14] The iPhone 4S: has Tim Cook started his tenure as Apple CEO with a dud? http://theconversation.edu.au/the-iphone-4s-has-tim-cook-started-his-tenure-as-apple-ceo-with-a-dud-3713, Accessed on 17 October 2011.

Curiously, people seemed to be most disappointed that the shape of the phone hadn't changed. What seemed to go completely unnoticed was a new feature that promises not only to revolutionise the way we interact with mobile phones but also with computers, tablets and potentially all other smart electronic devices.

The feature has also introduced a new word to our vocabulary: Siri.

5.2.1   Q: Siri, What Are You? A: I Live to Serve

Siri needs to be used to be believed, and also to begin to understand why this has been described as a revolutionary change.[15] It is easy to dismiss Siri as voice control for the iPhone. Most smart phones have had a voice control feature where using a number of preconfigured voice commands, you can ask the phone to dial a number.

But Siri is more than that. It is, in essence, a piece of software with voice recognition and sophisticated artificial intelligence (AI) capabilities.

Voice recognition translates your spoken commands into text. The AI then uses a combination of techniques that include natural language processing[16] to interpret the text and propose a spoken answer. A lot of the processing gets done on the phone but Siri also communicates with a server and a number of services such as Bing, Google, Wolfram Alpha[17] and Yelp.[18]

5.2.2   Q: Siri, What Can You Do? A: I'll Show You...

You can ask Siri to do most routine phone functions. Send a text, email or place a call, for example. You can create appointments and set an alarm. This would be clever enough, but Siri understands enough for the requests to be quite sophisticated.

For example, at the "Let's Talk iPhone[19]" event, Siri was asked three different questions about the weather:

1) "What is the weather like today?" (Siri answered: "Here's the forecast for today"),
2) "What is the hourly forecast?" (Siri answered: "Here is the weather for today"), and
3) "Do I need a raincoat today?" (Siri answered: "It sure looks like rain today").

---

[15] Apple's Siri Is as Revolutionary as the Mac, http://blogs.hbr.org/cs/2011/10/apples_siri_is_as_revolutionar.html, Accessed on 17 October 2011.

[16] Natural language processing, http://en.wikipedia.org/wiki/Natural_language_processing, Accessed on 17 October 2011.

[17] Wolfram Alpha, http://www.wolframalpha.com/, Accessed on 17 October 2011.

[18] Yelp, http://www.yelp.com/, Accessed on 17 October 2011.

[19] Apple Events, http://events.apple.com.edgesuite.net/11piuhbvdlbkvoih10/event/index.html, Accessed on 17 October 2011.

The point here is not just the accuracy of the voice recognition, but also the accuracy of the meaning analysis.

Actions that would normally take a number of clicks, interactions with applications and typing can be done with a single command, and they can be done hands-free.

Communicating with Siri is not simply a process of command and response, though. Siri understands that a series of commands are related, and understands the context. It learns from each interaction. This makes more complex operations possible.

For example, you can ask Siri to read a recently arrived text message that asks for an appointment. You can then ask Siri to check if you are free at a particular time and then ask to create an appointment and send a reply. All without touching your phone.

5.2.3 Q: Siri, Where Did You Come from? A: I Was Designed by Apple in California

Actually Siri, that's not quite true. Apple bought the company[20] that invented Siri in 2010. Siri was a spin-off company from SRI International's Artificial Intelligence Center[21] which originated from a 5-year project called CALO. The original aim of CALO was to create a personal assistant that could be used by the military (CALO was based on the Latin word "calonis" which means "soldier's servant").

The voice recognition is believed to be[22] from Nuance Communications,[23] whose products include DragonSpeak.[24]

Before Apple bought Siri (the company), Siri (the app) had been launched on the iPhone 3GS. The intention was to take the application to other phone platforms. But once it bought the technology, Apple integrated it seamlessly into the iPhone to transform something originally novel and useful into world-changing technology.

---

[20] Apple buys virtual assistant app maker Siri, http://news.cnet.com/8301-31021_3-20003671-260.html, Accessed on 17 October 2011.

[21] SRI International's Artificial Intelligence Center, http://www.ai.sri.com/, Accessed on 17 October 2011.

[22] Co-Founder of Siri: Assistant launch is a "World-Changing Event" (Interview), http://9to5mac.com/2011/10/03/co-founder-of-siri-assistant-is-a-world-changing-event-interview/, Accessed on 17 October 2011.

[23] Nuance, http://australia.nuance.com/, Accessed on 17 October 2011.

[24] Dragon NaturallySpeaking, http://en.wikipedia.org/wiki/Dragon_NaturallySpeaking, Accessed on 17 October 2011.

5.2.3.1   Q: Siri, What Are You? A: I'm Your Virtual Assistant

It is fair to say the original iPhone redefined our relationship with the phone. It allowed us to do many of the things that could previously only have been done on a PC.

It even made some of these things enjoyable. So much so that people have formed a symbiotic relationship with their phone.[25]

The advent of technology such as Siri takes the relationship between people and their mobile computing device to a new level that is not simply anthropomorphising an inanimate object.

More directly, it is replacing typing and touch with a more natural type of interaction. As companies like Microsoft scramble to bring touch to all platforms[26] such as the desktop PC with Windows 8,[27] the world has changed and technology will move to "conversational control".

It is easy to ascribe something more to the AI capabilities when in response to questions like "What do you look like?" Siri answers, "In the cloud, no one cares what you look like."

The developers obviously had a lot of fun developing answers to questions like the meaning of life ("42") and the famous quote from 2001, A Space Odyssey: "Open the pod bay doors" ("I'm sorry David, I'm afraid I can't do that. Are you happy now?").

There are now sites popping up everywhere of Siri witticisms[28] and insights,[29] but the enjoyment is in discovering them for yourself.

5.2.4   Q: Siri, What Does the Future Hold? A: I Can't Answer That. But I Could Search the Web for It, If You Like

The immediate question about Siri is whether the technology will appear on the iPad and then on the Mac. Technically, there is no reason for this but, as with all things Apple, the process will be controlled. When it happens, it will work and will not leave users frustrated through unmet expectations.

In the meantime, we are witnessing another truly radical technological shift.

---

[25]Love or addiction? What's your iPhone relationship? http://abclocal.go.com/kgo/story?section=news/technology&id=8392871, Accessed on 17 October 2011.

[26]Will Windows 8 Take the Touchscreen PC Mainstream? http://news.cnet.com/8301-33200_3-20107829-290/will-windows-8-take-the-touchscreen-pc-mainstream/, Accessed on 17 October 2011.

[27]Windows 8, http://windows.microsoft.com/en-US/windows-8/meet, Accessed on 17 October 2011.

[28]Siri Funny - Funniest Siri iPhone messages, http://www.sirifunny.com/, Accessed on 17 October 2011.

[29]Siri says, http://sirisays.org/, Accessed on 17 October 2011.

5.3   Paranoid Android: Does Carrier IQ Mean Your Phone Is Spying on You?

2 December 2011

What can only be described as "growing consternation" has resulted from revelations[30] by a developer, Trevor Eckhart,[31] that a large number of mobile phones are secretly monitoring users' actions on the phone and sending the data back to the phone provider.

The software, which has been dubbed "The Rootkit of All Evil[32]" after both its secretive operations and the seemingly unlimited access it has on the phone, is produced by a company called Carrier IQ.[33] Ostensibly, the software collects data that allows carriers and phone manufacturers to monitor how their phones are used, and detect problems and issues with the phones or the network.

But the capabilities of the software allow for much more, including the ability to record keystrokes and so perform a data logging function.

Although the software had been highlighted some time ago,[34] the matter came to the public's attention when Carrier IQ sent Eckhart a cease-and-desist letter[35] threatening legal action if Eckhart didn't retract his claims that the software was a "rootkit" and didn't take down training manuals from his site that he had obtained publicly from Carrier IQ's own site.

5.3.1   Rootkit

The use of the term "rootkit" is normally used to refer to software that is maliciously installed on a computer at the system level and assumes control of the system. Eckhart maintained that this was an accurate description of the Carrier IQ software as that was in essence what it did.

On November 21, the Electronic Frontier Foundation provided legal assistance to Eckhart and responded[36] to Carrier IQ stating that Eckhart's claims were protected under free speech.

---

[30] CarrierIQ, http://androidsecuritytest.com/features/logs-and-services/loggers/carrieriq/, Accessed on 2 December 2011.

[31] Trevor Eckhart's Home page, http://trevoreckhart.com/, Accessed on 2 December 2011.

[32] The Rootkit Of All Evil – CIQ, http://www.xda-developers.com/android/the-rootkit-of-all-evil-ciq/, Accessed on 2 December 2011.

[33] CarrierIQ, http://www.carrieriq.com/, Accessed on 2 December 2011.

[34] HTC Sensation and EVO 3D revealed to be spying on users, http://bgr.com/2011/09/01/htc-sensation-and-evo-3d-revealed-to-be-spying-on-users/, Accessed on 2 December 2011.

[35] Mobile 'Rootkit' Maker Tries to Silence Critical Android Dev, http://www.wired.com/threat-level/2011/11/rootkit-brouhaha/, Accessed on 2 December 2011.

[36] Link no longer goes to specified page, https://www.eff.org/sites/default/files/eckhart_c%26d_response.pdf, Accessed on 2 December 2011.

Realising they had—classically—increased attention to their activities rather than what they had set out to achieve in keeping it quiet, Carrier IQ then issued a retraction[37] of its demand for Eckhart to cease-and-desist and apologised to him for the letter.

Since then, of course, the story has been picked up globally and the company has come under increasing scrutiny. As always with these stories, it has been sometimes difficult to distinguish the fact from exaggeration and wildness of the claims. Stories with headlines such as "Carrier IQ Tracking Scandal Spirals Out of Control[38])" suggest that "nearly all Android devices" have the software installed and that it has "huge implications for user privacy".

5.3.2   Well, Actually, Not Really

Even though the software seems to have the capability[39] of recording the content of SMS messages and track the websites you have visited, it's not clear that this is necessarily sent back to the Carrier IQ servers or that it is then passed on to the phone providers or anyone else.

The Carrier IQ software is also installed on iPhones[40] but doesn't seem to be active unless the user enables "Diagnostics and Usage". In this case the information collected is more limited than in the case of the HTC phones tested running Android.

The major complaint is that Android users are not told about the monitoring or given an option to opt out. It's very difficult to stop the software or remove it from the phone without technical knowledge. In the US at least, this has led to the suggestion[41] that users may launch a class action suit against carriers and/or phone manufacturers (even possibly Google) for breaking the Wiretap Act (Electronic Communications Privacy Act, 1986[42]) and illegally collecting information without the users' consent.

---

[37] Link no longer goes to specified page, http://www.carrieriq.com/company/PR.EckhartStatement.pdf, Accessed on 2 December 2011.

[38] Carrier IQ Tracking Scandal Spirals Out of Control, http://mashable.com/2011/12/01/carrier-iq/?utm_source=feedburner&utm_medium=feed&utm_campaign=Feed%3A+Mashable+%28Mashable, Accessed on 2 December 2011.

[39] Carrier IQ Part #2, http://www.youtube.com/watch?v=T17XQI_AYNo&feature=player_embedded, Accessed on 2 December 2011.

[40] Carrier IQ is on iOS, http://blog.chpwn.com/post/13572216737?fe250de0, Accessed on 2 December 2011.

[41] Phone 'Rootkit' Maker Carrier IQ May Have Violated Wiretap Law In Millions Of Cases, http://www.forbes.com/sites/andygreenberg/2011/11/30/phone-rootkit-carrier-iq-may-have-violated-wiretap-law-in-millions-of-cases/, Accessed on 2 December 2011.

[42] Electronic   Communications   Privacy   Act,   http://en.wikipedia.org/wiki/Electronic_Communications_Privacy_Act, Accessed on 2 December 2011.

Already companies such as Nokia have issued statements[43] denying their handsets are loaded with the Carrier IQ software. Of course, this doesn't necessarily mean Nokia doesn't have its own version of the software that actually allows it to do the same thing.

Phones that are either free of Carrier IQ software or have the facility to control whether it is run or not include the Google-specific versions of the Android phone (Google Nexus One, Nexus S, Galaxy Nexus), the iPhone, and Windows Phone 7 phones.

Verizon[44] in the US has detailed[45] what information they collect and what they use it for—apparently for targeting "relevant ads" to the user. They offer an opt-out clause, but not a way for disabling the software on the phone.

Andrew Coward, Carrier IQ's VP Marketing, has insisted[46] the company might "listen[47]" to a smartphone's keyboard, but only for very specific diagnostic information, and that it isn't doing anything sinister with people's text messages. "We don't read SMS messages. We see them come in. We see the phone numbers attached to them. But we are not storing, analysing or otherwise processing the contents of those messages."

Trouble ahead.

As with all issues around privacy and confidentiality, it is not necessarily what is currently being done with our personal information that is the issue but rather what "could" be done in the future.

The possibility exists, for example, that governments and law enforcement agencies could co-opt the key-logging capabilities pre-installed on all handsets to actively log everything someone was doing. As with the recent revelations[48] that the German Government is using Trojan software installed on PCs to spy on its citizens, the convenience of having this software pre-installed on all phones is obviously huge.

There is already evidence[49] of the US security agency NSA working with the telephone carrier AT&T to carry out warrantless wiretaps on domestic communications.

---

[43]Link no longer goes to specified page, http://online.wsj.com/article/BT-CO-20111201-701491. html?mod=WSJ_ComputerSoftware_middleHeadlines, Accessed on 2 December 2011.

[44]Verizon Wireless, http://www.verizonwireless.com/b2c/index.html, Accessed on 2 December 2011.

[45]Important notice about how Verizon Wireless uses information. https://email.vzwshop.com/servlet/ website/ResponseForm?OSPECC_9_0_9hg_eLnHs_uhmpJLE, Accessed on 2 December 2011.

[46]Carrier IQ Speaks: Our Software Ignores Your Personal Info, http://allthingsd.com/20111201/ carrier-iq-speaks-our-software-monitors-service-messages-ignores-other-data/, Accessed on 2 December 2011.

[47]Pattern matching, http://en.wikipedia.org/wiki/Pattern_matching, Accessed on 2 December 2011.

[48]Ein spy: is the German government using a trojan to watch its citizens? http://theconversation. edu.au/ein-spy-is-the-german-government-using-a-trojan-to-watch-its-citizens-3765, Accessed on 2 December 2011.

[49]NSA Spying on Americans, https://www.eff.org/nsa-spying, Accessed on 2 December 2011.

Many other countries have set up monitoring facilities to carry out country-wide surveillance of their citizens, in many cases[50] using technology that was obtained from western companies prohibited from dealing with those countries.

In the meantime, should you be concerned? Well, it depends if you still hold a view that we are capable of living a private life. The answer to this question, increasingly, is probably not. Certainly not from companies whose services we use, nor from our governments or their agencies.

But it's possible to make active choices to limit the potential for "privacy leakage"—in this case by not using phones that have the software enabled by default with no option to switch it off.

This might persuade companies to be more open with their customers.

Read more on Carrier IQ here.[51]

5.4 Killing the Kodak Moment … Is the iPhone Really to Blame?

9 January 2012

According to the Wall Street Journal,[52] camera manufacturer Kodak is preparing to file for Chapter 11 bankruptcy,[53] following a long struggle to maintain any sort of viable business.

The announcement has prompted some commentators to claim[54] that Kodak's near-demise has been brought on by:

- a failure to innovate, or
- a failure to anticipate the shift from analogue to digital cameras, or
- a failure to compete with the rise of cameras in mobile phones.

Actually, none of these claims are true. Where Kodak *did* fail is in not understanding what people take photographs for, and what they do with photos once they have taken them.

---

[50] Trade in surveillance technology raises worries, http://www.washingtonpost.com/world/national-security/trade-in-surveillance-technology-raises-worries/2011/11/22/gIQAFFZOGO_print.html, Accessed on 2 December 2011.

[51] Carrier IQ knows everything you do on your phone … but why? http://theconversation.edu.au/carrier-iq-knows-everything-you-do-on-your-phone-but-why-4557, Accessed on 2 December 2011.

[52] Kodak Teeters on the Brink, http://online.wsj.com/article/SB10001424052970203471004577140841495542810.html, Accessed on 9 January 2012.

[53] Chapter 11 bankruptcy reorganization: what is it and how does it work, http://www.moranlaw.net/chapter11.htm, Accessed on 9 January 2012.

[54] Death By Smartphone: How Mobile Photography Helped Kill Kodak, http://readwrite.com/2012/01/05/death_by_smartphone_how_mobile_photography_helped, Accessed on 9 January 2012.

Before looking at what people actually take photos for, and how Kodak got it wrong, let's look at the two reasons others have given for Kodak's failure: that the camera in phones has replaced the stand-alone camera, and that Kodak failed to innovate.

'The dedicated camera is dead'

In an article for ReadWriteWeb[55] tech columnist John Paul Titlow claims Kodak is failing because of the dominance of camera phones.

In the article, Titlow uses a graph (see below) from photo sharing site Flickr,[56] showing the growth in popularity of the iPhone camera over several digital single-lens reflex (SLR) cameras.[57]

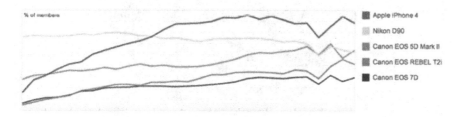

Flickr

Unfortunately this graph doesn't tell the whole story.

I downloaded Flickr data[58] and analysed the number of items uploaded to Flickr over the past year for several popular camera and phone manufacturers.

The charts below show that images taken with camera phones only represent approximately 3 % of the total. The actual number may be a little higher because Flickr can't always identify the type of camera that has taken the image, but it's still a very small percentage of the overall whole.

---

[55]Death By Smartphone: How Mobile Photography Helped Kill Kodak, http://readwrite.com/2012/01/05/death_by_smartphone_how_mobile_photography_helped, Accessed on 9 January 2012.

[56]Welcome to Flickr - Photo Sharing, http://www.flickr.com/, Accessed on 9 January 2012.

[57]Digital single-lens reflex camera, http://en.wikipedia.org/wiki/Digital_single-lens_reflex_camera, Accessed on 9 January 2012.

[58]Flickr: Camera Finder, http://www.flickr.com/cameras, Accessed on 9 January 2012.

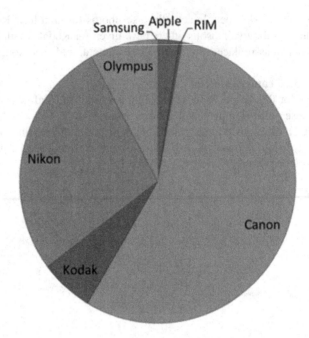

Origin of Flickr.com photos, by camera manufacturer. David Glance

The other thing to note is that Kodak cameras are only responsible for 6 % of images overall and that Canon and Nikon are by far the most dominant players in this market.

(Admittedly, the number of images on Flickr is about 5 % of that on[59] Facebook. It would be interesting to repeat this analysis using Facebook data, but there is no reason to believe the results would be substantially different.)

---

[59] The Number of Photos on Facebook is Exploding [Infographic], http://www.photoweeklyonline. com/the-number-of-photos-on-facebook-is-exploding-infographic/, Accessed on 9 January 2012.

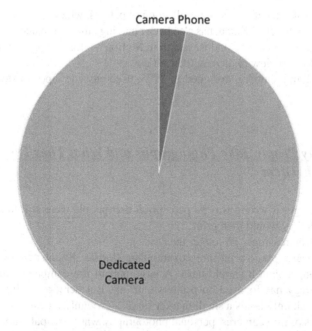

Origin of Flickr.com photos, by camera type. David Glance

5.4.1 'Kodak Failed to Innovate'

Kodak's financial problems[60] aren't necessarily due to a failure to innovate, or a failure to recognise the shift from print to digital photography. In fact, Kodak has been involved in the rise of digital cameras at virtually every step:

- Kodak electrical engineer, Steve Sasson, actually "invented" the digital camera[61] in 1975.
- Kodak partnered with Nikon[62] in 1991 to produce a professional-grade digital camera with a whopping 1.3 Megapixels (you can buy 12 Megapixel cameras[63] for under $100 now).
- In 1995, Kodak released[64] their first "point-and-shoot" camera.

---

[60] Get Quotes Results for EK, http://uk.finance.yahoo.com/lookup?s=EK#symbol=ek;range=1y;co mpare=;indicator=volume;charttype=area;crosshair=on;ohlcvalues=0;logscale=off;source=; Accessed on 9 January 2012.

[61] Bits Pics: Kodak's 1975 Model Digital Camera, http://bits.blogs.nytimes.com/2010/08/26/bits-pics-kodaks-1975-model-digital-camera/, Accessed on 9 January 2012.

[62] History of the Digital Camera, http://inventors.about.com/library/inventors/bldigitalcamera.htm, Accessed on 9 January 2012.

[63] 12.2MP Style Camera Silver ES80, http://www.samsung.com/au/consumer/camera-camcorder/compact-cameras/style/EC-ES80ZZBPBAU, Accessed on 9 January 2012.

[64] 1990–1999, http://www.kodak.com/ek/US/en/Our_Company/History_of_Kodak/Milestones_-_chronology/1990-1999.htm, Accessed on 9 January 2012.

One of Kodak's chief assets is its collection of patents, which company executives have been trying to sell.[65] Kodak has also been pursuing other companies[66]—including phone manufacturers Apple and Research in Motion[67]—for infringing their patents on the ability to preview photos on their phones.

The first digital camera, designed in 1975, used cassette tapes to store images. Kodak

5.4.2 Why People Take Photographs and What They Do with Them

Where Kodak got it wrong was its perception that people were still taking photographs which they would then print.

But this is increasingly no longer the case.

From dedicated photo print shops to automated kiosks, Kodak persisted with this notion for longer than it should have. A large part of the company's more recent business strategy has focused on printers and ink. But here, as with their digital cameras, Kodak only holds a small market share[68]—roughly 2.6 %.

In the days of film cameras, personal photography was principally about holding on to personal memories, with photos usually ending up in a shoebox.

Photography was once about saving personal memories. deflam

But recent research[69] by anthropologists, sociologists and psychologists suggests personal photography has moved from being mostly a tool for remembering, to one of emphasising communication and our individual identities.

As with most change, researchers have noted this switch most prominently in teenagers and young adults.

This shift has been supported by the changes in underlying technology and the advent of "frictionless[70]" sharing of photos and video via social network platforms. In the context of photography, "frictionless sharing" means minimising the number of steps between taking a photo and sharing it via a social network platform.

---

[65] Kodak Teeters on the Brink, http://online.wsj.com/article/SB10001424052970203471004577140841495542810.html, Accessed on 9 January 2012.

[66] Patent wars: Kodak sues Apple, RIM for patent infringement, http://www.zdnet.com/blog/btl/patent-wars-kodak-sues-apple-rim-for-patent-infringement/29558, Accessed on 9 January 2012.

[67] RIM Company - Learn about Research In Motion, http://www.rim.com/, Accessed on 9 January 2012.

[68] Kodak Teeters on the Brink, http://online.wsj.com/article/SB10001424052970203471004577140841495542810.html, Accessed on 9 January 2012.

[69] Digital photography: communication, identity, memory, http://vcj.sagepub.com/content/7/1/57.short, Accessed on 9 January 2012.

[70] Facebook Hasn't Ruined Sharing, It's Just Re-Defined It, http://readwrite.com/2011/11/20/facebook_hasnt_ruined_sharing_its_just_re-defined_it, Accessed on 9 January 2012.

But in terms of technology, the real shift came when camera phones (in particular) reached a certain quality.

Many of the cameras found on today's phones are at least five Megapixels. For people making a decision between using their phone and bringing along a dedicated point-and-click camera, this five Megapixel resolution probably represents the tipping point in favour of the phone.

But as we have seen with the data from Flickr, the move to the camera phone is still gathering momentum and other digital cameras are still popular.

5.4.2.1 Frictionless Photo Sharing

The real accelerator for frictionless sharing of photos has been the ability to instantly upload photographs to social networking platforms such as Facebook and Twitter, and to blog software such as Posterous and Tumblr. The iPhone, in particular, has popularised specialised photo sharing apps such as Instagram[71] and Hipstamatic.[72]

iPhone apps, such as Hipstamatic, are driving a change in the way we share photos. itspaulkelly.

Sharing a photo in this way is more about communication and less about remembering. The photo usually has some commentary ("Miserable in New York today.[73]") and is "liked" and commented on by friends and others with whom it is shared.

Another important part of photography's shift from memory tool to communication medium is that the photos are purposely temporary. The sheer volume of photographs taken and uploaded by individuals limits the shelf-life of these photos.

Of course this may change with features such as Facebook's timeline,[74] which attempts to make it much easier to access photos for the purpose of remembering.

(It's worth noting that in 2011, approximately 70 billion[75] photographs were uploaded to Facebook, with some estimates[76] putting that figure closer to 100 billion photographs. Either way, Facebook is the largest photo sharing[77] site by a considerable margin.)

It is hard to see a role for Kodak in all of this. Even with a company restructure, they would still be competing with companies such as Nikon and Canon; companies which are much stronger in the hardware and technology markets.

---

[71] Meet Instagram, http://instagram.com/, Accessed on 9 January 2012.

[72] Hipstamatic - Digital photography never looked so analog, http://hipstamatic.com/, Accessed on 9 January 2012.

[73] Hipstamatic, http://www.flickr.com/photos/mgh500/5647473299/, Accessed on 9 January 2012.

[74] Introducing timeline, https://www.facebook.com/about/timeline, Accessed on 9 January 2012.

[75] How many photos have ever been taken? http://blog.1000memories.com/94-number-of-photos-ever-taken-digital-and-analog-in-shoebox, Accessed on 9 January 2012.

[76] The Number of Photos on Facebook is Exploding [Infographic], http://www.photoweeklyonline.com/the-number-of-photos-on-facebook-is-exploding-infographic/, Accessed on 9 January 2012.

[77] The Number of Photos on Facebook is Exploding [Infographic], http://www.photoweeklyonline.com/the-number-of-photos-on-facebook-is-exploding-infographic/, Accessed on 9 January 2012.

The real value in photography today is the software and platforms used for sharing and distribution. Kodak would need to pull off a miracle to become a major player in this space.

In all likelihood, Kodak's moment might have passed.

5.5   Dream appzzz: Can the iPhone Help You Sleep?

5 March 2012

Sleep matters—and yet many of us know how difficult it can be to get enough unbroken slumber.

Research[78] has shown that getting less than 7–8 h sleep daily is associated with increased risk of:

- cardiovascular disease and diabetes
- depression
- car and workplace accidents, and
- learning and memory problems.

Given this, it's worrying that, in the US, approximately 28 % of people[79] get less sleep than this each night. Australian adults do slightly better according to one study,[80] with approximately 15 % of adults reporting 6 or fewer hours a night.

There are more than 80 different sleep disorders,[81] with estimates suggesting 20–33 % of the US population having suffered from insomnia. Estimates[82] put the prevalence of adult obstructive sleep apnea[83]—where a person momentarily stops breathing during his or her sleep—at 3–7 % of the population, with increasing evidence[84] of a link between sleep apnea and Type 2 diabetes.[85]

---

[78] Sleep Duration in the United States: A Cross-sectional Population-based Study, http://aje.oxford-journals.org/content/169/9/1052.full.pdf+html, Accessed on 5 March 2012.

[79] Sleep Duration in the United States: A Cross-sectional Population-based Study, http://aje.oxford-journals.org/content/169/9/1052.full.pdf+html, Accessed on 5 March 2012.

[80] Journal of Sleep Research, http://onlinelibrary.wiley.com/doi/10.1111/j.1365-2869.2011.00993.x/full, Accessed on 5 March 2012.

[81] The Prevalence, Cost Implications, and Management of Sleep Disorders: An Overview, http://link.springer.com/article/10.1007%2Fs11325-002-0085-1, Accessed on 5 March 2012.

[82] The Epidemiology of Adult Obstructive Sleep Apnea, http://pats.atsjournals.org/content/5/2/136.abstract, Accessed on 5 March 2012.

[83] Adult obstructive sleep apnea: pathophysiology and diagnosis, http://www.ncbi.nlm.nih.gov/pubmed/17625094, Accessed on 5 March 2012.

[84] Obstructive Sleep Apnea and Type 2 Diabetes: Interacting Epidemics, http://journal.publications.chestnet.org/article.aspx?articleid=1085691&issueno=2, Accessed on 5 March 2012.

[85] Type 2 Diabetes, http://www.diabetesaustralia.com.au/Understanding-Diabetes/What-is-Diabetes/Type-2-Diabetes/, Accessed on 5 March 2012.

The starting point for dealing with a sleep issue is to recognise there is one. To do so, people need a way of measuring the amount and quality of sleep they are getting. That's where the iPhone comes in.

5.5.1 Measuring Brain Waves with the iPhone: The Zeo

The Zeo[86] is essentially a headband that can be worn at night and feeds data to the iPhone. The headband contains sensors[87] that pick up electrical signals from the brain as well as information about eye movements.

The information is sent to the phone and analysed to produce a graph showing when you slept, when you were awake and how long you spent in each phase of sleep.

Sleep can be split into two types: REM[88] and non-REM[89] sleep. REM is named after the rapid eye movements that occur during this phase.

Zeo uses, appropriately enough, an artificial intelligence mechanism called neural networks[90] to take the brain's electrical activity and classify it into light sleep, REM sleep, deep sleep and wakefulness.

Click to enlarge.

Using the data the Zeo provides, the iPhone application then rates your night's sleep with a score called the ZQ[91] between zero and 120—the higher the number, the better the sleep. The data can then be uploaded to the myZeo website,[92] which provides a range of tools, including various assessments and a sleep journal.

Zeo's accuracy is actually quite high. When compared with polysomnography[93]— the gold standard for assessing sleep –researchers found[94] the Zeo was only slightly less accurate in detecting sleep phases, and just as accurate at detecting when people woke up and went back to sleep.

---

[86] Zeo, http://www.myzeo.com/sleep/, Accessed on 5 March 2012.

[87] Behind the Headband (1): How Zeo Works, http://www.youtube.com/watch?v=jmOG7RNlAUg &feature=related, Accessed on 5 March 2012.

[88] Rapid eye movement sleep, http://en.wikipedia.org/wiki/Rapid_eye_movement_sleep, Accessed on 5 March 2012.

[89] Non-rapid eye movement sleep, http://en.wikipedia.org/wiki/Non-REM_sleep, Accessed on 5 March 2012.

[90] Neural Networks in Plain English, http://www.ai-junkie.com/ann/evolved/nnt1.html, Accessed on 5 March 2012.

[91] Cracking the ZQ Code, http://www.myzeo.com/sleep/knowledge-center/articles/what-is-zq, Accessed on 5 March 2012.

[92] myZeo, http://mysleep.myzeo.com/, Accessed on 5 March 2012.

[93] Polysomnography, http://en.wikipedia.org/wiki/Polysomnography, Accessed on 5 March 2012.

[94] Validation of an automated wireless system to monitor sleep in healthy adults, http://onlinelibrary.wiley.com/doi/10.1111/j.1365-2869.2011.00944.x/full, Accessed on 5 March 2012.

5.5.2   Sleep Hacking

So let's imagine you've collected some sleep data on your iPhone. What can this tell you?

First and foremost, it's worth noting that this process doesn't replace seeing a doctor and getting a professional sleep assessment.

Although the information may be useful in pointing to a problem, it will probably not allow you to self-diagnose any of the specific sleep disorders, including obstructive sleep apnea.

For this, a sleep or respiratory physician may perform a more detailed assessment using polysomnography. This involves more equipment than just the Zeo headband.

But your sleep data *will* increase self-awareness about how long you are sleeping and how many times you are waking up. With that awareness comes an appreciation of how dramatically factors such as coffee, alcohol, exercise and TV and computer use affect how you sleep.

You can then modify your behaviour and get direct feedback on the results, hopefully with an improvement to your sleep.

One of the features of devices such as the Zeo is that they create a social network[95] of people willing to share their experiences, concerns and strategies regarding sleep.

In and of itself, that's important in dealing with sleep issues and reinforcing support for making life-changes that will improve health outcomes.

5.5.3   Measuring Sleep Through Movements

The Zeo headband isn't the only approach to measuring sleep quality. A popular iPhone application called the Sleep Cycle[96] professes to be able to do this by measuring the amount of movement during sleep. The concept is relatively simple.

You put the iPhone under your pillow and the accelerometers[97] in the phone track any movement. This movement is then correlated with four phases: falling asleep/dreaming/waking up, light sleep, medium/deep sleep, and deep sleep.

Click to enlarge

According to an online post citing[98] a professor of sleep medicine at Harvard Medical School, there is no evidence of movement being used to accurately determine sleep phases; other than potentially being able to distinguish between being asleep and being awake. Even in that regard, it may not be that accurate.[99]

---

[95] Zeo on Facebook, https://www.facebook.com/myZeo?sk=wall, Accessed on 5 March 2012.

[96] Sleep Cycle alarm clock, http://www.sleepcycle.com/, Accessed on 5 March 2012.

[97] A beginner's guide to accelerometers, http://www.dimensionengineering.com/info/accelerometers, Accessed on 5 March 2012.

[98] Sweet Dreams: iPhone apps claim to measure sleep – but do they work? http://s7.zetaboards.com/Apnea_Board/topic/8279222/1/, Accessed on 5 March 2012.

[99] Comparison between subjective and actigraphic measurement of sleep and sleep rhythms, http://onlinelibrary.wiley.com/doi/10.1046/j.1365-2869.1999.00155.x/full, Accessed on 5 March 2012.

This has not deterred other manufacturers from making the same claims. A bracelet device called the UP[100] also feeds movement data into the iPhone, and presents a graph of hours slept and light and deep sleep.

5.5.4   Personal Health Monitoring: The Future

The use of the iPhone as a data collection and analysis platform is set to become more common. The next step is to alert wearers—or people monitoring the health of wearers—when there are potential problems.

One recent experiment[101] used heart rate monitors and motion sensors to monitor nurses for episodes of stress. This provided the potential to intervene when someone was experiencing prolonged stress that was adversely affecting their health.

Many of us are unaware of the impact our environment, job and lifestyle are having on our health. As a result we're unable to intervene before lasting damage has been done.

Sleep is central to our wellbeing. In this, and other health areas going forward, the iPhone may be able to help.

5.6   Verizon Wireless Vs. Telstra: The Great Mobile Rip-Off Continues

12 July 2012

Will ACMA's new code of practice be enough to give Australian telcos a wake-up call? *Source*: Miki Yoshihito CC0[102]

---

[100] UP, https://jawbone.com/up, Accessed on 5 March 2012.

[101] Link no longer goes to specified page, http://tshrove.selfip.com/downloads/Real-time_ Monitoring_of_Occupational_Stress_of_Nurses.pdf, Accessed on 5 March 2012.

[102] Yoshihito M., Flickr, http://www.flickr.com/photos/mujitra/4757724124/, Accessed online 21 December 2012.

Does the recent announcement by the Australian Communications and Media Authority (ACMA)[103] of a new code of practice[104] to prevent bill shock[105] for "long-suffering telco customers", and improve product marketing practices, bring Australia up to par with its international cousins?

In a word: no.

Bill shock, as the name suggests, is the reaction customers have to unexpected charges on their mobile phone bills. A public enquiry[106] held by ACMA, with the final report released in September 2011, found that telecommunication companies write off up to A$113m annually in bad debts related to bill shock.

The latest ACMA announcement is a major step forward but the government and ACMA have to act urgently to fix the great Australian mobile rip-off.

The problem of the international roaming charges rip-off[107] is yet to be directly addressed by either.

Have you heard about "data share"[108] and why it is being promoted as a major step forward by Verizon Wireless USA[109]?

No? Read on and learn how Australian telecommunication companies are ripping-off mobile users with excessive data charges and failure to implement more flexible multi-device accounts.

5.6.1   The ACMA Announcement

After several years of record complaints to the Telecommunication Industry Ombudsman (TIO)[110] the ACMA finally decided to act.

---

[103] Australian Communications and Media Authority, http://www.acma.gov.au/, Accessed online 12 July 2012.

[104] C628:2012 Telecommunications Consumer Protections (TCP) Code, Communications Alliance, http://www.commsalliance.com.au/?a=2912, Accessed online 12 July 2012, new link http://www.commsalliance.com.au/about-us/newsroom/2012-8   or   http://www.commsalliance.com.au/Documents/all/codes/c628

[105] Moses A., Crackdown on telcos will ban misleading ads and 'bill shock', Fairfax, 1 June 2012, http://www.smh.com.au/technology/technology-news/crackdown-on-telcos-will-ban-misleading-ads-and-bill-shock-20110601-1ffi7.html, Accessed online 12 July 2012.

[106] Reconnecting the customer, Australian Communications and Media Authority, http://www.acma.gov.au/WEB/STANDARD..PC/pc=PC_312222, Accessed online 12 July 2012.

[107] Gregory M.A., Are Australian international roaming charges the greatest rip-off in history?, The Conversation, 30 November 2011, https://theconversation.edu.au/are-australian-international-roaming-charges-the-greatest-rip-off-in-history-4340, Accessed online 12 July 2012.

[108] Fingas J., Verizon's Share Everything data plans go live June 28th, let you add family (or a tablet) for a little extra, engadget, 12 June 2012, http://www.engadget.com/2012/06/12/verizon-share-everything-data-plans-go-live-june-28/, Accessed online 12 July 2012.

[109] Verizon Wireless, http://www.verizonwireless.com/, Accessed online 12 July 2012.

[110] Telecommunication Industry Ombudsman, http://www.tio.com.au/, Accessed online 12 July 2012.

Its 102-page code of practice—Telecommunications Consumer Protection (TCP)[111]—will be enforced from September 1[112] and phased in over the next 2 years. The top 10 "wins" for mobile consumers can be found here.[113] Among its many proposed benefits, customers will:

- be "empowered" to comparison shop
- better understand what they've actually signed up for
- receive notifications at 50, 85 and 100 % of call and data usage, meaning there will be "no excuse for unexpected bill shock when they return from overseas holidays"

The telecommunication industry body Communications Alliance[114] prepared the code after ACMA indicated it was not going to "roll over" to industry resistance for change.

The ACMA chair Chris Chapman was quoted yesterday[115] as saying:

My own discussions with the chief executives of the major telcos have convinced me that they get it [the need for a code of practice]. I think they know that in this increasingly technology driven environment [...] there is only one outcome for them—that is to change their business practices and to own their customer is a way that is materially rewarding.

In another article, Teresa Corbin, CEO of the Australian Communications Consumer Action Network (ACCAN)[116] was quoted as saying[117]:

[We] are hopeful that its [the new code of practice] adoption will result in clearer advertising, easier comparison of products, better information about contracts and better tools to help consumers avoid bill shock.

ACCAN is concerned that ACMA needs to be given greater powers of enforcement. Corbin argues:

The ACCC, for example, has much stronger powers and its issuing of fines has sent a strong message to the telecommunications industry that its advertising cannot be misleading.

---

[111]C628:2012 Telecommunications Consumer Protections (TCP) Code, Communications Alliance, http://www.commsalliance.com.au/?a=2912, Accessed online 12 July 2012, new link http://www.commsalliance.com.au/about-us/newsroom/2012-8 or http://www.commsalliance.com.au/Documents/all/codes/c628

[112]Fair call—new telco code to benefit consumers, Australian Communications and Media Authority, http://engage.acma.gov.au/reconnecting/fair-call-new-telco-code-to-benefit-consumers/, Accessed online 12 July 2012.

[113]Top 10 customer wins, Australian Communications and Media Authority, http://www.acma.gov.au/webwr/_assets/main/lib410251/TCP_code-Top_ten_consumer_wins.pdf, Accessed online 12 July 2012.

[114]Communications Alliance, http://www.commsalliance.com.au/, Accessed online 12 July 2012.

[115]Battersby L., Telco code moves to end 'confuseopoly', Fairfax, 11 July 2012, http://www.businessday.com.au/business/telco-code-moves-to-end-confuseopoly-20120711-21uzf.html, Accessed online 12 July 2012.

[116]Australian Communications Consumer Action Network, http://accan.org.au/, Accessed online 12 July 2012.

[117]Osman H., ACMA to register revised TCP code, ARN, http://www.arnnet.com.au/article/430228/acma_register_revised_tcp_code/#closeme, Accessed online 12 July 2012.

5.6.2   *Data Share*

Verizon Wireless USA[118] has introduced "data share"[119]—an initiative under which customers share their plan's data allowance across multiple mobile devices, including smartphones and tablets.

The Verizon Wireless data-share plans have been described as expensive for US mobile customers, but a sign of the future,[120] as American telecommunication companies try to wean customers off unlimited data plans in the move to 4G networks.[121]

Let's compare Telstra's current offering with the Verizon Wireless data share plans—bearing in mind Telstra Mobile[122] leaves the Australian competition in its wake for cost, coverage and network quality.

The current Telstra unlimited talk/MMS, text, with 3GB data plan costs A$100 per month. For three devices on the Telstra network, the cost is therefore A$300 a month, with 9 GB of data—3 GB per device, that cannot be shared.

The Verizon Wireless unlimited talk, text and share data plan with 4 GB data will cost US$40 (A$40) a month for a smartphone and US$70 (A$70) a month for 4 GB of shared data.

For a Verizon Wireless account with three devices (two smartphones and one basic phone) sharing a monthly allowance of unlimited talk, text and 4 GB of data would cost US$180 (A$180) a month (excluding taxes and surcharges).

To get a comparison we need to add 5 GB of data to the Verizon Wireless plan. Verizon Wireless charges for extra data at a rate of US$10 (A$10) a month for 2 GB. For an additional 6 GB of shared data a Verizon Wireless customer would pay US$30 (A$10) a month.

So the total cost to the Telstra customer is A$300 per month for three devices and 9 GB of data that cannot be shared across devices; the total cost for the Verizon Wireless customer is US$210 (A$210) for three devices and 10 GB of data that can be shared across the devices.

---

[118] Verizon Wireless, http://www.verizonwireless.com/, Accessed online 12 July 2012.

[119] Fingas J., Verizon's Share Everything data plans go live June 28th, let you add family (or a tablet) for a little extra, engadget, 12 June 2012, http://www.engadget.com/2012/06/12/verizon-share-everything-data-plans-go-live-june-28/, Accessed online 12 July 2012.

[120] Olivarez-Giles N., Verizon's Shared Data Plans Aren't Cheap, But They Are the Future, Wired, 12 June 2012, http://www.wired.com/gadgetlab/2012/06/verizons-shared-data-plans-arent-cheap-but-they-are-the-future/, Accessed online 12 July 2012.

[121] King H., You, me and 4G: the future is in our hands, The Conversation, 14 July 2011, https://theconversation.edu.au/you-me-and-4g-the-future-is-in-our-hands-884, Accessed online 12 July 2012.

[122] Mobile Phones & Plans, Telstra, http://www.telstra.com.au/mobile-phones/, Accessed online 12 July 2012.

5.6.3   Use or Lose

One of the most frustrating aspects of mobile devices is paying for data that's not used one month and then paying an exorbitant amount for going over the plan allowance the next month.

The Telstra website provides the following advice[123]

> If you use more than this [your agreed] amount each month you pay for that extra browsing at a reduced Pay As You Go (PAYG) rate—so you get more for your money.

Sounds great.

Yet the Telstra additional usage charges are described as A$0.10 per MB used, which means A$100 per GB used. To put that in context, a standard 10-min YouTube video is about 25 MB in size, so would cost the customer A$2.50.

What a rip-off!

The old arguments in defence of high data charges in Australia cannot be justified. Telecommunication companies in the US and Australia have mature 3G networks and have commenced rolling out 4G (LTE) networks targeting areas of high population density initially.

Technology costs have continued to fall. Backhaul,[124] core and international bandwidth costs[125] have continued to fall and are now similar to costs in the US and Europe.

Verizon Wireless's additional usage charges are described as US$15 (A$15) per 1 GB of data whenever customers go over their plan allowance.

A Telstra customer with three devices will pay A$85 (US$85) per month more than a Verizon Wireless customer for a similar plan—and for a 1 GB data overage, a Telstra customer will be charged A$85 (US$85) more than a Verizon Wireless customer.

Add to this injury the advantages of data share enjoyed by Verizon Wireless customers.

The Verizon Wireless customer will be able to share data use across their multiple devices; by doing so they will be better able to manage data use and potentially reduce the plan cost by moving to a lower shared-data plan.

For Australian families shared data plans are a must. It's time for the government to act and force telecommunication companies to introduce shared data plans immediately.

---

[123]Mobile Phone Data Packs, Telstra, http://www.telstra.com.au/mobile-phones/data-packs/, Accessed online 12 July 2012.

[124]Backhaul, Wikipedia, http://en.wikipedia.org/wiki/Backhaul_(telecommunications), Accessed online 12 July 2012.

[125]Cost of International Bandwidth, Whirlpool, http://forums.whirlpool.net.au/archive/99517, Accessed online 12 July 2012.

5.6.3.1   Further Reading

Are Australian international roaming charges the greatest rip-off in history?[126]

5.7   Why Conroy Needs to Do More on Roaming Rip-Offs

29 August 2012

Telecommunications companies already make mammoth profits from international roaming charges and these profits have only increased with the introduction of smart phones. Telcos now not only apply international roaming charges to phone calls, but to other popular services like SMS, email, web browsing and social media use as well.

Given this, and the fact that international roaming charges appear to change for every different country that you visit, it's no wonder that communications minster Stephen Conroy labelled the whole situation around mobile roaming as "frankly obscene" and has moved to **act on the issue**[127]—by tackling mobile roaming charges in New Zealand.

New Zealand and Australian have formed a committee to look into the problem of the international roaming charges for travellers between the two countries.

But it's hard to see that there is an international roaming problem between Australia and New Zealand. If you think about it, it's a bit like someone in Sydney being exponentially charged for making a call from Hobart.

It's just two islands with a cable running between them—how expensive can it be?

What makes it more baffling is the fact that no US or European telcos are involved in the connection between Australia and New Zealand. Our telcos have argued for years that they are the cause of higher international roaming costs.

So with this in mind, here's what Senator Conroy had to say about the government's approach to our New Zealand mobile roaming crisis on ABC News 24's Breakfast program.

- "We're announcing two things today. We're releasing a discussion paper which we've worked on for the last couple of years with the New Zealand government which is saying we need to act now"
- "We've done a study and what we found was at the beginning of the study the mark-up, the margin for international cost calls between here and New Zealand was 1,000 %"

---

[126]Gregory M.A., Are Australian international roaming charges the greatest rip-off in history?, The Conversation, 30 November 2011, https://theconversation.edu.au/are-australian-international-roaming-charges-the-greatest-rip-off-in-history-4340, Accessed online 12 July 2012.

[127]Polites H., Australia, NZ join forces to cut excessive mobile roaming charges, Technology Spectator, 23 August 2012, http://www.technologyspectator.com.au/australia-nz-join-forces-cut-excessive-mobile-roaming-charges, Accessed online 29 August 2012.

- "With the spotlight on, it's come down to 300 % but that is not good enough."
- "I'm directing the ACMA to put in place a standard which will see mobile phone companies notifying their customers when they're overseas of the cost of a call, the cost of sending a text, the cost of going online, and giving them the option to opt out."

Senator Conroy's announcement is a good small first step.

Unfortunately, telecommunication companies will pass on the cost of the new notification and opt-out system to customers and the announcement does not tackle the root cause of the problem.

It's a meagre step compared to what The European Union legislated back in 2007 to curb international roaming charges They recently **announced**[128] that from July 2012 there would be more regulation of roaming costs for EU citizens when travelling in EU countries.

The **move**[129] is expected to save EU families over 200 each year and business travellers over 1,000.

The European Union Commission Vice President Neelie Kross said that "by putting price caps on data we have created a roaming market for the smart phone generation. More than that, we have ended the rip-offs familiar to anyone who has used a mobile phone while travelling abroad. I am pleased that year after year the European Union is putting money back in the pockets of citizens".

What a sentiment. It's one that we're unlikely to experience anytime soon given the fact is that regulation of the trans-Tasman international roaming charges is still years away.

The **Association of South East Asian Nations (ASEAN)**[130] has, according to Ovum research director David Kennedy, expressed an interest to create an agreement similar to that in the EU.

Kennedy **says**[131] "that's at a much earlier stage than these negotiations, but if that were to come to pass, the next step would be combining the agreement with one between Australia and New Zealand."

Senator Conroy should implement wholesale and retail prices caps with New Zealand immediately and give the Australian Competition and Consumer

[128] More transparency and cheaper roaming prices for EU citizens, European Commission, http://ec.europa.eu/information_society/activities/roaming/regulation/archives/current_rules/index_en.htm, Accessed online 29 August 2012.

[129] Digital Agenda: New price caps for mobile data roaming expected to save families over 200 each year and business travellers over 1000., Europa, http://europa.eu/rapid/press-release_MEMO-12-316_en.htm, Accessed online 29 August 2012.

[130] Association of South East Asian Nations, http://www.aseansec.org/, Accessed online 29 August 2012.

[131] Stafford P., Conroy calls for submissions on trans-Tasman roaming charges, but international agreements still years away, SmartCompany, 23 August 2012, http://www.smartcompany.com.au/telecommunications/051379-conroy-calls-for-submissions-on-trans-tasman-roaming-charges-but-international-agreements-still-years-away.html, Accessed online 29 August 2012.

Commission (ACCC) the power to investigate and set prices in conjunction with the
New Zealand government.

The EU prices set a benchmark that could be immediately implemented between
Australia and New Zealand and could form the starting point for an agreement with
ASEAN.

As for an agreement with US and EU telecommunication companies, well this is
where we find out who our friends really are. There is no hope in the foreseeable
future of an international roaming agreement with telecommunication companies in
the US and EU unless their governments step in.

It's time for Senator Conroy to start calling his counterparts in the US and Europe
and tell them that the Australian public are sick of being ripped off.

5.8   Explainer: What Is 4G?

12 September 2012

You'll be hearing a lot more about 4G networks in the years to come. *Source*: Beau Giles[132]

If you're looking to buy a new smartphone or computer you've probably seen
advertisements and offers for 4G-compatible devices. You might even own a
4G-compatible device already.

But just what is 4G? How does it compare to existing 3G networks? And what is
the current availability of 4G networks in Australia?

---

[132]Giles B., Flickr, http://www.flickr.com/photos/beaugiles/6945452409/, Accessed online 21
December 2012.

5.8.1 4G: The Basics

Simply, "4G" is a marketing term that describes a fourth-generation mobile wireless cellular network. Telstra first offered 4G services in mid-2011[133] and now offers a range of 4G-compatible handsets, tablets and modems.

In August 2012 Optus began switching on 4G services[134] in some cities—Sydney, Perth and Newcastle, with more to come[135]—and in doing so became Australia's second 4G supplier.

5.8.2 Is 4G Much Better Than 3G/NextG?

Mobile cellular networks evolve and a good example has been the way the initial 3G offering evolved with the introduction of high-speed data services.

In Australia, Telstra launched a 3G network called the NextG network[136] in October 2006 with data download speeds between 550 Kbps and 1.5 Mbps. Over the next couple of years Telstra successively upgraded their network to provide improved data download and upload speeds.

In December 2008 Telstra boosted the speed of the NextG network to 21 Mbps, utilising the Evolved High-Speed Packet Access (HSPA+)[137] and Dual-Carrier HSPA[138] standards.

4G networks will evolve in a similar way.

5.8.3 Evolving 4G

In 2007 the International Telecommunication Union's Radiocommunication Sector (ITU-R)[139] defined a new global standard called International Mobile

---

[133] LeMay R., Telstra's 4G network goes live, Delimiter, 27 September 2011, http://delimiter.com.au/2011/09/27/telstras-4g-network-goes-live/, Accessed online 12 September 2012.

[134] Falconer J., Australia's Optus launches 4G network in Sydney, Perth & Newcastle, The Next Web, 3 September 2012, http://thenextweb.com/au/2012/09/03/australias-optus-launches-4g-network-sydney-perth-newcastle/, Accessed online 12 September 2012.

[135] Falconer J., Australia's Optus launches 4G network in Sydney, Perth & Newcastle, The Next Web, 3 September 2012, http://thenextweb.com/au/2012/09/03/australias-optus-launches-4g-network-sydney-perth-newcastle/, Accessed online 12 September 2012.

[136] Next G, Wikipedia, http://en.wikipedia.org/wiki/Next_G, Accessed online 12 September 2012.

[137] Evolved HSPA, Wikipedia, http://en.wikipedia.org/wiki/Evolved_HSPA, Accessed online 12 September 2012.

[138] High-Speed Downlink Packet Access, Wikipedia, http://en.wikipedia.org/wiki/Dual-Carrier_HSPA, Accessed online 12 September 2012.

[139] Radiocommunication Sector, International Telecommunication Union, http://www.itu.int/ITU-R/index.asp?category=information&rlink=rhome&lang=en, Accessed online 12 September 2012.

Telecommunications-Advanced (IMT-Advanced).[140] The standard contains a list of features required before a network can be marketed as being "4G". Such features include (to quote the ITU):

- compatibility of services within IMT and with fixed networks
- capability of interworking with other radio access systems
- high quality mobile services
- worldwide roaming capability
- enhanced peak data rates to support advanced services and applications.

What this means is that IMT-Advanced will be an internet protocol (IP)[141] packet-switched[142] network that incorporates Voice-over-IP (VoIP)[143] rather than the separate telephone call channels used in 3G networks.

Another IMT-Advanced feature will be seamless connectivity and roaming across multiple network types including Wi-Fi[144] with smooth handover.[145]

Simply, a smooth handover means your device will access the fastest available network to you. If you're on a phone call and move into range of a Wi-Fi hotspot your device will move from the 4G network to the Wi-Fi hotspot without dropping your phone connection and you will remain connected to your mobile provider while in the Wi-Fi hotspot. When you leave Wi-Fi range, your device will smoothly move you back to the 4G network and you will not lose your phone connection.

3G does not provide seamless connectivity and roaming across multiple network types because this functionality relies upon the all-IP nature of IMT-Advanced.

5.8.4   What Do We Have Now?

In Australia, thanks to Telstra and now Optus, we currently have 4G networks that utilise a technology called Long Term Evolution (LTE).[146] The key feature of 4G LTE is improved data speeds when compared to 3G networks—up to 40 Mbps[147] for upload and download.

---

[140] IMT Advanced, Wikipedia, http://en.wikipedia.org/wiki/IMT_Advanced, Accessed online 12 September 2012.

[141] Internet Protocol, Wikipedia, http://en.wikipedia.org/wiki/Internet_Protocol, Accessed online 12 September 2012.

[142] Packet switching, Wikipedia, http://en.wikipedia.org/wiki/Packet_switched, Accessed online 12 September 2012.

[143] Voice over IP, Wikipedia, http://en.wikipedia.org/wiki/IP_telephony, Accessed online 12 September 2012.

[144] Wi-Fi Alliance, http://www.wi-fi.org/, Accessed online 12 September 2012.

[145] Handover, Wikipedia, http://en.wikipedia.org/wiki/Handover, Accessed online 12 September 2012.

[146] Long Term Evolution, Wikipedia, http://en.wikipedia.org/wiki/LTE_(telecommunication), Accessed online 12 September 2012.

[147] Megabit per second, Wikipedia, http://en.wikipedia.org/wiki/Mbps#Megabit_per_second, Accessed online 12 September 2012.

Australian 3G/NextG networks currently provide download speeds up to 21 Mbps and upload speeds of up to 5.8 Mbps. That said, typical 3G/NextG download speeds range from 550 Kbps to 8 Mbps and upload speeds range from 300 Kbps to 1 Mbps.

Reporting in The Australian[148] on September 11, Chris Griffith provided the results of 4G LTE data download speed tests completed in six locations around Sydney. Griffith used 4G modems on the Telstra and Optus networks to show that the former is slightly faster across the board. Both networks managed download speeds in excess of 30 Mbps in several locations.

Telephone calls over 4G LTE are still done using a separate voice channel similar to 3G.

5.8.5   What's Next?

On August 8 this year a South Korean telecommunication provider SK Telecom launched[149] what is thought to be the world's first Voice over LTE (VoLTE)[150] service that moves closer to a full VoIP solution rather than using a separate telephone channel.

By processing phone calls over an LTE network (as opposed to a 3G or even 2G network), VoLTE allows considerably faster call connections and considerably better audio quality. This technology will be available in future Samsung LTE smart phones.[151]

In the US, Verizon Wireless,[152] which launched an LTE network in December 2010, has commenced work[153] with AT&T[154] and several equipment vendors to develop a VoLTE standard. Enhanced LTE networks that include VoLTE are not likely to be available in the US until late 2013 or 2014.

In Europe the first LTE networks are just being turned on, with the UK's first 4G network expected to be operating later this year.

---

[148] Griffith C., Bandwidth and quality of 4G hold up well, The Australian, News Limited, 11 September 2012, http://www.theaustralian.com.au/australian-it/exec-tech/bandwidth-and-quality-of-4g-hold-up-well/story-e6frgazf-1226471369013, Accessed online 12 September 2012.

[149] Brodkin J., World's first Voice over LTE launches in Korea; US stuck with 3G calls, ARS Technica, 8 August 2012, http://arstechnica.com/information-technology/2012/08/worlds-first-voice-over-lte-launches-in-korea-us-stuck-with-3g-calls/, Accessed online 12 September 2012.

[150] Voice over LTE, Radio-Electronics.com, http://www.radio-electronics.com/info/cellulartele-comms/lte-long-term-evolution/voice-over-lte-volte.php, Accessed online 12 September 2012.

[151] Sung-Mi K., SKT Launches World's First HD Voice over LTE, Korea IT Times, 7 August 2012, http://www.koreaittimes.com/story/22840/skt-launches-world%25E2%2580%2599s-first-hd-voice-over-lte, Accessed online 12 September 2012.

[152] Verizon Wireless, http://www.verizonwireless.com/, Accessed online 12 September 2012.

[153] Reed B., Verizon not launching voice over LTE anytime soon, Network World, 8 May 2012, http://www.networkworld.com/news/2012/050812-ctia-volte-259079.html, Accessed online 12 September 2012.

[154] AT&T, http://www.att.com/, Accessed online 12 September 2012.

Australian carriers are likely to follow their US counterparts and move to VoLTE in 2014 at the earliest.

The final two key requirements for a network that meets IMT-Advanced will be increasing data rates to 100 Mbps and seamless roaming mobility between networks including 4G, Wi-Fi and other possible future networks. It is not likely we will see solutions to all of the IMT-Advanced requirements before 2016 or 2017.

In Australia the technology that is likely to be deployed to meet the IMT-Advanced standard will be known as LTE-Advanced.[155]

5.8.6 International Roaming and 4G

Last year the Australian Competition and Consumer Commission (ACCC)[156] took Apple[157] to court[158] because the latter was selling a new product (the new iPad[159]) in Australia with the term "4G" in the product marketing.[160]

In fact, due to different implementations of 4G around the world the iPad operates with 4G LTE in the US and existing 3G networks in Australia. As a result of the litigation Apple changed the name of the product in Australia and removed all references to 4G.

The lesson to be learned is that "4G" can mean different things in different parts of the world. Your Australian 4G device may not work when you go overseas so, if you are travelling, be sure to contact your carrier before you go to see if your device will work at your destination.

5.8.7 4G Spectrum

4G networks are new and are still being rolled out around Australia. As well as having to pay for the infrastructure, carriers also have to purchase sections of the radio spectrum from the government for 4G.

---

[155]LTE Advanced, Wikipedia, http://en.wikipedia.org/wiki/LTE_Advanced, Accessed online 12 September 2012.

[156]Australian Competition and Consumer Commission, Australian Government, http://www.accc.gov.au/, Accessed online 12 September 2012.

[157]Apple, http://www.apple.com/, Accessed online 12 September 2012.

[158]ACCC to seek orders against Apple for alleged misleading iPad "4G" claims, Australian Consumer and Competition Commission, 27 March 2012, http://www.accc.gov.au/content/index.phtml/itemId/1042020/fromItemId/142, Accessed online 12 September 2012.

[159]Glance D., Apple's new iPad is no game-changer … but does that really matter?, The Conversation, 8 March 2012, https://theconversation.edu.au/apples-new-ipad-is-no-game-changer-but-does-that-really-matter-5767, Accessed online 12 September 2012.

[160]Glance D., Is Apple being ultrafast and loose with the truth?, The Conversation, 27 March 2012, https://theconversation.edu.au/is-apple-being-ultrafast-and-loose-with-the-truth-6097, Accessed online 12 September 2012.

Telstra and Optus use the 1,800 MHz band for their 4G networks, however Optus does not have enough 1,800 MHz spectrum available in regional areas.

Carriers are also keen to purchase spectrum at 700 MHz—a portion of the spectrum currently used by analog TV. The 700 MHz spectrum will be auctioned off by the Australian Communications and Media Authority[161] in 2013 under the government's digital dividend program.[162]

That said, Optus is concerned the 700 MHz spectrum won't be available for use until early 2015, giving Telstra a 3-year head-start on building a 4G network.

Optus is currently offering 4G modems in several cities on a limited number of plans[163] but is unlikely to be able to launch a proper national roll-out until it can get access to more spectrum[164] suitable for use in regional areas.

In 2011 Optus completed trials[165] of 4G LTE using the 700 MHz band in Bendigo and achieved download speeds of 70 Mbps.[166]

5.8.8   4G Costs

Telstra's current mobile plans[167] reflect the increase in mobile customer data usage year on year. Mobile data usage is expected to increase[168] still further with the faster 4G network.

Given the telcos will be keen to recoup the cost of purchasing more spectrum, we can expect 4G to be more expensive than 3G.

That said, Australian carriers typically offer plans and devices that are backwards-compatible so if a 4G network is not available the device will utilise the 3G network. This allows carriers to offer plans that are network independent and include costs to cover the 4G network rollout.

---

[161] Australian Communications and Media Authority, http://www.acma.gov.au/, Accessed online 12 September 2012.

[162] Digital dividend, Department of Broadband, Communications and the Digital Economy, Australian Government, http://www.dbcde.gov.au/radio/radiofrequency_spectrum/digital_dividend, Accessed online 12 September 2012.

[163] Optus Mobile, Optus, https://www.optus.com.au/shop/broadband/mobilebroadband/4g, Accessed online 12 September 2012.

[164] Battersby L., Optus 4G ready to take on Telstra, Fairfax Media, 5 September 2012, http://www.smh.com.au/business/optus-4g-ready-to-take-on-telstra-20120904-25cj8.html, Accessed online 12 September 2012.

[165] Australia's first 700 MHz call marks next step in LTE journey, Optus, 2011, http://www.optus.com.au/aboutoptus/About+Optus/Media+Centre/Media+Releases/2011/Australia%E2%80%99s+first+700+MHz+call+marks+next+step+in+LTE+journey, Accessed online 12 September 2012

[166] Hutchinson J., Optus calls for faster digital dividend rollout, ITNews, 16 March 2012, http://www.itnews.com.au/News/293998,optus-calls-for-faster-digital-dividend-rollout.aspx, Accessed online 12 September 2012.

[167] Telstra Mobile, https://onlineshop.telstra.com.au/, Accessed online 12 September 2012.

[168] Market Perspectives and Cisco Visual Networking Index, NBN Co, http://www.nbnco.com.au/assets/documents/k-m/market-perspectives-april-2012.pdf, Accessed online 12 September 2012.

While 4G networks have been in operation for several years elsewhere in the world, they're still in their infancy in Australia. One thing's for sure: you'll be hearing plenty more about 4G in the years to come.

Further Reading

- Australian 4G frequencies explained—Alex Kidman and Luke Hopewell, Gizmodo[169]
- Telstra's 4G isn't 4G—but it is the future—Alex Kidman, ABC Technology & Games[170]

5.9   International Roaming Charges Rip-Off: The ITU Gets Involved ...

20 September 2012

It's good news for customers, but there are limits to what the ITU can achieve. *Source*: rayand[171]

---

[169] Kidman A., Australian 4G Frequencies Explained, Gizmodo, 9 March 2012, http://www.gizmodo.com.au/2012/09/australian-4g-frequencies-explained-updated/, Accessed online 12 September 2012, new link http://www.gizmodo.com.au/2012/03/australian-4g-frequencies-explained/

[170] Kidman A., Telstra's 4G isn't 4G – but it is the future, Australian Broadcasting Corporation, 28 September 2011, http://www.abc.net.au/technology/articles/2011/09/28/3327530.htm, Accessed online 12 September 2012.

[171] Rayand, Flickr, http://www.flickr.com/photos/27478478@N00/3868086106, Accessed online 21 December 2012.

The International Telecommunications Union (ITU)[172] has entered the debate about excessive international roaming charges by recommending[173] measures that will improve consumer awareness and encourage operators to lower tariffs.

On September 14 in Geneva, ITU Secretary General Hamadoun I Touré said[174]:

> We recommend that governments and regulators explore ways to protect and empower consumers. Consumers need to be able to make their best choices among the array of options available to them in the rapidly evolving mobile marketplace.
>
> Carriers should make information on international mobile services clearer and more transparent, and it should be easier for consumers to choose a network abroad that offers the best value.
>
> In addition, alerts should be sent to consumers as they approach a certain cost limit for roaming, with a block placed on further usage unless authorised by the user.

The ITU is the United Nations[175] agency for information and communication technologies and is committed to connecting people from all over the world. It allocates global radio spectrum,[176] satellite orbits, develops the technical standards that ensure networks and technologies seamlessly interconnect, and acts to improve worldwide access to information and communication technologies.

But importantly, the ITU cannot compel telecommunications operators to lower international roaming costs. Nonetheless, by releasing the above recommendations the ITU is encouraging regional operators and regulators to enter into cooperative agreements that would include lowering wholesale tariffs for international roaming calls, SMS and data.

5.9.1   A Small Step Forward

In an earlier article on The Conversation,[177] I highlighted the excessive roaming charges between Australia and New Zealand as an example of the problem consumers faced when overseas.

---

[172] International Telecommunications Union, http://www.itu.int/, Accessed online 20 September 2012.

[173] D.98: Charging in international mobile roaming service, International Telecommunication Union, September 2012, http://www.itu.int/rec/T-REC-D.98-201209-P/en, Accessed online 20 September 2012.

[174] ITU acts to cut roaming charges, International Telecommunication Union, 14 September 2012, http://www.itu.int/net/pressoffice/press_releases/2012/57.aspx, Accessed online 20 September 2012.

[175] United Nations, http://www.un.org/en/, Accessed online 20 September 2012.

[176] Radio spectrum, Wikipedia, Accessed online 20 September 2012, Accessed online 20 September 2012.

[177] Gregory M.A., Are Australian international roaming charges the greatest rip-off in history?, The Conversation, 30 November 2011, https://theconversation.edu.au/are-australian-international-roaming-charges-the-greatest-rip-off-in-history-4340, Accessed online 20 September 2012.

More recently the federal communications minister Stephen Conroy stated the whole situation around mobile roaming was "frankly obscene"[178] and has started developing a regional agreement with New Zealand to reduce roaming charges across the Tasman.

Senator Conroy said on ABC News 24's Breakfast program[179] on August 24:

> We're announcing two things today: we're releasing a discussion paper which we've worked on for the last couple of years with the New Zealand government which is saying "we need to act now".
>
> We've done a study and what we found was, at the beginning of the study, the mark-up, the margin for international cost calls between here and New Zealand was 1,000 %. With the spotlight on, it's come down to 300 % but that is not good enough.
>
> I'm directing the Australian Communications and Media Authority[180] to put in place a standard which will see mobile phone companies notifying their customers when they're overseas of the cost of a call, the cost of sending a text, the cost of going online, and giving them the option to opt out.

Senator Conroy's announcement can now be seen to reflect the new ITU recommendations for regional agreements and actions to force operators to provide more information to customers about costs being incurred while overseas.

5.9.2 World Treaty

The first major agreement to tackle excessive international roaming charges was put in place in 2007 by the European Union (EU)[181] which legislated to curb international roaming charges among member states. The EU reduced roaming costs further[182] in July 2012 and indicated the process of roaming cost reduction would continue until costs were reduced to a minimum.

The rest of the world has yet to act but there is hope.

In December this year there will be a World Conference on International Telecommunications (WCIT-12)[183] in Dubai.

---

[178] Gregory M.A., Why Conroy needs to do more on roaming rip-offs, Technology Spectator, 29 August 2012, http://www.technologyspectator.com.au/why-conroy-needs-do-more-roaming-rip-offs, Accessed online 20 September 2012.

[179] Telcos ordered to end roaming 'rip-off', Australian Broadcasting Corporation, 24 August 2012, http://www.abc.net.au/news/2012-08-23/telcos-ordered-to-end-roaming-rip-off/4216862, Accessed online 20 September 2012.

[180] Australian Communications and Media Authority, http://www.acma.gov.au/, Accessed online 20 September 2012.

[181] European Commission roaming regulations, Wikipedia, http://en.wikipedia.org/wiki/European_Commission_roaming_regulations, Accessed online 20 September 2012.

[182] Essers L., EU roaming charges to be sharply capped starting in July, PCWorld Australia, 11 May 2012, http://www.pcworld.idg.com.au/article/424275/eu_roaming_charges_sharply_capped_starting_july/, Accessed online 20 September 2012.

[183] World Conference on International Telecommunications (WCIT-12), International Telecommunications Union, http://www.itu.int/en/wcit-12/Pages/default.aspx, Accessed online 20 September 2012.

The ITU has raised for discussion the possibility of including international roaming in the International Telecommunications Regulations (ITRs).[184] The outcome would be roaming price transparency, immediate access to price information, greater competition and prices that are based on the actual costs incurred by the operator when providing the roaming service.

5.9.3 Done Deal? No Way

The only way the EU countries were able to achieve regulation of the international roaming charges was to legislate and force local operators to lower costs. The EU left nothing to chance and prescribed the roaming charges that EU operators must adhere to for EU consumers who take their phones with them around the EU.

Apart from the successful EU legislation no other international agreement or treaty has been put in place.

International telecommunication operators are expected to argue against any inclusion of international roaming regulation in the ITRs at WCIT-12. This is hardly to be unexpected—excessive international roaming charges have become a river of gold.

If a miracle should occur (and the ITU is not known for miracles as its members include international telecommunication companies that typically vote against anything not to their advantage) and international roaming regulation *is* added to the ITRs in a meaningful way at WCIT-12 then it can be expected that international telecommunication companies may ignore that section of the ITRs or argue for an implementation delay that could stretch out to a decade or more.

5.9.4 The Way Forward

The EU legislation to reduce excessive international roaming charges has been successful and Australia must follow the EU lead.

Senator Conroy needs to wrap up an agreement with New Zealand this year. Australia and New Zealand should pass legislation before the end of this year to regulate international roaming charges across the Tasman.

Last month Ovum research director David Kennedy was reported in SmartCompany[185] as saying that the Association of South East Asian Nations

---

[184] International Telecommunication Regulations, International Telecommunications Union, http://www.itu.int/ITU-T/itr/, Accessed online 20 September 2012.

[185] Stafford P., Conroy calls for submissions on trans-Tasman roaming charges, but international agreements still years away, SmartCompany, 23 August 2012, http://www.smartcompany.com.au/telecommunications/051379-conroy-calls-for-submissions-on-trans-tasman-roaming-charges-but-international-agreements-still-years-away.html, Accessed online 20 September 2012.

(ASEAN)[186] has expressed an interest to create an agreement similar to that in the EU:

> That's at a much earlier stage than these negotiations, but if that were to come to pass, the next step would be combining the agreement with one between Australia and New Zealand.

An agreement with the US and EU to regulate international roaming charges is not likely in the foreseeable future. Why? The world's largest international telephone companies are located in the US and EU and for them international roaming charges remain a cash cow.

5.9.5 Will It Make a Difference?

The ITU action to highlight the international roaming problem is a positive step forward. But there are limits to what the ITU can achieve. Considerable effort is required by world governments to tackle excessive international roaming charges.

Senator Conroy can let our major international partners know of the Australian consumer's outrage and the need for urgent action. Senator Conroy should start by calling his counterparts in the US and Europe, discussing the problem and publicly identifying a timetable for a joint Australian, US and EU treaty.

For now you should take care when travelling overseas and ensure you turn international roaming off before you leave. Think about purchasing a pre-paid SIM or phone when you arrive at your destination and look for free Wi-Fi hotspots on your travels.

For more information on how to ensure you don't end up with bill shock after a holiday look at the international roaming guide[187] and tips to prevent data roaming from ruining your holiday[188] provided by the Australian Communications and Media Authority.[189]

Further Reading

- Are Australian international roaming charges the greatest rip-off in history?—Mark Gregory, The Conversation[190]

---

[186]Association of South East Asian Countries, http://www.aseansec.org/, Accessed online 20 September 2012.

[187]What is roaming, Australian Communications and Media Authority, http://www.acma.gov.au/WEB/STANDARD/pc=PC_1715, Accessed online 20 September 2012.

[188]Don't let data roaming ruin your holiday, Australian Communications and Media Authority, http://www.acma.gov.au/WEB/STANDARD/1001/pc=PC_410269, Accessed online 20 September 2012.

[189]Australian Communications and Media Authority, http://www.acma.gov.au/, Accessed online 20 September 2012.

[190]Gregory M.A., Are Australian international roaming charges the greatest rip-off in history?, The Conversation, 30 November 2011, https://theconversation.edu.au/are-australian-international-roaming-charges-the-greatest-rip-off-in-history-4340, Accessed online 20 September 2012.

5.10   How Safe Is Your Smartphone?

20 September 2012

Smartphones have been in the news a lot lately and not just because of the arrival of the new iPhone 5. Over the past couple of months stories have begun to surface on **data retention,**[191] **mobile roaming charges**[192] and **bill shock.**[193] The one thread that these stories all have in common is that they all revolve around the smartphone, which might be your best friend but could also do you harm.

5.10.1   The Best Spying Tool

Your smart phone is being used to spy on you. Everything from your voice, address book, photos, browsing history and any other personal details on the smart phone are being uploaded by either the phone manufacturer, operator or by one or most of the apps that you have loaded onto your phone.

The reasons that your personal data is being uploaded by one of the organisations that have found a way to get access to your smartphone vary. Your carrier collects information to ensure your phone can be restored if something goes wrong, and to comply with Australian cybercrime and other laws.

Other organisations collect your personal data so that they can sell it or use the data to impersonate you and carry out fraud or another crime. It is possible to get details on how to access e-commerce sites from your smartphone. With this information criminals can purchase goods and leave you with the bill.

Your smart phone provides a snapshot of who you are and what you do. Everything you do with your smartphone is of interest to data mining companies that ultimately sell snapshots of information gleaned from smart phones and apps to marketing companies.

US company, Flurry Analytics is an example of one of these data collection and mining organisations. It collects data from 1.4 billion app sessions per day from more than 600 million smart phones and tablets in the US.

---

[191]Gregory M.A., Why data retention laws won't work, Technology Spectator, 12 September 2012, http://www.technologyspectator.com.au/why-data-retention-laws-won-t-work, Accessed online 20 September 2012.

[192]Gregory M.A., Why Conroy needs to do more on roaming rip-offs, Technology Spectator, 29 August 2012, http://www.technologyspectator.com.au/why-conroy-needs-do-more-roaming-rip-offs, Accessed online 20 September 2012.

[193]Gregory M.A., The great Australian mobile rip-off, Technology Spectator, 13 July 2012, http://www.technologyspectator.com.au/industry/telecommunications/great-australian-mobile-rip, Accessed online 20 September 2012.

Worrying trends are now appearing where more and more companies are signing up app manufacturers who then provide information about what you're using for smartphone for. Some smartphone apps have been found to be accessing data on the smart phone for which the app has no reason to access.

5.10.2   Bill Shock

Smartphones cause bill shock for a couple of reasons including confusing plans, high excess data charges and the ongoing international roaming rip-off.

More recently, parents have been lending smartphones to children or alternatively buying them their own smartphone. More often than not, these children then proceed to purchase these so-called "free apps" from the app store. Most of which are games.

Many of the new smart phone game apps entice players to carry out "in-app purchases". Some of the apps use techniques that create anxiety or unfavourable game play unless in-app purchases are made.

For example, one of these apps is free to download and then allows in-app purchases of up to $100 with just two taps on the screen of the device.

Children are being **targeted by this phenomenon**[194] and advocacy groups are concerned that children are being targeted in the same way that adults are targeted by the gambling industry. It is possible that smart phone and tablet game apps are utilising practices developed over many years by the gambling industry to tap into an individual's competitiveness and introduce a pleasure-reward aspect to the game that causes some level of addiction.

Action is being taken in the US through a **class action against**[195] Apple over iTunes bill shock.

People who use iTunes need to be aware that if an iTunes purchase is made on the device then for the next 15 min purchases can be made without re-entering the iTunes account password. Hypothetically, if you make an iTunes purchase and then give your smart phone or table to a child, that child can download free game apps and make in-app purchases within the next 15 min without the need for the iTunes account password. Every time the child makes an in-app purchase the timer resets.

What is of concern is that restricting in-app purchases is turned off by default. This feature is one of several parental controls that must be turned on manually. To enable parental controls on an Apple device tap on settings > general > restrictions, and enter a passcode (this should be different to your iTunes account password). Many may not know that this parental control function exists.

---

[194] Smith S., Kids racking up huge bills on mobile games, Australian Broadcasting Corporation, 18 September 2012, http://www.abc.net.au/news/2012-09-17/kids-racking-up-huge-bills-on-mobile-games/4266632?section=business, Accessed online 20 September 2012.

[195] Associated Press, Apple sued over bills children rack up, boston.com, 20 April 2011, http://www.boston.com/business/technology/articles/2011/04/20/apple_sued_over_bills_children_rack_up/, Accessed online 20 September 2012.

5.10.3 What's Being Done?

The Australian Competition and Consumer Commission (ACCC) and the consumer group Australian Communications Consumer Action Network have voiced concerns about the ways that smart phones and tablets are being used by unscrupulous app providers to fleece users of smart phones and tablets and to steal personal information for on selling and financial gain.

There is a balance that must be achieved between consumer protection and the rights of the multi-national companies that make and sell smart devices to maximise profit for shareholders without exploiting their users. The Australian government will work with the ACCC to update consumer protection laws. But until they do, take heed, your smartphone and tablet are not benign devices. They have the potential to deal you some damage and must be closely managed, especially around children.

5.11 Hold Off on 4G for Now

27 September 2012

By now everyone has read about the benefits of 4G-enabled smartphones including the iPhone 5 and Samsung Galaxy S3 4G.

The **key change**[196] from 3G is the increased data connection speeds possible with 4G. Early adopters may achieve connection download speeds of more than 30 Mbps and upload speeds of more than 20 Mbps.

But before you jump head first into one of the telcos new 4G plans, consider what's happening in the US.

The US is further along in their 4G endeavours than Australia. Carriers offer 4G plans that range from 200 MB through to 20 GB per month.

A quick comparison shows that in the US customers should expect to get 2–3 GB per month data allowance for the same cost that Australians will pay for 200–250 MB. For the cost of the average Australian 4G per month data plans customers in the US can expect to get 16–20 GB per month.

What does this mean? Don't sign up for a 1 or 2 year 4G contract!

We should expect rapid change to Australian 4G plans and with each revision we should expect to see the included monthly data allowances increase significantly.

Any plan that includes less than 3 GB monthly data allowance is likely to be far too small for typical 4G smart phone usage. US carriers offering 12–16 GB per month are in the ball park for 4G.

Remember that 4G offers faster data speeds than ADSL2+ and most people have ADSL2+ data plans that include 20 GB or more per month. The difference is that

---

[196]Gregory M.A., Explainer: what is 4G?, The Conversation, 12 September 2012, http://theconversation.edu.au/explainer-what-is-4g-9448, Accessed online 27 September 2012.

ADSL2+ is only at home, whereas our smart phones go with us everywhere we go. It is logical that we would want to use the 4G smart phone more than our home ADSL2+ connections.

5.11.1   The Trap of Bill Shock

Low data allowances and increased speed has added yet another danger to Australia's 4G plans—it's increased the chances of being stuck by bill shock.

Keeping track of data usage is difficult and with the smartphone offering so many internet enabled features, it's easy for users fall into the trap of exceeding their monthly data allowance.

It is important to realise that with a 4G phone everyone should expect to use more data than they did with older 3G phones.

The Australian Communications and Media Authority (ACMA) and the Australian Consumer Network are **concerned**[197] that people using 4G phones will exceed data allowances and be faced with bill shock in coming months.

ACMA said: "users could use more data than they're used to and may experience bill shock as a result".

To complicate matters, a new voluntary industry code will commence on October 27 and under this code carriers will offer standard pricing information similar to the changes to pricing information that occurred in super markets so consumers could more easily compare product prices.

However, the introduction of the voluntary code will be slow and carriers will not be required to offer detailed information on consumer plans until 1 March 2013.

Despite this, some of the carriers have commenced providing customers with data usage warnings that were detailed in the new code.

A Telstra spokesman told **Fairfax**[198]: "Our post-paid mobile customers receive usage alerts when they reach 80 % and 100 % of their data allowance. iPhone and android customers can also access the Telstra 24×7 app which shows at a glance how much data they've used compared with their allowance."

Optus also told Fairfax: "that its customers received a text message when they've used 50, 85 and 100 % of their included value and data allowances. It also has the My Optus app which allows customers to check their use and recharge their credit."

---

[197] Polites H., 4G bill shock fears escalate after iPhone 5 launch, Technology Spectator, 26 September 2012, http://www.technologyspectator.com.au/4g-bill-shock-fears-escalate-after-iphone-5-launch, Accessed online 27 September 2012.

[198] Moses A., Faster, more addictive: a recipe for 4G bill shock, Fairfax Media, 25 September 2012, http://www.theage.com.au/digital-life/mobiles/faster-more-addictive-a-recipe-for-4g-bill-shock-20120925-26ie3.html, Accessed online 27 September 2012.

5.11.2   *Avoiding a 4G Sting*

The best way to avoid the sting is to not sign up to 4G at all. Not yet at least.

But if you must have the fastest mobile internet around, hunt around. Find a low cost handset provider and buy your handset before looking for a carrier. Discussion on where to purchase a handset can be found on **whirlpool.net.au**.[199]

Another approach is to wait until the Windows 8 phones hit the market later this year and the extra competition should force suppliers to reduce handset prices.

Where possible make sure you utilise free Wi-Fi hotspots and remember to turn your phone off when it is not in use. Unless you really need to, turn off all apps that utilise location information, as they will be constantly reporting your location and this means more data usage.

Also, download an app that will monitor and report your data usage and remember to keep track of what you're using your smartphone for so that you can identify activities that use too much data.

Australian customers should demand at every opportunity that the carriers offer more realistic plans. The low cost 4G plans should start with 3 GB included data per month and typical plans should offer 10 GB included data per month.

5.12   The Future of Smartphone Marketing

9 November 2012

The introduction of smartphones has been a catalyst for the innovative use of technology to bring business and customers closer together. With Australian start-ups competing on the international stage to make the most of the smartphone revolution, they certainly have what it takes to give their well-funded overseas rivals a run for their money.

5.12.1   *The Rise of Location-Based Advertising*

Location based advertising is one of the key avenues for connecting businesses with prospective customers, armed with their smartphones and on the lookout for bargains. The location based concept has been with us for many years, Google Maps was one of the most successful of the early entrants and is still a category leader that many of us rely upon for directions.

Google Maps provided an opportunity for business to register their location on the maps and in an associated searchable directory.

---

[199] Whirlpool, http://whirlpool.net.au/, Accessed online 27 September 2012.

Recently, Apple launched a map application with the introduction of iOS 6. Apple identified that Google Maps was an important application utilised regularly by nearly all smartphone users.

Apple decided to introduce a competing map product on Apple iOS products to increase revenue.

However, Google Maps is a benign application that relies upon a smartphone user opening the map application to find businesses.

It wasn't long before innovators identified that smartphone users wanted to be told about specials being offered by businesses and also to be told about specials being offered nearby.

Groupon[200] quickly entered this area by providing a platform for businesses to offer time limited specials directly to customers. Through Groupon a business can offer a special deal on a product or service and customers can sign on to the deal and get a coupon that can be displayed at the business when the customer goes to purchase the product or service.

Groupon also utilises social media to propagate deals and customers assist with this process by "sharing, liking and twittering" about a deal.

5.12.2 Australia's Answer to Groupon

A further innovation has been introduced by the Australian smartphone application **myPype**[201] which utilises the smartphone's internal GPS to identify the phones location and then to push product and service specials offered by businesses up to 25 km from the phone using on screen messages.

myPype fully utilises technology including on screen messages, real time location based advertisements, use of social media, directions to businesses offering specials and a more traditional fee structure for business where a flat fee is charged per month rather than the percentage of sales adopted by competitors.

The next big innovation will be the use of information collected about the habits of people that use applications like myPype and Groupon to identify products and services that closely match with their buying habits.

This is known as **"targeted marketing"**[202] and the data collected is called **"Big Data"**.[203]

Over time the information collected about the millions of people using smartphone applications to find and buy products and services will grow into a size that

[200]Groupon, http://www.groupon.com.au/, Accessed online 9 November 2012.

[201]MyPype, http://mypype.com.au/, Accessed online 9 November 2012.

[202]Target market, Wikipedia, http://en.wikipedia.org/wiki/Target_market, Accessed online 9 November 2012.

[203]Big data, Wikipedia, http://en.wikipedia.org/wiki/Big_data, Accessed online 9 November 2012.

is hard to imagine today. Data mining techniques are being developed today to provide companies with key information about their customers purchasing habits.

Smartphone users already see their phones as an important tool that provides access to work and entertainment capabilities. Australians have embraced the smartphone revolution.

5.12.3   But What About Privacy and Security?

Innovative companies like myPype are competing with international companies that have greater access to venture capital and will therefore be looking to earn revenue from every aspect of their business.

Already Australia has quite stringent privacy and security legislation by world standards, however, there are areas that need improvement.

The information captured by product and service marketing companies about their customers will become very valuable over time and there will be the temptation to sell this information.

The advent of 'Big Data' increases privacy and security concerns and has yet to be adequately addressed by the government.

While we wait for legislation to catch up, it is important to be aware of your rights and to check how your data will be used before signing up with a smartphone based marketing application.

We should expect more innovation by Australian companies and if myPype is an example of the innovation being introduced by Australian entrepreneurs then Australia should be satisfied to know that we're not being left behind in the smartphone revolution.

Chapter 6
Applications

Social media has become a driving force behind Internet growth and the companies behind the applications have become some of the largest technology companies in the world. Google, Facebook, Twitter and others enjoy market-share and the prestige of being best in their application category.

For Internet users security and privacy are a real concern as the corporations look to leverage customer information. The increasing use of automated target marketing systems demonstrates the value that can be found from customer information.

Competition between the big technology application corporations has increased and the race is on to provide customers with a single Internet location for their online needs.

Government has, at the same time, advocated greater customer security and privacy whilst quietly participating in and permitting the greatest collection of information about people, companies and organisations in history.

Concern is growing among privacy advocates about what the long term effects of the personal information gathered will be. If a person was being followed at all times of the day they would become concerned and may seek help from the police or the courts to prevent the intrusion into their private lives, but no such protection exists online.

6.1 Google+ Requires Real Name, or Else...

26 July 2011

A fresh storm has blown into Google's new Google+ service. The company has been suspending[1] accounts because they contravene Google's Community Standards[2]—ostensibly to stop fake or spam accounts being created.

---

[1] Blue, Violet, Google Plus Deleting Accounts En Masse: No Clear Answers, http://www.zdnet. com/blog/violetblue/google-plus-deleting-accounts-en-masse-no-clear-answers/567, Accessed online 1 July, 2013.

[2] Google+ Profile Names Policy, https://support.google.com/plus/answer/1228271, Accessed online 1 July, 2013.

M.A. Gregory and D. Glance, *Security and the Networked Society*,
DOI 10.1007/978-3-319-02390-8_6, © Springer International Publishing Switzerland 2013

This means any name Google has determined is not the person's real name has resulted in an automatic suspension.

The suspension has also, in some cases, removed access to all other Google services, including email.

Exactly how many users have been affected by this action is not known but it is enough to have mobilised Google+ users to voice their displeasure.

One of the more high-profile suspensions was of Limor Fried,[3] also known as Ladyada or Adafruit Industries.

Fried was recently featured on the front cover of Wired magazine with an article in that issue about DIY electronics.

In addition to selling electronic kits, her business's website[4] features videos which show how to "hack" electronics to do everything from creating a remote that switches off any television, to creating glowing cufflinks from Apple Mac power buttons.

After a brief outcry, Fried's account was reactivated with no explanation. Others, it seems, have not been so fortunate.

6.1.1 Say My Name

The issue of enforcing "real names" is a contentious one on the internet. In South Korea, for example, there's a policy requiring all users of sites that allow online comments to be identity-checked.

Google, along with many other internet companies, bowed to this policy on its sites, including YouTube, and blocked people from uploading videos unless they had verified their names.

Facebook also courted controversy recently when the company closed the account of a Chinese commentator called Michael Anti and told him he needed to use the name on his Chinese Government ID card.

The irony of this is that, allegedly, Mark Zuckerberg's dog[5] has a Facebook account under an alias (yes, this is the real case of "on the internet, nobody knows you are a dog").

6.1.2 Mixed Identity

Like all things, the argument is not simple. Governments and services will argue that using a Real Name policy will help cut down spam, internet trolling[6] and general bad behaviour.

---

[3]Doctorow, Cory, Limor Fried on the cover of Wired, http://boingboing.net/2011/03/16/limor-fried-on-the-c.html, Accessed online 1 July, 2013.

[4]Adafruit Industries, Unique & fun DIY electronics and kits, http://www.adafruit.com/, Accessed online 1 July, 2013.

[5]About Beast, https://www.facebook.com/beast.the.dog?sk=info, Accessed online 1 July, 2013.

[6]Troll (Internet), http://en.wikipedia.org/wiki/Troll_%28Internet, Accessed online 1 July, 2013.

But there are many legitimate reasons for using a pseudonym or "non-de-plume" that are mixed in with people's profession, identity and safety.

The issue quickly escalates to one of suppression of free speech and, as such, makes its enforcement one more example of companies trying to create an internet that is, in essence, simply commercial.

Another difficulty that Google, in particular, faces with the implementation of this policy is that it does so using a computer program that uses an algorithm to determine what is real and what is fake.

Google's reliance on automating these decisions is bound to lead to indiscriminate mistakes. Given this can then lead to an automatic suspension of your email account with no warning, the consequences are severe.

This is especially the case with the UN's recent declaration that internet access is a human right.[7]

Companies such as Google and Facebook face an ongoing public relations juggling act between achieving their commercial goals and providing a service supporting a major social infrastructure.

At the end of the day, it will always be about business, so discussions about Google's apocryphal mantra—"Don't be evil"—are moot.

6.2   The Name Game: Is Google+ Building a Cathedral or a Bazaar?

1 August 2011

The phrase "The Cathedral and the Bazaar" was coined by American computer programmer Eric S. Raymond[8] to distinguish two different approaches to the development of software.

The Bazaar was likened[9] to the slightly chaotic but powerful collective approach behind the development of open source[10] software.

The Cathedral represented the traditional, closed, corporate approach to software development.

In many ways, what we are seeing with Google's birthing pains[11] of its new social network of Google+[12] is the tension between Google wanting Google+ to be the Cathedral and a vocal section that would be happier to see it operate more as the Bazaar.

---

[7]Kravets, David, U.N. Report Declares Internet Access a Human Right, http://www.wired.com/threatlevel/2011/06/internet-a-human-right/, Accessed online 1 July, 2013.

[8]Eric S. Raymond, http://rationalwiki.org/wiki/Eric_S._Raymond, Accessed online 1 July, 2013.

[9]S. Raymond, Eric The Cathedral and the Bazaar, http://catb.org/~esr/writings/homesteading/, Accessed online 1 July, 2013.

[10]What is open source? http://www.webopedia.com/TERM/O/open_source.html, Accessed online 1 July, 2013.

[11]Glance, David, Google+ requires real name, or else … http://theconversation.com/google-requires-real-name-or-else-2493, Accessed online 1 July, 2013.

[12]Share and discover, all across Google, http://www.google.com/+/learnmore/, Accessed online 1 July, 2013.

Advocates of the Bazaar view of social networks would allow pseudonyms for example. They see their identity determined by how people know them in a particular environment or medium.

If all of your friends know you as your avatar from Second Life,[13] then that is the name you would use on a social network.

Likewise you may have an identity as a game character, blogger, actor, musician ... the list goes on.

Google sees Google+ very much in terms of the Cathedral model of social networks:

- It is ordered and controlled. Google knows who you are, where you are, what you are doing, and with whom at any point in time.
- It is a safe environment for businesses to communicate with their customers.
- Business people who want to interact with other business people can do so in a cloistered environment, protected from the social network anarchy of the general public, or a drunken nephew.

Google has unwittingly highlighted the tensions between these two approaches to social networks with its recent mass suspension[14] of accounts.

The anti-Googlers have started a campaign that has been tagged the "nymwars[15]" after the central issue of Google banning of the use of pseudonyms for Google+ accounts.

An open letter[16] to Google from GrrlScientist (whose Google+ account was suspended), published in the Guardian lays out possible legal issues under US, UK, Australian and European Union law of Google's terms and conditions.

Other campaigners, such as Australian Kirrily "Skud" Robert,[17] a former Google employee and ex-Google+ user (her account is still under suspension), have been talking to the press with articles appearing in mainstream media and sites such as Wired.

The number of campaigners is long, from Violet Blue,[18] the blogger who broke the story of the suspensions on ZDNET,[19] to the Geek Feminists[20] and the Electronic Frontier Foundation.[21]

---

[13] Second Life, Your World. Your Imagination, http://secondlife.com/, Accessed online 1 July, 2013.

[14] Taylor, Josh, Google+'s account suspension compromise, http://www.zdnet.com/googles-account-suspension-compromise-1339319258/, Accessed online 1 July, 2013.

[15] Twitter Trends, http://www.twitter-trends.de/, Accessed online 1 July, 2013.

[16] GrrlScientist, Google+ and pseudonymity: An open letter to Google, http://www.guardian.co.uk/science/punctuated-equilibrium/2011/jul/28/google-open-letter-google, Accessed online 1 July, 2013.

[17] Infotropism - Alex "Skud" Bayley's blog, http://infotrope.net/, Accessed online 1 July, 2013.

[18] Lack of hyperlink.

[19] Blue, Violet, Google Plus Deleting Accounts En Masse: No Clear Answers, http://www.zdnet.com/blog/violetblue/google-plus-deleting-accounts-en-masse-no-clear-answers/567, Accessed online 1 July, 2013.

[20] Link no longer available, http://geekfeminism.wikia.com/wiki/Who_is_harmed_by_a_%22Real_Names%22_policy%25, Accessed online 1 July, 2013.

[21] York, Jillian C, A Case for Pseudonyms, https://www.eff.org/deeplinks/2011/07/case-pseudonyms, Accessed online 1 July, 2013.

The latter two campaigners have listed all of the groups of people who will be potentially harmed by Google's policies.

So how has Google responded?

Well, allegedly by gagging any employees from discussing or advocating the issue.[22] Other than a communication[23] from Google VP Brad Horowitz on Google+ on the matter of pseudonyms, the company has been quiet.

For Google, the stakes are high. The company derives much of its revenue from advertising.[24] To grow this market, it needs to stop people spending time in closed environments, such as social networks where Google has no direct access (such as Facebook).

Google is also trying to compete against business-oriented social networks such as LinkedIn.[25]

LinkedIn is the epitome of the Cathedral model of social networks. The user interface is clean and absent of frills. People use LinkedIn to network with business contacts for the purpose of recruitment, soliciting and providing services and, to a lesser extent, sharing business-related information.

Google is hoping it can compete with LinkedIn by allowing for the separation of personal from business on Google+ through the use of its Circles feature.

To a certain extent, this is like the approach being adopted by BranchOut[26] and BeKnown[27] on Facebook. Both of these services are concerned with using Facebook contacts for job networking purposes.

They do this by running as applications within Facebook and they cordon off information and activities in their environments from the rest of your Facebook activities (and vice versa).

Google is always striving for cleaner and more comprehensive information about consumers, their preferences, connections and habits. The company collects all of its information using computer software executing sophisticated algorithms.

The more you control the way the information is presented and, more importantly, the links between that information (i.e. people's identifiers), the easier that information is to collect.

The last thing Google wants is the messy, anarchic environment of the Bazaar, where people can be anonymous, have multiple identities, interact with anyone they please, and remain unobserved.

---

[22] Skud, Google is gagging user advocates, http://infotrope.net/2011/07/29/google-is-gagging-employees/, Accessed online 1 July, 2013.

[23] Horowitz, Bradley, Robert Scoble - Google+, https://plus.google.com/+BradleyHorowitz/posts/VJoZMS8zVqU, Accessed online 1 July, 2013.

[24] Google's Business Model, http://internetbusinessmodels.org/googlebusinessmodel/, Accessed online 1 July, 2013.

[25] LinkedIn - World's Largest Professional Network, http://www.linkedin.com/, Accessed online 1 July, 2013.

[26] BranchOut - Career Networking on Facebook, http://branchout.com/, Accessed online 1 July, 2013.

[27] Link no longer available, http://www.beknown.com/landing, Accessed online 1 July, 2013.

6.3   LinkedIn, Twittered Out: The Business and Pleasure of Social Media

14 September 2011

This week, the American National Labour Review Board[28] ruled to reinstate five workers fired for complaining about a co-worker[29] on Facebook.

The board decided writing about work on Facebook was equivalent to talking about work in person—it was not inherently different just because it was via a social network.

This, of course, raises several issues.

6.3.1   Work/Life Balance

The lines between our work and personal lives are becoming blurred. With smartphones now pervasive, surveys have shown[30] 72 % of Americans are likely to be checking work email in the evenings, on weekends and on holidays.

Illness doesn't stop people from checking in (42 % of Americans will still check their email when off sick), nor does being in the bedroom, bathroom, or pretty much anywhere else.[31]

When not checking email, we're spending an increasing amount of time playing games, an activity the majority of women in one survey[32] reportedly preferred to sex.

But by far the most dominant activity online is the use of social networks.[33]

Some 65 % of adult American internet users[34] say they use a social networking site—Facebook being the most popular.

But this work/pleasure deal doesn't cut both ways.

---

[28] National Labour Relations Board, http://www.nlrb.gov/, Accessed on 14 September 2011.

[29] Link no longer goes to specified page, http://www.forbes.com/sites/mobiledia/2011/09/08/employees-cant-be-fired-for-facebook-complaints-judge-says/, Accessed on 14 September 2011.

[30] Link no longer goes to specified page, http://blog.xobni.com/2010/09/02/xobni-survey-70-of-us-email-outside-of-biz-hours-50-of-americans-email-on-vacation/, Accessed on 14 September 2011.

[31] Checking Email in the Bathroom? You're Far From Alone, http://mashable.com/2008/07/30/email-addiction/, Accessed on 14 September 2011.

[32] Women play computer games just as much as men - and they prefer gaming to sex, survey reveals, http://www.dailymail.co.uk/femail/article-2014821/Women-play-games-just-men--prefer-gaming-sex-survey-reveals.html, Accessed on 14 September 2011.

[33] What Americans Do Online: Social Media And Games Dominate Activity, http://blog.nielsen.com/nielsenwire/online_mobile/what-americans-do-online-social-media-and-games-dominate-activity/, Accessed on 14 September 2011.

[34] 65 % of online adults use social networking sites, http://pewinternet.org/Reports/2011/Social-Networking-Sites.aspx, Accessed on 14 September 2011.

In a world-wide survey, web security company ClearSwift[35] found 56 % of employers blocked access to social networks. Some 68 % monitored employee internet access.

Managers cited concerns about security and time-wasting as reasons for these restrictions.

The relationship between employers and their workers' use of social media outside work is an even greater challenge to the rights and responsibilities on both sides.

When is a "friend" not a friend?

Social networks have blurred distinctions between different types of friends, acquaintances, work colleagues, work contacts and organisations.

Sites such as Diaspora,[36] Google+[37] and even Facebook have a means of separating out these contacts into different groups.

But whether these mechanisms are used is unclear[38]—the default is sharing with the general public (in the style of Twitter) or with a specific group of friends, as is more common with Facebook.

Even when such mechanisms are in place, the difficulty of separating what we share with whom has been one of the problem areas with social networks.

We're also in a situation in which adding someone we've met once as a friend on Facebook will generally result in that person "friending" you in turn.

6.3.2 Business-Oriented Social Media

It was for these reasons that LinkedIn,[39] launched in 2003, sought to establish a social platform aimed specifically at work-related networking.

With approximately 100 million users, LinkedIn seeks to address a different aspect of social networking aimed at job opportunities.

For those who don't know, it offers a way for individuals to maintain an online CV coupled with recommendations from other LinkedIn users.

Separating the professional from personal allows users to manage their public profile with work contacts and colleagues, but the evidence is that, beyond the online CV aspect of LinkedIn, there's limited use of the network for social purposes.[40]

---

[35] Link no longer goes to specified page, https://info.clearswift.com/express/clients/clearhq/papers/Clearswift_report_WorkLifeWeb_2011.pdf, Accessed on 14 September 2011.

[36] Diaspora, https://diasp.org/, Accessed on 14 September 2011.

[37] Google+, https://accounts.google.com/ServiceLogin?service=oz&continue=https://plus.google.com/?gpsrc%3Dgplp0&hl=en-GB, Accessed on 14 September 2011.

[38] When social networks cross boundaries: a case study of workplace use of facebook and linkedin, http://dl.acm.org/citation.cfm?id=1531689, Accessed on 14 September 2011.

[39] LinkedIn, http://www.linkedin.com/, Accessed on 14 September 2011.

[40] When social networks cross boundaries: a case study of workplace use of facebook and linkedin, http://dl.acm.org/citation.cfm?id=1531689, Accessed on 14 September 2011.

In a survey conducted by market research company Lab42,[41] only 35 % of respondents logged in to LinkedIn every day. Job searching and hiring were the largest reason for doing so, followed by industry networking.

6.3.3 Newbies

Two other services—BranchOut[42] and BeKnown[43]—are now available as Facebook applications.

BranchOut started as a service to allow users to see where friends and friends-of-friends worked—the idea being: if you want a job at a particular company, you're only a couple of degrees of separation away from a contact who could help you.

BeKnown, launched in June, is another professional networking service, owned by the jobs site Monster.[44]

Whether BranchOut and BeKnown will pose any threat to LinkedIn is unclear—it may be that they end up serving different markets or demographics.

Judging by the slightly social gaming style of awarding merit badges for filling in profiles, making recommendations and so on (in the style of location-based networking site Foursquare[45]), BranchOut is obviously looking for a younger audience.

6.3.4 Socialising Your Work

A growing reason for using social networks is specifically to market or "socialise" your work, opinions or ideas.

In academia, for example, there is increasing competition for funding, visibility of publications and future students and collaborations.

Academics are increasingly turning to social media and Twitter in particular to publicise themselves and their work. There are guidelines being offered[46] as to optimal ways of doing this, as well as stories of research announcements going "viral" after mentions on Twitter.[47]

---

[41] The Linkedin Profile, http://blog.lab42.com/the-linkedin-profile, Accessed on 14 September 2011.

[42] BranchOut, http://branchout.com/, Accessed on 14 September 2011.

[43] BeKnown, http://www.beknown.com/landing, Accessed on 14 September 2011.

[44] Monster, http://www.monster.com/geo/siteselection, Accessed on 14 September 2011.

[45] Foursquare, https://foursquare.com/, Accessed on 14 September 2011.

[46] Top twitter tips for academics, http://www.scribd.com/doc/60642119/Top-Twitter-Tips-for-Academics, Accessed on 14 September 2011.

[47] Going viral: Using social media to publicise academic research, http://www.guardian.co.uk/higher-education-network/blog/2011/apr/11/communications-marketing-management-admin-and-services, Accessed on 14 September 2011.

Socialising work is not just about self-promotion—it also builds contacts and collaborations, and allows people to receive input from a global, diverse network.

Social networks are redefining interactions in our private, public and work lives. Comparisons to the way things work "in real life" are becoming harder to justify, as relationships and forms of communication carried out on social networks evolve into something new.

As our private lives increasingly intertwine with life online, our work lives will follow, whether organisations or governments like it or not.

6.4   #OccupyWallStreet…? I'll Be There, but on Twitter

19 September 2011

On Saturday, hundreds of protestors congregated in the Wall Street area of New York at the start of a protest dubbed #OccupyWallStreet.

The aim? To "flood into lower Manhattan, set up tents, kitchens, peaceful barricades and occupy Wall Street for a few months".

"Once there, we shall incessantly repeat our one simple demand until Barack Obama capitulates."

And the demand? Well …

Initially organised by Vancouver-based media activists Adbusters,[48] the campaign has set out to establish a protest presence in Wall Street for an extended period.

Adbusters was joined in August[49] by hacktivist group Anonymous[50] in rallying supporters for the start of the action and spreading the word through websites and social media.

Although the aim was to replicate[51] the protests of Egypt's Tahrir Square, it's clear NYC is not Cairo.

What was similar, and possibly of more importance though, was the activism that accompanied the protest being played out on social media.

---

[48] OCCUPY WALL STREET: DAY 480, http://www.adbusters.org/campaigns/occupywallstreet, Accessed on 19 September 2011.

[49] Anonymous Joins #OCCUPYWALLSTREET, http://www.adbusters.org/blogs/adbusters-blog/anonymous-joins-occupywallstreet.html, Accessed on 19 September 2011.

[50] Are Anonymous hackers really on trial, or is FBI payback misdirected? http://theconversation.edu.au/are-anonymous-hackers-really-on-trial-or-is-fbi-payback-misdirected-3205, Accessed on 19 September 2011.

[51] Campaigns, http://www.adbusters.org/campaigns, Accessed on 19 September 2011.

6.4.1   September 17: Wall Street

As protestors started congregating in Manhattan, police closed Wall Street and, in a slightly comic way, moved to protect the bronze icon of Wall Street, the Charging Bull.[52]

Fears for the Charging Bull of Wall Street appear to have been unfounded. Twitter

The bull was never in any danger: the protest began, and continued, peacefully with speeches, chanting, yoga and tai chi.

Probably the most serious problem the protesters faced, and reflective of the media-supported nature of the event, was when police allegedly switched off the power in one location restricting protestors from recharging laptops, phones and cameras.

Although not reaching the initial target of 20,000 protestors, it's estimated between 1,000 and 2,000 protesters attended on the first day with fewer staying through the night, camping in Lower Manhattan's Zuccotti Park.[53]

Meanwhile, online …

---

[52] Charging Bull, http://en.wikipedia.org/wiki/Charging_Bull, Accessed on 19 September 2011.

[53] Zuccotti Park, http://en.wikipedia.org/wiki/Zuccotti_Park, Accessed on 19 September 2011.

6.4.2   September 17: The Internet

Tens of thousands of people started following and interacting with the protestors via Twitter, live streaming, chat rooms and blogs. Organisers were coordinating the protest via the Twitter hashtags #OccupyWallStreet[54] and #Sep17.[55]

Concerned that Twitter was effectively blocking the tag #OccupyWallStreet from appearing in the top trending list, they switched to #TakeWallStreet,[56] which then went into the top trending list.

Protestors and supporters monitored police radio[57] and provided live streaming coverage[58] of events not only in NY but at other parallel protests in Spain, Greece and other locations.

By 9:30 p.m. EST, #OccupyWallStreet had nearly 71,000 tweets with 18,000 contributors and approximately 105 million views.

Chat rooms set up by Anonymous and livestream were buzzing with global dialogue. The #hashtag distribution of #OccupyWallStreet is a global and virtual phenomenon as much as a physical protest in NY City.

A global snapshot of #OccupyWallStreet activity on Twitter, September 18 http://trendsmap. com/

---

[54] Get instant updates on #occupywallstreet, https://twitter.com/search/%23occupywallstreet, Accessed on 19 September 2011.

[55] Get instant updates on #Sep17, https://twitter.com/search/%23Sep17, Accessed on 19 September 2011.

[56] Get instant updates on #TakeWallStreet, https://twitter.com/search/%23TakeWallStreet, Accessed on 19 September 2011.

[57] NYPD Manhattan Precincts 1–23 Live Audio Feed, http://www.radioreference.com/apps/audio/?action=wp&feedId=8905, Accessed on 19 September 2011.

[58] Globalrevolution, http://www.livestream.com/globalrevolution, Accessed on 19 September 2011.

6.4.3 *Mainstream Media's Silence*

This activity on global social media was not matched by traditional media. Apart from a few exceptions, such outlets have so far chosen not to cover the protest.

Following events as they unfolded on Twitter, it appeared there were only three mainstream journalists in Wall Street: a crew from Al Jazeera's The Stream,[59] Julianne Pepitone[60] of CNN Money and Colin Moynihan of the New York Times Cityroom Blog.[61]

Articles that have started appearing on sites such as MSNBC[62] appear to be taken from secondary sources.

The issue of lack of coverage by mainstream media has continued to dominate on Twitter, even though the reasons for this may be more prosaic than conspiratorial. They include:

1. The protest happened on a weekend, when it's conceivable mainstream media hadn't paid journalists to cover it, or had staff on standby pending "developments".
2. The protest was peaceful and, so far, non-disruptive, which lessens the newsworthiness.
3. The organisers had not done the journalists' jobs for them by sending copy/press releases to them.

---

[59] The Stream, http://stream.aljazeera.com/, Accessed on 19 September 2011.

[60] Hundreds of protesters descend to 'Occupy Wall Street', http://money.cnn.com/2011/09/17/technology/occupy_wall_street/, Accessed on 19 September 2011.

[61] Wall Street Protest Begins, With Demonstrators Blocked, http://cityroom.blogs.nytimes.com/2011/09/17/wall-street-protest-begins-with-demonstrators-blocked/, Accessed on 19 September 2011.

[62] Protesters invade NYC Financial District, http://today.msnbc.msn.com/id/44564317/ns/us_news-life/#.UOzQIHd_U24, Accessed on 19 September 2011.

Protestors aim to turn mixed messages into "one demand", *Source*: **David Shankbone**[63]

The question has been raised[64] as to why there should have been so much interest by organisers and others on Twitter about the involvement of mainstream media.

Perhaps there's a misguided belief that coverage in this way somehow legitimises the protest and would cause politicians, corporate executives or the public at large to take more notice.

Tied in with the above is an assumption that if the mainstream media does cover the occupation, they will do so in a way that reflects the protest accurately and in a positive light.

But this type of coverage is more likely to come, as it is increasingly does for events such as these, from bloggers, independent media sites and social media—principally Twitter.

Concerns over lack of mainstream media coverage may yet have a secondary effect, which is to prompt online attacks. Potential targets as part of #OccupyWallStreet were being discussed for just this reason.

---

[63] D. Shankbone, Flickr, http://www.flickr.com/photos/shankbone/6251296811/sizes/z/in/phones-tream/, Accessed online 19 September 2011.

[64] Link no longer goes to specified page, http://www.presstorm.com/2011/09/occupy-wall-street-day-one/, Accessed on 19 September 2011.

Has the peaceful nature of the protest been a turn-off for mainstream media? *Source:* **Michael Fleshman**[65]

6.4.4 What Are We Fighting for?

A further aspect of the protest that prevents realistic comparisons with those in the Middle East is that the aims, although legitimate, are much more amorphous.

The Adbusters' website claims there is one demand[66] to be agreed on by the end of the process and made to the US Government.

This demand has been variously translated into:

- reducing the undue influence of corporate lobby groups on Washington
- regulating the finance industry
- addressing the disproportionate ownership of wealth in the hands of the few
- punishing banks and corporations for their part in the Global Financial Crisis.

Finding people in the US who are happy with the political and economic situation is becoming increasingly difficult; finding consensus on what to do about it even more so.

We will need to wait and see whether the protestors of #OccupyWallStreet achieve a consensus over the coming days and weeks.

If they do, it won't just be a product of those that are physically in Wall Street but the tens of thousands participating online.

---

[65]M. Fleshman, Flickr, http://www.flickr.com/photos/fleshmanpix/6840361918/sizes/c/in/photo-stream/, Accessed online 19 September 2011.

[66]Hey President Obama … Get ready for our one demand! http://www.adbusters.org/blogs/adbusters-blog/hey-president-obama-our-one-demand.html, Accessed on 19 September 2011.

In the words of American rapper **Lupe Fiasco**, who wrote **a poem for the occasion**:

> Hey Moneyman poor Moneyman you should slip out the back. Cuz the forces of greed are under attack. No bombs or bullets or rocks or guns. Just hashtags and voices at the tops of their lungs!

6.5   Facebook Has Changed: Will You Still Feel the Same?

23 September 2011

The world is currently embroiled in on- and offline discussions about changes that are affecting the lives of millions.

The subject is not climate change, the global financial crisis, political upheaval or the latest natural disaster. It's the new-look Facebook.

The modifications so far have been relatively minor, but even more radical changes[67] have been announced today at Facebook's developer conference, "f8"[68] in San Francisco.

Facebook recently made changes to the layout of its live feed, removing users' ability[69] to sort the feed by Most Recent posts and Top News. Status updates and other items have been moved into a real-time ticker to the right of the live feed.

But the big changes—as outlined below—are yet to come.

6.5.1   Timeline

The soon-to-be launched "Timeline" will allow users to sort information on a timeline and to post historic information and photos about your life.

The timeline will be opt-in initially but eventually it's expected to replace a user's current profile page.

It's not clear how this will interact with other's timelines but one can imagine being able to visualise our social interactions, or changes to our social graphs over time.

Of course, this provides even more information of value to companies wanting to understand its consumers, how they interact and how those interactions have changed over time.

Facebook Gestures

The limitation of just being able to "Like"[70] something has always been a bit of an anomaly on Facebook.

---

[67] The Facebook Blog, https://blog.facebook.com/, Accessed on 23 September 2011.

[68] f8, https://www.facebook.com/f8, Accessed on 23 September 2011.

[69] Facebook makes layout changes, http://www.telegraph.co.uk/technology/facebook/7164912/Facebook-makes-layout-changes.html, Accessed on 23 September 2011.

[70] re Facebook and Google+ limiting your opinions? http://theconversation.edu.au/are-facebook-and-google-limiting-your-opinions-2375, Accessed on 23 September 2011.

It's hard sometimes to say you like something when what you are really just trying to do is indicate you found it interesting.

Facebook Gestures[71] will bring us other verbs in a button form that will allow users to share what they are reading, watching, cooking, etc—basically any verb can be turned into a button—yes, even possibly a "Dislike" one.

6.5.2 Sharing in Real-Time

The new ticker will allow you to click a link and share an experience with a friend in real-time. So you'll be able to watch a movie, listen to a song or read a news article at the same time as any of your friends.

6.5.3 Why Change?

The changes have been introduced for a number of reasons.

First, there is the threat of competition from Google, which opened its social media offering, Google+,[72] to the general public earlier this week after an invitation-only trial.

Facebook has rushed to counter features that were heralded as "game changers" [73] in Google+, such as Google's Circles.

Despite a much-hyped start, interest in Google+ has waned,[74] but it's clear Google will persist with Google+ because it simply has no choice in the matter.

Its search and advertising business is increasingly threatened by Facebook's hold[75] on the public's online attention and, through this, access to advertisers.

This brings us to the second reason for Facebook's changes. Put bluntly, the company needs to more effectively monetise users' social interactions.

Of course, none of the social media companies will put things quite like that. Mark Zuckerberg has said that Facebook is helping people to "tell the story of their life".[76]

---

[71] How Facebook Will Fix Its Like Button Problem, http://mashable.com/2011/09/22/facebook-gestures/, Accessed on 23 September 2011.

[72] Google+, https://accounts.google.com/ServiceLogin?service=oz&continue=https://plus.google.com/?gpsrc%3Dgpplp0&hl=en-GB, Accessed on 23 September 2011.

[73] 10 reasons why Google+ will never be Facebook, http://theconversation.edu.au/10-reasons-why-google-will-never-be-facebook-2073, Accessed on 23 September 2011.

[74] Google+ Witnesses Traffic Growth Decline: Aberration or Early Sign of Fatigue? http://www.ibtimes.com/google-witnesses-traffic-growth-decline-aberration-or-early-sign-fatigue-841647, Accessed on 23 September 2011.

[75] LinkedIn, Twittered out – the business and pleasure of social media, http://theconversation.edu.au/linkedin-twittered-out-the-business-and-pleasure-of-social-media-3307, Accessed on 23 September 2011.

[76] Facebook as Tastemaker, http://www.nytimes.com/2011/09/23/technology/facebook-makes-a-push-to-be-a-media-hub.html?_r=2&smid=tw-nytimestech&seid=auto, Accessed on 23 September 2011.

6.5.4   Will It Work?

Facebook's popularity and penetration has continued unabated despite criticisms from some of its users and surveys suggesting a degree of user dissatisfaction.[77]

Facebook has now passed the 800 million users mark[78] and has had 500 million users visitors to its site on 1 day.

In a survey, the Pew Internet and American Life Project has shown[79] a number of social and wellbeing benefits that Facebook brings to its users.

It's clear we have moved firmly into a new phase of interaction—both with others and the internet in general.

Companies and advertisers are scrambling to take advantage of these changes—much to Facebook's and its (potential) shareholder's delight.

Whatever your first impressions, the world has changed, and it won't be going back to the old days (that is, yesterday).

6.6   Google Has Lost Its Buzz and Missed the Wave, but Is There a Plus?

21 October 2011

It's hard to know what to think about Google these days. Financially, the company is booming, but its reputation has suffered following the lukewarm reception for Google+, and an embarrassing outburst by an employee.

Recently, Google exceeded analysts' expectations with its third Quarter 2011 financial results.[80]

Revenues have increased 33 % over the same period last year and, for the first time, Google has reported it is on track to earn $2.5 billion[81] for the year from mobile ad revenue.

---

[77] User satisfaction study shows Facebook vulnerable to Google+, http://www.infoworld.com/d/applications/user-satisfaction-study-facebook-vulnerable-google-386, Accessed on 23 September 2011.

[78] Facebook Changes Again: Everything You Need To Know, http://mashable.com/2011/09/22/facebook-changes-roundup/, Accessed on 23 September 2011.

[79] Social networking sites and our lives, http://www.pewinternet.org/Reports/2011/Technology-and-social-networks/Summary.aspx, Accessed on 23 September 2011.

[80] Google Announces Third Quarter 2011 Financial Results, http://investor.google.com/earnings/2011/Q3_google_earnings.html, Accessed on 21 October 2011.

[81] Google Posts Strong Earnings and Exceeds Expectations, http://www.nytimes.com/2011/10/14/technology/google-reports-strong-earnings-topping-expectations.html?_r=3&, Accessed on 21 October 2011.

6.6.1 A One-Trick Pony?

Nearly all of Google's revenue is from advertising and most of what Google does is as a vehicle for that. This has led some analysts to ask whether[82] Google is a "one-trick pony", albeit one with a pretty lucrative trick. The problem with this, of course, is that if this is all Google can do, at some point growth is going to taper off, with nothing in the pipeline to be the "next big thing".

It is not that Google hasn't tried. Since February 2001 it has purchased[83] about 100 companies. Some of these, like Android,[84] YouTube,[85] DoubleClick[86] and a few others have gone on to be successful.

The great proportion of the other companies, however, have either been subsumed into Google or shut down. Slide,[87] a social application company (responsible for the application Photovine[88]), was purchased by Google in 2010 for $200 million and shut down this year.[89]

And then there are the products Google launched itself, especially the predecessors of Google+,[90] like Google Wave and Buzz, which were closed down last week.[91] Ostensibly, killing off a large range of products is Google house-cleaning and focusing the company on fewer things: presumably those that will earn revenue.

Bradley Horowitz, Google's Vice President of Product Management has said[92] Google is "throwing fewer things against the wall". He argues the company is maturing and "acting more responsibly"; more so to the shareholders, presumably, than the customers.

---

[82] What If Google Is Just a One-Trick Pony? http://www.businessweek.com/technology/content/jan2011/tc20110128_084457.htm, Accessed on 21 October 2011.

[83] List of mergers and acquisitions by Google, http://en.wikipedia.org/wiki/List_of_acquisitions_by_Google, Accessed on 21 October 2011.

[84] Link no longer goes to specified page, http://en.wikipedia.org/wiki/Android_%28operating_system, Accessed on 21 October 2011.

[85] YouTube, http://www.youtube.com/, Accessed on 21 October 2011.

[86] DoubleClick, http://www.google.com/doubleclick/, Accessed on 21 October 2011.

[87] No longer available, http://www.slide.com/, Accessed on 21 October 2011.

[88] Link no longer goes to specified page, http://photovine.com/, Accessed on 21 October 2011.

[89] Link no longer goes to specified page, http://www.scribbal.com/2011/08/google-shuts-down-slide-founder-max-levchin-leaves-company/, Accessed on 21 October 2011.

[90] Google+, https://plus.google.com/up/?continue=https://plus.google.com/&type=st, Accessed on 21 October 2011.

[91] Link no longer goes to specified page, http://www.scribbal.com/2011/10/google-kills-off-buzz-to-focus-on-google/, Accessed on 21 October 2011.

[92] Google's Bradley Horowitz: 'we're throwing fewer things against the wall', http://www.engadget.com/2011/10/20/googles-bradley-horowitz-were-throwing-fewer-things-against/, Accessed on 21 October 2011.

6.6.2   The Rise and Fall of Google+

Part of the newly-focused Google strategy[93] is that Google+ "is a social layer built into all of its products".

It appears, however, that even though Google executives are talking the product up, things may not be going as well as claimed.

Despite an initial frenzy of interest about Google+, the social networking site hit problems early on with its very widely publicised exclusion of a range of users in the so-called "nymwars [94]". These came about due to Google's insistence its users use their real name on the site.

It didn't help that Google's chairman went on to explain[95] Google's aim was to create an online ID service where everything a user did could be linked to a clearly identified person.

This was followed by analysts' reports[96] that after Google+ was opened to the general public there was a spike of interest followed by an almost equal decline. And there it has sat.

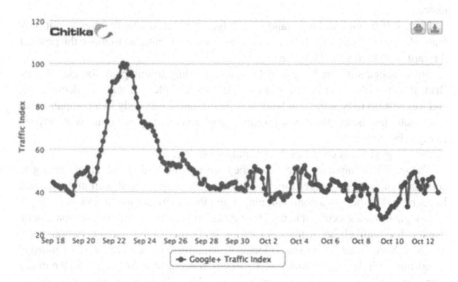

Chitika

---

[93] Sergey Brin & Vic Gundotra on Pseudonyms, Apps Users & the Google Plus Platform, http://readwrite.com/2011/10/19/sergey_brin_vic_gundotra_on_pseudonyms_apps_users, Accessed on 21 October 2011.

[94] Google+ requires real name, or else… http://theconversation.edu.au/google-requires-real-name-or-else-2493, Accessed on 21 October 2011.

[95] Google Confirms It Aims to Own Your Online ID, http://www.businessweek.com/technology/google-confirms-it-aims-to-own-your-online-id-08292011.html, Accessed on 21 October 2011.

[96] Report: Google+ Traffic Fails to Rebound After Dip, http://insights.chitika.com/2011/report-google-traffic-fails-to-rebound-after-dip/, Accessed on 21 October 2011.

CEO Larry Page has said Google+ now has 40 million users who have uploaded 3.4 billion photos. So it seems that people are using Google+ more for sharing things privately than publicly.

6.6.3 A Complete Failure?

Probably most damning for Google, however, was a 4,000-word rant accidentally posted[97] by Google employee Steve Yegge. It branded Google+ a "complete failure".

Yegge eventually took the post down after he realised he had made it public on Google+ (a reflection in itself, perhaps, about the usability of the product).

Yegge's criticism was mainly focused on Google's lack of vision. He wrote, "Google+ is a knee-jerk reaction, a study in short-term thinking". He compared Google's approach to products to Amazon's, where he previously worked, and to the approach Facebook had taken with its platform. There was nothing compellingly new in Google+, he argued, to make people leave Facebook and use Google+ instead.

Indeed, Facebook did not stand still. It has introduced new features to not only match features (like Circles) that Google+ introduced, but also to move the product forward with their new Timeline feature.

Steve Yegge still has his job at Google according to company founder Sergey Brin. But it is clear the honchos at Google were not pleased with the declaration, and Yegge's options at the company will be limited. Everybody in a company may appreciate that the emperor is not wearing any clothes; they just don't want anyone to say it in public.

Anything you can do, I can do not quite so well…

The trouble companies face when they are not innovating but simply trying to copy or match their competitors is that it is very hard to do it well and succeed. In each market there is a dominant player and then there are the "wannabes".

Google has not succeeded in matching Amazon in its control of the electronic book market. It is unlikely to displace Facebook or Twitter in the social network space. The New York Times has reported Google is planning to launch a music store aimed at competing with Apple and Amazon. To do this, it needs to strike deals with the music companies to license their music, and so far they have shown a reluctance to do so.

The launch of the new version and the Samsung Google Nexus, a phone positioned to rival the Apple iPhone 4S, has passed by largely unnoticed. The events don't generate the same level of excitement as an iPhone announcement and mainly appeal to a technical audience.

It is not likely that Google is going to disappear any time soon. Their dominance in search and online advertising will continue to bring in staggering revenues.

But if you are looking for a company that will change the world, it will probably not be Google.

---

[97]Link no longer goes to specified page, http://webhostdir.com/news/ShowItem.aspx?ID=90819, Accessed on 21 October 2011.

6.7 The Internet of Things: This Is Where We're Going

24 October 2011

In one vision of the future, every "thing" is connected to the internet. This "Internet of Things[98]" will bring about revolutionary change in how we interact with our environment and, more importantly, how we live our lives.

The idea of everything being connected to the internet is not new, but it's increasingly becoming a reality. The Internet of Things[99] came into being in 2008 when the number of things connected to the internet was greater than the number of people who were connected.

The technical utopians have portrayed the Internet of Things as a good thing that will bring untold benefits. They are supported by all the companies that stand to benefit by the increasing connectedness of everything.

Universal connectivity, sensors and computers that are able to collect, analyse and act on this data will bring about improvements in health, food production.[100] In a roundabout way, it might even alleviate poverty.[101] Even our efforts to battle global warming would benefit from the Internet of Things.

On the other side are the sceptics who warn of the dangers[102] inherent in not only having an ever growing Internet of Things, but our increasing reliance on it.

The problems range from the difficulties in actually scaling the internet to be capable of supporting the vast number of things, how these things (and the internet itself) are powered, through to issues of security, privacy and safety.

6.7.1 How Many Things Are Connected?

Today, there are nine billion devices connected[103] to the internet. By 2020, this will have increased to 24 billion[104] although some estimates[105] place the number at 100 billion.

---

[98] Internet of Things, http://en.wikipedia.org/wiki/Internet_of_Things, Accessed on 24 October 2011.

[99] Link no longer goes to specified page, http://www.cisco.com/web/about/ac79/docs/innov/IoT_IBSG_0411FINAL.pdf, Accessed on 24 October 2011.

[100] Link no longer goes to specified page, http://www.iteuropa.com/news/features/cows-under-cloud, Accessed on 24 October 2011.

[101] Link no longer goes to specified page, http://www.cisco.com/web/about/ac79/docs/innov/IoT_IBSG_0411FINAL.pdf, Accessed on 24 October 2011.

[102] The internet of hype http://www.economist.com/blogs/schumpeter/2010/12/internet_things, Accessed on 24 October 2011.

[103] Internet of things will have 24 billion devices by 2020, http://gigaom.com/cloud/internet-of-things-will-have-24-billion-devices-by-2020/, Accessed on 24 October 2011.

[104] Cellular devices to hit 24 billion by 2020, http://gigaom.com/2011/10/11/cellular-devices-to-hit-24-billion-by-2020/, Accessed on 24 October 2011.

[105] Link no longer goes to specified page, http://www.casaleggio.it/pubblicazioni/Focus_internet_of_things_v1.81 %20-%20eng.pdf, Accessed on 24 October 2011.

The parallel change is that the human-generated data being transported on the internet will be dwarfed by the data being generated by machines.

In fact, much of this communication will be between machines. Again, Cisco estimates[106] that by the end of this year, 20 typical households could generate more traffic than the traffic of the entire internet in 2008.

6.7.2 What Are We Connecting?

The Internet of Things is not just about devices that are directly connected to the internet. Sensors and identifiers such as RFID (radio frequency identification) tags[107] also provide data through an intermediary such as a mobile phone, RFID reader, or internet-connected base station.

This means an RFID-tagged cereal box may be considered as one of the "things" on the internet. Theoretically, the RFID would have been used in conjunction with other sensors to record the full life-history of that particular box of cereal, from the time it was manufactured to how it was transported and how long it took for it to be empty.

Sparked,[108] a company in the Netherlands, has developed[109] a sensor that measures a cow's vital signs as well as movement and interactions with other cows. The sensor will transmit approximately 200 MB of data per cow every year to allow farmers to monitor the health and wellbeing of their herds.

Sensors in the home and in cars are becoming ubiquitous. A modern car may have as many as 200 sensors,[110] measuring everything from engine performance to tyre pressures. The data are being collected and analysed by on-board computers connected to the car's internal network.

These data can now be communicated to the internet and made available to not only the driver of the car but also to companies that own or manage it on the driver's behalf. The sensor data can be used to detect problems but also to give statistics on the use of the car.

Tied in with real-time artificial intelligence, the car's network could be providing the driver with feedback and advice, and interacting with the internet for route information, for example.

---

[106]Ciscoinfographic, http://allthingsd.com/20110714/cisco-reminds-us-once-again-how-big-the-internet-is-and-how-big-its-getting/ciscoinfographic/, Accessed on 24 October 2011.

[107]Radio-frequency identification, http://en.wikipedia.org/wiki/Radio-frequency_identification, Accessed on 24 October 2011.

[108]Why Sparked? http://www.sparked.nl/Pages/default.aspx, Accessed on 24 October 2011.

[109]Link no longer goes to specified page, http://www.iteuropa.com/news/features/cows-under-cloud, Accessed on 24 October 2011.

[110]Automotive technology - The connected car, http://www.economist.com/node/13725743, Accessed on 24 October 2011.

6.7.3   Health-Related Sensors

Cars and houses are not the only things being wired up with sensors. There are numerous devices that monitor blood pressure, heart rate, levels of hormones and blood components and the like.

Sensors are now being connected directly to the internet or to a smart phone and stored in the Cloud[111] for monitoring and analysis. Again, the estimates are that there will be about 400 million wearable wireless sensors by 2014.[112]

6.7.4   And the Catch?

Everybody who has experienced that moment when a computer or phone has defeated all your attempts to do something basic such as connecting to a wireless network. At times like these, it's hard to imagine a technology-driven utopian world in which billions of devices are all communicating seamlessly and controlling everything around us to improve our lives.

But it really isn't as simple as that. The recent major outage of the BlackBerry Messaging Network[113] serves as a reminder that something as relatively simple as delivering messages from one phone to another, over a network that is supposed to be robust and fault-tolerant, can still be difficult to get right.

NetGear's Connected Lifestyle Survey[114] has recently shown that in Australia, there are 18 million internet-enabled devices that are not connected. These devices include TVs, games consoles, music and media players.

It's not clear from the report, though, if they are not connected because of the technical difficulty in connecting them or simply because the owners didn't know or care about the benefits of doing so. Clearly the growth and sustainability of the Internet of Things will not be able to rely on the ordinary consumer for connectivity and maintenance.

A recent blog on The Economist[115] highlights issues with the infrastructure, privacy and the danger of a catastrophic failure in an Internet of Things world.

---

[111] What cloud computing really means, http://www.infoworld.com/d/cloud-computing/what-cloud-computing-really-means-031, Accessed on 24 October 2011.

[112] Wearable Wireless Sensor Market To Grow By 400 Million Devices, http://www.fiercehealthcare.com/press-releases/wearable-wireless-sensor-market-grow-400-million-devices, Accessed on 24 October 2011.

[113] WRAPUP 2-Contrite BlackBerry co-CEOs go into damage-control, http://uk.reuters.com/article/2011/10/13/blackberry-idUKN1E79C0LF20111013?feedType=RSS, Accessed on 24 October 2011.

[114] It's time we connected at home, http://www.technologyspectator.com.au/industry/media/its-time-we-connected-home, Accessed on 24 October 2011.

[115] The internet of hype http://www.economist.com/blogs/schumpeter/2010/12/internet_things, Accessed on 24 October 2011.

Perhaps the most pressing of concerns Schumpeter raises is that of who will end up owning and controlling the data from the Internet of Things.

We are rapidly proceeding to a point where the range of data being collected can literally be used to reconstruct a person's life. The privacy issues brought about by the Internet of Things will make concerns about our interactions on social media giants such as Facebook seem trivial by comparison.

The recent furore over the German Government's use of spyware to watch its citizens[116] is also a harbinger of the amount of information that can be obtained by controlling connectedness to the internet.

The Internet of Things can ultimately be used for the benefit or detriment of individuals and society as a whole. Although business will argue a whole raft of benefits that include increasing efficiency, safety and health, these need to be balanced by safeguards and controls.

The ethics of mass connectivity have yet to be developed.

6.8 #QantasLuxury: A Qantas Social Media Disaster in Pyjamas

23 November 2011

By now, most people will have heard of the social media disaster which even provided its own hashtag: #QantasLuxury. Ironically, this was everything but a luxury for Qantas.

What it did illustrate was a marketing department that was totally out of touch with what the company was doing[117] and what it really needs to do to overcome the PR disaster that was the grounding[118] of the Qantas fleet on October 29.

So, how did the story unfold?

At 9:00 a.m. on the yesterday morning, the "social media team" at Qantas, as part of an ongoing "social media campaign", released details of a competition on Twitter:

---

[116]Ein spy: is the German government using a trojan to watch its citizens? http://theconversation. edu.au/ein-spy-is-the-german-government-using-a-trojan-to-watch-its-citizens-3765, Accessed on 24 October 2011.

[117]How might Qantas rebuild relations with its workforce? http://theconversation.edu.au/how-might-qantas-rebuild-relations-with-its-workforce-4264, Accessed on 23 November 2011.

[118]Qantas grounds entire fleet, http://www.abc.net.au/news/2011-10-29/qantas-locking-out-staff/3608250, Accessed on 23 November 2011.

QantasAirways Qantas Airways
To enter tell us 'What is your dream luxury inflight experience? (Be creative!) Answer must include #QantasLuxury.TCs qantas.com.au/travel/airline...
3 hours ago

QantasAirways Qantas Airways
Ever wanted to experience Qantas First Class luxury? You could win a First Class gift pack feat. a luxury amenity kit and our famous QF PJs.
3 hours ago

Twitter

They had run campaigns like this before. The prize? Well, as you can see from the photo at the top of this article, hardly something that would launch a Twitter frenzy of positive sentiment. The most notable part of the prize were the pyjamas ...

What they got—instead of a few tweets of marketing fodder—was a deluge of sometimes caustic, but at best sarcastic, vitriol reflecting more on the ongoing labour relations battles with the unions and the grounding of the fleet than the quality of the service.

Another interesting observation is that once a Twitter trend starts, it is self-feeding: supporting tweets appear that are self-referential, about the trend itself.

lehmo23   9 hours
#virginluxury **getting an exit row**
#tigerluxury **getting a biscuit**
#qantasluxury **getting a pilot, a plane, engineers and baggage handlers**
6+ recent retweets

ndrew10   11 hours
RT @kiwi_kali: #qantasluxury **Somewhere in Qantas HQ a middle aged manager is yelling at a Gen Y social media "expert" to make it stop. / LOL**
7+ recent retweets

rgcooke   12 hours
Can't wait to see the Air Crash Investigations episode on the #qantasluxury **hashtag disaster.**
6+ recent retweets

Twitter

The negative commentary took an even bigger dive when a parody of Downfall[119]—a film depicting the last days of Adolf Hitler—was posted on YouTube, as seen below.

The problem for Qantas was that the parody was very well written and pretty much summed up the sentiment of the public, and probably of CEO Alan Joyce himself.

An analysis of approximately 2,000 tweets gives a graphic illustration of the way the Twitter trend maintained the sentiment over the course of the day.

Wordle

Fortunately for Qantas, as the east coast of Australia went to bed the tweets died down. It will be interesting to see if this changes today (Wednesday) but the sentiment has been vented.

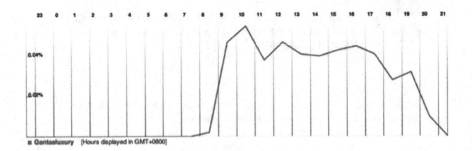

Trendistic

---

[119]Downfall, http://www.imdb.com/title/tt0363163/, Accessed on 23 November 2011.

On the positive side, Qantas has now received some fairly unambiguous market data about how the public feels (and it was free). It seems clear the Qantas "social media team" are astoundingly amateurish and probably reflects the low priority that Qantas puts on this.

A statement that Qantas had recently hired social media staff to monitor social media for sentiment about Qantas was denied on Twitter.

As Hitler says on the QantasLuxury Downfall parody: "With any luck someone will post a new funny cat video", otherwise he will "ground the whole internet".

6.9 The Future of News: Crowdsourced and Connected

29 November 2011

To paraphrase Mark Twain, reports of the death of newspapers are somewhat exaggerated. But traditional media is experiencing the "perfect storm" of declining circulations, collapsing advertising revenues and seismic changes in the way news is produced and consumed.

This is forcing change on an industry that has to-date largely resisted it.

Globally, changes in news production and consumption are not happening uniformly. Newspaper circulation declined by nine million worldwide in 2010[120] according to the World Press Trends report published by the World Association of Newspapers and News Publishers.[121]

Newspapers are still read by 2.3 billion people compared to 1.9 billion who read their news online.

The impact of the circulation fall has been greatest in the US with an 11 % overall decline—compared to an increase of 7 % in the Asia Pacific region.

At the same time, newspaper advertising revenues continue to nosedive, the biggest decline again happening in the US.[122]

The net result of declining revenue has seen the closure of newspapers[123] and the permanent move from paper to online for others. Even for those newspapers still in business, the fall in income has seen widespread layoffs of staff[124] and expectations

---

[120]Global circulation falls as readers become 'promiscuous', http://www.journalism.co.uk/news/global-circulation-falls-as-readers-become-promiscuous-/s2/a546340/, Accessed on 29 November 2011.

[121]Link no longer goes to specified page, http://www.wan-press.org/worldpresstrends/home.php, Accessed on 29 November 2011.

[122]Washington Post: the latest example of print ad plunge, http://blogs.reuters.com/mediafile/2011/11/04/washington-post-the-latest-example-of-print-ad-plunge/, Accessed on 29 November 2011.

[123]Google Now Bigger than U.S. Print Media Industry, http://newspaperdeathwatch.com/, Accessed on 29 November 2011.

[124]Link no longer goes to specified page, http://newspaperlayoffs.com/, Accessed on 29 November 2011.

of increased productivity from those who remain—the archetypical "doing more with less[125]"…and less.

Migration online for some news organisations has accompanied changes in the way the public consume the news.[126] The Pew Research Center's Project for Excellence in Journalism report showed that 46 % of Americans currently get news from 4 to 6 media platforms per day and 37 % contribute to news creation by commenting and sharing. Only 7 % get their news from a single media platform.

Daily news consumption patterns[127] have changed with the iPad being used in the morning and evening and mobile phones being used constantly throughout the day.

In all of this, the debate on what should happen next has raged. This is mainly because there's no single obvious solution, and what you consider to be the most important problem depends on your perspective. For the CEO and shareholder, the primary focus has been to try and reverse the fall of revenue, often through slash and burn.

For editors, journalists and the customers, the problem has been that the nature of news and the relationship between the producers and consumers has fundamentally changed. News is no longer produced for a passive audience to consume. As mentioned previously, 37 % of internet users[128] have contributed to the creation of news, commented on it or shared it with others. Information sourced from social media, blogs and video sites often makes its way into reporting.

The issue with revenue can't be tackled without first adapting news organisations to these changes.

John Paton, CEO of the Journal Register Company has declared[129] that traditional journalism is dead. He sees that the "crowd knows more than we do and the crowd can do what we do". Once you reduce the cost of production of news to next to nothing, then everyone can produce "news" and can disseminate that news through social media, video and blogs.

Even investigative journalism is open to being crowdsourced for both funding—through sites such as Spot.us[130]—and for collecting data and reporting.[131]

---

[125]The Wire - It's a Bad Time for Newspapers, http://www.youtube.com/watch?v=gKM34ijnhzI, Accessed on 29 November 2011.

[126]Key Findings, http://stateofthemedia.org/2011/overview-2/key-findings/, Accessed on 29 November 2011.

[127]Link no longer goes to specified page, http://futureofjournalism.com.au/wp-content/uploads/2011/10/AU-IG-111016-02.jpg, Accessed on 29 November 2011.

[128]How internet and cell phone users have turned news into a social experience, http://www.journalism.org/analysis_report/understanding_participatory_news_consumer, Accessed on 29 November 2011.

[129]Another Tough Step, http://jxpaton.wordpress.com/, Accessed on 29 November 2011.

[130]Spot.us, http://www.spot.us/, Accessed on 29 November 2011.

[131]Crowdsourcing investigative journalism: a case study (part 1), http://onlinejournalismblog.com/2011/11/08/crowdsourcing-investigative-journalism-a-case-study-part-1/, Accessed on 29 November 2011.

The crowd is also blogging, along with expert analysis and opinion. Companies, think tanks, and academics are producing timely, informed and expert content, often at a speed and depth most news organisations find difficult to match.

Companies such as the Huffington Post[132] have tried to aggregate some of this content with contributions from more than 9,000 bloggers—some of whom are now suing the company[133] for what they allege is a lack of financial compensation—in addition to content from regular staff. Sites such as the Daily Kos[134] are also collections of contributed blog posts with a political leaning.

John Paxton is not the only CEO of traditional media organisations to recognise things have changed. News companies such as the Guardian,[135] Al Jazeera[136] and the New York Times[137] have adapted their own businesses to extend regular reports with blogs, video, Twitter and Facebook feeds, comment and community input.

The Guardian recently started an experiment where it has made public its newslists,[138] the articles and events that journalists are covering and working on. They also have a blog site, commentisfree[139] where community writers can contribute blog articles.

The New York Times and Al Jazeera have moved in a similar direction with equivalent features. All of the news organisations have allowed journalists and editors to interact with their readers and others on social media.

The New York Times has been declared[140] the "most social" of companies in the US—however, two relatively unknown tech companies, intuit[141] and juniper,[142] were second and third, so this should probably be taken with a grain of salt.

Al Jazeera is probably the leader[143] in its use of technology and social media to report, interact and incorporate content with and from the public.

---

[132] The Huffington Post, http://www.huffingtonpost.com/, Accessed on 29 November 2011.

[133] Bloggers sue Arianna Huffington after 'being treated like slaves', http://www.telegraph.co.uk/technology/8448234/Bloggers-sue-Arianna-Huffington-after-being-treated-like-slaves.html, Accessed on 29 November 2011.

[134] Daily Kos, http://www.dailykos.com/, Accessed on 29 November 2011.

[135] The Guardian, http://www.guardian.co.uk/, Accessed on 29 November 2011.

[136] Al Jazeera, http://www.aljazeera.com/, Accessed on 29 November 2011.

[137] The New York Times, http://www.nytimes.com/, Accessed on 29 November 2011.

[138] The Guardian is opening up its newslists so you can help us make news, http://www.guardian.co.uk/media/2011/oct/09/the-guardian-newslists-opening-up, Accessed on 29 November 2011.

[139] Comment is free, http://www.guardian.co.uk/commentisfree/uk-edition, Accessed on 29 November 2011.

[140] NYTimes, TV stations among 'most social' companies, http://lostremote.com/nytimes-tv-stations-among-most-social-companies_b20508, Accessed on 29 November 2011.

[141] Intuit: Going Beyond Innovation, http://about.intuit.com/, Accessed on 29 November 2011.

[142] Juniper, http://www.juniper.net/us/en/, Accessed on 29 November 2011.

[143] Covering Protest and Revolution: Lessons from Al Jazeera's Mobile and Citizen Media, http://www.mobileactive.org/covering-protest-and-revolution-lessons-al-jazeera-innovation-and-mobile-citizen-media, Accessed on 29 November 2011.

The organisation has used Audioboo[144] to record, upload and share audio content. It utilises live blogs to report on rapidly changing events such as the Egyptian protests.[145]

It uses Flickr[146] to share images and Scribble Live[147] to write, edit and share collaborative content. Al Jazeera is also very active on Twitter, using feedback to determine what to report and to help shape stories that are breaking.

Al Jazeera has adapted to working with citizen journalists. Ultimately, the entire organisation is working in this way, a key differentiator between organisations that will succeed in the digital world and those that will fail.

Other organisations are taking a different approach to collaboration between the public and professional journalists. This so-called "pro-am" (professional-amateur) process involves professional editors assisting public contributors to submit content to a set standard or quality.

This is the approach taken by The Conversation[148]—a site for which academics write articles in their area of expertise which are then polished by professional editors. Earlier attempts to effectively do this, such as "Assignment Zero[149]", a collaboration between Wired Magazine[150] and NewAssignment.net[151] did not succeed, mainly because of a lack of supporting technology and poor organisation.

NewAssignment.net is collaborating with the Huffington Post on OffTheBus.net[152] which will provide citizen journalist coverage of the US 2012 election campaign.

Clay Shirky,[153] author and academic at New York University, has discussed the transformation[154] news organisations are going through as a revolution where—like any revolution, perhaps—we don't know what the end result will be.

We can guess the production of news has irrevocably changed from being institution-based to a hybrid of institution/crowd. We don't know the business models that will support this and we can guess about the organisations that are most likely to succeed and fail.

We can also guess there is no reason that the quality of news reporting both from an immediacy aspect through to in-depth coverage should change—if anything, there is reason to believe it will improve.

---

[144] Audioboo - Because sound is social. http://audioboo.fm/, Accessed on 29 November 2011.

[145] Live blog 30/1 - Egypt protests, http://blogs.aljazeera.com/blog/middle-east/live-blog-301-egypt-protests, Accessed on 29 November 2011.

[146] Flickr, http://www.flickr.com/, Accessed on 29 November 2011.

[147] Scribble Live, http://www.scribblelive.com/, Accessed on 29 November 2011.

[148] The Conversation, http://theconversation.edu.au/, Accessed on 29 November 2011.

[149] Did Assignment Zero Fail? A Look Back, and Lessons Learned, http://www.wired.com/techbiz/media/news/2007/07/assignment_zero_final?currentPage=2, Accessed on 29 November 2011.

[150] Wired, http://www.wired.com/, Accessed on 29 November 2011.

[151] NewAssignment.net, http://newassignment.net/, Accessed on 29 November 2011.

[152] OffTheBus 2012, http://www.huffingtonpost.com/news/offthebus, Accessed on 29 November 2011.

[153] Clay Shirky, http://www.shirky.com/, Accessed on 29 November 2011.

[154] Why We Need the New News Environment to be Chaotic, http://www.shirky.com/weblog/2011/07/we-need-the-new-news-environment-to-be-chaotic/, Accessed on 29 November 2011.

6.10   Google Search Just Got Way More Personal … and That's a Problem

16 January 2012

In what has been labelled[155] a "bad day for the internet", Google last week[156] changed its search engine to include personalised results from Google+.

The introduction of Google Search plus Your World[157] has led some commentators to claim[158] the search giant has "changed the way search works", in favouring posts[159] from Google+ over relevancy.

But it's possible to argue that you can't break what has already been broken for some time.

In his book[160] The Filter Bubble, internet activist Eli Pariser[161] wrote about the increasingly personalised view of the world that search engines present. He noted that people may be struggling to access information because Google and others have made a decision about what an individual wants to see.

Of course, from Google's perspective, the more personalised the search, the more personalised and targeted the accompanying advertisements can be. And the more targeted the advertising, the more money Google is likely to make.

When you search for something on Google, the results depend on more than 200 factors[162] (or signals, as they are known within Google). The main signals affecting search are the country you are in and whether you are logged in to a Google product such as Gmail and/or Google+. Being logged in to a Google product then brings your search history[163] into play.

To illustrate the dramatic effect location has on search results, I conducted a simple experiment. Using a clean browser (with no page history, cookies or other existing data) and not logged into Google, I searched for the term "Human Rights".

---

[155] Link no longer goes to specified page, https://twitter.com/#!/amac/statuses/156811166738427906, Accessed on 16 January 2012.

[156] Search, plus Your World, http://googleblog.blogspot.com.au/2012/01/search-plus-your-world.html, Accessed on 16 January 2012.

[157] Search, plus Your World, http://www.google.com/insidesearch/features/plus/index.html Accessed on 16 January 2012.

[158] Google Just Made Bing the Best Search Engine, http://gizmodo.com/5875571/google-just-made-bing-the-best-search-engine, Accessed on 16 January 2012.

[159] Real-Life Examples Of How Google's "Search Plus" Pushes Google+ Over Relevancy, http://searchengineland.com/examples-google-search-plus-drive-facebook-twitter-crazy-107554, Accessed on 16 January 2012.

[160] The Filter Bubble: What the Internet Is Hiding from You, http://www.amazon.com/Filter-Bubble-What-Internet-Hiding/dp/1594203008/ref=pd_sim_b_1, Accessed on 16 January 2012.

[161] Eli Pariser: Beware online "filter bubbles", http://www.ted.com/talks/eli_pariser_beware_online_filter_bubbles.html, Accessed on 16 January 2012.

[162] Exclusive: How Google's Algorithm Rules the Web, http://www.wired.com/magazine/2010/02/ff_google_algorithm/all/1, Accessed on 16 January 2012.

[163] Google Accounts & Web History, http://www.google.com/goodtoknow/data-on-google/web-history/, Accessed on 16 January 2012.

Using virtual private networking (VPN)[164] software, I was able to conduct the search with Google thinking I was in Australia, and then in the US. Of the ten results returned on the first page, only three were the same. Even the news items from international news organisations (that is, not from the US) were different.

(Bear in mind that the default setting on Google is to search the entire web and there is an option to restrict the search to Australian sites only.)

Somewhat bizarrely, the ABC's page on human rights[165] was returned high in the list of search results. I hadn't asked Google specifically for information on human rights in Australia—something I could have done easily by adding "Australian" to the search term. The decision to display human rights information from an Australian site was made for me.

Google is not alone in this—search engines such as Bing return similar results in Australia.

To be fair to Google, creating a good search algorithm is very difficult. And when Google started in 1998, its algorithms were the best of any search engine at the time for returning relevant results. But in 2009, Google embarked[166] on an ongoing quest to personalise search results.

With the advent of Google+[167] last year, searches started including posts from Google+ and search results were influenced by the people you were following. The idea was[168] that relevance was going to be increasingly dictated by our likes and dislikes and through our social connections (or "social graph"[169]). In this way, Google assumes we are mostly looking for what our friends, colleagues and people we follow like and dislike.

According to Google,[170] people also want to use search to find information that is directly about themselves (known as "vanity searching[171]"). The example given[172] by Google Fellow and software engineer Amit Singhal[173] is when that he searches for his dog's name, he gets results about his dog and not the fruit it is named after.

---

[164] How VPNs Work, http://www.howstuffworks.com/vpn.htm, Accessed on 16 January 2012.

[165] Human rights, http://www.abc.net.au/civics/rights/enter.htm, Accessed on 16 January 2012.

[166] Personalized Search for everyone, http://googleblog.blogspot.com.au/2009/12/personalized-search-for-everyone.html, Accessed on 16 January 2012.

[167] Google+, https://accounts.google.com/ServiceLogin?service=oz&continue=https://plus.google.com/?gpsrc%3Dgplp0&hl=en-GB, Accessed on 16 January 2012.

[168] The Battle Against Info-Overload: Is Relevance or Popularity the Best Filter? http://readwrite.com/2011/01/26/the_battle_against_info-overload_is_relevance_or_popularity_the_best_filter, Accessed on 16 January 2012.

[169] Social Graph: Concepts and Issues, http://readwrite.com/2007/09/11/social_graph_concepts_and_issues, Accessed on 16 January 2012.

[170] Google "Search, Plus Your World" Makes Google More Personal Than Ever, http://www.webpronews.com/google-search-plus-your-world-2012-01, Accessed on 16 January 2012.

[171] Egosurfing, http://en.wikipedia.org/wiki/Egosurfing, Accessed on 16 January 2012.

[172] Search, plus Your World, http://googleblog.blogspot.com.au/2012/01/search-plus-your-world.html, Accessed on 16 January 2012.

[173] Amit Singhal, https://plus.google.com/+AmitSinghal/posts, Accessed on 16 January 2012.

Search plus Your World has taken the inclusion of Google+ content to a new level by promoting that content. Those who have been positive about this new development have used what are particularly banal examples, but essentially it comes down to "vanity" searches—a search[174] for the name of one person's dog, another search[175] for the word "Werewolf" that returned pictures of the author.

Not everyone is so positive.

The change was enough to make one tech writer switch to Bing[176] (even though—it should be pointed out—it's possible to disable personal results in Google.[177])

Hitler is, of course, upset[178] that he won't be able to find Britney Spears' Facebook page in Google any more. In a poignant comic, The Joy of Tech,[179] Google founder Larry Page meets his future self and is appalled at what his search has turned into.

More seriously, the move has also caught the attention of the US Federal Trade Commission, which is investigating Google[180] for antitrust violations through its search and mobile platform businesses. That investigation now includes[181] Google+.

If you're looking for objective search results, it might be time to look beyond Google. Gwyn Michael

The changes to Google's search platform have prompted discussions[182] about whether Google alternatives could soon be used more widely.

Microsoft's Bing search engine is one alternative, but it suffers from some of the same problems as Google with an attempt at "Filter Bubble"[183] search.

One Google alternative that has made a point of not allowing "bubble" searching[184] is DuckDuckGo.[185] This search engine aggregates searches from its own web crawler,[186] from crowd-sourced search sources and from other sites and search engines.

---

[174] Search, plus Your World, http://googleblog.blogspot.com.au/2012/01/search-plus-your-world.html, Accessed on 16 January 2012.

[175] Sharing a search story, http://www.mattcutts.com/blog/search-plus-your-world/, Accessed on 16 January 2012.

[176] Google Just Made Bing the Best Search Engine, http://gizmodo.com/5875571/google-just-made-bing-the-best-search-engine, Accessed on 16 January 2012.

[177] How (and Why) to Turn Off Google's Personalized Search Results, http://www.huffingtonpost.com/larry-magid/google-personal-search-results-_b_1206420.html, Accessed on 16 January 2012.

[178] Hitler Hears About Google Search Plus Your World, http://www.youtube.com/watch?v=ipkSRwgVtpA, Accessed on 16 January 2012.

[179] Tech Companies as Christmas icons, http://www.geekculture.com/joyoftech/, Accessed on 16 January 2012.

[180] FTC Sharpens Google Probe, http://online.wsj.com/article/SB10001424053111904823804576500544082214566.html, Accessed on 16 January 2012.

[181] Google+ Added to FTC Antitrust Probe, http://www.pcworld.com/article/248208/google_added_to_ftc_antitrust_probe.html, Accessed on 16 January 2012.

[182] The Most Annoying Thing About 'Google Search, Plus Your World' (Beyond Its Awful Name), http://www.forbes.com/sites/kashmirhill/2012/01/13/the-most-annoying-thing-about-google-search-plus-your-world-beyond-its-awful-name/, Accessed on 16 January 2012.

[183] Filter bubble, http://en.wikipedia.org/wiki/Filter_bubble, Accessed on 16 January 2012.

[184] Escape your search engine - Filter Bubble! http://dontbubble.us/, Accessed on 16 January 2012.

[185] DuckDuckGo, http://duckduckgo.com/, Accessed on 16 January 2012.

[186] Web crawler, http://en.wikipedia.org/wiki/Web_crawler, Accessed on 16 January 2012.

Google seems to be taking an increasingly perilous path with its move towards "socialising the web". It is fast gaining a reputation for having progressed rapidly through the ages of corporate development and straight into senility. The changes it is making are somewhat random and unpopular, and with every change Google asserts that it knows best.

Google Search plus Your World may be a case in point.

6.11 Teaching with Tech: Could iBooks Author Spark an Education Revolution?

23 January 2012

Late last week, Apple announced[187] the launch of a new piece of software, iBooks Author,[188] and a new version of its eBook reader, iBooks 2. It's a development that promises to accelerate the move to interactive eBooks, by radically simplifying their development.

iBooks Author does to eBooks what Apple's GarageBand[189] does to producing music—it makes the development of an interactive eBook as simple as dropping in a presentation or document. Videos, audio and other interactive elements can also be included, and the software automatically positions these elements, adjusting text and layout.

Once produced, eBooks can be distributed through Apple's iBooks store—after going through the Apple review process—for download onto iPads, iPhones and the iPod Touch.

iBooks 2, Apple's new eBook reader, has been updated to support the new textbook format and has launched in the US with a sample of beautifully crafted high school textbooks covering science and maths.

6.11.1 A Catalyst for Change?

It's an ironic feature of new technology—the social and cultural change that new tech brings is so unequal. Nowhere is this more clearly highlighted than in education.

Kids, living permanently connected and socially mediated lives, are transported into the dark ages the moment they step into a classroom. Although there are

---

[187] Apple Special Event January 2012, http://events.apple.com.edgesuite.net/1201oihbafvpihboijhp ihbasdouhbasv/event/index.html, Accessed on 23 January 2012.

[188] Apple - iBooks Author, http://www.apple.com/ibooks-author/, Accessed on 23 January 2012.

[189] Apple to announce tools, platform to "digitally destroy" textbook publishing, http://arstechnica. com/apple/2012/01/apple-to-announce-tools-platform-to-digitally-destroy-textbook-publishing/, Accessed on 23 January 2012.

examples of excellence and progress, there are many classrooms in which teaching and learning practices have remained unchanged for hundreds of years.

In the early 1980s, MIT Professor Seymour Papert[190] believed personal computers would bring about radical changes[191] in schools, both in the way students learned and how educators taught.

Using computers, Papert thought, students would be able to move at their own pace, learning, experimenting and testing themselves. Teachers would become facilitators and guides, and not the source of the content.

It's now 30 years later and progress has been slow. Teaching has barely scratched the surface of the potential integration of computers (especially mobile devices) into the classroom.

There are many reasons for this. Lack of funding, training and infrastructure play a large part, along with a fear of change and the potential scrutiny and criticism this change may spark off.

It is possible, though, that we are at a point where this might all change.

6.11.2 The Platform Is Right

One of the impediments to integrating computers into the classroom has been purely practical—in many schools, there was literally nowhere to put them. Even with notebooks, issues such as power and storage were enough to limit their use.

Tablets such as the iPad are an ideal platform because of their weight, size, battery life and versatility. Importantly, a tablet also doesn't form a physical barrier between student and teacher in the same way that a desktop or even notebook computer can.

The iPad's versatility is starting to be recognised, with roughly 1.5 million iPads[192] now used in educational establishments. Some universities[193] and schools[194] have even started issuing students with iPads.

6.11.3 The Content Is Coming

The second significant roadblock in the way of using computers in education has been the lack of content. More specifically, there has been a lack of electronic versions of textbooks that are tailored to a learning curriculum.

---

[190] Seymour Papert, http://web.media.mit.edu/~papert/, Accessed on 23 January 2012.

[191] Link no longer goes to specified page, http://crste.org/images/Halverson_Smith_How_New_Technologies.pdf, Accessed on 23 January 2012.

[192] Apple Special Event January 2012, http://events.apple.com.edgesuite.net/1201oihbafvpihboijhpihbasdouhbasv/event/index.html, Accessed on 23 January 2012.

[193] Link no longer goes to specified page, hubscher.org/roland/courses/hf765/readings/eJBEST_Murphy_2011_1.pdf, Accessed on 23 January 2012.

[194] Math That Moves: Schools Embrace the iPad, http://www.nytimes.com/2011/01/05/education/05tablets.html?pagewanted=all, Accessed on 23 January 2012.

Traditional publishers have not rushed into the eBook market, with Forrester Research estimating[195] that eBooks make up only 2.8 % of the US$8 billion textbook market in the US. Reasons for this include:

- the fear of sabotaging profits on print versions of the texts
- the cost of eBook production, and
- the fragmentation of publishing formats and platforms.

(Interestingly, eBook sales in general exceeded[196] print book sales on Amazon for the first time last year.)

Of course, publishers have now learned the inevitability of an electronic future for textbooks. The fear of not being part of this will drive the move from print.

The release of iBooks Author (a free application for Mac) opens up the production of educational material to anyone. It's not so much the ability to author the books simply—although this is significant—but the ability to distribute, and potentially get paid for, such works. As with its apps, Apple has created an ecosystem with critical mass that makes it worth the effort of producing books in this way.

Of course it's not just books that are important for content. Apple has for some time been delivering educational video and audio content through iTunes U.[197] This education-specific section of iTunes has seen 600 million downloads of educational video, audio and study material since it started in 2007. Stanford University and the Open University top the list of universities providing material, each with more than 30 million downloads.

Last week, Apple also announced the availability of a dedicated iTunes U app.[198] This app joins 200,000 educational apps[199] in the iTunes App Store.

6.11.3.1 Is Apple the Future of Education?

Every announcement from Apple seems to bring out the sceptics.

There is resentment[200] at the revenue cut that Apple takes when products are sold through their sales network. With iBooks Author, the License Agreement[201] prohibits

---

[195] Apple unveils iBooks 2 for textbooks, http://www.theaustralian.com.au/australian-it/apple-unveils-ibooks-2-for-textbooks/story-e6frgakx-1226248972719, Accessed on 23 January 2012.

[196] Kindle ebook sales exceed print sales in US, http://www.slashgear.com/kindle-ebook-sales-exceed-print-sales-in-us-19153084/, Accessed on 23 January 2012.

[197] iTunes U - Learn anything, anywhere, anytime. http://www.apple.com/education/itunes-u/, Accessed on 23 January 2012.

[198] 404 not found, http://www.engadget.com/2012/01/19/apple-revamps-itunes-u-and-intros-dedi-cated-app/, Accessed on 23 January 2012.

[199] Apple's new apps revealed, potential student reaction? http://www.zdnet.com/blog/igeneration/apples-new-apps-revealed-potential-student-reaction/14740, Accessed on 23 January 2012.

[200] iBooks Author end-user license agreement sparks controversy, http://9to5mac.com/2012/01/19/ibooks-author-end-user-license-agreement-sparks-controversy/, Accessed on 23 January 2012.

[201] Use iBooks Author, only Apple can ever publish the result, http://www.theregister.co.uk/2012/01/20/apple_ibooks/, Accessed on 23 January 2012.

the use of eBooks produced in this way to be distributed anywhere other than through the iBooks store, where Apple takes 30 % of the revenue. (This limitation doesn't seem to exist for content given away for free.)

What the critics haven't mentioned is that most textbook authors receive little financial return for their efforts from publishers. In most cases textbooks are written out of dedication or for academic recognition, with the financial returns rarely covering the time invested in the writing.

Further criticisms have been levelled[202] at Apple for creating a closed environment that forces people to use Apple products to access their content. This is in contrast to Amazon, Google and others that provide software that allows users to access their media purchases on any platform. Sites such as the Khan Academy[203] provide high quality instructional videos for free and there is a wealth of free educational websites available on the internet.

Finally, critics argue[204] that in American schools at least, the money for iPads would be better spent on recruiting and training teachers. Their argument is that there's little evidence to show iPads contribute to improved learning outcomes.

But a report[205] released last week about a pilot study found students using an algebra application on an iPad (instead of a printed textbook) performed 20 % better in California Standard Tests.[206]

6.11.3.2 What Next?

For anyone involved in education—whether a teacher, administrator, parent or student—the ability to produce and distribute educational material represents an exciting and pivotal moment. All of the necessary stars have aligned to spur the move to digital educational material.

Of course we haven't yet seen how Amazon, Google, Microsoft and others will respond to this, but the net result is sure to be positive for learners and teachers everywhere.

6.12 Gamification Status: You Score Ten Points for Reading This Article

1 February 2012

---

[202]iBooks Author end-user license agreement sparks controversy, http://9to5mac.com/2012/01/19/ibooks-author-end-user-license-agreement-sparks-controversy/, Accessed on 23 January 2012.

[203]Khan Academy, http://www.khanacademy.org/, Accessed on 23 January 2012.

[204]Math That Moves: Schools Embrace the iPad, http://www.nytimes.com/2011/01/05/education/05tablets.html?pagewanted=all, Accessed on 23 January 2012.

[205]Student Math Scores Jump 20 Percent with HMH Algebra Curriculum for Apple® iPad®; App Transforms Classroom Education, http://www.hmhco.com/content/student-math-scores-jump-20-percent-hmh-algebra-curriculum-apple-ipad-app-transforms-class, Accessed on 23 January 2012.

[206]CST Released Test Questions, http://www.cde.ca.gov/ta/tg/sr/css05rtq.asp, Accessed on 23 January 2012.

A white paper[207] was released this week stating that "Gen Y" employees could be better engaged and motivated by applying "game dynamics" to the workplace. Bunchball,[208] the company behind the paper, *would* say that of course, because it sells technology that allows other software vendors to "gamify" their products.

But what, exactly, is the argument?

Gamification[209] is the term used when game dynamics are applied to engage customers for business, or to engage the general public to solve problems.

To date it has been employed for everything from crowd-sourcing—to discover how proteins fold[210]—to motivating children[211] to exercise.

Given its origins in video and computer games, the mechanics of gamification will be familiar to gamers. They involve the use of points, levels of skill or mastery, and rewards.

6.12.1 *You Have Scored 20 Points and Earned the Principles of Gamification Badge*

Gamification really gained attention through its application in the social gaming network foursquare[212] which was established in 2009.

On foursquare, players can "check in" at any location and earn points. When someone has checked in more than anyone else, they become "mayor" of that location and are publicly acknowledged. The mayor also becomes eligible for discounts[213] and other specials where these are offered.

On passing the 15 million user[214] mark in 2011, foursquare had seen[215]:

- 4.7 million users check in on main streets in the US
- 6,230 users check in to sake bars in Japan, and
- 1,602 users check in to weddings in US city halls.

---

[207] Link no longer goes to specified page, http://info.bunchball.com/enterprisegamification/?utm_campaign=11-17-01-eg-heropanel&utm_source=website, Accessed on 1 February 2012.

[208] Bunchball – The Leader in Gamification, http://www.bunchball.com/, Accessed on 1 February 2012.

[209] Gamification, http://en.wikipedia.org/wiki/Gamification, Accessed on 1 February 2012.

[210] The Science Behind Foldit, http://fold.it/portal/info/science, Accessed on 1 February 2012.

[211] Zamzee, https://www.zamzee.com/, Accessed on 1 February 2012.

[212] Foursquare, https://foursquare.com/, Accessed on 1 February 2012.

[213] Mayors of Starbucks Now Get Discounts Nationwide with Foursquare, http://mashable.com/2010/05/17/starbucks-foursquare-mayor-specials/, Accessed on 1 February 2012.

[214] foursquare Hits 15 Million Users, Or Rather, 15 Million People You Can Avoid by Downloading foursquare, http://betabeat.com/2011/12/number-of-foursquare-users-2011-12052011/, Accessed on 1 February 2012.

[215] Foursquare has more than 10 million users, http://latimesblogs.latimes.com/technology/2011/06/foursquare-number-users.html, Accessed on 1 February 2012.

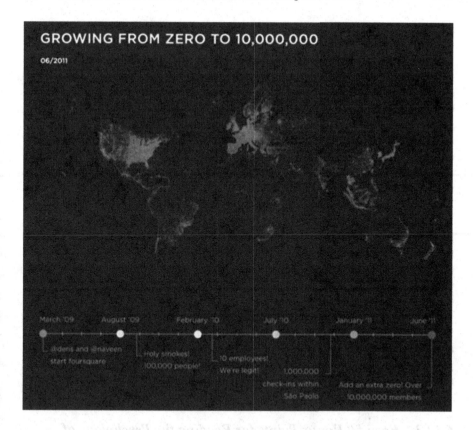

People check in to foursquare for no other reason than to receive points for their first sushi bar or foreign destination. Of course, there is a social element to foursquare—you can link your location to Facebook or Twitter to let your friends know where you are. Similarly, foursquare tells you who else is checked in at a particular location, so you could find out if you have friends at a concert, for example.

6.12.2   You Have Scored 30 Point and Reached Level 1: Novice of Gamification

The site Fun Theory[216] has examples of turning everyday activities into games to encourage positive behaviour. Turning a set of stairs into an interactive piano encouraged 66 % of people to use the stairs rather than the accompanying escalator.

Gamification's principle aim is to motivate people and to keep them engaged, whether the activity is visiting a website or improving their health. Its role in health

---

[216]The Fun Theory, http://www.thefuntheory.com/, Accessed on 1 February 2012.

is of special interest because keeping people motivated when dealing with preventative measures or maintaining treatments[217] has traditionally been very hard.

Zamzee[218] is a site promoting exercise to children by allowing them to record and upload activity data. The kids' activity is measured using the Zamzee device, a small digital pedometer. Points are awarded according to the level of activity and leader boards show the users with the most activity, best improvement, most consistent activity etcetera. The points can also be traded for actual physical gifts.

Research[219] by the founders of Zamzee has shown that participating in the site increased activity by 30 % over the course of the study.

MeYou Health[220] has created an application that sets a daily challenge[221] to promote improved wellbeing and better health—such as visiting the American Heart Association's website and learning how to avoid ordering fatty foods in restaurants.

In the case of gamification of the workplace, the distinction between so-called game dynamics and what already happens is subtler. According[222] to Bunchball, you need to provide continuous data about employees' activities (the game equivalent of points), acknowledge and reward elmployees when they achieve these goals (badges and moving staff to new levels) and foster an environment of competition (leaderboards).

One may argue that these are simply different labels for what is already happening: people have been promoted for good work behaviour for centuries. But, although the difference may be chiefly in the presentation, looking at the underlying psychological mechanisms of behaviour and motivation tells us presentation and timing is actually very important to the process.

6.12.3   Earn 50 Bonus Points for Reading the Psychology of Behaviour

Although there are many theories put forward around behaviour and motivation, the Behaviour Model[223] created by psychologist B.J. Fogg has been applied to the successful implementation of gamification.

---

[217] In Chronic Diseases - Poor compliance of Patients with drug treatment, http://www.bio-medicine.org/medicine-news/In-Chronic-Diseases---Poor-compliance-of-Patients-with-drug-treatment--2097-1/, Accessed on 1 February 2012.

[218] Zamzee, https://www.zamzee.com/, Accessed on 1 February 2012.

[219] Innovative Solutions: Zamzee, http://www.hopelab.org/innovative-solutions/zamzee/, Accessed on 1 February 2012.

[220] MeYou Health, http://meyouhealth.com/, Accessed on 1 February 2012.

[221] Gamification of Health Series (4 of 7): What does the Daily Challenge hope to accomplish? http://www.youtube.com/watch?list=PLD58A94DF3B762E80&feature=player_detailpage&v=4wcP6y_NpOE, Accessed on 1 February 2012.

[222] Link no longer goes to specified page, http://www.bunchball.com/enterprisegamification/?utm_campaign=11-17-01-eg-heropanel&utm_source=website, Accessed on 1 February 2012.

[223] BJ Fogg's Behavior Model, http://www.behaviormodel.org/index.html, Accessed on 1 February 2012.

The model describes three elements that interact to determine whether a behaviour will occur. These elements are "motivation", "ability" and "triggers".

Triggers are the opportunity or prompt to perform a behaviour. Whether the behaviour is performed or not depends on the difficulty of the action being carried out, the ability of the person carrying out the action and the motivation of that person.

If the behaviour is easy, the level of motivation required is low. If the desired behaviour is hard, the level of motivation required to carry it out will be high.

6.12.4   *You Have Scored 80 Points: 20 Points More Earns You the "Expert in Gamification" Level!*

Critics[224] of gamification range from people objecting to the horrible name, to those pointing out that the idea is not entirely new. Engaging customers with points, levels and rewards is the basis of every frequent flyer or loyalty programme. Trading stamps given to customers for purchases and redeemable against gifts date back[225] to 1896 in the US.

6.12.5   *Congratulations! You Have Earned 100 Points and Are Now at the "Expert in Gamification" Level*

Turning everyday activities into a game certainly has huge potential as it taps into the very essence of what motivates us to do things and to keep doing them—and our mobile-connected, socially-networked society provides the ideal platform for its implementation.

To paraphrase Confucius, find a job that feels like a game and you may never need to work again.

6.13   Facebook IPO: What It Means for Zuckerberg and You

2 February 2012

---

[224]Gamification has issues, but they aren't the ones everyone focuses on, http://radar.oreilly.com/2011/06/gamification-criticism-overjustification-ownership-addiction.html, Accessed on 1 February 2012.

[225]Green Shield Stamps, http://en.wikipedia.org/wiki/Green_Shield_Stamps, Accessed on 1 February 2012.

Apple	$415 billion
Google	$186 billion
McDonald's	$101 billion
Facebook	$100 billion
Amazon.com	$84 billion
Bank of America	$6 billion
Boeing	$6 billion
Hewlett Packard	$5 billion

Facebook's potential valuation compared to other companies. ABC

Of course, the thing that really matters is how much revenue Facebook can, and will, make. Part of the excitement around the IPO is that, once Facebook goes public, all of its internal financial workings become public. Until now, those workings have largely been a matter of speculation.

Estimates had previously put Facebook's revenue at between US$3.5 billion–US$7 billion.[226]

In fact,[227] Facebook made US$1 billion profit on revenue of US$3.7 billion in 2011, up from US$1.97 billion in 2010.

6.13.1 Does Facebook Make Enough Profit to Justify the Valuation?

Facebook currently has 845 million users and is expected to pass the 1 billion user mark in August.[228] Roughly half of those users are active on a daily basis. When you consider Facebook had 12 million active users in 2006,[229] this has been phenomenal growth.

Clearly, social network platforms—and Facebook in particular—are part of the fabric of the lives of most people with access to a computer and the internet. This is unlikely to change, just as email is still a fundamental part of how we communicate.

---

[226] Facebook IPO: six things you need to know, http://www.guardian.co.uk/technology/2012/jan/31/facebook-ipo-six-things, Accessed on 2 February 2012.

[227] Inside Facebook's S-1 Filing: 845 Million Users, $3.7 Billion In Revenues In 2011, http://www.fastcompany.com/1813364/inside-facebooks-s-1-filing-845-million-users-37-billion-revenues-2011, Accessed on 2 February 2012.

[228] Facebook to Hit 1 Billion User Mark in August [STUDY], http://mashable.com/2012/01/12/facebook-1-billion-users/, Accessed on 2 February 2012.

[229] Mapping Facebook's growth – Decoder, http://www.reuters.com/video/2012/02/01/reuters-tv-mapping-facebooks-growth-decoder?videoId=229447923&videoChannel=117772, Accessed on 2 February 2012.

The question is whether Facebook can continue to grow along with the evolution and emergence of other modes of communication and interaction. The expansion of the "like" feature to a range of gestures is just one example.

Of course, with every shared interaction, Facebook gains more data to use in targeting advertising, which is where most of the potential revenue opportunities lie. This is, of course, if Facebook can avoid extended battles over user privacy issues.

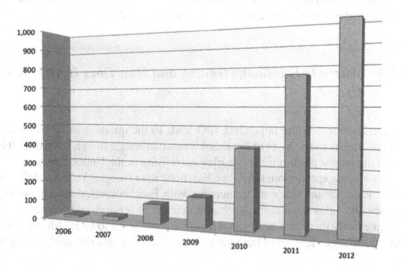

Facebook user growth, in millions of users by year. Reuters

6.13.2   Is Going Public Worth the Risks?

It's perhaps worth asking why Facebook wants to go public at all. Going public changes the way companies operate as their operations become more transparent to the public and shareholders sometimes have an increased say in how the company should run.

There's also the real possibility the IPO won't be as successful as hoped, in which case there could be a perception issue that could stay with the company.

There are a number of reasons a company goes public—the most obvious being that it allows employees to cash shares that they own in the company. Mark Zuckerberg alone could make $24 billion[230] from the sale. More than 1,000 employees[231] could become millionaires, on paper at least.

---

[230]Facebook IPO: Could Mark Zuckerberg Make $24 Billion? http://www.dailyfinance.com/2011/12/02/facebook-ipo-could-mark-zuckerberg-make-24-billion/, Accessed on 2 February 2012.

[231]Status update: I'm rich! Facebook flotation to create 1,000 millionaires among company's rank and file, http://www.dailymail.co.uk/news/article-2072204/Facebook-IPO-create-1-000-millionaires-companys-rank-file.html, Accessed on 2 February 2012.

Facebook's founder may do quite well. Peter Klaunzer/EPA

Facebook, as with all tech companies, faces competition in recruiting and retaining quality staff. Having actively traded shares that are (hopefully) increasing in value is a powerful employee incentive.

The other, and probably "official", reason for going public is to raise cash for the company itself. The cash generated by the IPO would give Facebook the ability to accelerate its expansion through the purchase of other companies. Or it could simply fund the development of new businesses or functionality.

6.13.3   Where Is Facebook Heading and How Does It Affect Its Users?

The announcement of the impending IPO leads to the question of where next for Facebook and its users. Most of Facebook's revenue comes from advertising. It has become the largest platform[232] for display advertising in the United States.

Users already spend more time[233] on Facebook than Google, Yahoo or Microsoft and this is something that's set to increase, with Facebook offering more services from directly within the website, such as purchases of services and products.

What exactly these new products and services are going to be is still a matter of speculation. Suggestions have been made[234] that Facebook will strengthen its mobile site.

vincos

Facebook's future is partially assured by the growing number of companies[235] using it as their mechanism for providing social networking functionality. One of the biggest strengths of Facebook is that it, along with Twitter, has become one of the easiest ways for companies to authenticate and register new users.

Facebook's "frictionless sharing[236]"—through gestures and its new Timeline[237] feature—allows companies to advertise in a very targeted way through users' direct sharing of activities with their friends.

Google is not used in this way because it is tied to its own network of products—and this will prove a major disadvantage when it tries to compete against Facebook.

---

[232]Personal Data's Value? Facebook Is Set to Find Out, http://www.nytimes.com/2012/02/01/technology/riding-personal-data-facebook-is-going-public.html?pagewanted=all&_r=1&, Accessed on 2 February 2012.

[233]comScore: Facebook Keeps Gobbling People's Time, http://techcrunch.com/2011/02/07/comscore-facebook-keeps-gobbling-peoples-time/, Accessed on 2 February 2012.

[234]Facebook IPO: six things you need to know, http://www.guardian.co.uk/technology/2012/jan/31/facebook-ipo-six-things, Accessed on 2 February 2012.

[235]70 % of Local Businesses Use Facebook For Marketing, http://readwrite.com/2011/02/18/70-of-local-businesses-use-facebook-for-marketing, Accessed on 2 February 2012.

[236]Missing hyperlink.

[237]Introducing timeline, https://www.facebook.com/about/timeline, Accessed on 2 February 2012.

Even though Google+ has just reached the 100-million-user-mark,[238] Google now automatically signs users up to Google+ when anyone registers with its other products, such as Gmail. But getting users to utilise Google+ in the same way they do with Facebook is going to continue to be a challenge.

6.13.3.1 Should I Buy Shares in Facebook?

That's probably a question for your financial adviser. But there's no reason why Facebook shouldn't reach the same or greater valuation as Google in the future. I believe Facebook has more opportunities than Google and is making the right moves for every wrong move that Google makes.[239]

Of course, anything could happen and the next Mark Zuckerberg could be sitting in his or her bedroom developing the next Facebook as we speak.

6.14 Words With Friends, Draw Something... Are You Addicted to Social Gaming?

3 April 2012

They are everywhere: people in cafés or supermarket queues, staring at their smartphones with determined concentration, occasionally shuffling yellow tiles of letters to use all of them in a killer move. Or, like actor Alec Baldwin, trying to make a move before a plane takes off (he didn't and got thrown off[240] the plane for not switching off his phone). Even if this isn't you, chances are you still know someone who uses their phone to play Words With Friends.[241]

Words With Friends is an addictive word game based on the popular board version, Scrabble. Unlike Scrabble, it can only be played by two people but is part of a broader phenomenom of Social Gaming[242]—online games that are played with others or allow interactions and sharing with others, usually through a social networking site such as Facebook.

According to social games metrics site AppData.com,[243] Words With Friends has 20.3m Monthly Average Users (MAU), although this is also likely to be an

---

[238] Analyst: Google+ Hits 100 Million Users, http://mashable.com/2012/02/01/google-plus-breaks-100m-users/, Accessed on 2 February 2012.

[239] Google search just got way more personal... and that's a problem, https://theconversation.edu.au/google-search-just-got-way-more-personal-and-thats-a-problem-4935, Accessed on 2 February 2012.

[240] Alec Baldwin's Words With Friends Addiction Gets Him Booted Off Plane, http://mashable.com/2011/12/07/alec-baldwin/, Accessed on 3 April 2012.

[241] Words With Friends, http://www.wordswithfriends.com/, Accessed on 3 April 2012.

[242] Social Gaming, http://en.wikipedia.org/wiki/Social_gaming, Accessed on 3 April 2012.

[243] AppData, http://www.appdata.com/, Accessed on 3 April 2012.

underestimate because AppData.com measures the number of users that log in using Facebook. With the mobile version, it's possible to login and bypass Facebook altogether.

If you're more of a visual person—as it seems a younger demographic are—a new social game called Draw Something[244] may be more your style. With 31.1m monthly average users,[245] Draw Something has eclipsed the popularity of Words With Friends.

Based on the game Pictionary, players use drawings to depict words that their opponents try to guess. Draw Something was downloaded 35m times in its first month alone. It also reached 1m users in 9 days, something Facebook took 9 months to achieve.[246]

A survey of UK and US social gamers found the average age was 43, and 55 % of gamers were female. Only 6 % of all social gamers were 21 or younger.

6.14.1   Reasons to Be Cheerful

Regarding the reasons why people play these games, a separate survey[247] showed connecting with others was actually not the most important reason. "Fun and excitement" (53 %) was the greatest motivation, followed by "stress relief" (45 %), "competitive spirit" (43 %), "mental workout" (32 %) and finally "connecting with others" (24 %).

Anecdotally, however, in the New York Times,[248] Seth Schiesel describes his relationship with a neighbour whose only contact with friends was through the chat function of Words With Friends.

The woman in question had disconnected her phone and only used the iPhone through its Wi-Fi connection. Eventually she reconnected with an old classmate, flirted through Words With Friends and finally met in person.

Social gamers view the their online activities[249] as being important in initiating, maintaining and enhancing their relationships both online and offline.

---

[244] Draw Something, http://omgpop.com/drawsomething, Accessed on 3 April 2012.

[245] Facebook Apps Leaderboard (statistics possibly outdated?), http://www.appdata.com/leaderboard/apps?metric_select=mau, Accessed on 3 April 2012.

[246] The 'dizzying' success of Draw Something: By the numbers, http://theweek.com/article/index/225921/the-dizzying-success-of-draw-something-by-the-numbers, Accessed on 3 April 2012.

[247] Social Games: What are the primary demographics (gender, age, ethnicity, etc) of the average social game enthusiast?, http://www.quora.com/Social-Games/What-are-the-primary-demographics-gender-age-ethnicity-etc-of-the-average-social-game-enthusiast, Accessed on 3 April 2012.

[248] Real Connections in Game Land, http://www.nytimes.com/2012/01/05/arts/video-games/the-electronic-games-that-now-connect-us.html?pagewanted=all, Accessed on 3 April 2012.

[249] Link no longer goes to specified page, http://ieeexplore.ieee.org/stamp/stamp.jsp?tp=&arnumber=5718722, Accessed on 3 April 2012.

Initiating relationships is as much about having someone to play a game with as actually starting a new friendship. In some games, advancement in the game is faster the more people you have in your network as "neighbours" and this is part of the motivation.

For other players, meeting new people is an important factor. Some 38 % of people playing Words with Friends said that they[250] would be more willing to "hook up" with someone if they were good at the game.

Of more importance is the ability of social games to maintain and enhance relationships. Staying in touch with distant friends and relatives even if there is no communication other than playing the game is an important feature. Women are more likely to play social games with a relative, which follows from their interest in maintaining relationships.

Following on from maintaining a relationship is enhancing relationships. This is mainly perceived as taking an acquaintance to "the next level" through interactions in social gaming. Of course, this is only going to happen if there's the ability to actually chat in the game. Draw Something, for example, doesn't have this facility, possibly a reason why it's favoured by a younger group of players.

6.14.2 The Dark Side

The interaction between social games and Facebook is interesting. Game companies such as Zynga,[251] which owns Words With Friends and Draw Something, could essentially create their own social network platform based around these games. But their dependency on Facebook for new users and payment, rewards and sharing aspects outweigh any benefits they would get from being independent.

Of course, not everything about social games is positive. While the majority of people playing social games report the games make them feel "more connected", playing games can also lead to increased stress and anxiety.

One person posting[252] on a social anxiety support site complained about playing with two players, one a non-native English speaker and another who "can't spell that good", and still consistently getting beaten. As someone with low self-esteem, this seemed too much for him to handle. He couldn't improve, no matter what tactics he applied.

Another niggle is that sharing updates about games with people who don't play can be extremely frustrating[253] for those that are not participating—an argument against the so-called "frictionless" sharing of everything in our lives.

---

[250]Meet Women Thanks To Words With Friends (Infographic), http://lowdownblog.com/2012/03/01/meet-women-thanks-to-words-with-friends-infographic/, Accessed on 3 April 2012.

[251]Zynga, https://zynga.com/, Accessed on 3 April 2012.

[252]words with friends is depressing, http://www.socialanxietysupport.com/forum/f35/words-with-friends-is-depressing-143182/, Accessed on 3 April 2012.

[253]Link no longer goes to specified page, http://ieeexplore.ieee.org/stamp/stamp.jsp?tp=&arnumber=5718722, Accessed on 3 April 2012.

Of course, a game such as Words With Friends is as much about tactics as it is about the luck of getting the right letters. There's also the possibility of "cheating" by using software to recommend the optimal solution. The approach you take is actually as much about the person you are playing with and the relationship you have with that person.

Play too aggressively or defensively and the game can be frustrating for a beginner. Some 35 % of Words With Friends players admit to[254] "letting" others win.

Like all social interactions, those in social games are multilayered and complex. After all, is the choice of words used in a Words With Friends game completely random, or are you sending subliminal messages to your partner?

6.15 An Invincible File-Sharing Platform? You Can't Be Serious

6 March 2012

Treats are great to share, provided you have the owner's permission. *Source*: **methodshop. com CC**[255]

A new version of the peer-to-peer sharing application Tribler[256] has created a buzz[257] online following claims by the software's lead developer that the app is impervious to attack.

---

[254] Meet Women Thanks To Words With Friends (Infographic), http://lowdownblog.com/2012/03/01/meet-women-thanks-to-words-with-friends-infographic/, Accessed on 3 April 2012.

[255] Methodshop.com, Flickr, http://www.flickr.com/photos/methodshop/8098221524/, Accessed online 21 December 2012.

[256] Tribler download, http://dl.tribler.org/download.html, Accessed online 6 March 2012.

[257] Tribler makes BitTorrent impossible to shut down, TorrentFreak, http://torrentfreak.com/tribler-makes-bittorrent-impossible-to-shut-down-120208/, Accessed online 6 March 2012.

In a recent interview with TorrentFreak,[258] Dr Johan Pouwelse[259] from the Delft University of Technology,[260] said "the only way to take [Tribler] down is to take the internet down[261]".

Tribler has been in development for 5 years and, as with many other file-sharing applications, is based on the BitTorrent protocol.[262] But unlike other BitTorrent platforms, Tribler is a decentralised system that works without the need for torrent sites—lists of links to files available for download through the BitTorrent protocol—and trackers.[263] Instead, Tribler has been designed to search the internet for hosts that contain the desired files.

Dr Pouwelse's claims of Tribler's invincibility are simply amazing. If he is to be believed, peer-to-peer file-sharers finally have a tool that can't be turned off nor attacked by government[264] and the music and movie industry.

Sadly, these are difficult claims to take seriously.

In the 1980s and 1990s, music and movie companies flooded the internet with hosts[265] containing music and movies that had been altered from their original form. The aim was to trick users into wasting time and bandwidth downloading a file that wasn't the file they were looking for.

One way files could be modified was with the addition of a cuckoo egg[266] (as we all know, the cuckoo lays its eggs in another bird's nest to trick the victim bird into tending the cuckoo egg).

A cuckoo egg[267] is a file that looks the same as the file a user is searching for—in filename and filesize—but is actually a totally different file.[268]

---

[258] Tribler makes BitTorrent impossible to shut down, TorrentFreak, http://torrentfreak.com/tribler-makes-bittorrent-impossible-to-shut-down-120208/, Accessed online 6 March 2012.

[259] Dr Johan Pouwelse, Delft University of Technology, http://pds.twi.tudelft.nl/~pouwelse/, Accessed online 6 March 2012.

[260] Delft University of Technology, http://home.tudelft.nl/en/, Accessed online 6 March 2012.

[261] Could Anonymous really shut down the internet?, The Conversation, https://theconversation.edu.au/could-anonymous-really-shut-down-the-internet-5573, Accessed online 6 March 2012.

[262] BitTorrent, Wikipedia, http://en.wikipedia.org/wiki/BitTorrent_(protocol), Accessed online 6 March 2012.

[263] BitTorrent tracker, Wikipedia, http://en.wikipedia.org/wiki/BitTorrent_tracker, Accessed online 6 March 2012.

[264] 'To take it down, you have to take down the internet': New file-sharing technology is IMMUNE to government attacks, Daily Mail, http://www.dailymail.co.uk/sciencetech/article-2098759/Tribler-New-file-sharing-technology-IMMUNE-government-attacks.html, Accessed online 6 March 2012.

[265] Host (Network), Wikipedia, http://en.wikipedia.org/wiki/Host_(network), Accessed online 6 March 2012.

[266] Sabotaging files with Cuckoo Eggs, http://filesharingbook.uw.hu/filesharing0093.html, Accessed online 6 March 2012.

[267] While you are browsing. The Eggs are Hatching., Cukoo's Egg Project, http://www.hand-2-mouth.com/cuckooegg/, Accessed online 6 March 2012.

[268] Example file with cuckoo egg, http://www.hand-2-mouth.com/cuckooegg/cuckooeggsound.mp3, Accessed online 6 March 2012.

Tribler 5.5.20

Sorry: limited website due to high popularity.

Windows	**Mac OS X**	**Ubuntu Linux**
Tribler 5.5.20 for Windows	Tribler 5.5.20 for Mac OS X	Tribler 5.5.20 for Linux
Windows XP, Windows Vista, and Windows 7		Ubuntu 10.10 - 11.10
		latest code.

Tribler Makes Great Claims … and Is Popular. *Source*: **tribler.org**[269]

Watermarks can also be added to music and movies, allowing the files to be tracked across the network.[270] This allows organisations such as PeerMedia Technologies[271]—who provide this service to the music and movie industries—to identify people who have breached copyright.

As countries move towards implementing traffic filters and systems to prevent cyberattack,[272] it has become easier to identify and then disrupt, stop or distort Tribler traffic streams.

The process of distorting, altering or substituting a different stream is not complex and in some ways may occur much as a "man-in-the-middle attack"[273] is used to penetrate secure systems. (In such an attack, a third party intercepts traffic between two users, creating a fake stream of data, while making one—or both—users believe they are communicating with the other).

Another approach is to filter[274] the Tribler stream and if a copyrighted music or video stream is found, the source and destination IP addresses[275] could be added to a blacklist, blocked by filters or blocked from essential network services such as the

---

[269] Tribler, http://www.tribler.org/, Accessed online 6 March 2012.

[270] Bloom, J.A., Polyzois, C., Watermarking to Track Motion Picture Theft, http://videote-chresearch.com/Jeffrey_Bloom/research/bloom04-asilomar.pdf, Accessed online 6 March 2012.

[271] Peer Media Technologies, http://peermediatech.com/, Accessed online 6 March 2012.

[272] Cyber Security Operations Centre, Defence Signals Directorate, http://www.dsd.gov.au/infosec/csoc.htm, Accessed online 6 March 2012.

[273] Man-in-the-middle attach, Wikipedia, http://en.wikipedia.org/wiki/Man-in-the-middle_attack, Accessed online 6 March 2012.

[274] Deep packet inspection, Wikipedia, http://en.wikipedia.org/wiki/Deep_packet_inspection, Accessed online 6 March 2012.

[275] The end of the internet? IPv4 versus IPv6, The Conversation, https://theconversation.edu.au/the-end-of-the-internet-ipv4-versus-ipv6-145, Accessed online 6 March 2012.

Domain Name System (DNS).[276] (DNS is the service used to translate web address names—such as amazon.com—to IP addresses—such as 72.21.214.128.)

Late last year a group of Australian ISPs—including Telstra and Optus—proposed a copyright infringement policy that would allow ISPs to send users a warning[277] after five illegal downloads. The policy[278] lists a range of consequences for customers that fail to comply with the warning notice, such as providing the copyright holder with access to the customer's details upon request.

Over time, we're likely to see music, movie and media companies developing closer links with network carriers and ISPs because the internet is becoming the medium of choice for distributing this content. For carriers and ISPs, revenue from access systems is decreasing due to competition,[279] leading to a decrease in the number of ISPs.[280] At the same time, we're seeing an increase in revenue from bundled products including music, movie and media distribution.

Carriers and ISPs will increasingly want to reduce the amount of pirated content on their networks as copyright infringement reduces income from customers subscribing to IPTV[281]—television delivered over the internet—video on-demand and music-streaming services.

This symbiotic relationship between ISPs and media companies should be a cause for concern for peer-to-peer file-sharers. We shouldn't be surprised if we even see music and movie companies buying ISPs in the near future.

Regardless, claims about Tribler's invincibility are almost certainly overblown, and it's clear the battle between file-sharers and copyright holders is far from over.

6.16   Viral Video, Gone Bad: Kony 2012 and the Perils of Social Media

There have been enough social media disasters of late to make one thing clear: manipulating sentiment through social networks is next to impossible.

---

[276]Domain Name System, Wikipedia, http://en.wikipedia.org/wiki/Domain_Name_System, Accessed online 6 March 2012.

[277]ISPs propose new anti-piracy warning scheme, Delimiter, http://delimiter.com.au/2011/11/25/isps-propose-new-anti-piracy-warning-scheme/, Accessed online 6 March 2012.

[278]A Scheme to Address Online Copyright Infringement, Communications Alliance, http://www.commsalliance.com.au/__data/assets/pdf_file/0019/32293/Copyright-Industry-Scheme-Proposal-Final.pdf, Accessed online 6 March 2012.

[279]Telstra warns ISPs to expect "aggressive" competition, ITNews, http://www.itnews.com.au/News/224372,telstra-warns-isps-to-expect-aggressive-competition.aspx, Accessed online 6 March 2012.

[280]Number of Internet Service Providers (ISPs), Australian Bureau of Statistics, http://www.abs.gov.au/ausstats/abs@.nsf/mf/8153.0, Accessed online 6 March 2012.

[281]IPTV, Wikipedia, http://en.wikipedia.org/wiki/IPTV, Accessed online 6 March 2012.

The McDonald's #McDStories campaign[282] in January was supposed to allow the public to share fond memories of eating at McDonald's. Instead, responses quickly became abusive and negative.

Qantas famously made the same mistake[283] with their ill-fated #QantasLuxury campaign in November of last year.

At first glance, the Kony 2012[284] film seemed an undeniable social media success.[285] Purporting to raise awareness about the use of children in the Lord's Resistance Army[286] guerilla group, the film agitated for the hunting-down and arrest of the group's leader, Joseph Kony.

The film and its director, Jason Russell, were blatant in their intention to use social media to propel the campaign. Analysis[287] of Twitter and YouTube traffic showed how Invisible Children,[288] the charity behind the Kony 2012 video, used its existing social networks to initiate and drive the viral growth of attention to the video.

The obsession of media and marketing with "virality" is something Arianna Huffington—co-founder of the Huffington Post—has commented on.[289] While not mentioning the Kony video explicitly, Huffington suggested that when something attains "viral" status, this can signify a positive or negative outcome. But more often than not, it signifies both.

This is exactly what happened in the case of the Kony 2012 video.

For every celebrity that endorsed the film[290] there seemed to be someone publishing criticism.[291] These criticisms have been unpacked elsewhere,[292] including on The Conversation.[293]

[282] Abject Lessons Learnt from McDonald's Social Media Disaster, http://socialmediatoday.com/david-amerland/434385/abject-lessons-learnt-mcdonald-s-social-media-disaster, Accessed on 28 March 2012.

[283] #QantasLuxury: a Qantas social media disaster in pyjamas, https://theconversation.edu.au/qantasluxury-a-qantas-social-media-disaster-in-pyjamas-4421, Accessed on 28 March 2012.

[284] KONY 2012, http://www.youtube.com/watch?feature=player_embedded&v=Y4MnpzG5Sqc, Accessed on 28 March 2012.

[285] Kony 2012: Anatomy of a Social Media Sensation, http://www.huffingtonpost.com/patricia-vanderbilt/kony-2012_b_1344050.html, Accessed on 28 March 2012.

[286] Q&A: Joseph Kony and the Lord's Resistance Army, http://www.guardian.co.uk/world/2012/mar/08/joseph-kony-lords-resistance-army, Accessed on 28 March 2012.

[287] [Data Viz] KONY2012: See How Invisible Networks Helped a Campaign Capture the World's Attention, http://blog.socialflow.com/post/7120244932/data-viz-kony2012-see-how-invisible-networks-helped-a-campaign-capture-the-worlds-attention, Accessed on 28 March 2012.

[288] Invisible Children, http://invisiblechildren.com/, Accessed on 28 March 2012.

[289] Virality Uber Alles: What the Fetishization of Social Media Is Costing Us All, http://www.huffingtonpost.com/arianna-huffington/social-media_b_1333499.html, Accessed on 28 March 2012.

[290] Kony 2012 campaign gets support of Obama, others, http://www.washingtonpost.com/blogs/blogpost/post/kony-2012-campaign-gets-support-of-obama-others/2012/03/08/gIQArnHkzR_blog.html, Accessed on 28 March 2012.

[291] The problem with Kony 2012, http://thestar.com.my/lifestyle/story.asp?file=/2012/3/19/lifefocus/10901832&sec=lifefocus, Accessed on 28 March 2012.

[292] Unpacking Kony 2012, http://www.ethanzuckerman.com/blog/2012/03/08/unpacking-kony-2012/, Accessed on 28 March 2012.

[293] In defence of the bandwagon: Kony 2012 makers should check their facts, but so should critics, https://theconversation.edu.au/in-defence-of-the-bandwagon-kony-2012-makers-should-check-their-facts-but-so-should-critics-5773, Accessed on 28 March 2012.

Criticism of the campaign would have been alright but the campaign did as much to turn the spotlight on Invisible Children as it did on the problem of the children in Uganda. The charity and director were forced to defend[294] not only the film but their operations and past record.

Most damning of all were the criticisms of Invisible Children being made by Ugandans[295] and by former "invisible children" themselves.

Kony 2012 bracelets[296] and T-shirts[297] became the signifiers of a US Christian organisation that didn't even have the support of the people they were allegedly trying to help. Ugandan Prime Minister Amama Mbabazi even created his own video[298] to refute allegations made in the Kony 2012 video.

In the video Mbabazi invited the celebrities who promoted the Kony 2012 video—including Rihanna, Bill Gates and Kim Kardashian—to come to Uganda and see the situation for themselves.

All of this would have been bad enough … but it got worse.

Late last week Kony 2012 director Jason Russell was arrested[299] in San Diego after police received reports of a man running through the streets and traffic naked, vandalising cars and "masturbating".

Invisible Children CEO Ben Keesey issued a statement[300] claiming Russell had been admitted to hospital suffering from exhaustion, dehydration and malnutrition. Unfortunately, a video[301] has been released seemingly showing Russell in the midst of a psychotic episode[302] of some sort.

Although there have been statements of compassion[303] about Russell's condition, members of the twittersphere have not been as kind. A new hashtag, #Horny2012, was created with tweets ridiculing him, Invisible Children and the film.

---

[294] Questions & answers, http://invisiblechildren.com/critiques/, Accessed on 28 March 2012.

[295] Ugandan forces capture key Kony ally, http://www.aljazeera.com/indepth/spotlight/konydebate/, Accessed on 28 March 2012.

[296] Kony Bracelet, http://shop.invisiblechildren.com/advocate-it/kony-2012/kony-bracelet/, Accessed on 28 March 2012.

[297] Link no longer goes to specified page, http://invisiblechildrenstore.myshopify.com/collections/bracelet-stories, Accessed on 28 March 2012.

[298] Uganda scathing of Kony 2012 video, http://www.abc.net.au/news/2012-03-18/uganda-responds-to-kony-2012-video/3896476, Accessed on 28 March 2012.

[299] Kony 2012 campaigner Jason Russell detained for public rampage, http://www.guardian.co.uk/world/2012/mar/16/kony-2012-campaigner-detained, Accessed on 28 March 2012.

[300] Statement from CEO Ben Keesey, http://blog.invisiblechildren.com/2012/03/16/statement-from-ceo-ben-keesey/, Accessed on 28 March 2012.

[301] New Jason Russell, Naked Meltdown of 'Kony 2012' Mastermind, From Up Close, http://www.tmz.com/2012/03/18/jason-russell-video-naked-meltdown-kony/#.T2XYSXj0Wec, Accessed on 28 March 2012.

[302] Sharing Public Breakdowns: What We Can Learn From Jason Russell, http://www.theatlantic.com/health/archive/2012/03/sharing-public-breakdowns-what-we-can-learn-from-jason-russell/254659/, Accessed on 28 March 2012.

[303] Sharing Public Breakdowns: What We Can Learn From Jason Russell, http://www.theatlantic.com/health/archive/2012/03/sharing-public-breakdowns-what-we-can-learn-from-jason-russell/254659/, Accessed on 28 March 2012.

The tragedy of all this is what started out as a probably well-intentioned plan has ended with:

- the central message of the film getting lost
- a charity losing its credibility, and
- a man suffering a breakdown and having a personal incident "go viral".

Worse still, Russell made his 5-year-old son, Gavin Danger, the centrepiece of the film. Ironically, in a pale reflection of the Invisible Children themselves, Danger was made to take part in something he would have had no say in; something he will now have to deal with for the rest of his life.

This whole debacle serves to remind us we are still barely coming to terms with the nature of what it means to be massively connected on a global scale.

As we saw in attempts to spread the Kony 2012 film, grossly oversimplifying the way social networks function is always going to lead to unpredictable results; results that are often damaging.

6.17 Why Is Telstra Next G Serving Your Data to Netsweeper in America?

28 June 2012

Information gleaned from data mining is a prized delicacy in certain circles. *Source*: **Philippe Put CC[304]**

---

[304]Philippe Put, Wikimedia, http://commons.wikimedia.org/wiki/File:%22Italian_Data%22_-_ Photo_by_Philippe_Put.jpg, Accessed online 21 December 2012.

Telstra representatives[305] have this week admitted to collecting data for a new internet filtering product and sending this data to the USA office of Netsweeper Inc.

Netsweeper Inc.,[306] based near Toronto, Canada, provides web content filtering and web threat management solutions. Web threat management solutions are designed to reduce email and web based threats such as phishing, viruses, malware and include the capability to do content filtering.

Telstra spokeswoman Nicole Mckenzie told the ABC[307]:

> "We were trying to classify internet sites as part of a new tool to help parents and kids when they're surfing the net."
>
> "[…] Cyberspace safety is a really important issue to address but we're obviously conscious of individual rights in that as well and we are going to be talking with key industry bodies to determine how next best to proceed."

Concerns identified by users of the Whirlpool broadband forum,[308] where this Telstra product development was publicly identified—in a thread aptly named "Are Telstra hackers?"—included the lack of notification by Telstra that customers' internet usage would be monitored and that the monitoring would occur from the USA.

It's worth pointing out in this context that the USA does not have the same level of privacy protection as either Europe[309] or Australia[310]—a point not lost on many of those so far commenting on this development at Telstra.

Basic mistakes made by Telstra include its failure to notify its Next G customers of the work taking place for its "new internet filtering product" and its failure to invite customers to take part in a development trial.

---

[305] Ockenden W., Telstra accused of tracking Next G internet use, ABC News, 27 Jun. 2012, http://www.abc.net.au/news/2012-06-27/telstra-accused-of-tracking-internet-use/4094692, Accessed online 28 June 2012.

[306] Netsweeper Inc., http://www.netsweeper.com/, Accessed online 28 June 2012.

[307] Ockenden W., Telstra accused of tracking Next G internet use, ABC News, 27 Jun. 2012, http://www.abc.net.au/news/2012-06-27/telstra-accused-of-tracking-internet-use/4094692, Accessed online 28 June 2012.

[308] Are Telstra hackers?, Whirlpool, 18 June 2012, http://forums.whirlpool.net.au/archive/1935438, Accessed online 28 June 2012.

[309] Sullivan B., 'La difference' is stark in EU, U.S. privacy laws, NBC News, 19 Oct. 2006, http://www.msnbc.msn.com/id/15221111/ns/technology_and_science-privacy_lost/t/la-difference-stark-eu-us-privacy-laws/, Accessed online 28 June 2012.

[310] US-Australia Agreements Create Opportunities for Privacy Violation, Extradition, Slashdot, 5 May 2012, http://politics.slashdot.org/story/12/05/06/0147248/us-australia-agreements-create-opportunities-for-privacy-violation-extradition, Accessed online 28 June 2012.

The Telstra boo-boo will raise a few hackles and ultimately could lead to a Telstra apology to the customers concerned. But will the company's offshore development effort end? Probably not—and this will mean more data from Australian customers being sent to the US.

6.17.1   Real-Time Tracking of Individuals

Nicole McKenzie of Telstra stated: "We were trying to classify internet sites as part of a new tool to help parents and kids when they're surfing the net." Currently

---

[311] Imamon, Flickr, http://www.flickr.com/photos/imamon/283894146/, Accessed online 21 December 2012.

Telstra utilises the Nominum[312] Domain Name Server (DNS)[313] solution for ensuring family safety online.[314]

So why is the company working with Netsweeper—a company known for content filtering—to develop a new family safety product?

Current family internet safety systems rely upon static lists of banned webpages. The webpage blacklists are published by organisations such as Interpol.[315]

What is different is the way the new application appears to work.

When a targeted Next G customer browses a webpage the IP[316] is sent to a server in the USA which then immediately browses the same webpage. The purpose of the activity is apparently to identify the webpage and ultimately to identify those pages that should be blocked.

What we can identify about this new system is that it is not just blocking access to blacklisted webpages but includes individual customer tracking and appears to be near real-time testing of the webpages accessed.

Why? One possibility is that a simple test is being carried out to see if the webpage exists. This would be a useful step that would be carried out to ensure the webpage in question still exists before blocking further access to the webpage. But that's unlikely to be the only reason.

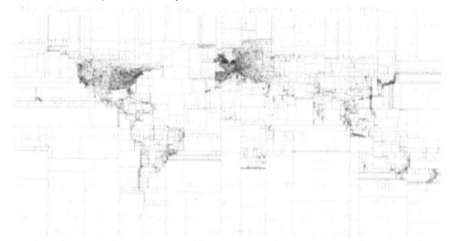

Source: **Eric Fisher**[317]

[312] Nominum, http://www.nominum.com/, Accessed online 28 June 2012.

[313] Domain Name System, Wikipedia, http://en.wikipedia.org/wiki/Domain_Name_System, Accessed online 28 June 2012.

[314] Nominum Offers Australian ISPs the Most Effective and Responsible DNS Solution for Ensuring Family Safety Online, Nominum, 21 December 2009, http://www.nominum.com/company/news-center/press-releases/nominum-offers-australian-isps-the-most-effective-and-responsible-dns-solution-for-ensuring-family-safety-online/, Accessed online 28 June 2012.

[315] Access Blocking, Interpol, http://www.interpol.int/Crime-areas/Crimes-against-children/Access-blocking/The-INTERPOL-%22Worst-of%22-list,Accessed online 28 June 2012.

[316] IP address, Wikipedia, http://en.wikipedia.org/wiki/IP_address, Accessed online 28 June 2012.

[317] Fisher E., Flickr, http://www.flickr.com/photos/walkingsf/6159680639/, Accessed online 21 December 2012.

It seems more likely what we're seeing is the first step in a new system that will ultimately:

1. identify customers
2. track their browsing
3. send the IP addresses of the webpages browsed to a separate application server for further processing

It has been confirmed by Mark Newton,[318] formerly a senior engineer with Australian internet company Internode,[319] that the application server, upon receiving the details of a webpage, proceeds to browse the same webpage.

6.17.2   What's Going on?

Given the purpose of this automated visit to the webpage has not, as yet, been explained by Telstra, I will speculate. In doing so, I am not suggesting this is what Telstra is doing—simply what could be possible in a similar scenario.

The next step of this type of product development could be an automated process that utilises deep packet inspection[320] techniques.

Deep packet inspection is an automated process that captures copies of IP packets and identifies what's inside them as they move across the internet. Assuming the content is not encrypted, the deep packet inspection system will identify what is in the packet in some detail.

The individual that accessed any given webpage would be known and the authorities could be notified whenever deemed appropriate.

Technology is now rapidly reaching a point where real-time internet tracking and traffic data mining will be carried out by carriers, Internet Service Providers (ISP)[321] and multi-national website providers.

This information gained is the Holy Grail[322] for companies offering services over the internet and will become a major source of revenue for carriers and ISPs.

Behavioural-targeted advertising[323] is the technologies, techniques and processes involved in providing advertising that has been tailored to individual customers.

---

[318] Are Telstra hackers?, Whirlpool, http://forums.whirlpool.net.au/archive/1935438, Accessed online 28 June 2012.

[319] Internode, http://www.internode.on.net/, Accessed online 28 June 2012.

[320] Wawro A., What is deep packet inspection, PCWorld, 1 Feb 2012, http://www.pcworld.com/article/249137/what_is_deep_packet_inspection_.html, Accessed online 28 June 2012.

[321] Internet service provider, Wikipedia, http://en.wikipedia.org/wiki/Internet_service_provider, Accessed online 28 June 2012.

[322] Chen J., Stallaert, J., An Economic Analysis of Online Advertising Using Behavioral Targeting, http://infosys.uncc.edu/CIST2011/Papers/cist2011_submission_41.pdf, Accessed online 28 June 2012.

[323] Drell L., 4 Ways Behavioral Targeting is Changing the Web, Mashable, 26 April 2011, http://mashable.com/2011/04/26/behavioral-targeting/, Accessed online 28 June 2012.

Source: **Michael Coghlan**[324]

The focus for behavioural-targeted advertising products has been multinational website providers. Information is collected every time a person accesses a website or carries out a search and this information is used to develop a behavioural targeted advertising strategy for the customer.

The customer is identified by his or her IP address, which for most residential and business customers does not change often—but mobile device users have a different IP address every time the device is used. The only way a website provider can link such a device to its user is with the help of cookies or the carrier/ISP because it is they who can identify the IP, the device and subsequently the owner.

---

[324]Coghlan M., Flickr, http://www.flickr.com/photos/mikecogh/8121683770/, Accessed online 21 December 2012.

6.17.3   Australia and Privacy

In Australia the Privacy Act[325] places limits on the way information can be gathered and sold.

Companies looking to become National Broadband Network (NBN)[326] retail service providers (RSP) (most of the existing carriers and ISPs) will all pay the same price per customer to NBN Co.[327]

The RSPs will differentiate themselves by bundling products and seeking ways to tap into the large revenue stream that can be generated by providing data that can be used for behavioural-targeted advertising.

Targeted marketing[328] by online advertisers in the USA will rise to more than US$2.6 billion in 2014. The value to Australian RSPs could be in the range of A$10 million to more than A$100 million annually.

RSPs may start looking for ways to appear to comply with, yet subtly circumvent the Privacy Act. Mel Gibson played Jerry Fletcher in Conspiracy Theory[329] and I can hear him now saying: "Rumours are that this process may have already started."

Is this what Telstra is really doing? Surely not.

But let's be clear: a real-time customer computer or mobile device tracking and webpage monitoring system incorporating deep packet inspection that was developed as an improved new family safety product could quite readily be adapted for use as a real-time data mining system that would provide information that could be used by behavioural targeted advertising systems.

It is important that Telstra be asked to explain in some detail.

It is also time that all carriers and ISPs be required to disclose to customers all filtering, proxy servers[330] or data mining products being used and commercial arrangements with all third-party companies that may be involved in the provision of these services or may be paying for information retrieved from these products.

---

[325] Privacy Act, Office of the Australian Information Commissioner, http://www.privacy.gov.au/law/act/, Accessed online 28 June 2012.

[326] Opperman I., Explainer: the National Broadband Network (NBN), The Conversation, https://theconversation.edu.au/explainer-the-national-broadband-network-nbn-207, Accessed online 28 June 2012.

[327] NBN Co, http://www.nbnco.com.au/, Accessed online 28 June 2012.

[328] Chen J., Stallaert, J., An Economic Analysis of Online Advertising Using Behavioral Targeting, http://infosys.uncc.edu/CIST2011/Papers/cist2011_submission_41.pdf, Accessed online 28 June 2012.

[329] Conspiracy Theory, IMDB, http://www.imdb.com/title/tt0118883/, Accessed online 28 June 2012.

[330] Proxy.org, http://proxy.org/, Accessed online 28 June 2012.

Source: **Alan Cleaver**[331]

How do we slow down the advance of behavioural-targeted advertising and the associated tracking of what we do on the internet? A few suggestions:

1. Ban carriers, ISPs and NBN Co from having systems that carry out tracking, monitoring, filtering real time data mining etcetera. But, while such a ban is possible, carriers, ISPs and NBN Co are required to provide this capability to police and therefore the capability would always be within the organisation. Naturally, it would be difficult to monitor and ensure the capability was not used for non-police related purposes.

---

[331] Cleaver A., Flickr, http://www.flickr.com/photos/alancleaver/4105726930/, Accessed online 21 December 2012.

2. Stipulate that all websites and mail systems are to use Secure Socket Layer (SSL)[332] encryption, which would effectively defeat existing deep packet inspection systems. A side benefit is that by utilising SSL between mail servers and when connecting to a mail server it is possible to reduce SPAM.[333]
3. Utilise Virtual Private Network (VPN)[334] connections to defeat existing deep packet inspection systems. VPN provides a point-to-point encrypted traffic tunnel.

Systems such as TOR[335] and the Darknet[336] were built around the use of VPNs and private servers not visible on the internet.

6.17.4   Deep Impact

The issue of internet tracking and monitoring is a complex one.

One aspect of this is governments wanting to reduce cybercrime and terrorism. Recently the UK government announced[337] that, under new legislation to be introduced soon, it will be able to monitor calls, email, SMS and website visits.

As anticipated, civil liberties groups have come out hard against the British government's announcement.

The Director of the Big Brother Watch Campaign[338] group Nick Pickles said[339]:

> "This is an unprecedented step that will see Britain adopt the same kind of surveillance seen in China and Iran. This is an absolute attack on privacy online and it is far from clear this will actually improve public safety, while adding significant costs to internet businesses."

There is an urgent need for the government to update the Privacy Act and to fully consider the impact of the rapid technology change that is driving the internet.

In the interim, Telstra has some explaining to do.

---

[332] The Transport Layer Security (TLS) Protocol Version 1.2, IETF, http://tools.ietf.org/html/rfc5246, Accessed online 28 June 2012.

[333] You've got mail – how to stop spam and reduce cyber crime, The Conversation, https://theconversation.edu.au/youve-got-mail-how-to-stop-spam-and-reduce-cyber-crime-2029,   Accessed online 28 June 2012.

[334] Framework for Layer 2 Virtual Private Networks (L2VPNs), IETF, http://tools.ietf.org/html/rfc4664, Accessed online 28 June 2012.

[335] Tor, https://www.torproject.org/, Accessed online 28 June 2012.

[336] The dark side of the internet, The Guardian, http://www.guardian.co.uk/technology/2009/nov/26/dark-side-internet-freenet, Accessed online 28 June 2012.

[337] Email and web use 'to be monitored' under new laws, BBC News, http://www.bbc.co.uk/news/uk-politics-17576745, Accessed online 28 June 2012.

[338] Big Brother Watch, http://www.bigbrotherwatch.org.uk/, Accessed online 28 June 2012.

[339] Email and web use 'to be monitored' under new laws, BBC News, http://www.bbc.co.uk/news/uk-politics-17576745, Accessed online 28 June 2012.

The Australian Communications and Media Authority[340] should carry out an inquiry into this matter and publish a report on exactly what the state of tracking, monitoring and data mining is within Australian carriers and ISPs.

6.18 Sick of Paying for Textbooks? Get Them Now, Free and Online

18 July 2012

In the same way that free open online courseware[341] is threatening to disrupt traditional universities, open textbook initiatives such as OpenStax[342] College from Rice University threaten to do the same to the traditional textbook market.

OpenStax College has taken five of the most popular topics taught in American universities and produced high quality peer-reviewed textbooks that are available for anyone to download for free.

OpenStax College aims to try and save students[343] at least $90 million over 5 years by capturing 10 % of the US textbook market.

But this is not the first open access textbook venture. Sites like Bookboon[344] and Flat World Knowledge[345] offer free online and downloadable versions of their texts with print versions available at a price. But the difference is that these sites have strong associations with publishers, whereas OpenStax College is run through a university.

Authors of textbooks in Flat World Knowledge receive a royalty on sales of printed versions of their textbooks, whereas authors contributing towards Rice University's venture are volunteering their efforts. Bookboon funds open access through the inclusion of advertising in the books.

The move to electronic textbooks is something that students have adopted with gusto. In a summary of research[346] at Indiana University over 1,700 students were surveyed for their attitudes and use of e-Textbooks: 87 % of students reported reading e-Texbooks over paper versions, while 68 % of students never printed any part of their texts, reading everything digitally.

---

[340] Australian Communications and Media Authority, ACMA, http://www.acma.gov.au/, Accessed online 28 June 2012.

[341] Will free online courseware from the US mean the end of (most) universities elsewhere?, https://theconversation.edu.au/will-free-online-courseware-from-the-us-mean-the-end-of-most-universities-elsewhere-8016, Accessed on 18 July 2012.

[342] about OpenStax College, http://openstaxcollege.org/about, Accessed on 18 July 2012.

[343] Why Pay for Intro Textbooks?, http://www.insidehighered.com/news/2012/02/07/rice-university-announces-open-source-textbooks, Accessed on 18 July 2012.

[344] Bookboon, http://www.bookboon.com, Accessed on 18 July 2012.

[345] Personalization & Affordability Changes Everything. http://www.flatworldknowledge.com/, Accessed on 18 July 2012.

[346] Dennis A., e-Textbooks at Indiana University: A Summary of Two Years of Research, Indiana University, August 2011, http://etexts.iu.edu/files/eText%20Pilot%20Data%202010-2011.pdf, Accessed on 18 July 2012.

The survey also revealed that the primary reading device was their laptops and only 1 % used a mobile device or an e-Reader (this may be a reflection of the time of the study which covered 2009–2011, as iPads were relatively new in 2009).

In 2012, MIT teamed up[347] with Flat World Knowledge to provide textbooks for their OpenCourseWare courses. Presumably this will continue with the edX[348] venture.

With the average textbook costing between $50 and $300, the availability of free textbooks would be extremely attractive to students. There is certainly anecdotal evidence that students are resorting to using pirated copies of electronic textbooks to avoid the large financial outlay. Certainly, it wasn't hard to find a pirated copy of the first textbook I looked for on the internet.

Given that free textbooks are available and that they are at least of equal quality as those available from commercial publishers, the question could be raised as to why they are not more commonly used by academics.

On the assumption that most academics would care about students having to pay for a textbook, there are probably a number of reasons they are not more commonly used. The primary reason is that academics don't know they are available. Another reason might be time pressures in preparing a course.

Spending time searching for a free textbook is probably not a priority. The practice of making a university course revolve intimately around a text would also make changing textbooks an effort for some academics -especially if they wrote the textbook!

The open textbook's American focus might also be a disincentive for academics (and students) in some subjects. This is more likely to be an issue in the humanities than in the sciences or engineering.

Aside from the benefits to students, the move to open access textbooks released under creative commons licenses is an important development in education. The ability to use content without worrying about copyright issues is a big advantage, especially when making the courses developed in this way open access themselves.

A considerable amount of effort is spent by universities locking away content on so-called learning management systems simply to avoid copyright issues when non-original content is used. This also allows for academics to modify content and incorporate it with their own to customise the way it is used in their course.

Of more importance, however, is that the world simply doesn't need 9,603 introductory texts to Sociology[349] that can currently be found on Amazon. Of course, we have so many variants of textbooks because this is the only way that publishers can make money out of books that sell small numbers of copies each (a long tail[350] business model).

---

[347] MIT OpenCourseWare teams up with Flat World Knowledge to combine free texts and free course materials, http://web.mit.edu/newsoffice/2012/ocw-flat-world-knowledge.html, Accessed on 18 July 2012.

[348] edX, https://www.edx.org/, Accessed on 18 July 2012.

[349] Link no longer goes to specified page, http://www.amazon.com/ref=nb_sb_noss_null#/ref=sr_pg_2?rh=i%3Aaps%2Ck%3Aintroduction+to+sociology&page=2&keywords=introduction+to+sociology&ie=UTF8&qid=1341927673, Accessed on 18 July 2012

[350] The long tail of academic publishing and why it isn't a bad thing, https://theconversation.edu.au/the-long-tail-of-academic-publishing-and-why-it-isnt-a-bad-thing-8126, Accessed on 18 July 2012.

Wikipedia has demonstrated the power of a crowdsourcing model in the development of mostly high quality content. Applying this to introductory texts as in the OpenStax College model benefits from a collaborative model of development that can be sustained with constant updates.

The move to open education models of open courseware and content is only going to be of enormous benefit to students. For universities, there is the opportunity of contributing to this movement and reaping the reputational benefits as a consequence.

By making their textbooks free, a university can extend its reach enormously, to hundreds of thousands of potential readers. It can also monetise free textbooks, by selling associated question-and-answer sheets, by incorporating subject related advertising, or by selling a related physical product (such as a calculator, a titration set, or an anatomy lab coat).

Traditional publishers may not be happy with this move. A group of them are trying to sue[351] another open access textbook company Boundless Learning.[352]

But at the end of the day, it is going to be hard to argue against "free" in the world of learning.

6.19 Is Origin Smart Sleepwalking Into a Shocking Personal Data Breach?

3 September 2012

The origin smart portal provides customers with an estimate of future electricity bills.
Source: **Quinn Dombrowski**[353]

---

[351] Publishers Sue As Boundless Learning Grabs $8 M For An Open Alternative To Textbooks, http://techcrunch.com/2012/04/05/publishers-sue-as-boundless-nabs-8m/, Accessed on 18 July 2012.

[352] Boundless, https://www.boundless.com/, Accessed on 18 July 2012.

[353] Dombrowski Q., Flickr, http://www.flickr.com/photos/quinnanya/8042337565/, Accessed online 21 December 2012.

Early last week, Origin Energy,[354] Australia's pre-eminent energy retailer, launched an online energy-use monitoring portal Origin Smart[355] to much fanfare.[356] All good—but what about the privacy and security of the data being collected and made available?

Origin Smart is a website that lets Origin's Victorian customers to see their home electricity usage updated every half hour. The electricity usage information comes from the new smart meters[357] that were rolled out over the past 6 years.

Victorian customers (and then customers nationally) will be able to view their electricity usage for up to 24 h prior to the current half-hourly reading.

Other energy companies, including United Energy,[358] are in the final stages of testing[359] a portal similar to Origin Smart.

6.19.1 What You're Getting

The Origin Smart portal provides customers with an estimate of future electricity bills and the capability to set daily electricity consumption targets.

But the value of Energy Smart is yet to be identified because customers may need to see historical energy usage data—beyond the current 1-day provided—to gain an understanding of their energy usage over time and to be able to make informed decisions.

Customers will be also able to compare their usage with households of a similar size and occupancy.

This all sounds fine, right? I mean, who wouldn't want to know how much energy they're using? But, as mentioned above, there are bigger issues at play here, involving privacy and security.

---

[354] Origin Energy, http://www.originenergy.com.au/, Accessed online 3 September 2012.

[355] Origin Smart, Origin Energy, http://www.originenergy.com.au/originsmart, Accessed online 3 September 2012.

[356] Wells R., Half-hourly checks to monitor smart meters, Fairfax Media, 27 August 2012, http://www.brisbanetimes.com.au/environment/energy-smart/halfhourly-checks-to-monitor-smart-meters-20120826-24ulb.html, Accessed online 3 September 2012.

[357] Smartmeters, Victorian Government, http://www.dpi.vic.gov.au/smart-meters, Accessed online 3 September 2012.

[358] United Energy, http://www.unitedenergy.com.au/, Accessed online 3 September 2012.

[359] Wells R., Half-hourly checks to monitor smart meters, Fairfax Media, 27 August 2012, http://www.brisbanetimes.com.au/environment/energy-smart/halfhourly-checks-to-monitor-smart-meters-20120826-24ulb.html, Accessed online 3 September 2012.

6.19.2   Risk of a Cyber-Attack?

In recent weeks I have written on The Conversation about cybercrime and cyber-terrorism laws. The Cybercrime Legislation Amendment Bill 2011[360] increases the scope of customer data that carriers and internet service providers (ISPs) must collect when notified by police or security organisations.

Proposed changes to cybersecurity laws[361] include a provision for a 2-year internet data retention requirement for all Australians.

How is this relevant to Origin Smart? Well, I've received several requests for an example of a national network-related privacy and security problem.

I submit Origin Smart.

Origin Smart has all the characteristics of an information store that will be a target for hackers.

Knowledge is power and information about customers' electricity usage is a saleable commodity. Information about electricity usage for business, government, defence and national infrastructure is of value to hackers and terrorists. (Origin Energy hasn't made it clear whether Origin Smart will be available only to residential customers.)

Will Anonymous[362] target Origin Smart as part of its current Operation Australia[363] campaign? I don't see why not.

Victorian customers can access the portal from any internet-connected computer. The portal does not utilise two-step authentication[364]—that is, a second layer of security (such as being sent a password by text message) that makes a security breach less likely.

By contrast, most Australian banks and many online services, including Google[365] and Dropbox, *do* use two-step authentication.

Failure to utilise these additional security measures is a potential flaw that makes Origin Smart more of a target than it needs to be.

---

[360] Cybercrime Legislation Amendment Bill 2011, Australian Government, 22 August 2012, http://parlinfo.aph.gov.au/parlInfo/search/display/display.w3p;query=Id:%22legislation/billhome/r4575%22, Accessed online 3 September 2012.

[361] Gregory M.A., Why is Anonymous hacking Australia?, The Conversation, 31 July 2012, https://theconversation.edu.au/why-is-anonymous-hacking-australia-8480, Accessed online 3 September 2012.

[362] Anonymous, http://anonymous.pysia.info/, Accessed online 3 September 2012.

[363] Lee J., Operation Australia Anonymous, Cyber War News, 12 August 2012, http://www.cyber-warnews.info/timelines/time-line-of-attacks-from-operation-australia-opaustralia/, Accessed online 3 September 2012.

[364] Two-factor authentication, Wikipedia, http://en.wikipedia.org/wiki/Two-factor_authentication, Accessed online 3 September 2012.

[365] Two step verification, Google, http://support.google.com/accounts/bin/answer.py?hl=en&answer=180744, Accessed online 3 September 2012.

6.19.3 Collection

At the most basic level, Origin Smart is collecting critical information about customers putting it all into internet-connected systems and making it available to customers from any internet-connected computer around the world.

Why would a Victorian Origin Energy customer need to see their half-hourly energy usage while on holiday in Russia?

More concerning is the fact the Origin Smart: Initial Privacy Consent[366] provides a list of organisations that customers agree, when signing up to the service, to allow access to their data.

That list includes:

> ... relevant contractors which may include installers, mail houses, data processing analysts, IT service providers and smart energy technology providers, debt collection agencies and credit reporting agencies, relevant Government authorities...

Why would I want to share my half-hourly electricity usage data with a debt collector? Or a credit reporting agency for that matter?

Is Origin Smart being set up as a dual-purpose portal that will allow a range of companies to log in and access the complete energy usage history of one or more customers? No-one as yet is saying so, but it would be reassuring to have such issues clarified.

6.19.4 Offshoring Data

The Origin Smart Terms and Conditions[367] indicate customer information will be sent to a "third-party smart energy technology provider" located in Colorado, USA.

The Australian government should be very concerned that potentially most (Origin Energy currently has 4.4m customers nationwide[368]) of Australia's residential, business and corporate energy usage is being sent to the USA—a country that does not have strict privacy and security rules.

The Origin Smart Terms and Conditions read:

> The USA does not have laws that provide the same level of protection for an individual's personal information as in Australia, however, the Third Party Provider is required to comply with any applicable privacy legislation.

---

[366] Origin Smart: Initial Privacy Consent, Origin Smart, https://www.originenergy.com.au/osregister/?_qf_p1_display=true, Accessed online 3 September 2012.

[367] Terms and Conditions, Origin Smart, Origin Energy, http://www.originenergy.com.au/originsmart/support/origin-smart-terms-and-conditions, Accessed online 3 September 2012, New link http://www.originenergy.com.au/4122/Terms-and-conditions?rt=y

[368] Who We Are, Origin Energy, http://www.originenergy.com.au/1758/Who-we-are, Accessed online 3 September 2012.

But let's be clear: the US company is not subject to Australian law and would never agree to being subject to Australian privacy laws.

This statement in the Origin Energy Terms and Conditions should be investigated by the relevant authorities immediately.

6.19.5   Data Breach?

Are we in danger of inadvertently paving the way for the largest personal data breach in Australian history? And all without having been attacked by Anonymous, by cyber-terrorists or a potential enemy nation carrying out an act of cyber-warfare.

Origin Energy has stated it will send customer data to a company in a country that does not require that company to keep the data secure and permits the company to on-sell the data to whomever they please. I'm gobsmacked.

Can Origin Energy guarantee the data sent to the USA will be destroyed at some point in the future? When would this be?

We all should remember Google making a similar promise[369] to the Australian Privacy Commissioner[370] in the context of the Google Street View controversy.[371]

Google admitted to collecting Wi-Fi data when capturing information for Google Steet View. After assuring the Australian Privacy Commissioner that all of the data collected had been destroyed, Google later admitted to finding more data[372] that had not been destroyed.

To summarise, my concerns about Origin Smart are the following:

1. **Poor security**. Without two-step authentication the system could be a juicy hacking target
2. **Poor privacy**. The list of organisations that can be provided with access to customer data is extraordinary and access for many is unnecessary and unwarranted
3. **National security**. The data of everyone who signs up to Origin Smart will be sent to the USA.

The Origin Smart Initial Privacy Consent requirement and the Terms and Conditions were red flags for me. As an Origin Energy customer I chose not sign up to Origin Smart.

I strongly recommend you refrain from doing so as well.

---

[369] Google ordered to destroy personal data, AAP, 8 August 2012, http://news.smh.com.au/breaking-news-national/google-ordered-to-destroy-personal-data-20120808-23ubc.html, Accessed online 3 September 2012.

[370] Office of the Australian Information Commissioner, http://www.privacy.gov.au, Accessed online 3 September 2012.

[371] Orlowski A., Google KNEW Street View cars were slurping Wi-Fi, The Register, 30 April 2012, http://www.theregister.co.uk/2012/04/30/google_slurp_ok/, Accessed online 3 September 2012.

[372] Google finds more data not destroyed, NineMSN, http://news.ninemsn.com.au/technology/8513051/google-ordered-to-destroy-personal-data, Accessed online 3 September 2012, new link http://www.theregister.co.uk/2012/10/09/google_oz_street_view_data_slurp/

6.20   MOOC and You're Out of a Job: Uni Business Models in Danger

11 October 2012

Academics and universities might need to be careful of what they wish for with free online education. *Source*: **Koka Sexton**[373]

Consider this scenario.

There are 36 universities employing 36 academics who each offer a first year mathematics course. The 36 universities collaborate and develop a single first-year mathematics course which is available to all students online and for free.

Do the universities need the 36 academics?

Does the government need 36 universities?

The answer to both questions, of course, is no. Academics and universities have been quick to jump on the Massive Open Online Course (MOOCs) bandwagon, but they may become less enthusiastic as we begin to see the dramatic, and perhaps unintended consequences in store for higher education.

6.20.1   Why Academics Should Be Wary of MOOCs

At the moment, academics already use technology to create and host courses, usually through a Learning Management Systems (LMS). Unlike a MOOC which is offered by brand name universities for free online, the LMS is only accessible by

---

[373] Sexton K., Flickr, http://www.flickr.com/photos/ikoka/7324887986/, Accessed online 21 December 2012.

university staff and students. Job promotions and university income depend on this course development, particularly through book publications later on.

So if most academics already use an LMS, why should the use of MOOCs be any different?

The problem is that MOOCs change several dynamics associated with course delivery; changes academics may have not considered.

One of the first reasons academics should be worried is the potential for completed MOOCs to count toward "prior learning credits",[374] which include working, training, volunteering and activities in the community that can count towards a formally recognised qualification.

So far only a small number of universities worldwide have offered credits for MOOC courses, and if they do, students are required to undergo additional university examinations.

But prior learning credits could be awarded to students who have completed a MOOC without additional university assessment.

Chari Kelley, vice president for LearningCounts.org, which is a subsidiary of the US Council for Adult and Experiential Learning (CAEL),[375] recently said[376] regarding prior learning credits based on MOOCs "we are set up to do that. The infrastructure is there."

This gives MOOCs the potential to be recognised in university programs—allowing for greater competition between them and traditional universities.

6.20.2   Slippery Slope to Outsourced Education

Another issue is the way open, online education could affect the privatisation of higher education and the role of academics.

Already technology has facilitated a move away from chalk-and-talk lectures toward more project based learning,[377] workshops (sometimes online) and online forums and meetings. Many academics have also embraced multiple choice or online examinations through their LMS.

This shift in course delivery has also seen the academic's role change, becoming more akin to course coordinators. Universities are hiring casual staff to manage student projects, workshops and online activities. Academics are now primarily responsible for setting and marking examinations.

---

[374] Credit transfer and recognition of prior learning (RPL), Victorian Tertiary Admissions Centre, http://www.vtac.edu.au/courses-inst/credit-transfer.html, Accessed online 11 October 2012.

[375] Centre for Adult and Experiential Learning (CAEL), http://www.cael.org/, Accessed online 11 October 2012.

[376] Fain P., Making It Count, Inside Higher Ed, http://www.insidehighered.com/news/2012/06/15/earning-college-credit-moocs-through-prior-learning-assessment, Accessed online 11 October 2012.

[377] Project-based learning, Wikipedia, http://en.wikipedia.org/wiki/Project-based_learning, Accessed online 11 October 2012.

The next logical step along the MOOC pathway is for universities to collaborate and develop examinations that are based on the MOOC courseware. The examinations can then be centralised and outsourced.

Students would attend examination centres, be verified and carry out multiple-choice or quiz-type questions that are machine mark-able. With this achieved, the academic no longer has a role in course delivery and is too expensive to keep on as a course coordinator.

Not possible?

It's already happening in the world of multinational companies. They offer industry qualifications and training by private education providers. The final qualification examination is carried out through local accredited testing centres. Non-technical people verify the identity of the person completing the examination, oversee the person carry out an online, multiple-choice examination, and issue a certificate if the person is successful.

6.20.3 Research-Only Universities

Several Australian universities already identify academics as "research-only" or "teaching-only". Earlier this year it was reported[378] that Monash University has identified 196 teaching-only jobs, 1,058 research-only jobs and 1,444 jobs in teaching and research.

Other universities reported to have teaching-only roles include Melbourne (107), Swinburne (164) and Newcastle (156).

The number of academics identifying with teaching-only roles has increased[379] over the past decade to between 10 and 15 %.

With the potential for undergraduate education to be outsourced, does this mean teaching-only academics will become redundant?

With courses run through MOOCs and centralised outsourced examinations, many universities will have already answered the question: do we need all the academics we have?

But then comes the next question: do we need all the universities?

Australian universities with low research profiles and high undergraduate and vocational teaching focus will be identified and asked to justify their future.

Private industry will argue for university closures and low-cost examination testing centres to be opened in their place.

---

[378]Lane B., Rise in teaching-only roles bucks tradition, The Australian, News Limited, 16 November 2011, http://www.theaustralian.com.au/higher-education/rise-in-teaching-only-roles-bucks-tradition/story-e6frgcjx-1226196058746, Accessed online 11 October 2012.

[379]Rhiannon L., Senate Estimates: Australian Research Council – Higher Education standards, The Greens, http://lee-rhiannon.greensmps.org.au/content/estimates/senate-estimates-australian-research-council-higher-education-standards, Accessed online 11 October 2012.

6.20.4   Raising the Alarm

Speaking at a high-speed broadband and higher education forum[380] last month, Australian National University Vice-Chancellor Professor Ian Young warned MOOCs could be Australian universities' "own worst enemy". "Once you have given away something," he said, "it is very difficult then to make people pay for it".

At the same conference the Minister for Broadband and Communications, Senator Conroy said:

> It's only taken us 112 years to get a national curriculum, I don't think we've got 112 years to work out what we want to provide in the globalised digital education world.... What is a lecture worth if the best lecturer in the world at MIT is online for free for all to access?

Senator Conroy's call for more rapid change highlights an urgent need for academics to get involved in the online learning discussion now.

For academics, the advent of MOOCs may be the beginning of a perfect storm where technology will provide a means to centralise courseware and provide for automated assessment for undergraduate courses.

Of course, we can't know for certain but time may well prove that academics joining MOOCs now could be the first lemmings off the cliff.

We'd love you to take part: leave your comments, join the discussion on twitter. com/conversationEDU, facebook.com/conversationEDU.

This is part four of our series on the Future of Higher Education.[381] **You can read other instalments by clicking the links below:**

Part one: Online opportunities: digital innovation or death through regulation?, Jane Den Hollander[382]

Part two: MOOCs and exercise bikes—more in common than you'd think, Phillip Dawson & Robert Nelson[383]

Part three: How Australian universities can play in the MOOCs market, David Sadler[384]

---

[380] High-speed broadband and higher education seminar, Melbourne University, 27–28 September 2012, http://www.cshe.unimelb.edu.au/research/res_seminars/major_events/nbn_forum/program. html, Accessed online 11 October 2012.

[381] Future of Higher Education, The Conversation, https://theconversation.edu.au/pages/future-of-higher-education, Accessed online 11 October 2012.

[382] Den Hollander J., Online opportunities: digital innovation or death through regulation, The Conversation, 8 October 2012, https://theconversation.edu.au/online-opportunities-digital-innovation-or-death-through-regulation-9736, Accessed online 11 October 2012.

[383] Nelson R. and Dawson P., MOOCs and exercise bikes – more in common than you'd think, The Conversation, 9 October 2012, https://theconversation.edu.au/moocs-and-exercise-bikes-more-in-common-than-youd-think-9726, Accessed online 11 October 2012.

[384] Sadler D., How Australian universities can play in the MOOCs market, The Conversation, 10 October 2012, https://theconversation.edu.au/how-australian-universities-can-play-in-the-moocs-market-9735, Accessed online 11 October 2012.

6.21 Australia Post's Digital Delivery Scheme May Yield Few Returns to Spender

12 October 2012

Australia Post have every reason to be pleased with their role in the online shopping revolution. They are central to the process by providing a means of converting the virtual into the real, by delivering online shoppers' purchases to their doorstep or mail locker. This has resulted in Australia Post "posting"[385] a $281 million profit for 2011/2012. This was despite a $148 million loss in the traditional mail business.

On the back of this success — and perhaps over confident in its mastery of the Internet — Australia Post has announced a $2 billion investment in upgrading its national parcel network and in providing a service called the "Digital MailBox".[386]

6.21.1 Mail Re-imagined in the Digital World

The Digital MailBox is due to launch in the next few weeks. Details are sketchy at this point. It will be a service that provides the ability to receive secure communications from companies and organisations also using the service. It will also allow you to receive and pay bills.

The "secure" portion of Digital MailBox will be provided by Telstra's Australian-based cloud. There will also be two-factor authentication,[387] which provides extra security when people log into the site. This will presumably be via a text message that provides a time-based one-off password in addition to the user's regular password.

Australia Post may also require some sort of identification process in order to set up an account so that the account identifiers can be used in the confidence that they are actually linked to the people they are supposed to be linked to.

6.21.2 A Good Idea: But Hasn't It Been Done Before?

The idea of providing this type of service is not necessarily a bad one, given that there are already successful services that already do much of what it is proposing. To a large extent, it is an extension of what the banks and Australia Post themselves

---

[385] Australia Post announce $2bn 'future ready' strategy, http://www.businessspectator.com.au/bs.nsf/Article/Australia-Post-to-spend-2b-on-parcels-YY252?OpenDocument&src=pm&utm_source=exact&utm_medium=email&utm_content=115975&utm_campaign=pm&modapt=news, Accessed on 12th October 2012.

[386] Digital Mailbox, https://digitalmailbox.auspost.com.au/, Accessed on 12th October 2012.

[387] Two-factor autehtication, http://en.wikipedia.org/wiki/Two-factor_authentication

are already providing with online access to services such as BPay[388] and Australia Post's own POSTbillpay.[389]

The subtle difference (possibly too subtle) with Digital MailBox is that the service can theoretically be used beyond just paying bills. Dealing with government agencies could be done through this mechanism because the communication is both secure, the party's identities can be verified and, possibly more importantly, the communication can be tracked. The service will be free of spam and thus reduce the likelihood of important messages going missing or being missed in the general flow of other communications.

The challenge for Australia Post in launching this service is twofold. The first challenge is as previously mentioned: the competition from existing and new services that largely provide some or all of what they are proposing to offer. The second and probably crucial issue is convincing the public and organisations that the service is necessary at all.

6.21.3   The Competition

Australia Post faces challenges from the banks—who already provide the ability to pay bills from their online services—and from direct competitors in the secure mailbox space.

One such competitor is Computershare, who has proposed a similar service called Digital Post.[390] Digital Post is almost identical to the Digital MailBox, so much so that Australia Post took Computershare to court to try and prevent is using the name Digital Post. It lost[391] the battle, leaving the coast clear for a race to see who can provide the service in Australia first.

Here, Computershare may have the advantage, having already launched a service publicly in the US in partnership with Zumbox.[392] It has also launched the service in Australia in a limited private release.

6.21.4   A Solution to a Non-existent Problem?

The big question however is whether digital mail is a solution looking for a problem that hasn't already been solved. Here, I am not convinced. The technology to achieve

---

[388] BPay, http://www.bpay.com.au/

[389] Postbill Pay, http://postbillpay.com.au/

[390] Digital Post, http://www.computershare.com/au/business/ccs/Documents/Fact%20Sheets/Digital%20Postal%20Mail%20Fact%20Sheet.pdf

[391] Court finds Digital Post joint venture by Salmat and Computershare does not infringe Australia Post's trademark, http://www.smartcompany.com.au/information-technology/051307-court-finds-digital-post-joint-venture-by-salmat-and-computershare-does-not-infringe-australia-post-s-trademark.html

[392] Zumbox, https://www.zumbox.com/

a digital mailbox using ordinary email with digital signatures and encryption has been around for a very long time. Despite improvements in infrastructure and the ease of use, it has never really taken off, mostly because there has never been the perception that it was really needed in the first place.

Another big problem has been that digital signatures and identity services were fine as long as you were dealing with the purely digital, but never really quite accommodated the need to also operate in the physical world. One immediate irony is that to prove identity, you often have to present paper copies of bills sent to a postal address!

Even Computershare CEO Stuart Crosby had a hard time[393] convincing a slightly sceptical Alan Kohler of ABC's Inside Business that Digital Post Australia was a viable business proposition. He said "One of the exciting things about these sorts of businesses [...] is that you don't know the answers".

I expect that Australia Post is none the wiser. Fortunately for them, they don't have shareholders asking those questions, including what part of the $2 billion is going to be invested in this scheme. If they did, I expect they would be prepared to never see that money again.

6.22 Telstra's Revised Cyber-Safety Service Could (and Should) Be Better

9 November 2012

Telstra listened to customer complaints about data privacy, but they could have done more. *Source*: **gailjadehamilton**[394]

---

[393] Lines   set   for   digital   mailbox   war,   http://www.abc.net.au/news/2012-09-02/ lines-set-for-digital-mailbox-war/4238548

[394] Gailjadehamilton, Flickr, http://www.flickr.com/photos/29881930@N00/2086639404/in/pho- tostream, Accessed online 21 December 2012.

Telstra's first attempt to introduce a cyber-safety service for mobile customers in June was a flop of significant proportions.[395]

Customers and concerned members of the public reacted strongly[396] to the collection and offshoring of user data that was part of the "Smart Controls" cyber-safety service and the service was eventually scrapped.[397]

But earlier this week, Telstra representatives apologised[398] for the first version of Smart Controls and announced the service would be re-introduced in late November 2012 following a suite of revisions.

6.22.1   Privacy Concerns

The Smart Controls service was originally introduced to help parents ensure their children were only visiting appropriate websites when surfing the net via a mobile phone.

The service allowed parents to block certain web pages, allow access to other pages, manage the amount of time spent online and a number of other options.

Despite these noble aims, there were many concerns about how the service would be implemented, including:

- data collection for Smart Controls would be compulsory for all Telstra mobile customers
- telstra offered no explanation about what data was collected
- the collected data was sent[399] to a Canadian-based web-content-filtering company Netsweeper Inc.[400]

It was the last of these that caused the greatest concern, with a thread on the Whirpool broadband forum addressing these issues given the title "Are Telstra hackers?".[401]

---

[395] Gregory M.A., Why is Telstra Next G serving your data to Netsweeper in America?, The Conversation, 28 June 2012, https://theconversation.edu.au/why-is-telstra-next-g-serving-your-data-to-netsweeper-in-america-7939, Accessed online 9 November 2012.

[396] Are Telstra Hackers, Whirlpool, http://forums.whirlpool.net.au/archive/1935438, Accessed online 9 November 2012.

[397] Clarke D., Update on Telstra's mobile cyber-safety tool, Telstra, 27 June 2012, http://exchange.telstra.com.au/2012/06/27/update-on-telstras-mobile-cyber-safety-tool/, Accessed online 9 November 2012.

[398] Ruddock N., A smart way to keep kids safe on their mobiles, Telstra, 5 November 2012, http://exchange.telstra.com.au/2012/11/05/a-smart-way-to-keep-kids-safe-on-their-mobiles/, Accessed online 9 November 2012.

[399] Gregory M.A., Why is Telstra Next G serving your data to Netsweeper in America?, The Conversation, 28 June 2012, https://theconversation.edu.au/why-is-telstra-next-g-serving-your-data-to-netsweeper-in-america-7939, Accessed online 9 November 2012.

[400] Netsweeper Inc., http://www.netsweeper.com/, Accessed online 9 November 2012.

[401] Are Telstra Hackers, Whirlpool, http://forums.whirlpool.net.au/archive/1935438, Accessed online 9 November 2012.

6.22.2   Smart Controls 2.0

The process of checking webpages accessed by Smart Controls users has changed little from the original version to the revised version.

That is, when a customer using the service accesses a webpage via their mobile, Telstra checks the requested website against its database of known websites to see if the site is appropriate for minors or not.

And while this process is the same in the revised version of Smart Controls, there are some subtle changes.

One change is the fact that Telstra is only sending data to Netsweeper Inc.[402] if a website accessed by the customer is not listed in the Telstra database.

That is, if the requested page isn't in Telstra's database, it then sends the page request to Netsweeper's more-extensive database to retrieve the page's classification.

If the page isn't in Netsweeper's database then the target site is assessed using an automated process and, if necessary, by Netsweeper staff. Information about the page's suitability for minors is then sent to Netsweeper's and Telstra's databases.

This is in contrast with the original version in which all mobile phone customer data was sent offshore to Netsweeper, albeit with variables and other extra information stripped from URLs first.[403]

Telstra Smart Controls Process *Source*: **Copyright © 2012 Telstra**

Furthermore, and importantly, the revised Smart Controls service is opt-in. As Peter Symons from Telstra Innovation told me via email:

> Telstra has re-engineered the product so that only customers subscribed to Smart Controls have URLs they visit compared with a database of classified sites held by Telstra on Telstra local servers.
>
> If the Telstra database does not recognise the website visited by the Smart Controls subscriber, the URL will be stripped of any parameter information in Australia [e.g. from telstra.com.au/index.html?mydata to telstra.com.au/] and sent to a database managed by Telstra's technology vendor Netsweeper.
>
> Subscribers to the Smart Controls service will need to consent to these arrangements via the product terms.

---

[402] Netsweeper Inc., http://www.netsweeper.com/, Accessed online 9 November 2012.

[403] Goonan A., Further update – Telstra 'Smart Controls' Cyber-Safety Tool, Telstra, 28 June 2012, Netsweeper Inc., http://www.netsweeper.com/, Accessed online 9 November 2012, Accessed online 9 November 2012.

6.22.3 That's Good, but …

These changes are a step in the right direction but concerns still remain.

Despite requiring customer opt-in, data is still being sent offshore to Netsweeper. Offshoring is a concern because different countries have different privacy laws and US laws are lax compared to Australian privacy laws.

The second concern is the question of what Netsweeper is doing with customers' information. Is Netsweeper on-selling Telstra customers' data or information derived from that data?

There is also no explanation offered by Telstra of how Netsweeper is classifying websites.

How is Netsweeper relating websites, content and the legislation concerning what is and what isn't legal or child-friendly in each country?

6.22.4 Cyber-Safety Is Important

Netsweeper should set up an office in Australia and the three main Australian mobile phone companies (Optus, Telstra and Vodafone) should work together to offer a cyber-safety service that is developed here based on Australian censorship laws.

Companies that have had a website added to the Smart Controls banned list should have the right of appeal—an issue Telstra doesn't appear to have addressed.

Telstra's apology for the misstep with the first version of Smart Controls should be accepted and Australians should appreciate that Telstra has worked towards a revised version.

But there are still questions that need to be answered about this service.

Cyber-safety is important and it would be great if Telstra, Optus and Vodafone could work together to build a comprehensive suite of Australian-based cyber-safety services that protect all users.

These services should comply with Australian legislation, society standards and ensure privacy and security are at the forefront of this effort.

6.23 Facebook's Privacy Tightrope

14 December 2012

Facebook is a commercial entity that is navigating a path fraught with danger with the multitude that inhabits the social network left exposed with a bullseye on their backs.

The executive director of US Centre for Digital Democracy Jeffrey Chester was recently told the Los Angeles Times that "Facebook's vision of its member base is a bunch of people naked, exposed and targeted at will by anyone who wants to do so." But isn't this what people sign on for when they opt to join Facebook?

People join Facebook because it is there, it is free and it simplifies the process of connecting with family and friends. There are alternatives but the ease of access and availability of Facebook makes it a compelling choice. It's still possible to get a family domain name and to setup a family portal for photos, messages, email, and so on but this costs about $200 per annum and takes some time to master. The success of Facebook is built on the capability to connect with people quickly and to be able to access a range of features in the one internet based location.

For Facebook then privacy is at odds with the corporate goal of maximising revenues. The recent changes to privacy announced by Facebook are subtle shifts that facilitate new revenue opportunities while providing customers with some visibility over what is happening—but is this enough?

Earlier this month Facebook ran a vote about the proposed privacy changes and about 600,000 of the ten billion Facebook users voted against the proposed changes. The vote fell short of the 300 million votes needed to reject the privacy changes under the current Facebook rules. With more than ten billion registered users the chances of getting 300 million to all vote the same way were always slim and unsurprisingly, there will be no more votes on privacy changes.

6.23.1   What Do the Votes Say?

About 600,000 Facebook users voted to reject the privacy changes proposed by Facebook. This is a significant number by any standard and Facebook would be wise to heed the advice that this outcome provides. Facebook is well aware that people are fickle and will move on to the next big thing as they did when they migrated to Facebook from MySpace. Facebook is relying on remaining the social media platform of choice for the foreseeable future, especially now that it has competitors on its tail.

The privacy changes are the latest changes proposed to partly address user concerns, but also to make it easier for advertisers and Facebook application developers to learn about the network's users and to target marketing for individual users.

These changes include:

1. New options that can be used to untag photos
2. A simple pop-up privacy shortcut selector
3. The capability to block people with one click
4. User profiles will now become searchable
5. The capability to hide or remove posts that appear of the searchable Timeline

The changes will be subject to the requirements that formed part of the US Federal Trade Commission settlement reached in April 2012 when Facebook agreed to get user consent for certain changes to privacy settings and to be independently audited regarding privacy provisions for 20 years.

Facebook has warned customers that information on the website needs to be closely monitored as the Timeline profile page is not the only personal information that may be viewed by others. This warning was reiterated[404] by the Facebook Director of Product Sam Lessin who warned that: "when users don't understand the concepts and controls and hit surprises, they don't build the confidence they need. Our number one priority is to not surprise users with our controls."

6.23.2   Gunning for the Top

What Facebook should be aware of is that Google, Microsoft and Apple, currently locked in combat in the devices space, will inevitably turn their attention to social media as a way to consolidate application, game, email, chat and talk features of their current offerings.

Google has already taken steps to enter into the social media fray with Google+ and it is only time before Microsoft and Apple do the same. The reason that this will occur is pragmatic more than any particular desire to destroy Facebook. Customers want a reason to purchase a device from Google, Microsoft or Apple and one key reason for Apple's success to date has been the integration of apps with entertainment purchases.

Facebook bought Instagram in September 2012 and this acquisition provides Facebook with a stranglehold on the photo sharing space. More than one billion photos have been shared with Instagram. This tie-up was always going spark a response from other social media organisations and Twitter has fired off its own salvo this week with the launch a photo sharing application to compete with the Facebook/Instagram combination. The shift by Twitter will not immediately hurt Facebook as it has plans to more closely integrate Instagram into the Facebook platform. However, the question that needs to be asked now is will Facebook retaliate and create a competitor to Twitter?

A sleeper in the pack is Microsoft for little is known about Microsoft's plans for Skype. Skype provides a huge customer base and by subtly and slowly adding to Skype, Microsoft could build an alternative ecosystem to Facebook. However, Microsoft will need to show flare and innovation to do this and the current management team has not demonstrated a great deal of either lately—but there is always 2013.

---

[404]Reuters, Facebook unveils new privacy controls, Technology Spectator, 13 December 2012, http://www.technologyspectator.com.au/facebook-unveils-new-privacy-controls, Accessed online 14 December 2012.

Chapter 7
Predictions

Technology change has an increasing effect on our lives and on business prosperity so it is vital to identify what is coming next and how we might benefit from it.

There is a broad range of change occurring to the digital world from infrastructure, systems, and cloud computing through to devices and user applications that range from entertainment, social media to education and health.

Business applications have also significantly benefited from the growth of the digital economy. Business to business and machine to machine applications are both experiencing an explosion of growth and the growth rate for automated systems should continue to increase.

7.1 Top Ten Tech Predictions for 2012...
and How to Interpret Them

4 January 2012

Around this time of year you see plenty of articles (such as this one) reflecting on notable technologies and events of the year now gone. Such pieces will also attempt to predict the events of the year just started.

When reading these articles, it's worth considering how the technologies being described are never taken in isolation. Instead, these technologies always need to be seen in terms of how they interact with and impact our personal and social lives. How technology does this, however, can be subtle and extremely complex.

In fact, there is a significant amount of research—past and present—that focuses on why we do or don't use software and technology. Most researchers agree that the reasons are sociotechnical[1]—a complex mish-mash of technological and societal factors. The study of these factors is increasingly becoming the realm of social scientists and psychologists, rather than engineers or computer scientists.

---

[1] Sociotechnical system, http://en.wikipedia.org/wiki/Sociotechnical_systems, Accessed on 4 January 2012.

That's important because individual technologies appear in the context of larger sociotechnical trends. Whether a technology is significant or revolutionary will depend, in part, on its role in facilitating, or more rarely, being the catalyst behind such trends.

One such trend is the move from the PC to the use of mobile technology. Early smartphones set the groundwork for heralding the move to mobile but it took the iPhone and apps delivered from the App Store to act as the catalyst. Even then, it wasn't until the iPhone 3—and the Android equivalents appearing shortly afterwards—that we could truly say the era of the smartphone had begun.

In many cases, identifying the particular "tipping point" for a technology or trend is really only possible after the fact. We certainly had no idea at the launch of Facebook that social networks would become so important in our lives. But a tipping point was reached and it became widely acknowledged that social networks were part of the general fabric of society.

Predictions may be hard to make but that doesn't stop us all from trying. Unfortunately the research done in this area only gives us pointers to reading tea leaves, and not a robust and reliable formula.

Looking back at 2011, the notable technical events were part of two major sociotechnical trends. The post-PC, move to mobile trend and the social hyper-connectedness trend. The technical events included the continued roll-out of mobile phones with new functionality, in particular the iPhone 4S and its onboard artificial intelligence Siri.[2]

In the world of social networking, we saw the advent of Google+[3] and the role of social media in the Arab Spring[4] and OccupyWallStreet[5] movements. These two trends will continue this year.

Here are my ten predictions for next year:

1) **Social networks**

   Facebook and Twitter will continue to dominate as social network platforms. The lacklustre Google+[6] will continue to struggle to get past its predominantly US, white, tech-oriented and male audience. This struggle will continue despite Google's attempts to insinuate it into everything they do.

2) **Email**

   Contrary to recent predictions,[7] email will continue to be the primary mode of electronic communication in the non-personal world.

---

[2] Apple's iPhone 4S is a game changer … Siri-ously, https://theconversation.edu.au/apples-iphone-4s-is-a-game-changer-siri-ously-3880, Accessed on 4 January 2012.

[3] 10 reasons why Google+ will never be Facebook, https://theconversation.edu.au/10-reasons-why-google-will-never-be-facebook-2073, Accessed on 4 January 2012.

[4] Arab spring, https://theconversation.edu.au/pages/arab-spring, Accessed on 4 January 2012.

[5] OccupyWallStreet, https://theconversation.edu.au/pages/occupywallstreet, Accessed on 4 January 2012.

[6] 10 reasons why Google+ will never be Facebook, https://theconversation.edu.au/10-reasons-why-google-will-never-be-facebook-2073, Accessed on 4 January 2012.

[7] Should we send work email to the trash? https://theconversation.edu.au/should-we-send-work-email-to-the-trash-4603, Accessed on 4 January 2012.

3) **Smartphones**
Android will continue as the dominant smart phone OS. Blackberry and the Symbian[8] will continue their decline into eventual irrelevance and Windows Phone 7[9] will fail to become relevant. The pairing of Nokia and Microsoft[10] will ultimately not be successful and Nokia will bring out Android phones.

4) **Apple**
Apple will survive the loss of Steve Jobs[11] and release the iPad 3 and iPhone 5. Siri will appear on the iPad and Apple TV and her capabilities[12] will extend into further integration with apps, including third-party apps.

5) **Apps vs. web**
Contrary to some predictions,[13] apps will not disappear any time soon and will not be replaced with HTML 5 web applications[14] (at least not in 2012).

6) **TV**
Apple will release a TV in 2012. The convergence of TVs as network-enabled media devices will see the adoption of Android as an alternative platform to Apple's forthcoming TV.[15]

The convergence of TV and the computer will allow TV to become integrated with social networks. This will extend the real-time interaction with talk shows that are increasingly displaying viewer Twitter and Facebook comments. It will also allow viewers to share their TV watching on their social networks.

Of course, advertising will become increasingly personalised on TV, moving from its current broadcast format.

7) **The PC**
The demise of the desktop computer will continue. It will be replaced with laptops, ultra-portables, tablets and phones, with data in the cloud.[16]

Windows 8[17] will be released towards the end of 2012 and will find its way to tablets. It will be universally shunned by businesses and will see only

---

[8] Symbian, http://symbian.nokia.com/, Accessed on 4 January 2012.

[9] Meet the new Windows Phone, http://www.windowsphone.com/en-nz, Accessed on 4 January 2012.

[10] Microsoft Buying Nokia's Phone Business For $19 Billion – TWEET, http://articles.businessinsider.com/2011-06-01/tech/29981525_1_nokia-tweet-microsoft, Accessed on 4 January 2012.

[11] RiP Steve Jobs – the CEO we felt we knew, https://theconversation.edu.au/rip-steve-jobs-the-ceo-we-felt-we-knew-3733, Accessed on 4 January 2012.

[12] Something about Siri: has the iPhone virtual assistant become the Apple of our eye? https://theconversation.edu.au/something-about-siri-has-the-iphone-virtual-assistant-become-the-apple-of-our-eye-4817, Accessed on 4 January 2012.

[13] No app for that? No apps, period, http://www.thestar.com/business/article/1089184--no-app-for-that-no-apps-period, Accessed on 4 January 2012.

[14] HTML 5.1 Nightly, http://www.w3.org/html/wg/drafts/html/master/browsers.html#history-1, Accessed on 4 January 2012.

[15] Apple readying 'iTV' connected TV set for 2012, http://www.digitalspy.com.au/tech/news/a353231/apple-readying-itv-connected-tv-set-for-2012.html, Accessed on 4 January 2012.

[16] Cloud computing, https://theconversation.edu.au/pages/cloud-computing, Accessed on 4 January 2012.

[17] Windows 8 Features & Release Date, http://www.thetechlabs.com/tech-news/windows-8-features/, Accessed on 4 January 2012.

slow adoption among consumers. Microsoft will make the new Metro user interface[18] optional.

8) **The news media**

Although strictly speaking not a technological issue, traditional news companies will continue to struggle to make money from either paper or online sales.

Paywall experiments will continue but at least one paywall exercise will be abandoned because of severely diminishing circulations.

9) **Legislation and legal**

Patent battles will continue and specific judgements will determine companies' strategies. Defensive purchasing of patents similar to the syndicate of companies that purchased patents[19] belonging to Nortel will continue. The participants of the patent wars will get more entrenched and their methods more convoluted.

One example of things to come is Apple's passing of patents to a shell company Cliff Island and subsequent arrangement with Digitude.[20] Getting others to do your dirty work.

Attempts to introduce legislation around online piracy[21] will fail. The realisation that law enforcement agencies (in the US in particular) can already shut down supposedly infringing sites without warning, renders new legislation giving these powers to copyright holders largely unnecessary.

10) **Cybersecurity**

Hacking and cyber-warfare/cyber-vandalism will continue. I initially thought that hacking by the hacking collective Anonymous[22] would stay focussed on real-life protests such as the Occupy Movement.[23] However, the recent hacking[24] of security intelligence firm Stratfor has shown that hacks in the name of Anonymous will continue to surprise, and for some, vex, next year.

---

[18] Microsoft to developers: Metro is your future, http://www.zdnet.com/blog/microsoft/microsoft-to-developers-metro-is-your-future/10611, Accessed on 4 January 2012.

[19] Nortel patents sold for $4.5bn, http://www.guardian.co.uk/technology/2011/jul/01/nortel-patents-sold-apple-sony-microsoft, Accessed on 4 January 2012.

[20] Digitude Innovations, http://www.digitudeinnovations.com/, Accessed on 4 January 2012.

[21] Stop Online Piracy Act draws battle lines for 'control' of the internet, https://theconversation.edu.au/stop-online-piracy-act-draws-battle-lines-for-control-of-the-internet-4366, Accessed on 4 January 2012.

[22] Anonymous, https://theconversation.edu.au/pages/anonymous, Accessed on 4 January 2012.

[23] Occupy movement, https://theconversation.edu.au/pages/occupy-movement, Accessed on 4 January 2012.

[24] Link no longer goes to specified page, http://myresearchspace.grs.uwa.edu.au/dglance/2011/12/27/the-ongoing-insurrection-anonymous-hacks-intelligence-firm/, Accessed on 4 January 2012.

7.2   Top Ten Tech Predictions for 2013

21 December 2012

The past 12 months have been a rather turbulent period for the technology sector. On the quirky side, we've seen robots land on Mars,[25] exoskeletons making wheel chairs reduntant,[26] and the rise of people creating their own plastic figurines with 3D printing technology.[27]

But it hasn't been all fun and games. The major technology players have made some significant moves this year. Microsoft launched its landmark Windows 8 operating system, Apple caved to rumours and launched its iPad Mini, and telcos around the world are diving into 4G networks and LTE technology.

And that's not to mention all the advances in smartphones, cameras, GPS, game consoles and tablets.

All of this has framed 2013 as a key year for technological change, which begs the question: what is going to happen in 2013?

Here's my top ten predictions for the next year:

1. **Wi-Fi the big winner**
   The shift away from the desktop to mobile platforms will continue in 2013. Already positive and negative trends are emerging. Recent changes to mobile carrier plans to reduce data allowances[28] bodes ill for mobile customers in 2013 hoping to increase their smart phone and tablet use. The move to increase charges on mobile customers continues Australia's mobile rip-off[29] and poses the problem for regulators—how to increase competition[30] with such a skewed mobile landscape where Telstra is dominant, Optus seems to be asleep and Vodafone still reals from the Vodafail[31] episode. The big winner in 2013 will be Wi-Fi. The mobility market is growing rapidly and customers are increasingly looking to Wi-Fi as an alternative solution to overcome the high cost of mobile plans. Expect to see an explosion of Wi-Fi in 2013 as this technology matures as

---

[25] Curiosity, The Conversation, https://theconversation.edu.au/pages/curiosity, Accessed online 21 December 2012.

[26] Strickland E., Good-bye, Wheelchair, Hello Exoskeleton, IEEE Spectrum, January 2012, Accessed online 21 December 2012.

[27] Hill D.J., 3D Printing Robot Produces Chairs And Tables From Recycled Waste, SingularityHub, 23 April 2012, http://singularityhub.com/2012/04/23/3d-printing-robot-produces-chairs-and-tables-from-recycled-waste/, Accessed online 21 December 2012.

[28] Hutchinson J., Telstra price hikes a premium play, it news, 6 July 2012, http://www.itnews.com.au/News/307779,telstra-price-hikes-a-premium-play.aspx, Accessed online 21 December 2012.

[29] Gregory M.A., Verizon Wireless vs Telstra: the great mobile rip-off continues, The Conversation, 12 July 2012, https:/theconversation.edu.au/verizon-wireless-vs-telstra-the-great-mobile-rip-off-continues-8132, Accessed online 21 December 2012.

[30] McDuling J., Bring on great mobile competition: Vodafone, Financial Review, 16 November 2012, http://www.afr.com/p/technology/bring_on_great_mobile_competition_a1BjuuTWuYA3C-1QWbbuDSK, Accessed online 21 December 2012.

[31] Vodafail, http://www.vodafail.com/, Accessed online 21 December 2012.

a commercial alternative to 4G. The successful Queensland train Wi-Fi system[32] should provide the impetus for Victoria and New South Wales to introduce train Wi-Fi systems in 2013.

2. **NBN in the balance**

The 2013 federal election promises to be a pivotal moment for NBN Co and the National Broadband Network (NBN). If the government is returned the NBN will move ahead as planned—albeit with faults including the glacial pace of the rollout, the ban on the NBN connecting with planes, trains, buses and other vehicles and continuing to use Alcatel-Lucent as a sole supplier of the fibre system.[33]

If the opposition wins government we should expect to see immediate change. Key changes if the opposition wins government are likely to include a reduction in the fibre rollout—with the new mix of customer access being 60 % fibre to the home, 30 % fibre to the node, 7 % fixed wireless and 3 % satellite. Also note that the 30 % fibre to the node will consist mainly of multi-dwelling buildings—many of which now utilise a fibre to the building solution.

3. **Mobile advertsing will take centre stage**

The gradual shift towards mobile devices is set to have a drastic impact on the internet next year. As the rise of smartphones, tablets and the big mover for 2013, cyber-glasses[34] will become the focus for internet developments and marketing will attempt to overcome the perception that it is difficult to advertise effectively through mobile devices. Research and advisory firm Gartner predicts[35] that mobile app downloads will top 81 billion in 2013, an increase of about 45 % over 2012.

4. **E-commerce becomes an election issue**

Australians will further embrace[36] online shopping and in 2013 we are expected to spend more than $37 billion online. The government will face increasing pressure to do something about the widening competitive gap between traditional store front retailers and online international retailers. The loss of GST revenue and the flow of capital out of Australia will reach a level that will make this an

---

[32] Queensland Rail Free Wi-Fi, http://www.queenslandrail.com.au/RAILSERVICES/CITY/Pages/wifi.aspx, Accessed online 21 December 2012.

[33] Foo F., Alcatel-Lucent named key NBN supplier, The Australian, 24 June 2010, http://www.theaustralian.com.au/australian-it/alcatel-lucent-named-key-nbn-supplier/story-e6fr-gakx-1225883962536, Accessed online 21 December 2012.

[34] Simonite T., Google's Glasses Gets a Competitor, MIT Technology Review, 20 November 2012, http://www.technologyreview.com/news/507666/googles-glass-gets-a-competitor/, Accessed online 21 December 2012.

[35] Gartner Says Free Apps Will Account for Nearly 90 Percent of Total Mobile App Store Downloads in 2012, Gartner, 11 September 2012, http://www.gartner.com/it/page.jsp?id=2153215, Accessed online 21 December 2012.

[36] Analysis of Australian Ecommerce Statistics [Infographic], Competitions.com.au, 16 July 2012, http://blog.competitions.com.au/infographics/australian-ecommerce-statistics-infographic/, Accessed online 21 December 2012.

election issue. A recent survey[37] by SLI Systems identifies that retailers will focus their e-commerce priorities on search engine optimisation, mobile commerce, e-commerce platforms and improving website search capabilities.

5. **Cyber-crime hits a new high**

   Criminal activity over the internet will reach a new peak in 2013. Cyber-crime[38] may reach the $2 billion mark in 2013. Government will come under increasing pressure to take steps to reduce cyber-crime and this may finally lead to the introduction of technologies to improve privacy and security[39] on the internet. Companies operating on the internet are likely to focus their attention on the cyber-crime problem and improve the security of their online presence through smart design.[40]

6. **The IT world will "get real" about the Cloud**

   The cloud should become a dominant feature[41] of our online experience in 2013. Analyst firm, Forrester, predicts[42] that the IT world will finally "get real about cloud" in 2013. Applications such as Dropbox, Apple iCloud, Google Apps and Microsoft Office 365 will become central to our online experience by improving productivity and reducing organisation technology costs. The move away from desktop computing to the cloud will accelerate for many of our routine activities such as collaboration, email and document processing. There will be growth in the construction and use of date centres to match the need for ever expanding cloud capability. We can only hope that new Australian data centres are required to be built using environmentally sustainable technologies.[43]

---

[37] Benton J., Australian and New Zealand Retailers Reveal 2013 E-Commerce Priorities, Power Retail, 14 December 2012, http://www.powerretail.com.au/technology/australian-new-zealand-retailers-reveal-2013-ecommerce-priorities/, Accessed online 21 December 2012.

[38] Gregory M.A., Cybercrime bill makes it through – but what does that mean for you?, The Conversation, 23 August 2012, https:/theconversation.edu.au/cybercrime-bill-makes-it-through-but-what-does-that-mean-for-you-8953, Accessed online 21 December 2012.

[39] Gregory M.A., The dark side to data retention, Technology Spectator, 4 October 2012, http://www.technologyspectator.com.au/dark-side-data-retention?utm_source=exact&utm_medium=email&utm_content=112963&utm_campaign=kgb&modapt=commentary, Accessed online 21 December 2012.

[40] Phair N., Cutting cybercrime is a question of smart design, The Conversation, 12 September 2012, http://theconversation.edu.au/cutting-cybercrime-is-a-question-of-smart-design-9013, Accessed online 21 December 2012.

[41] Darrow B. and Higginbothamm S., What we'll see in 2013 in cloud computing, Gigaom, 14 December 2012, http://gigaom.com/2012/12/14/what-well-see-in-2013-in-cloud-computing/, Accessed online 21 December 2012.

[42] Staten J., 2013 Cloud Predictions: We'll Finally Get Real About Cloud, Forrester, 3 December 2012, http://blogs.forrester.com/james_staten/12-12-03-2013_cloud_predictions_well_finally_get_real_about_cloud, Accessed online 21 December 2012.

[43] Google Green, Google, http://www.google.com.au/green/efficiency/, Accessed online 21 December 2012.

7. **Big Data, bigger business opportunities**

Big business is turning its attention[44] to big data[45] and investing considerable sums to mine data repositories. This activity will expand rapidly in 2013 and organisations are learning that big data can be a source of increasing revenue through trading or resale of data and targeted marketing[46] opportunities. A Gartner report[47] published in October 2012 states that by 2015 big data will support 4.4 million IT jobs. Australian companies have been late to explore the opportunities provided by big data but we should expect that to change in 2013.

8. **The tech giants will turn to social media**

Increased competition, better privacy and improved security are likely to be key ingredients for the social media scene in 2013. The big three—Apple, Google and Microsoft—went head to head in the mobility market in 2012 and should turn their attention to unified social media offerings in 2013. The Facebook versus Twitter war is hotting up and we should expect to see new and existing social media organisations duke it out in 2013.

9. **Broadband applications rise as Australians continue to resist Geoblocking**

Next year will be a watershed period for broadband applications. Expect to see a huge growth in consumer and business broadband applications including IPTV, eHealth, eLearning, 3-D interactive games and business applications such as machine to machine (M2M) and business to business (B2B). We will see the start to an explosion of sensor networks[48] and vehicles[49] connected to the internet. Australian's will increasingly turn to technologies[50] that overcome regional[51] and digital format[52] restrictions.

---

[44] Head B., Big data blasts off in 2013, itwire, 14 December 2012, http://www.itwire.com/business-it-news/technology/57925-big-data-blasts-off-in-2013, Accessed online 21 December 2012.

[45] What is big data?, IBM, http://www-01.ibm.com/software/data/bigdata/, Accessed online 21 December 2012.

[46] Targeted advertising, Wikipedia, http://en.wikipedia.org/wiki/Targeted_advertising, Accessed online 21 December 2012.

[47] Gartner Says Big Data Creates Big Jobs: 4.4 Million IT Jobs Globally to Support Big Data By 2015, Gartner, 22 October 2012, http://www.gartner.com/it/page.jsp?id=2207915, Accessed online 21 December 2012.

[48] Wireless sensor network, Wikipedia, http://en.wikipedia.org/wiki/Wireless_sensor_network, Accessed online 21 December 2012.

[49] Digital Agenda: Commission takes first step to ensure life-saving emergency call system for road accidents in place by 2015, European Union, 8 September 2011, http://europa.eu/rapid/press-release_IP-11-1010_en.htm?locale=en, Accessed online 21 December 2012.

[50] Why do I need a personal VPN, VyprVPN, http://www.goldenfrog.com/vyprvpn/why-vpn, Accessed online 21 December 2012.

[51] Geolocation software, Wikipedia, http://en.wikipedia.org/wiki/Geolocation_software, Accessed online 21 December 2012.

[52] Digital rights management, Wikipedia, http://en.wikipedia.org/wiki/Digital_rights_management, Accessed online 21 December 2012.

10. **Regulators will need to grow some teeth**

Australians demand a better experience online and for this reason pressure will build in the lead up to the 2013 federal election. The internet is a fast moving space and the major issues[53] facing people on the internet today appear to be daunting to the slow moving government bureaucracy. Government agencies including the Australian Communications and Media Authority, Australian Competition and Consumer Commission, Australian Federal Police and the Australian Privacy Commissioner are seen to be too slow to react, toothless[54] or hesitant to take action.

Several issues that are of significant concern to Australians are the tech rip-off,[55] excessive global roaming charges,[56] cyber-crime[57] and the failure of large international multi-nationals to pay tax.[58] 2013, being an election year, must surely be the year that government stops the endless cycle of committees and inquiries and takes action.

---

[53]Gregory M.A., The UN's internet gabfest, Technology Spectator, 30 November 2012, http://www.technologyspectator.com.au/uns-internet-gabfest, Accessed online 21 December 2012.

[54]Moses A., Telstra's 734,000 account privacy blunder breached multiple laws: regulators, Fairfax, 29 June 2012, http://www.theage.com.au/it-pro/security-it/telstras-734000-account-privacy-blunder-breached-multiple-laws-regulators-20120629-2165z.html, Accessed online 21 December 2012.

[55]Polites H., Husic vs tech goliaths, Technology Spectator, 1 May 2012, http://www.technology-spectator.com.au/industry/it/husic-vs-tech-goliaths, Accessed online 21 December 2012.

[56]Gregory M.A., Are Australian international roaming charges the greatest rip-off in history?, The Conversation, 30 November 2012, http://theconversation.edu.au/are-australian-international-roaming-charges-the-greatest-rip-off-in-history-4340, Accessed online 21 December 2012.

[57]Cybercrime, Australian Federal Police, http://www.afp.gov.au/policing/cybercrime.aspx, Accessed online 21 December 2012.

[58]AAP, Panel named on multinational tax avoidance, The Australian, 10 December 2012, http://www.theaustralian.com.au/news/breaking-news/panel-named-on-multinational-tax-avoidance/story-fn3dxiwe-1226533548609, Accessed online 21 December 2012.

Printed in the United States
By Bookmasters